FDR's Ambassadors and the Diplomacy of Crisis

What effect did personality and circumstance have on US foreign policy during World War II? This incisive account of US envoys residing in the major belligerent countries – Japan, Germany, Italy, China, France, Great Britain, USSR – highlights the fascinating role played by such diplomats as Joseph Grew, William Dodd, William Bullitt, Joseph Kennedy, and W. Averell Harriman. Between Hitler's 1933 ascent to power and the 1945 bombing of Nagasaki, US ambassadors sculpted formal policy – occasionally deliberately, other times inadvertently – giving shape and meaning not always intended by FDR or predicted by his principal advisors. From appeasement to the Holocaust and the onset of the Cold War, David Mayers examines the complicated interaction between policy, as conceived in Washington, and implementation on the ground in Europe and Asia. By so doing, he also sheds needed light on the fragility, ambiguities, and enduring urgency of diplomacy and its crucial function in international politics.

David Mayers teaches at Boston University, where he holds a joint professorship in the History and Political Science departments. His previous books include *Cracking the Monolith: US Policy Against the Sino-Soviet Alliance, 1949–1955* (1986), *George Kennan and the Dilemmas of US Foreign Policy* (1988), *The Ambassadors and America's Soviet Policy* (1995), *Wars and Peace: The Future Americans Envisioned, 1861–1991* (1998), and *Dissenting Voices in America's Rise to Power* (2007).

FDR's Ambassadors and the Diplomacy of Crisis

From the Rise of Hitler to the
End of World War II

David Mayers

CAMBRIDGE
UNIVERSITY PRESS

CAMBRIDGE UNIVERSITY PRESS

Cambridge, New York, Melbourne, Madrid, Cape Town,
Singapore, São Paulo, Delhi, Mexico City

Cambridge University Press
The Edinburgh Building, Cambridge CB2 8RU, UK

Published in the United States of America by
Cambridge University Press, New York

www.cambridge.org
Information on this title: www.cambridge.org/9781107031265

First published 2013

Printed and bound in the United Kingdom by the MPG Books Group

A catalogue record for this publication is available from the British Library

Library of Congress Cataloguing in Publication data
Mayers, David, 1951–
    FDR's ambassadors and the diplomacy of crisis : from the rise of Hitler to the end of
World War II / David Mayers.
        p. cm.
    ISBN 978-1-107-03126-5 (Hardback)
    1. United States–Foreign relations–1933–1945. 2. Ambassadors–United States–
History–20th century. 3. World War, 1939–1945–Diplomatic
history. 4. Roosevelt, Franklin D. (Franklin Delano), 1882–1945. I. Title.
    E806.M424 2012
    973.917–dc23

                                                              2012024352

ISBN 978-1-107-03126-5 Hardback

To Elizabeth,
To Peter

CONTENTS

LIST OF ILLUSTRATIONS

ACKNOWLEDGEMENTS

This study draws upon the research of numerous scholars, memoir literature, published government documents – above all the invaluable *Foreign Relations of the United States* (*FRUS*) series – and archival materials housed in repositories in North America and elsewhere. The archivists and librarians with whom I dealt were uniformly gracious. My thanks to the excellent staffs of the archives listed in this book's bibliography and the people of Boston University's Mugar Library and the Saluda Public Library.

I spent much of 2008 as a Fellow (Haniel) at the American Academy in Berlin (AAB). My German and American comrades were unfailingly helpful as I worked on this book. I am grateful to the AAB's energetic impresario, Gary Smith, to his courteous staff, and to the engaging Fellows that I had the privilege to know. Additionally, Boston University's College of Arts and Sciences provided sabbatical relief and generous funds in support of travel to archival collections, without which this study could not have been written.

Professional associations and specialty groups let me present parts of this book as it developed to thoughtful audiences. I benefited from responses at meetings of the British International Studies Association (BISA), German-American Center/James Byrnes Institute in Stuttgart, International History Institute of Boston University, Society for Historians of American Foreign Relations, Transatlantic Studies Association, and the US Foreign Policy Working Group of BISA.

Portions of Chapter 2 appeared as an article in the March 2009 volume of *Diplomacy and Statecraft*: "Neither War Nor Peace: FDR's Ambassadors in Berlin and Policy toward Germany, 1933–1941." Parts of Chapter 7 appeared as an article in the June 2011 volume of *The International History Review*: "The Great Patriotic War, FDR's Embassy Moscow, and Soviet-U.S. Relations."

Friends, relatives, colleagues, and students have been crucial. They listened. They made good recommendations and saved me from stupidities and infelicities. I acknowledge with appreciation Susan Abel, John Archer, Andrew Bacevich, Brooke Blower, Donald Brand, David Clinton, Walter Connor, Frank Costigliola, Michael Cullen, Kathleen Dalton, Andrew David, Stephanie Fawcett, Joseph Fewsmith, Zach Fredman, Max Paul Friedman, David Fromkin, Irene Gendzier, Jonathan Harris, Gregg Herken, Takeo Iguchi, Robert Jackson, Detleff Junker, Peter Kenez, William Keylor, Warren Kimball, Martina Kohl, Vladislava Kukuy, Walter LaFeber, Fred Leventhal, David Levering Lewis, Igor Lukes, Marc Masurovsky, Marilyn Mayers, Peter Michael Mayers, Carol McHale, Richard Melanson, Charles Neu, Cathal Nolan, Suzanne O'Brien, Arnold Offner, Larry Plitch, the late Lucian Pye, J. Simon Rofe, Gina Sapiro, James Schmidt, Ruth Ann Stewart, Manfred Stinnes, Mark Stoler, Vladimir Vulovic, Jeremy Weiss, Jenny White, Peter Widdicombe, Graham Wilson, Gregory Winger, the late Howard Zinn.

As before, I am grateful to Michael Watson, the highly accomplished and supportive History editor at Cambridge University Press. Once more, working with him and his colleagues has been a delight from start to finish. Special thanks also to Laurence Marsh, masterful copy-editor.

This book is dedicated to my wife, Elizabeth Kirkland Jones, and our son, Peter Kirkland Mayers. Elizabeth has been my writing coach for years. She has also used her admirable literary and administrative skills on behalf of Harvard University's School of Public Health. Peter has inspired me by his commitment to humanitarian service. Through the United Nations High Commissioner for Refugees and the International Catholic Migration Commission, he has worked in Geneva and Bangladesh on behalf of refugees and displaced persons. Both of his grandfathers – John James Jones, Eugene David Mayers – served as officers in the United States army during World War II. They and their wives – Sarah Moore Jones, Odette Gilchriest Mayers – must in their heavenly bower sigh with satisfaction as Peter continues to help put right a world that, in the years of their vitality, was wildly out of joint.

DM
Saluda, North Carolina
6 June 2012

SELECTED UNITED STATES CHIEFS OF MISSION, 1933–1945

Japan

Ambassador Joseph C. Grew: Appointment 19 February 1932, Presentation of Credentials 14 June 1932, Termination of Mission 8 December 1941 (having been interned, Grew left Japan 25 June 1942).

Germany

Ambassador William E. Dodd: Appointment 13 June 1933, Presentation of Credentials 30 August 1933, Termination of Mission 29 December 1937.

Ambassador Hugh R. Wilson: Appointment 17 January 1938, Presentation of Credentials 3 March 1938, Termination of Mission 16 November 1938.

Chargé d'affaires ad interim Alexander C. Kirk served from May 1939 to October 1940.

Chargé d'affaires ad interim Leland B. Morris served from October 1940 to December 1941.

Italy

Ambassador Breckinridge Long: Appointment 24 April 1933, Presentation of Credentials 31 May 1933, Termination of Mission 23 April 1936.

Ambassador William Phillips: Appointment 4 August 1936, Presentation of Credentials 4 November 1936, Termination of Mission 6 October 1941.

George Wadsworth was chargé d'affaires ad interim when Italy declared war on the United States, 11 December 1941.

Ambassador Alexander C. Kirk: Appointment 8 December 1944, Presentation of Credentials 8 January 1945, Termination of Mission 5 March 1946.

China

Ambassador Nelson T. Johnson: Appointment 16 December 1929, Presentation of Credentials 1 February 1930, Termination of Mission 14 May 1941.

Ambassador Clarence E. Gauss: Appointment 11 February 1941, Presentation of Credentials 26 May 1941, Termination of Mission 14 November 1944.

Ambassador Patrick J. Hurley: Appointment 30 November 1944, Presentation of Credentials 8 January 1945, Termination of Mission 22 September 1945.

France

Ambassador Jesse Isidor Straus: Appointment 17 March 1933, Presentation of Credentials 8 June 1933, Termination of Mission 5 August 1936.

Ambassador William C. Bullitt: Appointment 25 August 1936, Presentation of Credentials 13 October 1936, Termination of Mission 11 July 1940 (Anthony J. Drexel Biddle acted as Deputy Ambassador during 13–25 June 1940).

Ambassador William D. Leahy: Appointment 29 November 1940, Presentation of Credentials 8 January 1941, Terminaiton of Mission 1 May 1942.

S. Pinkney Tuck was chargé d'affaires ad interim when Vichy authorities cut diplomatic relations with the United States, 8 November 1942.

Ambassador Jefferson Caffery: Appointment 25 November 1944, Presentation of Credentials 30 December 1944, Termination of Mission 13 May 1949.

United Kingdom

Ambassador Robert Worth Bingham: Appointment 23 March 1933, Presentation of Credentials 23 May 1933, Termination of Mission 19 November 1937.

Ambassador Joseph P. Kennedy: Appointment 17 January 1938, Presentation of Credentials 8 March 1938, Termination of Mission 22 October 1940.

Ambassador John Gilbert Winant: Appointment 11 February 1941, Presentation of Credentials 1 March 1941, Termination of Mission 10 April 1946.

Soviet Union

Ambassador William Bullitt: Appointment 21 November 1933, Presentation of Credentials 13 December 1933, Termination of Mission 16 May 1936.

Ambassador Joseph E. Davies: Appointment 16 November 1936, Presentation of Credentials 25 January 1937, Termination of Mission 11 June 1938.

Ambassador Laurence A. Steinhardt: Appointment 23 March 1939, Presentation of Credentials 11 August 1939, Termination of Mission 12 November 1941.

Ambassador William H. Standley: Appointment 14 February 1942, Presentation of Credentials 14 April 1942, Termination of Mission 19 September 1943.

Ambassador W. Averell Harriman: Appointment 7 October 1943, Presentation of Credentials 23 October 1943, Termination of Mission 24 January 1946

Source: United States Department of State, *Principal Officers of the Department of State and Chiefs of Mission 1778–1988* (Washington, DC, 1988).

INTRODUCTION

In this book I delve into the effects of personality and circumstance on foreign policy and the outcomes of war. More specifically, I explore the interaction between policy conceived in Washington during World War II, defined as 1937 (Nanjing) to 1945 (Nagasaki), and the lived experience of US diplomats residing in the major belligerent countries. There American ambassadors sculpted formal policy – occasionally deliberately, other times inadvertently – giving it shape and meaning not always intended by FDR or predicted by his principal advisors. As such this book belongs to an expanding genre in diplomatic studies, centered on those activities undertaken by a cast of characters outside the limelight but who have served national leaders.[1]

Popular and scholarly interest in World War II has generated an immense literature. It continues to grow without signs of abating as audiences try to grasp the war's many facets. These include the conflict's deep origins and immediate causes, aims of the belligerents, strains within alliances, weapon technologies, life on the home fronts, genocides. Related postwar events have been evaluated too from diverse standpoints – the convening of international military tribunals at Nuremberg and Tokyo to mete out justice to Axis leaders, rumblings of Cold War confrontation, first flushes of decolonization in Africa and Asia.

Treatment of US aspects of the Second World War has also ranged broadly. Among topics of interest are isolationism's allure and adherents, the drift into hostilities, the failure to rescue European Jewry, the Pacific campaigns, the D-Day landings, the Manhattan Project and use of atomic bombs, the internment of Japanese-Americans, the feminization of the industrial work force, and the reinvigoration of the drive for African-American civil rights. Neither has the diplomatic side of the US effort been neglected. Analyses have centered on presidential performances at summit conferences of the Big Three, where grand strategy and postwar plans were devised and ratified: Tehran, Yalta, Potsdam. Yet a crucial feature of American wartime diplomacy has been given shorter shrift by historians, namely, that having to do with US embassies and ambassadors during the crisis years, from Hitler's capture of power to Japan's 1945 capitulation.

This neglect partly stems from the fact that Franklin Roosevelt had little time for his senior diplomat, the hapless Cordell Hull. FDR kept him around primarily to maintain links with Capitol Hill, where he was respected owing to his previous congressional career, having served terms in the House and Senate where he specialized in international trade relations. The president was otherwise not solicitous of his secretary of state, whom he tolerated as a cross between Tennessee rube and Wilsonian fundamentalist. Hull had good reason to complain when he blurted early in his State Department tenure: "[Roosevelt] never tells me anything."[2]

Like many presidents before and since, FDR preferred to play the part of foreign minister. Moreover, he had scant regard for State Department professionals, whom he considered a blend of incompetent and snooty.[3] Except for Undersecretary of State Sumner Welles, whom FDR esteemed but let go (September 1943) to mollify Hull's accumulating resentment and in light of Welles's alleged homosexual escapades, he rarely sought out the department's people.[4] Roosevelt cared little for their ideas. He instead relied on his own inner circle for advice, notably his confidante Harry Hopkins, or men in uniform, preeminently General George Marshall.

A presumption has developed that because FDR largely ignored the formal apparatus through which US foreign relations is conducted, and deployed special emissaries for delicate missions, its wartime functioning was correspondingly dull or trivial. The main action and grappling with grave matters took place elsewhere – on the battlefields, in the factories, in cabinet and Allied meetings – while State Department machinery clunked along with meager direction. Diplomats posted abroad purportedly fell into secondary routine while hoping dimly that a return to peacetime would salvage ambassadorial dignity and deliver them from the ignominy of playing bit roles in a surpassing drama; younger officers, meanwhile, labored under the popular suspicion that they were sons of privilege who had shirked military obligations by scurrying into Foreign Service cushiness. But such interpretations distort the record. Cumulatively they give a misleading portrait, practically a cartoon, of America's diplomatic front in World War II.

The account here of FDR's ambassadors provides for a fuller understanding of the scope, intention, and controversies that marked US foreign policy. Thus, for example, the split in FDR's administration between people who – before 7 December 1941 – wanted to accommodate Japan and those who wanted to confront it was intensified by the disagreements between two distinguished envoys: conciliatory Joseph Grew in Tokyo versus tougher-minded Nelson Johnson in China. The depth of dispute between Americans who wanted to avoid involvement in European troubles ("isolationists") and people who feared the consequences of prolonged aloofness ("interventionists") was vividly illustrated by the two successive heads of Embassy London: Joseph Kennedy versus John Winant. W. Averell Harriman, to cite another case, helped stabilize the uneasy Soviet–US wartime alliance. Later, as Harry Truman's tutor, he had tangible impact on the president as he tried from April 1945 onward to understand Stalin's ways and goals.

Concomitantly, occupation of the ambassadorial office by irresponsible or naïve people was not a trite problem or simply more fodder for satirists in their ridiculing of diplomats as pompous functionaries who swill champagne and consume caviar. The posting of ill-qualified men abroad did mischief. They hindered the attainment of US ends. William Bullitt in Paris, for instance, inadvertently misled FDR's cabinet in 1940 about the resilience of French society and the robustness of its military forces. At the same time, he assured the French government of US determination to provide abundant materiel at the hour of need, when in fact the administration had neither the means nor will to send decisive help. The overall result of Bullitt's mission was to confuse officialdom in both Washington and Paris during a portentous moment. In China during 1944–1945 Patrick Hurley, to mention another sad instance, disparaged his staff – excellent in the main – and misunderstood a central political reality: abiding antipathy between Chiang Kai-shek (Jiang Jieshi) and Mao Zedong. This did not

1 Left to right: General George Marshall, W. Averell Harriman, Admiral William Leahy, FDR. Yalta 1945.

allow for civil peace or China's playing a role as one of the world's policemen, an assignment blithely devised by FDR and endorsed by the uncomprehending Hurley.

An appreciation of the ambassadorial ledger of achievements and fumbles is integral to understanding the US record in World War Two. Diplomacy, for good or ill, was much more than just FDR.[5]

The first section of this study is centered on ambassadors posted to the Axis capitals – Tokyo, Berlin, Rome – before direct US involvement in hostilities. These people monitored the currents racing toward war and suggested methods for containing them or, failing that, preparing for national emergency. The focus of the Japanese chapter is on the period of 1937–1941, from the resumption of Sino-Japanese violence to Pearl Harbor, and probes the question of whether a plausible alternative existed to war in the Pacific. The German chapter takes up the story at an earlier date, with the Nazis coming to office in 1933 and William Dodd's warnings against them, and ends in December 1941, by which time Hitler's armies had overrun most of Europe. The tale of diplomats in Germany during the 1930s throws into relief those dilemmas posed by the Third Reich to FDR's America and its equivocal response. The main question in the Italian chapter turns on whether a more adept US policy could have prevented Mussolini's developing an exclusive orientation on Germany.

I devote the book's second section to Axis victims. The China chapter pivots on the record of American officials in the mauled Middle Kingdom. The matter for them was twofold, hinging on whether Chiang might contribute significantly to the anti-Japanese struggle and assessing prospects for China's assuming a greater international part in the future under US tutelage. The French chapter deals with the only great power in the European war to collapse during the first year of combat. The June 1940 surrender presented dilemmas to Americans regarding the collaborationist Vichy regime. They hoped it might maintain a modicum of independence from the Third Reich and, perhaps, be dislodged from the German sphere. At a minimum, Washington expected that the Vichy contribution to Germany could be weakened or otherwise played to US–British advantage. Realization of these military-diplomatic imperatives clashed with a humanitarian imperative. A few diplomats, exemplified by the chargé d'affaires S. Pinkney Tuck, wanted in mid-1942 to aid thousands of Jews at risk of deportation by Vichy and delivery to German custody. With the dissolution of Vichy in 1944 and France's return to belligerency against Germany, the United States acquired another ally, but only marginally better positioned than China to contribute to Axis defeat.

Section three of the book deals with America's two most important coalition partners. The Britannia chapter concentrates on the vicissitudes of the US–British relationship from the 1938 Munich conference to victory in 1945. That period was marked by the fateful weakening of the British empire and US rise to dominance in the English-speaking world. As developed in the Soviet chapter, by war's end the USSR, alone among nations, occupied a spot from which to challenge America's emergent global writ. The main outlines of the postwar Soviet–US contest of wills ("Cold War") took shape during the anti-German alliance of 1941–1945.

The concluding chapter combines several elements: reflections on FDR's statecraft and the nature of the US diplomatic corps in the World War II era; an evaluation of ambassadorial diplomacy with emphasis on the intersection between Washington conceptions of exalted policy and lived experience overseas; ruminations (not too tangential, I hope) on the long shadow cast by the Second World War. Regarding this last item, these words of William Faulkner apply: "The past is never dead. It's not even past."[6]

Irrespective of their place of residence and the specificity of each mission, FDR's envoys dealt with common puzzles. They went beyond the ordinary requirement of producing reliable reportage (embassy as "relay station") or leading orderly life in alien settings. Foremost among difficulties, the president's representatives had to divine Roosevelt's elusive mind, prerequisite for giving an intelligible account of US concerns to host governments. The difficulty in this discernment was further aggravated by the brittleness of White House–State Department communication. Authorized ambassadors, moreover, had to take precautions to preserve their usefulness whenever the president graced foreign governments with visitations by roving emissaries. They typically presumed much, not infrequently "scooped" the embassies by acquiring useful information first, and got quick entrée to personages, who thereafter required persuasion that the local diplomats were worth knowing. Too often, not without reason, the suspicion shared by ambassadors and potentates alike was that FDR more dearly valued analysis acquired by his "utility players" than by long-term retainers assigned to distant stations. Yet despite these handicaps, several of America's ambassadors acquitted themselves well. They added materially to the US cause and to the sum of diplomacy's moderating purpose. The bungling of other people must be read as a cautionary tale.

This history of World War II envoys is meant as more than a study of a discrete topic in twentieth-century US foreign relations. It is a vehicle to investigate broad questions of diplomacy and international relations within the context of a specific crisis. Diplomacy normally aims to advance the national interest by nonviolent means. By its very existence, diplomacy fosters procedures and a semblance of community, however incipient, among competitive states and anxious peoples.

The Second World War's immense violence did not obviate diplomacy. It is an ameliorative activity, premised on recognition that the problems afflicting states – born of insecurity, competition, self-regard – constitute a condition that cannot be fixed but only managed. Diplomats do not aim at perfect peace or absolute justice but settle for, and count themselves lucky when they have achieved, approximations of such ends. Secretary of War Henry Stimson was incontrovertibly right when he stated in 1947: "The face of war is the face of death … [War] has grown steadily more barbarous, more destructive, more debased in all its aspects."[7] Incomprehensible to "progressivist theory," war since Stimson's time has continued to derange global society.[8] Yet the diplomatic vocation, in tandem with its sturdy helpers – international law and organizations, treaty regimes, regional associations – can slow the war reflex and purchase respite from disaster.

By retrieving salient elements in the careers of FDR's ambassadors, one can better grasp not just "lessons" of the past, such as they are, or the modalities of modern foreign policy, but also better comprehend the fragility, ambiguities, and enduring urgency of diplomacy. This study argues implicitly for the primacy of diplomacy, even during violent times, a useful orientation for Americans and other peoples as they pick their way through the twenty-first century's hazards. The local knowledge, intuitions, compromises, and tact that compose the essence of diplomacy – velvet covering the mailed fist – are even more vital in stirred eras than in placid ones.

Part I

Axis

1 RISING SUN

The Japanese attack (7 December 1941) on military and naval installations in Hawaii shoved the United States into the general violence that had rocked international life since the late 1930s but Americans had heretofore avoided, at least in an immediate sense. In the absence of Pearl Harbor, followed by Berlin's obliging war declaration, US immersion in the fight against Germany would have been delayed, albeit not ultimately averted.

After France's June 1940 downfall, Washington officials looked anxiously at Germany's reconfiguration of Europe and pondered the problems, immediate and long-term, that they posed to New World safety. Japan's behavior in East Asia, especially aggression against China, had long unsettled FDR's cabinet officers. They had not placed Japan in the same category with Germany of menace to the Americas, however. Adroit diplomacy, some thought, notably Cordell Hull, would preclude Japanese–US hostilities. Failing that, war against Japan should be postponed as long as feasible while the main problem – surging German power – was checked and British survival, West European wellbeing, and US security thereby ensured.

The above considerations point to fundamental but rival interpretations. According to one, a durable modus vivendi could have been crafted between Tokyo and Washington, thereby escaping the bitter Pacific war and allowing for concentration upon the European situation. Not so, another historical school has contended; the intensity of Japanese–US rivalry in Asia disallowed diplomatic solution. The catalogue of Tokyo's misdeeds, as read in Washington, was too ominous to downplay or otherwise dismiss. Phrased differently, the quest for empire by dissatisfied Japan placed it on a collision course with the status quo-oriented United States that outstripped the ability of leaders in either country to redirect. The notion that Japan and the United States might avoid a clash was, in other words, a fantasy unworthy of attention by Washington in the era of General Tojo Hideki. Tokyo's alignment with the European Axis powers in particular, solemnized by the signing (27 September 1940) of the Tripartite Pact, meant certain trouble with FDR's America.

Despite cooperation during the Great War with Japan, by 1941 Washington's view of Tokyo's external policy underscored its seeming rapaciousness. Successive Japanese administrations since the early 1900s, according to this line, had, via conquests and predatory diplomacy, created a bristling empire at the expense of unoffending Asian neighbors and weakening European states. The component parts of this empire included Formosa, the Pescadores, Korea, southern Sakhalin, an ostensibly independent Manchuria – rechristened Manchukuo – and swaths of Chinese territory below the Great Wall. Japanese military forces occupied parts of French Indochina in September 1940. Tokyo governments in the meantime had committed other transgressions: withdrew from the League of Nations in 1933 after it condemned (Lytton Report) the Manchurian venture; violated international prohibitions – detailed in the 1922 Nine Power Treaty, to which Japan was party – on gaining unilateral advantages in China; provoked and then tangled with Soviet armed forces in border skirmishes; upheld a provocative imperial idea, embodied in the Greater East Asia Co-Prosperity Sphere. Couched in the language of Asian grievance against Western trespass and in modernization aspirations, this doctrine proclaimed a new East, to be rejuvenated by a spiritually energized Japan.[1] Matsuoka Yosuke, foreign minister in 1940–1941, explained Japan's variant of *mission civilisatrice*: "We are endeavoring to initiate an era of enduring peace and unlimited prosperity, based on justice, equity and mutuality in ... Asia, where we firmly believe we have a great mission as the civilizing and stabilizing force. We stand for peace and order."[2] Matsuoka admitted that the violence involved in organizing this improved order was regrettable. Still, he insisted, one should not lose sight of the brilliance to be achieved: "[Japan's] employment of armed force is an act looking beyond the immediate present. The sword she has drawn is intended to be nothing other than a life-giving sword that destroys evil and makes justice manifest."[3]

To Matsuoka and other apologists, Japan's proposed new order, as applied to China, meant the people of that enormous but palsied country should ally themselves with the dynamo of the East. Their cooperation would hasten a glad day that would benefit all Asians while routing Western intruders and scattering their conceits.[4] The West, as implied in Amo Eiji's 1934 statement and subsequent (more authoritative) iterations, should keep a correct political distance from China, a place of primary concern to Japan and intimately related to its future welfare. Western missionary and business interests were welcome, in theory, to fair shares of China. That country, though, had also to be seen as bound by mystical cords of fate to Japan and of overriding strategic-military-economic interest to Tokyo. China functioned as buffer against the USSR and its communist contagion, was a potentially lucrative market, contained investment opportunities, and had become a favored destination for industrious emigrants. Matsuoka reflected a core Tokyo conviction when, in December 1940, he pronounced: "The fate of China is largely a question of sentiment to the Americans, but to us it constitutes a truly vital issue affecting, as it does, the very existence of our Empire."[5] Japanese authorities had earlier recognized Wang Jingwei as head of the Chinese government, a proxy for Tokyo rule as "legitimate" as Puyi, titular emperor of Manchukuo.

Violent changes to the East Asian status quo dismayed Secretary of State Henry Stimson. He proclaimed America's non-recognition in 1932 of Japanese presumption in China and decried Tokyo's sponsorship of the Manchukuo regime ("puppet"). These were anathema, said he, to America's Open Door policy, insulted the 1928 Kellogg–Briand outlawry of war, and defied the provisions of the Nine Power Treaty. Five years later, in response to Japan's assault upon China in undeclared war, FDR promoted an informal embargo on warplanes to Tokyo and invoked his "quarantine" that – like Stimson before – sought to check aggression by censure.[6] Verbal condemnations, coupled with increased unhappiness about the exclusion of US enterprises from Japanese-controlled China, triggered Washington's escalating actions and a stiffening containment line.[7] Among them was the administration's decision in July 1939 to abrogate the 1911 Japan–US trade treaty (done 26 January 1940). A ban on the sale of scrap iron and metals followed in September. More stingingly in July 1941 – following Japan's seizure of all of France's Indochina possessions and

in light of continuing military operations against China – FDR issued
an executive order that froze Japanese assets in America. He also
placed a lid on the sale of oil and aviation fuel to Japan. To him, in
language that he once used for Joseph Grew's edification, the main
players in Tokyo had "fail[ed] to speak as civilized twentieth century
human beings."[8] Now, evidently, they should pay the price.

Grew worked against the prevailing trend. He hoped from
1932, when he arrived on the Tokyo scene amidst the Manchurian
turmoil, to prevent an implosion of Japanese–US relations, a project
that became his absolute preoccupation after the 1937 commencement
of Sino-Japanese violence. He later counted the onset of Japanese–US
fighting as his own failure, likening his lost labors to "having been
wiped out as if by a typhoon."[9]

Grew and Embassy Tokyo

Grew personified the Foreign Service as it had evolved during the
interwar period, melding elements of meritocracy with aristocratic
ethos. Scion of a prominent Boston business family, he had prepped
at Groton. There he imbibed the tenets of "manly" Christianity and the
imperative of shouldering civic duty, defined as a version of noblesse
oblige.[10] Adhering to family tradition, he attended Harvard University
(class of 1902), where he specialized in the Fly Club, athletics, and the
Crimson. He was satisfied with grades of the gentleman C type. He did
not permit academic studies to interfere with his social life. He differed
not at all in these respects from his fellow Grotonian and *Crimson*
colleague, Franklin Roosevelt, two years Grew's junior. Handsome,
and an avid outdoorsman (golf to hunting), Grew took a post-graduation
tour around the world. His adventures included the stalking and shooting of a tiger in China. This exploit won the admiration of President
Theodore Roosevelt who then championed the young man through the
early stages of his diplomatic career.[11] Marriage to the elegant Alice de
Vermandois Perry brought Grew into closer contact with American
wealth and anchored him even more securely in upper society. He
accepted uncritically, as a matter of family legacy, the mild strictures
of the Episcopal Church and the Republican party's precepts.

As a personality, Grew was blessed with optimism, averse to
flamboyance, unfailingly polite. Albeit slightly distracted at times, he

was not drawn to abstract ideas or given to theorizing. He preferred physical exercise and light fiction (mysteries, adventure stories) to systematic or deep reflection.[12] Partial deafness rendered him hesitant in conversations, poor material for high-table repartee. A streak of social snobbery inhibited him from inquiring more closely than he might into the attitudes or conditions of common folk in America or elsewhere. Yet he was not indifferent to faults of the privileged class, particularly its sense of entitlement. He dedicated himself to the ideal of a professional Foreign Service – a pooling of genuine talent – with uniform standards and integrity, unencumbered by dilettantes, party donors, or cronies of the White House occupant.[13] Christened by analysts as "father" of the career Foreign Service, Grew made its rise to respectability his cause, the third part of his personal trinity (along with Groton and Harvard).[14]

His pre-Japan career, with allowance for minor slips, went from strength to strength. He entered the diplomatic corps in 1904 and, after a series of junior-grade assignments (in Cairo, Mexico City, St. Petersburg, Berlin), obtained the rank of chargé d'affaires in Vienna, where he served at the moment when the United States and Austria-Hungary severed relations (9 April 1917). He afterwards briefly headed the State Department's division of West European affairs.

Grew assumed a secondary but useful part at the 1919 peace conference in Paris. There, with equivalent rank of minister, he applied his administrative skills to the daily requirements of the US delegation. His widely admired competence in Paris helped him win appointment as minister to Denmark in 1920, then minister to Switzerland (where he dealt discreetly with aspects of the informal League of Nations–US relationship). As American delegate to the Lausanne conference, he helped smooth the way for the July 1923 treaty between Turkey and the Allied powers, which formally ended belligerency between them. He also negotiated a treaty at the time that would have advanced US railroad and oil interests in Turkey (but failed Senate ratification). Grew next served as undersecretary of state, 1924–1927, during which time he helped implement the 1924 Rogers Act whose purpose was to reform the diplomatic service, combining the diplomatic and consular bureaucracies into a single Foreign Service.[15] His dealings with Secretary of State Frank Kellogg were poor, spoiled by policy differences (regarding China) and personal incompatibility. Grew was plainly glad to accept his first full-fledged ambassadorship (1927–1932), to Mustafa Kemal's modernizing Turkey.[16]

President Herbert Hoover validated the professional idea when he selected Grew for Tokyo in 1932, the first such assignment of a career man to a world-class power. He presented his credentials in June of that election year. Lest replaced by an FDR appointee in 1933, Grew wrote a timely letter to his Groton–Harvard classmate, "Dear Frank." It gently reminded him of their common ties (Fly Club too) and pledged Grew's willingness to stay in harness for however long the new president wanted.[17] Roosevelt was glad not to disturb matters, as a satisfactory person led the Tokyo mission during tense times. Grew remained at this post until Pearl Harbor.

His diplomatic experience, solid though it was, prepared him little for an East Asian errand. Grew was proficient in French and German, but knew not a word of Japanese and, in his Tokyo years, acquired only a smattering. He did enjoy a few distinct advantages, however. First, his wife ("my teammate"), who had earlier lived in Japan with her scholar-father, knew the language. She was also sufficiently familiar with local customs and mores that she could instruct her husband in them. Related to Commodore Matthew Perry, whose 1853 visit inaugurated Japanese–US relations, Alice Grew enjoyed uncommonly high standing in Tokyo society that in subtle ways benefited her husband.[18]

The embassy possessed a staff of fifty-three Americans by December 1941, from radio operator upward. Grew's people included accomplished Japanese language officers, notably Eugene Dooman. Born in Osaka of Protestant missionaries, and reared in Japan, he served as counselor of embassy during 1937–1941. Opinionated, exacting of subordinates, and fully at ease in Japanese company, he was alter-ego to Grew, practically his co-ambassador ("my fidus Achates"). Dooman shared his chief's overarching goal: the preservation of Japanese–US amity.[19] As for other embassy officers, Grew did not seek their affection but treated them fairly. They brimmed with loyalty. Charles Bohlen, who served briefly as the embassy's Soviet expert, admired Grew as "a thorough professional." John Emmerson, an officer with impressive Japanese language credentials, judged Grew "distinguished," the exemplar of an ambassador "of the old school."[20]

Consistent with State Department creed, Grew held that diplomacy constituted America's "first line of national defense."[21] Its success meant the achievement of national ends by means other than violent. An accredited envoy, to this end, should concentrate heart and mind on

fostering sympathetic understanding between hosts and home government.[22] Intellectual flexibility, imperturbability, and psychological
suppleness were required of an ambassador, not legalism or literal mindedness. Sanctimoniousness or reliance on any brand of supposed universal ethics also constituted a dead-end, Grew felt.[23] These attitudes, plus
faith that diplomats and political leaders could funnel history's "blind
forces" into safe channels, stamped his approach to Japan: "constructive
conciliation." He hoped thereby to contribute to the stability of East
Asia, an area, in his view, organically connected to the economic-political
flourishing of the United States. Nothing, he believed, could be more
"utterly futile" or tragic than a US–Japanese war.[24]

Peace quest

Grew was well practiced in diplomacy's ceremonial and social side and
viewed it as useful lubricant to that serious business transacted between
governments. His attentiveness to this matter in Tokyo meant that, by
the start of Sino-Japanese combat, he was familiar to the political class
and resident foreigners.[25] He, in turn, had come to feel at home among
Japan's elites (court set, ranking naval/military officers, *Gaimusho*
ministers, *zaibatsu* captains). Through them he came to appreciate
the exalted position enjoyed by the emperor – sacred object and foun-
tainhead of national unity, point of justification for people eager to
enhance Japan's status.[26] Grew's Japanese education also encompassed
the nation's contradictory attitude toward US policies. It mixed gratitude for relief assistance after the 1923 earthquake (which killed more
than 100,000 people) with disquiet. The latter being born of Woodrow
Wilson's blocking a racial equality clause in the League of Nations
covenant, passage of the 1924 Immigration Act that discriminated
against would-be Japanese newcomers, and implementation of the
1930 Smoot–Hawley Tariff (which reduced Japanese silk imports, thus
harming Tokyo's economy during a period of downturn)
     Grew termed himself to Japanese officials as a stalwart "friend"
of their island nation. His efforts to humanize the Washington–Tokyo
connection involved recruitment of Japanese chums to share his golfing
passion; he once praised the country to Emperor Hirohito as "a golfer's
paradise."[27] Grew escorted baseball stars – Babe Ruth, Lefty O'Doul – in
their 1934 tour of Japan. He wryly admitted that the Bambino, swarmed

2 Joseph C. Grew.

by admirers, was "a great deal more effective Ambassador that I could ever be."[28] Grew tried in vain to grasp the ritual and appeal of Sumo wrestling. He expressed warm gratitude for Japanese help in the attempt to locate and rescue Amelia Earhart after she and her plane mysteriously disappeared (1937) over the Pacific.[29] He was moved by the cordial reception that Tokyo personalities accorded Helen Keller when she visited Japan as part of a crusade to heighten awareness of people afflicted by deafness and blindness.[30] He helped organize in 1939 the transfer by US warship to Japan of the remains of Ambassador Saito Hiroshi, who had died in the United States, and participated in the Buddhist rites of Saito's funeral.[31] As doyen of the diplomatic corps, Grew offered that body's congratulations in 1940 on the occasion of the 2,600th anniversary of Japan's founding. He, meanwhile, cultivated relations within the diplomatic community. He got on well with Britain's envoy, Sir Robert Craigie. Despite distaste for the Nazis, Grew even had tolerable dealings with Hitler's ambassador, the obtuse Herbert von Dirksen.[32]

Grew perceived Japan in the 1930s as politically unstable ground. Upon it forces of moderation and decency (identified by him with Arita Hachiro, Prince Konoye Fumimaro, Admiral Viscount Saito Makoto, Yonai Mitsumasa) struggled with those of militarism and chauvinism, led by Tojo.[33] The former, Grew thought, looked hopefully to cooperation with the democratic West while the latter's proclivity was dictatorial and instinctively sought cooperation with the Third Reich, per the November 1936 Anti-Comintern Pact. The pendulum swing (Grew's imagery) between these two Japanese groupings was continuous. The United States in this circumstance, then, had to take actions helpful to the moderates and, whenever possible, frustrate the cause of militant nationalism lest it hijack the state.[34] Washington, meantime, should – with reference to the balance of power and the needs of commerce and Christian missionaries – take diplomatic steps to secure America's Pacific possessions and East Asian flank. Calibrated adjustments in this circumstance did not equal abject submission. Grew averred that these were the only plausible devices to employ in a difficult setting, which he likened to "living on a volcano."[35]

The assassinations that occurred in Tokyo during the 1930s demonstrated, as nothing else could, Japan's political volatility. They unnerved civilian leaders and appalled Grew. The most notorious instance occurred in February 1936, when young army officers (plus their 1,400 men) occupied government buildings and murdered previous officials or ones actually serving, including a former prime minister and the incumbent finance minister, Takahashi Korekiyo. "These (rampages) have stirred us terribly," Grew recorded in his diary.[36] After anonymous threats were made upon his life, he took the precaution of packing a pistol.[37]

Smoldering Sino-Japanese relations, meanwhile, burst into flame as Chiang refused in autumn 1936 to comply with Tokyo's demands: to attach Imperial troops to Chinese units engaged against local communists, to admit "advisers" into Chinese ministries, to cede "autonomy" to northern (Japanese-penetrated) provinces. Mutual recriminations and thickening suspicion led to the Marco Polo bridge "incident," July 1937, and the eruption of full-scale hostilities. By the end of the month, Japanese forces had seized Tientsin and Beijing. Shanghai fell in November. The capital, Nanjing, succumbed in December. The emperor's navy also imposed a blockade of the entire Chinese coastline. Grew counseled that the US response to this intensified violence should be one of neutrality – not an easy position to defend as Shanghai was bombed, Nanjing terrorized, and American lives and property lost. He himself thought Japan culpable.[38]

Grew reasoned that the United States, preoccupied with its own economic-social woes, had neither the means nor stamina for influencing the course of this new Asian war. Better, therefore, for Washington not to preach or pretend to have solutions for ending it. A transparently flimsy stance would only aggravate matters and bring discredit upon Roosevelt's administration. The world did not need another version of platitudinous non-recognition policy. Americans, for their part, should bide their time until saner elements in the Diet regained the upper hand. They would surely terminate, or at least limit, the militarists' China adventure, one that over time could only sap national strength and alienate Japan from global society. Even as Tokyo's armies were bound to confront problems in China of boundless space and gritty resistance (ingredients for quagmire), and pay a steep financial price for waging an imprudent war, US interests did not – Grew advised State Department superiors – lie in Japanese setback. That country, not China, torn by warlords and communist insurgents, was better able to ensure order in northeastern Asia and blunt Soviet influence.

Furthermore, Japan was America's leading trade partner in the Far East and likely to remain so into the deep future, not China of wretched poverty and political shambles.[39] Grew reminded Washington in 1938 that US exports to Japan during the previous year exceeded by more than five times that sold to China. Imports were double those from China. Japan was America's third best customer in the world, China a lowly sixteenth. In fact, he noted approvingly, commerce with Japan equaled US exports to all of South America.[40] Imperial Japan, in effect, was not only a pillar of geopolitical stability, but also a major player in America's trading economy. China was a minor economic-political factor, its theoretically huge market a pipedream.

Grew's preferred approach confronted increasingly severe tests in 1937. The first sprang from FDR's so-called quarantine declaration on 5 October. Grew interpreted it and the commotion stirred by Roosevelt's remarks as prelude to the leveling of stiff penalties against Japan. They would entail, he guessed, economic sanctions, international ostracism, and an irreversible degrading of Washington–Tokyo relations. "There goes everything I have tried to accomplish in my entire mission to Japan," Grew grumbled after reading the text of FDR's speech.[41] He responded sharply to Hull and the White House: the imposing of sanctions on Japan would cause more grief than good. They would, he argued, strengthen the rhetorical appeal of militarists in Tokyo and deal a body blow to moderates. Luckily, from Grew's standpoint, FDR's proposed "quarantine" of aggressor states proved a chimera. It dissolved into vagueness while Congress's iterations of neutrality legislation inhibited an activist policy.

The Japanese bombing of Shanghai shocked people everywhere, not yet psychologically hardened to aerial assaults upon lightly defended urban centers. Grew called it "one of the most horrible episodes in modern times."[42] Among the 1,700 people killed were an American sailor aboard the USS *Augusta* and a young scholar, Robert Reischauer (son of missionaries and brother to the future historian/ diplomat Edwin Reischauer). Other Americans peacefully residing in the city were wounded, including eighteen sailors aboard the *Augusta*, or lost property. The US government by late October had evacuated more than 4,500 citizens (businessmen, educators, Protestant/Catholic proselytizers) from the expanding zone of Sino-Japanese fighting.[43] Grew's concern, one that he repeatedly shared with Japanese officials, was that these damages were exciting US opinion. It could leap into vengeful mood should a substantial US enterprise or ship be again hit. In this connection, he reminded the *Gaimusho* of the USS *Maine*'s explosion in Havana harbor and concatenation of events that led to the 1898 Spanish–American war.[44]

The sinking of the US gunboat *Panay* on the Yangtze (plus three Standard Oil tankers crowded with Chinese evacuees) by warplanes on 12 December climaxed a year in which American nationals suffered as incidental victims of Japanese actions. Stationed near Nanjing during that city's siege, the *Panay* had been operating as a floating office of the US embassy and site of refuge.[45] Washington seethed with rage upon learning of the ship's destruction and of its naval/civilian casualties. A rupture in Japanese–US relations seemed imminent. Grew prepared mentally to leave Tokyo.

Without instructions but at his own initiative, he sought a conference with Foreign Minister Hirota Koki upon learning of the *Panay*'s fate. The distraught minister apologized profusely for the vessel's loss and toll in human lives. Thereupon both men determined to calm the situation. The Japanese envoy in Washington, Saito, also assured Hull of the emperor's sorrow over the event and eagerness to make amends. These were subsequently made in accordance with FDR's demands. Japan promised to pay indemnities (more than $2,220,000), to discipline those people responsible for the attack, and pledged to prevent similar happenings in future.[46]

Though gratified to have played a role in defusing the *Panay* crisis, Grew remained anxious lest the Tokyo government misunderstand the depth of US alarm. He consequently denounced the naval and air assaults on Shanghai, the injuries visited upon Nanjing, and later (June 1938) the aerial bombardment of Canton. Not only were US interests and lives in these cities put in jeopardy, he explained, but also the suffering of Chinese innocents offended American opinion. "Japan's reputation can never recover from these things," he privately concluded.[47]

Despite these discouragements, Grew did not lose sight of his main objective: to maintain a semblance of trust between Tokyo and Washington. He also managed to persuade himself, although supporting evidence was scant, that Japanese advocates of empire-in-China were starting to lose the public's confidence and tempting Hirohito's disfavor; moderate personalities might eventually seize the government's top portfolios in the wake of protracted fighting against Chiang. After a 1939 furlough and meeting with FDR, Grew gave notice to Japanese political/business leaders of thinking in Washington.

He delivered (19 October 1939) a tightly composed speech to the America–Japan Society (AJS) in Tokyo. Grew hoped by his remarks to bolster the resistance of moderates to those military-minded people who were tugging the country in the direction of Germany and confrontation with European empires (British, French, Dutch) in Asia. The time seemed auspicious to him; the revolving door of Japanese governments had stopped, at least momentarily. Ten prime ministers, incidentally, served during the span of his ambassadorship. The political leanings of the current incumbent, Abe Nobuyuki, were not overtly one thing or another. Admiral Nomura Kichisaburo, thought to be friendly toward the United States, was foreign minister. Additionally, the recently concluded Molotov–Ribbentrop nonaggression treaty (August 1939), wholly unanticipated in Tokyo, suggested that Germany could not be counted upon should Japan find itself plunged into full-scale conflict with its old nemesis, Russia.[48]

Referring to war's outbreak in Europe, Grew in high tone taught his AJS audience: "When the structure of international good faith, when the reliance of mankind and government upon the inviolability of the pledged word becomes undermined and collapses, when might makes right and force becomes an instrument of national policy rather then discussion and settlement of disputes by peaceful means, then civilization crumbles."[49] He also dwelt at length upon the bewilderment felt in the White House over Japan's actions in China, especially those causing harm to US interests and in contravention of the universally recognized principle of equality in commercial opportunity. American enterprises had become circumscribed by restrictive policies in zones under Imperial sway. Japan seemed intent, he suggested, in establishing a closed economy on mainland Asia at the cost of legitimate US desiderata. Moreover, he stressed, the trampling of treaties by Japan and its reported brutalities "shocked" popular opinion, to say nothing of the hardships suffered by US citizens in China.[50] He closed his remarks with this admonition on the need for Tokyo–Washington cooperation: "In a world of chaos I plead for ... a relationship which, if it can be preserved, can bring only good to Japan and the United States."[51]

Most of the US press praised Grew's speech. Editors hailed it as useful for placing Japan on notice that US patience was not infinite or to be abused. Roosevelt offered congratulations too. Copies of Grew's remarks, meantime, made their way to government departments in Tokyo and were read by the prime minister and cabinet officers. Despite divided opinion within the *Gaimusho* and complaints from various Japanese news media, Nomura indicated to the embassy a willingness to review outstanding matters.[52] Grew surmised that his AJS address had made a dent on Japanese thinking and so informed FDR:

My speech ... has at least started people thinking, talking and writing about the present parlous state of American-Japanese relations. Many influential Japanese have welcomed it as having come at the right moment. Some of the newspapers have ... intimate[d] in veiled language that there may be some merit in the American point of view. One prominent Member of Parliament said to me: "Your speech started the ball rolling and we shall keep it rolling."[53]

Subsequent Grew–Nomura talks, alas, did not break the impasse. Matters only worsened. Japanese soldiers in the course of China campaigns humiliated Americans (with slapping, desecrations of the US flag) living in isolated areas. Even worse, the numbers of wounded – a few fatally – piled higher. Understandably, US businessmen and missionaries felt squeezed and vulnerable in Japanese-occupied zones. Ambassador Nelson Johnson in China recorded numerous harrowing episodes for Washington's edification. Then conveyed to Grew, these formed the basis of his markedly vigorous protests to Tokyo officialdom, itself becoming palpably authoritarian ("New Structure"). The last political party was dissolved in August 1940.[54]

Grew's optimism in diplomacy had noticeably faded, but not disappeared, by September 1940. He was disconcerted as Japanese leaders showed themselves giddy over German victories in Europe, which implied fresh opportunities in Asia against the defeated French (Indochina) and Dutch (Indonesia), and the embattled British (Hong Kong).[55] Having come to share the determination of FDR and Stimson to shore up Britain and preserve the Pacific status quo, Grew dropped his opposition to the use of sanctions to slow Japanese expansion.[56] He sent (12 September 1940) what he dubbed his "green light" telegram to Secretary Hull: only unwavering US resolution and, if necessary, the application of force would impress upon ministers, such as mercurial Foreign Secretary Matsuoka, the limits of US indulgence and Tokyo's concomitant need for self-restraint.[57] The United States should, therefore, gradually impose economic measures on Japan that would supersede the existing moral embargo (announced in 1938) on the export of warplanes and spare parts.[58] Japan might, then, adopt a less aggressive line in Asia, distance itself from Germany, and become more circumspect toward the United States. The alternative, Grew predicted, would be a growing number of Japanese–US confrontations. They might culminate in a sudden war led by swaggering soldiers of the Kwantung Army type, who had already led their country into the China maze. In December 1940, to the just-reelected FDR, Grew restated his aim: "If ... we can bring about the eventual discrediting of [Tokyo's] present leaders, a regeneration of thought may ultimately take shape in [Japan], permitting the resumption of normal relations with us and leading to a readjustment of the whole Pacific problem."[59]

Just two weeks passed between Grew's "green light" message and Japan's adherence to the Tripartite Pact, signed by Matsuoka in

Berlin.[60] The event upset Grew, who had lobbied Japanese officials, successfully he thought, against getting cozy with Germany (and Italy). Nevertheless, he soon saw through the cloud of his disappointment to the pact's main import, to forestall US intervention in either the European or Asian wars.[61] Not privy to the treaty's secret clauses that qualified German and Japanese commitments to each other should either party find itself at war with the United States, he did guess that the alliance was a hollow one, based on expediency but devoid of shared strategy. He believed that Japan could be detached from Germany (and Italy), in which connection he told Tokyo ministers that their link to Germany boded ill for themselves; it placed them at direct odds with the United States. Japan, he warned Matsuoka, upon his return to Tokyo, might soon become a "satellite" of the Third Reich or – Grew mixing his metaphors – be thrown upon "the rocks." Germany, the ambassador observed, was not positioned to help Japan in East Asia in 1940 or later.[62]

However bleak the turn in international life – Japan looking covetously at Southeast Asia, Tokyo snug with Berlin, Germany and the USSR cooperating in eastern Europe, Britain in extremis – Grew could not rid himself of this idea. The ingenuity of diplomats like himself could yet untangle the Gordian knot of suspicion and spare the United States from the hazards of Pacific war.[63] In this task, he reasoned, one might be aided by unexpected events, as when Germany turned on its erstwhile Soviet ally in June 1941.

BARBAROSSA placed Prince Konoye's cabinet in a quandary as the Germans invaded a country with which Japan had recently signed (13 April 1941) a neutrality treaty.[64] How now Berlin's credibility and good faith, Grew insinuated to Matsuoka (and his successors Toyoda Teijiro, Togo Shigenori). Hitler had failed to consult with Japan, or even notify it in advance, about a momentous undertaking with far-reaching implications. Grew and Dooman also let *Gaimusho* officers know in spring/summer of 1941 that a Japanese attack upon the USSR or Britain's naval stronghold in Singapore would dash for good any chance of a sound Japanese–US future.[65] Might army and navy diehards, Grew calculated hopefully, therefore temper their ambition or get reined in by their sober brother officers and civilian betters?

Simultaneous with FDR's clamp down on trade with Japan in summer 1941 was the unfolding of negotiations in Washington between Hull and Tokyo's emissaries: the former foreign minister,

Admiral Nomura, and Kurusu Subaru, the latter sent to assist the genial but not entirely competent sailorman. Grew was a distant witness to these desultory proceedings. Only occasionally did the State Department consult him, never telling him, incidentally, about MAGIC and the decryption of Tokyo's coded diplomatic communications. He complained at length about being kept in the dark. Nevertheless, he followed the confidential talks as best he could with devouring interest; he prayed that a bargain could be struck.[66] It might have encompassed a formula involving the suspension of sanctions and restoration of normal trade. These would be swapped for Japan's de facto separation from the Axis and withdrawal from French Indochina and China, the schedules and completeness of which proved fatal sticking points. They were grounded in Chiang's objection to any deal that might abandon his country to Japan, and to anxiety in Tokyo about purported encirclement by the American, British, Dutch, and Soviet powers, none of which cared about the dependence of Japan's economy on foreign natural resources (oil, tin, rubber).

Unenthused by what he did glean of the Hull–Nomura talks, Grew encouraged FDR in September 1941 to pursue another initiative. Grew adopted as his own an idea first floated by a couple of Maryknoll priests (Bishop James Walsh, Father James Drought) and their Japanese associates: Roosevelt and Prime Minister Konoye should arrange a summit conference in the Pacific, perhaps in Hawaii or near the Alaska shoreline, to negotiate a comprehensive settlement.[67] The Hull–Nomura exercise was, so Grew's brief went, barren of results. Only a direct meeting between heads of state could revitalize the diplomatic moment before it slipped away. The Churchill–Roosevelt meeting (9–12 August 1941) aboard warships at Placentia Bay could serve as a model and might yield comparably good results. Impressed by Konoye's assurances to keep militants in check, Grew wrote to FDR on 22 September: "Prince Konoye ... in the face of bitter antagonism from extremist and pro-Axis elements in the country is [bravely] working for an improvement in Japan's relations with the United States ... I am convinced that he now means business and will go as far as possible, without incurring open rebellion in Japan, to reach a reasonable understanding with us."[68] Grew also ventured, with an eye to FDR's sense of flair: "The opportunity is here presented ... for an act of the highest statesmanship ... with the possible overcoming ... of apparently insurmountable obstacles to peace hereafter in the

Pacific."[69] Even Konoye, an indecisive and cautious personality, harried by army–navy zealots, recognized the wisdom of a Pacific conference. He secretly relayed his commitment to Grew and Roosevelt.[70] The president, at first, was captivated by the idea.

Hull had been incensed at his exclusion from the August Atlantic/Churchill meeting, which his *bête noire* Sumner Welles had attended. Hull may have reckoned that he would be similarly uninvited to a Pacific rendezvous, his work with Nomura discredited or tacitly dismissed as superfluous.[71] Hull did, in any case, supported by his Far Eastern affairs advisor, Stanley Hornbeck, warn FDR against a meeting with Tokyo leaders before the essentials of a Japanese–US agreement had been decided. Without the preliminaries in place, the possibilities for misunderstanding or embarrassment, according to the Hull–Hornbeck line, would be legion. Harmony in the Pacific could not be advanced by a failed conference – wiser to let the Washington talks take their course to produce something broad and durable.[72] The gradual economic stifling of Japan, meanwhile, was sure to have an impact on the thinking of Konoye (then Tojo, prime minister as of 18 October) and push him in the direction of meaningful accommodation. Roosevelt ultimately accepted this counsel; he dropped the idea in October of a Pacific summit. The Hull–Nomura conversations lumbered on to their end, past the 29 November date set by the Japanese government for a peaceful settlement with the United States. On 7 December the secretary spoke his last words of exasperation to Nomura (who had previously basked in his acquaintanceship with FDR) and – in bumbling fashion – had sought peace with the United States and distance from Germany.

Washington's rejection of the proposed Pacific conference left Grew incredulous. Nothing would have been lost, he felt, and potentially much salvaged, including – he must have whispered to himself – his long service in Tokyo. Yet a stubborn fact obtained, one that he faintly supposed but did not grasp until too late: he had neither voice nor credibility in Washington on how best to handle Japan.

One-time college teacher in China (1909–1913), and major influence on Hull's attitude toward East Asia, Hornbeck belittled Embassy Tokyo. It did not understand China's vast potential for economic development and outlet for US businesses. The embassy had become wooly-headed, overplaying the putative differences between moderates and expansionists and waiting for the ascendancy of the former.[73] The embassy was soft on Japanese expansionism, naïve to wager on a Berlin–Tokyo split, too tolerant of Japanese claims to being misinterpreted or the guiltless victim of Western bigotry.[74] Grew, so went Hornbeck's critique, was gullible, having harbored thoughts about an imagined Japanese–US rapprochement conjured by Konoye, whose record as prime minister (June 1937–January 1939, July 1940–October 1941) coincided both with Japan's war on China and pact with Germany.[75] Grew and his staff, Dooman especially, were guilty of having gone native, of being seduced by a politically trivial minority that spoke only for itself but exercised no control over the real power behind the Imperial throne: the naval and military cabal. It was, instances of internal bickering aside, united behind this idea, charged Hornbeck: a self-sufficient empire enjoying unimpeded access to plentiful raw resources. In short, Grew and colleagues had lost perspective. They had no inkling of the bigger picture as understood by attentive Washington:

> *The Embassy has over and over asked the American Government to deal gently with Japan or to make concessions to Japan in order not to discourage and in order to encourage the moderate element toward an achievement by that element of a preponderant influence – long represented as a possibility just around the corner – in the determining of Japanese policy. The White House and the Department of State have paid a great deal of attention to this line of advice and suggestion from the Embassy. This government has hoped that the talked-about "moderate element" might achieve some influence. But nothing tangible has come of our hopes in that direction. And, in my opinion, nothing will come of them ...*
>
> *Japanese policy has been made, is being made, and for a long time to come will be made by hardheaded ... leaders who are weighing and re-weighing every point of potential advantage or disadvantage to Japan in the international situation. Those leaders can be influenced to some extent by the views of Japanese persons who advocate caution and long-range foresight, but they are not going to be supplanted by or compelled to knuckle under to the small minority which constitutes the so-called "moderate element."*

The language which is being spoken in official circles in Japan today is the language of force – military force, economic force. The Japanese will give up their program of conquest by force only when their present leaders become convinced that they have more to lose by persisting in that program than to gain. They will yield not to persuasion but to fear.[76]

Hornbeck did not falter in his confidence. He *knew* in autumn 1941 that a Konoye–FDR conference would be a purposeless exercise.[77] He *knew* that the economic suffocating of Japan would become so unbearable that the country's leadership would finally desist from its China course, retreat from Indochina, shelve plans for an Indonesia lunge, and renounce the Axis alliance. And Japan would assiduously avoid war with the United States.[78] Nervous Nellies in Embassy Tokyo, panting about the need to negotiate with Tokyo and not push Japan into a corner, would learn that their worries were misplaced. Hornbeck assured Hull on 27 November: "The Japanese Government does not desire or intend or expect to have forthwith armed conflict with the United States. The Japanese Government ... will endeavor to avoid attacking or being attacked by the United States."[79]

Ten days later came the Pearl Harbor surprise. Vice Admiral's Nagumo's carrier strike force (*kido butai*) left 2,400 US servicemen and civilians dead; 1,200 were wounded. Eight battleships were sunk or severely damaged. Three light cruisers, three destroyers, plus other vessels were also sunk or suffered injury. A total of 165 planes were destroyed outright, another 130 disabled. Japanese naval and military forces meanwhile assaulted the Philippines, where they killed, captured, or routed the combined Filipino–US command of General Douglas MacArthur. On FDR's orders, he fled (12 March 1942) Corregidor with vows to return.[80]

***

Upon the issuance of Tokyo–Washington war declarations, armed guards restricted Grew and his staff to the embassy compound. They remained there for six months, until exchanged for Japanese diplomats interned in the United States.[81] Wives and children had earlier been evacuated, except for the spouse of the naval attaché and the ambassadress who had elected to stay on. The tedium of confinement was broken by play upon an improvised golf course. Once an errant ball, according to lore, had the good sense to bonk a passing German diplomat. Organized study of East Asian history and Japanese-language classes also helped to boost morale, otherwise eroded by uncertainty and loneliness. The Americans also tried to snatch reliable information from broadcasts by the local press and propaganda apparatus as they reveled in a string of Japanese feats: Bataan, Guam, Java, Singapore. From his embassy perch, Grew witnessed the first US air strike against Tokyo (18 April 1942), conducted by Colonel James Doolittle's B-25 bombers. The wing of a hospital, misidentified as a proper military target, was smashed when a bomb hit, evidently released from the plane piloted by Doolittle.[82]

Overall, the diplomats did not suffer at the hands of their Japanese keepers, many of whom were solicitous of their charges and treated them respectfully, although in conditions of mounting privation.[83] Grew and company were, meanwhile, struck by the somber mood and lack of demonstration in Tokyo streets after news of Pearl Harbor arrived (in contrast with the spontaneous expressions of pride that had followed the 1937 capture of Nanjing).[84] On the Swedish ship *Gripsholm*, which bore the diplomats (plus other formerly incarcerated Americans) back to the United States, a Methodist bishop taking passage asked for divine guidance in effecting Japanese–US reconciliation, not a request that won much assent from nerve-worn people just released from captivity. The United States, he intoned, had acted hastily after Pearl Harbor; he thought the embassy personnel, beginning with Grew, had been mistaken to endorse war against Japan.[85]

Whether a Pacific conference as envisioned by Grew, featuring FDR and Konoye, would have averted Japanese–US violence must remain a matter of conjecture. The ambassador himself had nothing specific to recommend by way of agenda at such a meeting. Yet he believed, from December 1941 to the end of his days, that direct talks between national leaders would have delayed war's onset or, perhaps, entirely cut the impasse in Japanese–US relations, ushering a new era of concord. Grew decided not to unburden himself on this subject to Roosevelt at any time after Pearl Harbor – thus retaining the president's favor – but did believe that pinched White House imagination and a dearth of courage resulted in an avoidable war. Konoye was prepared to accept US "terms whatever they might be," Grew had convinced himself, based on conversations with the prince in autumn 1941. In return for normalized commercial relations with America, an unfreezing of Japanese assets, and resumption of access to petroleum products, Tokyo would likely have agreed to withdraw troops from Indochina and most of China (except for a few "face-saving" garrisons in inner Mongolia and northern provinces). Konoye could have carried the Japanese nation, Grew maintained, including recalcitrant naval and military officers. Such a Japanese–US agreement would have had the added benefit of separating Japan from Germany, the Tripartite Pact becoming "a dead letter." He held that only Hitler, who wanted Japan and the US embroiled in war, would have been disappointed by a Pacific meeting. What was needed at the critical time was bold gesture, Grew privately fumed, not "quibbling" between Hull and Nomura over arid formulas.[86] The ambassador fired in an unsent letter to FDR (14 August 1942):

> *There are some things which can be sensed by the man on the spot which cannot be sensed by those at a distance, and I am completely convinced that my reports as to what the Japanese Government was prepared to do and was able to do and would have done had the meeting between yourself and Prince Konoye taken place were fundamentally accurate and sound. It seems to me pertinent to add that, even if, despite my belief, the Japanese Government had found it impossible to implement any agreement reached with the government of the United States, the longer war between the two countries could have been postponed the more it would have been to the advantage of our vital national interests. There was in my opinion, no possibility that the Japanese Government could have jockeyed us into a less favorable position than we were in when the meeting between you and Prince Konoye might have taken place, for we would certainly have relaxed our own economic measures against Japan only gradually and* pari passu *with Japan's loyal implementation of such commitments as she might undertake. The leverage would have remained constantly in our hands.*[87]

Not only did Grew choose not to confront FDR in the tone or substance of the above statement. Prudence also inhibited Grew from making any public comment during the war that could have been construed to indicate disagreement between himself and the administration on the desirability of a Pacific summit. Never more than a casual friend of FDR's, he was not about to jeopardize what line he did enjoy by openly questioning White House policies.[88]

Preservation of relations with Roosevelt allowed Grew to retain a responsible position in wartime Washington. During the first months of his post-Tokyo career, he served as special assistant to the secretary of state. This assignment centered on the making of speeches to diverse audiences (bankers, health professionals, educators) about Japan and the need for resolve to disable its militarist clique. A much-sought speaker, to whom romance attached as he had been recently in the enemy's clutches, Grew gave 250 talks to groups within the first year of his repatriation.[89] He refined on the certainty of US victory while condemning the harshness of Japanese rule in conquered lands. He delivered himself of opinions about the Japanese as immature, easily manipulated by political thugs, and being herd-like.[90] Despite these lapses into prejudice, common in the emotional atmosphere of wartime, he did resist popular vindictiveness. He explained that Americans would find many upright people in postwar Japan with whom one could enjoy mutually beneficial relations. Vengeance should form no part of the future but yield to a renewal of Japanese–US amity. He spoke admiringly of the Japanese as a nation of hardy warriors.[91] He also found time to compile selections from his voluminous diary, speeches, and correspondence to publish in book form: *My Ten Years in Japan*. It appeared in spring 1944 to mainly favorable reviews, despite its argument (modestly phrased) against a punitive peace.[92]

Grew accepted the directorship of the State Department's Office of Far Eastern Affairs in May 1944. From this position he made the case – neither popular nor compatible with FDR's unconditional surrender policy – for letting Japan retain the institution of the emperor after the war. Grew pressed too for Japan's keeping other national-cultural concepts and organizations. He strenuously objected to what he saw as misguided American radicalism that aimed to extinguish Shintoism or the *zaibatsu*. Their dismantling, he predicted, combined with the disorientation sure to follow in the wake of defeat, would foster anarchy from which only Japanese communists and their Soviet patrons could benefit. Victory over Japan, in other words, meant for him more than military defeat of the enemy. The political-diplomatic definition of victory entailed sensitivity to Japanese traditions and sufferance of them for the sake of US interests – short term (ending the war sooner rather than later) and long-term (encouraging a pro-US orientation in post-hostilities Tokyo).

At the end of 1944, after Hull's resignation and selection of Edward Stettinius as State Department head, Grew was again appointed undersecretary. He kept this position until replaced by Dean Acheson in mid-August 1945. During this second tenure as undersecretary, Grew told FDR – then Truman – that the intensity and duration of the Pacific war could be reduced by suspending the unconditional surrender policy and assuring Japanese leaders that the office of emperor could be retained by the nation, were that the popular preference. Grew and like-minded Japan hands in the State Department (Dooman, Joseph Ballantine, George Hubbard Blakeslee) were agnostic on whether Hirohito the man should be removed or tried on war crimes. But Grew and company were emphatic that the emperor institution should be kept.[93] Retention would not only fortify social calm in Japan, the royal personage (whoever it might be) could be employed too as a foil against resurgent militarism should it arise. This view of the emperor's prospective utility, though, remained a minority position during the final months of Japanese–US combat and Grew was ridiculed by pundits and government figures (among them James Byrnes and Archibald MacLeish). Acheson once referred to Grew as the "prince of appeasers," who failed to recognize that Japan required comprehensive reordering; its feudal-militaristic institutions had to be uprooted if the country were to become a peacefully inclined democracy.[94] Too forgiving as ambassador to Japan, so critics claimed, Grew was compounding his past errors by advocating leniency for a criminal regime.

The charge that Grew had been overly soft or witless in Tokyo ignored contrary evidence. He had reported in January 1941 that Japanese naval planners were rumored to have a scheme for attacking Pearl Harbor; he told Washington in November that hostilities might suddenly erupt.[95] He certainly was not blind to the deficiencies of Japanese statecraft and had no doubt that the manic Matsuoka, with whom he had several unpleasant encounters, was a mentally disordered person. Additionally, as Japanese brazenness became more pronounced, Grew had fallen in line with the sanctions idea. He never went native as Hornbeck and Acheson liked to say. Nor did Grew ever get anything so spectacularly wrong as Hornbeck's forecast in

November 1941 about the unlikelihood of war. In the end, of course, the emperor was retained for Japan by the occupation-authority under MacArthur (a decision that led Acheson to retract comments on Grew as a patsy).

Byrnes, secretary of state as of early July 1945, asked Grew in August whether he would like to join MacArthur's Tokyo staff to help manage the occupation. He declined. He did not want to face old friends as a vanquisher in the moment of their humiliation.[96] Perhaps, too, the obliteration of Hiroshima and Nagasaki, which he thought gratuitous, colored his decision to refuse the assignment: "[I] will always feel that had the President issued as far back as May 1945 the recommended categorical statement [advanced by Grew] that the Japanese dynasty could be retained ... [that] the atom bomb might never have been used at all."[97]

Grew trundled off into retirement in autumn 1945. Thereafter, he occasionally returned to advise the State Department, as when he championed the 1953 appointment of Bohlen as ambassador to Moscow against criticism by anticommunist fundamentalists. Correctly perceived as an ardent Cold Warrior – with credentials dating to his opposition to recognizing Moscow in 1933 – Grew testified in support of Bohlen, thus adding much to his successful confirmation battle.[98] Dooman, by the way, played a different hand in the McCarthy season of hysteria. He had disliked the New Deal, did not care for Jews, and recoiled from liberals. He lent himself to zany attempts to discredit Emmerson as communist sympathizer, who was, in fact, a faithful public servant.[99]

In the final analysis what stands out in Grew's ambassadorship – eclipsing his respect for subordinates, or carefully tended ties to FDR, or admiration of Japan as ancient civilization – was his conviction that US diplomacy is perdurable and naturally implicates patience and aversion to violence with the requirements of national safety. Hence his notion of a Pacific summit and other effort, epic in the circumstances of disintegrating Japanese–US relations, to prevent hostilities.

Grew could not have imagined anything so far-fetched as the United States waging an aggressive war ("preemption"), as in 2003 against Iraq.[100] He wondered aloud in 1942, during a grim moment for the Allied cause:

What would the American people have done if an American government, in the midst of diplomatic conversations, had

attacked another country wantonly and without notice?
Would not our people have raised a clamor against such a
government? In any event, would not large minorities – if
not the majority – have criticized, sabotaged, or even
revolted against such a policy of aggression and treachery?
And – to reveal the hypothesis in all its absurdity – could the
American people in the first place have elected a government
capable of conceiving such a deed?[101]

No political theorist, contending that republics bend toward diplomatic resolution of international problems, could fault this reasoning of Grew when he answered his own questions. The trust in which the United States has long been regarded rests upon "the humane, peaceful outlook of the people who elect the leaders, and on the democracy which makes all leaders responsible to the people." He underscored in 1942 without a quiver of doubt to the future and with this confidence in US sensibility: "We are constitutionally incapable of aggression."[102]

2 THIRD REICH

Germany had for generations been a site where originality flourished in philosophy, scientific investigations, poetry, and music. Achievements in intellectual life, plus the material wellbeing enjoyed by its inhabitants, assured the country an honored place in civilization. Germany also possessed traditions of tolerance and equality, indicated by the vibrancy of its Social Democratic party. These appreciations were deeply felt by FDR's principal envoy in Berlin, Professor William Dodd, who had earned (1900) his Ph.D. in History at the University of Leipzig. He lauded the rigorous standards of the German academy, shared its democratic yearnings, and was drawn to its theological intensity. He counted Dürer, Goethe, Kant, and Beethoven among his idols. The reason for Germany's slide from cultural eminence into its antithesis during Hitler's reign baffled Dodd.[1]

Scholarship since his day has sought to identify the mix of underlying forces and contingencies that created the Third Reich. The puzzle of Germany's descent might yet be grasped, whence may come steps to ensure that nothing like Nazi murderousness can arise again.[2]

Clearer in retrospect than to most people who lived through the 1930s, Germany's march to conquest – then to *Götterdämmerung* – was evident early in Hitler's rule. The Nazis accomplished what Gustav Stresemann's diplomacy had not. They burst the restrictions on national life imposed by the 1919 Versailles treaty and dared the status quo powers. Hitler arranged in 1933 for Germany's retirement from both the League of Nations and Geneva Disarmament Conference. The Third Reich in July 1934 ceased repayment to foreign creditors.

Its leaders successfully pressed via plebiscite in January 1935 for the Saar's return to Germany. They undertook national rearmament – covertly at first – that embraced the building of a modern air force and navy. They expanded the size of the army beyond Versailles stipulations, confirmed by the introduction in March 1935 of conscription. Germany defied France by occupying the Rhineland with thousands of Reichswehr troops (March 1936), entered into understandings with Japan against the USSR via the Anti-Comintern Pact, and with Italy intervened in the Spanish civil war. Annexation of Austria (*Anschluss*) in March 1938 and the absorption of Czechoslovakia's Sudetenland, dignified by the Munich meetings (September 1938), culminated in the occupation of Bohemia and Moravia (March 1939), Hitler's last conquest by measures short of war. Reconciliation with the USSR, marked by the Molotov–Ribbentrop agreement (23 August 1939), constituted a shrewd diplomatic maneuver. It paved Germany's path to breathtaking military offensives in 1939–1941.

Subjugation of Poland, Norway, Denmark, the Low Countries, France, Greece, Yugoslavia, and the Wehrmacht's sweep to the gates of Leningrad and Moscow remade Europe. Even Great Britain, nourished by its far-flung empire and buoyed by Winston Churchill's defiance, could not dislodge German preponderance from Europe but prayed only to survive.

From his Berlin post, 1933–1937, Dodd foresaw the likelihood of German domination over Europe before it occurred. He repeatedly issued dire predictions to White House and State Department superiors. After his ambassadorial tenure ended, he toured US cities to sound the tocsin: the Third Reich pursued racialist-dictatorial policies at home, and meant to subdue as many foreign lands as possible. Neither US political institutions nor safety could prosper in a Nazi-dominated world. Therefore, he emphasized, the United States had to act in concert with other European powers to contain Germany.

An introverted America, weakened by the Great Depression, still unrelieved by FDR's New Deal improvisations, tried to ignore Dodd or explain him away as an eccentric. To M. H. Carter, an Alabama businessman, Dodd's yapping about Nazi foibles showed the ambassador to be "naïve" and "a damn fool," who should have been shipped off to Timbuktu.[3] Dodd's friend and fellow historian, Charles Beard, was also not persuaded. He wrote, while Dodd was straining his utmost to alert the public: "Not until some formidable European power comes into the western Atlantic, breathing the fire of aggression and conquest, need the

United States become alarmed about the ups and downs of European conflicts, intrigues, aggressions, and wars."[4]

Contra Dodd, his successor in Berlin, Hugh Wilson, tried to enhance German–US relations and to mend the fraying that had occurred. He attributed important virtues to Hitler's regime. He chose not to dwell upon its ethical defects. Against his will – to his chagrin – he was obliged to return to the United States after Kristallnacht.[5]

Professor as diplomat

Dodd hardly fit the 1930s profile of an ambassador, his differences from Joseph Grew being illustrative. Whereas the latter sprang from a patrician background, Dodd (b. 1869) came from a hardscrabble farm near Clayton, North Carolina. While Grew glided through society as a matter of birthright, Dodd struggled to escape farm toil and rural poverty. Only thanks to financial aid was he able to attend the Virginia Agricultural and Mechanical College. He later petitioned a kinsman for loans to pursue advanced studies at Leipzig.[6] Resentment of privilege and inherited wealth, alien to Grew's notion of propriety, stamped Dodd's personality, shaping his preference for the laboring classes. His feeling for the disadvantaged did not, though, extend to southern blacks whose abilities Dodd questioned or other groups whose integrity he doubted: Jews, Catholics, hyphenate Americans.[7] Class feeling, nevertheless, did color the substance of his writings on US history, which concentrated on the socially stratified antebellum south.

Other experiences and temperament also separated the two men: Grew the Republican, outdoorsman, and lover of parlor games versus Dodd the Democrat, partaker of physical exercise as mental therapy, and disheveled academician, who made his teaching career at the University of Chicago. While Grew read light fiction or sought new golf greens to conquer, Dodd produced tomes on Thomas Jefferson's political theory, southern colonial economy, and Jefferson Davis's state-craft. Election to the presidency of the American Historical Association in 1934 gratified Dodd. His most cherished hope was to complete a projected four-volume study, *The Old South*. In the event, he published one volume of this magnum opus a few years before his death.[8]

Not only did Dodd win acclaim by scholars of his generation (the "New History" denomination) and delight in the affection of his

Ph.D. students, but also progressives in the Democratic party respected him as a stout Jeffersonian, who embraced the causes of Woodrow Wilson: domestic reform, internationalism. Eager to play a part in mending the post-Great War world, Dodd wrote a few research essays for Wilson's Inquiry – concerning the Monroe Doctrine, free trade, East Asian dilemmas. He became a champion of the League of Nations idea, on which subject he could be eloquent.[9] He collaborated with Ray Stannard Baker in editing a six-volume collection of *The Public Papers of Woodrow Wilson* that appeared in 1925–1927. Dodd also wrote a biography of Wilson – with the president's cooperation – that amounted to hagiography. The hero was unique, his ideals transcendent.[10]

Dodd maintained a modest involvement in local Democratic activities during the years of Republican White House incumbency, Warren Harding to Herbert Hoover. Dodd stayed in touch too with party insiders: Colonel Edward House, Henry Wallace, Cordell Hull, Josephus Daniels, Daniel Roper. Through these people, after FDR's 1932 election, Dodd made known his availability for renewed service. Evidently, he was interested in obtaining a diplomatic sinecure – perhaps the Netherlands or Belgium – where he could devote his remaining energy to *The Old South*.[11] The press of advancing years, distraction of administrative chores (he chaired Chicago's History Department), and classroom fatigue had made him hunger for a quiet government assignment. There he should finish his research project.

Roper, FDR's first secretary of Commerce, recommended Dodd for the Berlin assignment. By no means was he the president's first choice, however. Rights of refusal had earlier gone to James Cox (Democratic presidential candidate in 1920), Newton Baker (Woodrow Wilson's secretary of war), Owen Young (monetary expert), and Edward Flynn (New York Democratic operator). Roosevelt also toyed with the idea of sending a university president or prominent churchman to Berlin, such as Riverside's Reverend Harry Emerson Fosdick.[12] Still, FDR judged Dodd suitable: a faithful Democrat, the professor also knew Germany from first-hand experience. He was proficient in German. By his republican sturdiness, he could have a salutary effect on a people who might yet be rescued from beguiling Nazi promises. "I want an American liberal in Germany," the president opined.[13]

Berlin, admittedly, was not what Dodd had in mind when he advertised his wish for foreign assignment. Nothing about troubled Germany in 1933 suggested that he would have spare time for *The*

Old South. He had an inkling too that Nazis would prove disagreeable company, but nevertheless accepted FDR's offer.

Dodd persuaded himself that he could help smooth relations between his country and the adopted one of his youth.[14] Besides, he had for years nurtured (vaguely) ideas of performing public service. As a youngster he had dreamt of a military career, but missed an appointment to West Point. In the 1920s, fancying the idea of making history, not just writing it, he investigated possibilities of running for office in Illinois on a progressive-Democratic platform. Berlin, in effect, gave him a belated opportunity to realize ambition of long standing. Anyway, he respected FDR and professed to see in him several of Wilson's excellent qualities.[15]

Roosevelt's instructions struck Dodd as sound. The new envoy to Berlin had to improve the conditions and volume of German–US trade. He should encourage Berlin to make good on the repayment to US creditors of loans, valued at $1.2 billion. He must work to protect Jewish Americans in Germany from being harmed by anti-Semitic edicts.[16]

Soon after his installation in Berlin, Dodd discovered that at heart he was just another contemplative – happier to be with students and undisturbed in his studies. Intent on living within the ambassadorial salary ($17,500) allotted by the State Department, he did not host many entertainments at his residence. He found them obnoxious in the context of world economic crisis and they undermined his fading physical stamina (signaled by "digestive nervous difficulties").[17] He meantime chafed at the routines of diplomatic life. He disliked its recreations, unalloyed, as he saw such doings, by intellectual content. With few exceptions, the foreign ambassadors in Berlin offended him with what he deemed as their smugness and prickliness over protocol. His relations with Britain's Sir Eric Phipps were correct, but distant. Dodd thought the French ambassador, André François-Poncet, unctuous and suspected him of being "half-fascist."[18]

Dodd also failed to establish rapport with the Foreign Service officers or other professionals (commercial and agricultural attachés) on his staff. He perceived them as spoiled brats spawned by the idle rich, who had packed their sons off to polishing schools (Harvard, Yale, Princeton), where they had caroused for years but learned little. Badly educated and incurious, Dodd charged, these dandies either loafed or pursued silliness abroad – golf, polo, late-night dinners – at government expense but seldom exerted energy on behalf of US interests. George Gordon, counselor of the embassy, infuriated Dodd on first contact and discerned in him a martinet sensibility. Upon closer acquaintance, Dodd concluded that his embassy officers were exceedingly hostile to FDR, if not downright reactionaries. He suspected some were in league with that arch-villain in Dodd's demonology, publishing-magnate William Randolph Hearst, who Dodd felt never missed a chance to curry favor with Mussolini or the Nazis.[19] The military and naval attachés posted to Embassy Berlin, in Dodd's estimation, were also an uninspired lot, whose number should have been cut.[20]

If this sneering attitude were not enough to disaffect his subordinates, Dodd ensured their enmity by decreeing measures of frugality. He limited the number and length of telegrams sent to Washington. He reduced secretarial service. He slashed operational budgets. He gave unsolicited advice to State Department seniors on ways to remake the Foreign Service into a proper meritocracy. He recommended purging the diplomatic corps of its millionaires – beginning with Sumner Welles, whose hauteur affronted Dodd – and drilling diplomats in history, foreign languages, economics, political science.[21] On the whole, Dodd preferred the company of US journalists in Berlin, such as William Shirer, who, although not enamored of diplomats, made an exception for the peppery professor.[22] Unsurprisingly, his departure from Berlin in late 1937 caused relief among his officers, who then broadcast their regret that a clueless amateur had been visited upon a major embassy.[23]

Making matters worse, Dodd's underlings were scandalized by the amorous adventures of his daughter, Martha (b. 1908). Leaving behind a minor writing job with the *Chicago Tribune* and a moribund marriage, she had joined her father, mother, and scholarly-minded brother in Berlin. Of bohemian bent, and blessed with indulgent parents, she flung herself into an exciting life abetted by diplomatic privilege.

She was initially drawn to the dynamism of new Germany, which she professed had shed the despondency and impotence that hobbled the Weimar republic; the Nazis were high-minded, youth-oriented, and virile. This infatuation caused the ambassador to chide her for having become a "young Nazi."[24] She was, though, disabused of all enthusiasm upon closer scrutiny of German reality, encapsulated for her by the gory Night of the Long Knives (30 June–2 July 1934).

The regime's persecution of Jews also distressed her. It prompted her to compose *Through Embassy Eyes* (1939), a rebuke of people unworried about German fascism.[25]

Martha Dodd was destined ultimately for a checkered career on the far left, which involved philosophical naïveté and inconsequential espionage for the USSR (causing FBI investigation plus flight to Prague in 1957).[26] The elasticity of her early political commitments, in any case, permitted romantic affairs of varying seriousness that she conducted with an assortment of men in Germany. They ranged from Armand Berard (third secretary of the French embassy), to high-ranking Nazi functionaries (Ernst Hanfstaengl), to security chieftains (Rudolf Diels of the Gestapo), to military officers (General Ernst Udet of the Luftwaffe), to Hohenzollerns (Prince Louis Ferdinand), and to the dashing Boris Vinogradov. Purportedly first secretary in the Soviet embassy, Vinogradov was, in fact, an NKVD agent. Passion for him drove her to write to Stalin for permission to marry the man, a proposal undone by his execution (1938) during one of the purges of Moscow's intelligence apparatus.[27]

As occasional typist and courier for her father, his staff had plausible reason to suspect that Martha Dodd compromised via her Soviet liaison the confidentiality of mission business, beyond that already jeopardized by Nazi surveillance, telephone taps, and miscellaneous snoops.[28] Thus uneasiness aroused by her in Embassy Berlin, inevitably affecting views in Washington, aggravated the mutual incomprehension in which ambassador and staff beheld one another.[29]

Assessments of Dodd by Washington officials were mostly critical. Some sniped that a befuddled FDR had never meant to appoint him but had confused him with Harold Dodds, president of Princeton University.[30] Syndicated columnist Drew Pearson told readers in 1936 that Dodd was useless for any foreign assignment, much less a sensitive one like Berlin. Welles disliked the bookish egalitarian, hinting slyly (September 1937) to Germany's ambassador in Washington, Hans Heinrich Dieckhoff, that the diplomatic days of the "incomprehensible" man were numbered.[31] Insofar as FDR gave thought to Dodd, it was forgiving of his expostulatory missives, sometimes obsessively didactic (on the thirteen colonies, framers of the Constitution, Lincoln's wisdom) or marginally related to diplomatic-political questions at hand. Still, Roosevelt regarded Dodd with good humor, although not oblivious to embassy discontents or unconcerned by his daughter's nonconformity.[32] Hull, whose opinion anyway carried little weight, remained polite but agnostic concerning the qualities of his southern compatriot. Only R. Walton Moore, an indefatigable assistant secretary of state, exhibited genuine feeling for the ambassador. A sunnier personality than Dodd, he tried to bolster his spirits during bouts of gloom, when a return to writing and university routine constituted his main longing. From summer 1934 onward, Dodd played with ideas of fleeing Berlin for better districts (summer home at Round Hill in Virginia's Blue Ridge mountains or Chicago).[33]

Despite frustrations and doubts, Dodd took pride in performing his duty. He congratulated himself for shunning those frivolities to which he believed most diplomats surrendered. He once wrote to Moore: "It must be surprising to you to find any Ambassador really at work – not fishing, hunting and playing golf most of his time. But I can't excuse myself for such things."[34]

Among Nazis

Lack of intimacy with Washington's upper echelon, reservations regarding the Berlin diplomatic corps, and attenuated relations with his Foreign Service men narrowed the chance that Dodd would shine as ambassador. Still, the quality of his connection to superiors, brother envoys, and embassy subordinates sparkled compared to what passed for relations with the German leadership. These deteriorated by stages.

Only during the first months of his Germany stay did he experience anything like pleasure. He visited his former haunts in Leipzig. He traveled with family and friends to places of cultural interest: Martin Luther's Wittenberg, Oberammergau for the Passion Play. He looked up acquaintances from university days; a few had pursued enviable academic careers of their own. He managed to locate one of his former professors, who offered candid views on recent events. Dodd even traveled incognito, booking third-class train passage, to determine better the predilections of ordinary Germans.[35]

He believed that the Nazis in office would act more rationally for the sake of social-economic stability than their original stridency suggested; the Nazi revolution would necessarily moderate. Perhaps, he also speculated, Hitler was not so bad a chap as critics charged.[36] In this hopeful mood, Dodd looked forward to opportunities for

improving German–US trade/investment ties and resolving the knotti-
ness of German debts to American bondholders. Hoped-for Nazi moderation, alas, did not materialize. After a few months in Berlin, Dodd
despaired of prospects for success.[37] The question first formed: "Ought
I to resign?"[38]

His mission began coming apart when desultory talks on trade
quotas and indebtedness failed to advance. Neither Dodd nor Treasury
Department experts – nor Hjalmar Schacht of the Reichsbank – were
able to devise satisfactory solutions to these problems before Hitler
repudiated all German debt owed to foreigners. The resultant anger of
American financiers guaranteed that tariff adjustments downward were
rejected. Concomitantly, German–US trade and investment failed to
thrive at the level sought by the State and Treasury departments. While
technically complicated negotiations on these problems lurched into
impasse, other facts of German life pressed upon Dodd. Book burnings
discouraged him. Tramping youths and uniformed *Sturmabteilungen*
(SA) and *Schutzstaffeln* (SS) unnerved him. They sang their Horst Wessel
anthem or chanted jingoist verses, typically exhorting vengeance against
France.[39] The regime's attempts to instill military values in children,
glamorize war (in such films as *Unsere Wehrmacht*), and increase the
rate of armaments production further affected Dodd.[40]

His response to Reich officials varied. Encounters with Schacht
and Foreign Minister Konstantin von Neurath convinced Dodd, at first,
that Hitler's government contained reasonable men with whom one
could talk. Collectively, they were Germany's best bet for a return to
international respectability. The aged President Paul von Hindenburg
was too frail for Dodd ever to know but represented precisely that
conservative element in society that he hoped would hold steady
against Nazi zealotry. As for Nazi party activists, he met the chief of
the SA, Ernst Roehm, attended dinners with the propaganda minister,
Joseph Goebbels, and came to know his rival for Hitler's favor, Hermann Goering. The ambassadress found Goebbels witty. She had
tender feelings for Goering's wife, Emmy Sonnemann.[41] Even so, neither of the Dodds felt comfortable in such company and soon invented
excuses to avoid Nazi society. The couple's daughter, Martha, later
claimed, quite sensibly, that the emotional-physical health of her
parents suffered from having to socialize with Nazi chieftains.[42]

Dodd had two interviews with Hitler: 17 October 1933,
7 March 1934. In them, Dodd delved into the matter of German debts

and possible future US loans. He spoke against commercial discrimination. He protested street attacks by SA ruffians on US nationals. In most instances they were taken for being Jewish or had not returned the Nazi salute when greeted. Hitler promised to end these outrages and developed conciliatory themes – the desirability of peace, the inviolability of European borders, the merit of arms control. But when Dodd ventured that Berlin's withdrawal from the League of Nations and persecution of Jews were damaging to German–US relations, Hitler's calm broke. He blasted the Versailles "diktat." He derided the League of Nations. He castigated French perfidy. He blamed world Jewry for stirring prejudice in the United States against the Reich. Hitler swore that if Jews in Germany intrigued to wreck the country, "we shall make a complete end to all of them."[43]

On Hitler's last point, Dodd cautiously countered. Germany ought to study the US example in containing Jewish "over-activity." He mentioned, trying to be helpful, that unobtrusive barriers had been erected in America to limit the numbers and influence of Jews entering into elite circles. Consequently, he said, "we [Americans] had managed to [distribute] the offices in such a way as not to give great offense, and the wealthy Jews continued to support institutions which had limited the number of Jews who held high positions." Subtle discrimination in other words, not violence, might better serve the cause of checking Jewish influence in Germany while reassuring public opinion elsewhere about the Third Reich's wholesomeness. Hitler later called the ambassador unintelligible and referred facetiously to *"Der gute Dodd."*[44] He, for his part, found Hitler in the interviews to be peevish. After the Night of the Long Knives, Dodd decided to avoid meetings with the Führer, labeling him unendurable.[45] Thenceforth the two men met only on formal state occasions, where they exchanged perfunctory greetings. Dodd espied Hitler at the 1936 Berlin Olympic games as he touted contestants of the master race, but did not speak with him. The games themselves, said Dodd, were an uninhibited display of German chauvinism. He had earlier conveyed reservations to Washington about the wisdom of letting US athletes participate.[46]

The ditch between the ambassador and his hosts deepened as he declined all invitations to attend Nazi rallies in Nuremberg. He refused on the grounds that these were partisan party events, unrelated to the administrative machinery of the state to which he was assigned. He did not want to foster the mischievous fiction, as he saw it, that the

German government and nation were synonymous with the Nazi party. (Phipps and François-Poncet joined Dodd in this boycott of Nazi jamborees.) Nonattendance, in his mind, also showed solidarity with those anxious people, including Foreign Office personnel, who disapproved of the Nazis but were unable to wage resistance.[47] Besides, he once averred, justifying his absence: "I do not care to sit by quietly and listen to Hitler and Goebbels denounce democracies."[48]

Dodd's occasional public lecturing – before church forums, chambers of commerce, university assemblies – on the worth of bygone democratic polities and flaws of ancient tyrannies was seen by the Nazis for what it was: thinly veiled criticism of Hitler's regime. Dodd added to his sin of sermonizing by withholding support from German protests of the March 1934 mock trial of Hitler in New York (organized by the American Jewish Congress and American Federation of Labor). Neither did Dodd, to the annoyance of Berlin, evince objection as New York's Mayor La Guardia heaped scorn upon Hitler and his adherents. Nor did Dodd express sympathetic interest to Foreign Office officials when they registered anger for the boycotting of German goods by US consumer groups, Jewish and other.[49]

As mentioned, Dodd was not enamored of Jews. He made little attempt to conceal his disappointment in 1938 when his daughter married Alfred Stern, a philanthropically inclined Jewish businessman from the midwest.[50] Years earlier, on the eve of going to Germany as ambassador, Dodd had kept silent as Colonel House pronounced solemnly on purported Jewish influence: "The Jews should not be allowed to dominate economic or intellectual life in Berlin as they have done for a long time." Nor did Dodd in 1933 parry Charles Crane, a benefactor of the University of Chicago, after he stated in private conversation: "Let Hitler have his way [with the Jews]."[51]

Once in Berlin, Dodd did not inquire closely into the circumstances whereby he obtained a posh rental residence at bargain price. It belonged to a Jewish banker, Alfred Panofsky, in danger of being disinherited unless he leased his property at rates far below market value.[52] For all this, however, Dodd was not vehemently anti-Semitic. He merely held notions unexceptional to his day and place. He did meet with American Jews during the period of his embassy. They included such luminaries as Rabbi Stephen Wise, upset by the scale and tempo of Germany's anti-Jewish measures, exemplified by the 1935 Nuremberg Laws. Time in Berlin actually quickened

Dodd's feeling for Jews, especially those from Germany's learned classes who were hounded from their jobs.

Dodd devoted long days to monitoring the regime's evolving anti-Jewish campaign. Its continuance he told Nazi interlocutors would limit future Washington–Berlin intimacy. He dutifully remonstrated against fresh episodes in which American Jews were harassed in their conduct of normal business or came afoul of discriminatory legislation. He tracked the false ebb of anti-Semitic disturbances just before the Berlin Olympics, then their return to floodtide after foreign athletes and spectators departed.[53]

Dodd pleaded valiantly for clemency in the trial of Helmut Hirsch. This Jewish lad of US origin was twenty at the time of his June 1937 execution (beheading) in Berlin. He had been judged guilty by a Reich court of complicity in an aborted attempt to blow up government buildings and kill Nazi personages, including Julius Streicher, founder of the notorious tabloid *Der Stürmer*. Dodd's entreaties on Hirsch's behalf were resented by German authorities from Hitler downward. The Führer explained to Dodd, in a tersely worded letter, that leniency was impossible.[54]

The regime's anti-Jewish policy once directly touched Dodd. The wife of a Reich diplomat, away on a Balkans errand, asked for help. She needed to obtain documentation that would prove her parents, US-born Germans, were free of Jewish taint. Dodd referred the matter to a subordinate, commenting noncommittally: "The woman revealed no sign of non-Aryan blood."[55]

Dodd realized by the time he vacated Berlin that Hitler's aims went beyond the disenfranchisement of Jews or their expulsion from Germany. The logic of policy was more radical, premised on the superfluity of a category of people. Wherever Berlin's writ ran in Europe, he predicted, well before Wannsee conspirators clarified homicidal plans (January 1942), Jews would have no safety: Hitler wanted "to kill them all."[56]

Dodd had faint hope for the long-term peace of Europe where, he sighed, "folly rules." He concluded early in his Berlin tour that Hitler's professing of peaceful aims was a fraud.[57] He later wagered – in 1935 – that if the Führer remained in office for another five years, and the army stayed compliant, a European-wide war would ensue. Military conquest constituted Hitler's fixed purpose, the main goals being to humble France, absorb the Balkans, destroy the USSR.[58]

Dodd followed the failed Nazi coup in Vienna (July 1934) and subsequent attempts to coax Austria's Chancellor Kurt von Schuschnigg into closer connection with Germany.[59] Hitler's pressure on the Polish and Czech governments to revise their national borders with the Third Reich also boded ill for the future, Dodd acknowledged. He was most disheartened by the 1936 outbreak of the Spanish civil war, which he read – not inaccurately – as hastening the drift toward general collapse.[60] He felt that a Franco victory, aided by material support from Hitler and Mussolini, would result in a formidable concentration aimed against stagnating Western power: "Thus 'civilized' Europe offers a sad and barbaric picture."[61] Dodd advised FDR in 1936 that Germany stood poised to reap vast rewards at the expense of the demographically and politically desiccated Anglo-French states:

> The French nation is now on a definite decline ... her population at a standstill. Although she has her peace pact with Russia, it means little ... The English nation ... is beginning a similar decline, her population at a standstill and her relations with her colonies weakening ... But Germany's dictatorship is now stronger than ever. If she keeps the pace three more years, she can beat the whole of Europe in a war ... The 67,000,000 is expected to be 80,000,000 when Austria is annexed, including part of Czechoslovakia. With universal service ... and with a solid front never before enjoyed here or elsewhere, Europe can hardly escape [German] domination.[62]

Dodd believed that chances for the overthrowing of Hitler's regime were dim. He had originally thought that Protestant and Catholic churchmen, members of the intellectual class, and conservative activists (drawn from the aristocracy, naval/military officer corps, government bureaucracy) could somehow combine to loosen Hitler's grip on power. Just how these disparate groups might organize in common cause, Dodd never presumed to know. Instead, he bore witness to the Nazi state's lengthening reach. He watched as dissenters were incarcerated or executed, as propaganda distorted public discourse, as neo-paganism fueled the cult of Hitler. Dodd reluctantly decided that Germans lacked the courage of their better convictions and stumbled blindly behind anyone who flattered them or painted pictures of a radiant future.[63]

The only antidote to international instability and the hazards posed by Germany, Dodd informed Washington, lay in America's return to active engagement with European matters. Without it, the British could not overcome their aloofness, the French their divisions, or the Soviets their suspicion of the West – leaving Germans (with Italian and/or Japanese assistance) free to seize new territories and place a Nazi imprint on world politics. Against such a future, Dodd hoped for a renewal of intensive Anglo-US cooperation. Failing that, he recommended Washington's coordination with the League of Nations to block German expansion, with threatened economic boycott if necessary. He also held that a US alliance might be desirable with states bordering on Germany, especially Edvard Beneš's Czechoslovakia. Dodd offered that FDR should convene a conference of global leaders with the object of peaceably settling European problems. A "worthwhile" idea, FDR conceded in 1937, but unfeasible.[64]

Dodd implored Roosevelt to alert Americans to the dangers cresting abroad. The pedagogue did not shrink from lecturing the president, as in October 1935: "While the domestic situation must be your fundamental problem, world peace is not less important. If Italy, Germany, and Japan at some critical moment move at the same time in their spheres, I cannot see any way to stop the dictatorships."[65] Yet, Dodd recognized, pacifist sentiment and economic woes had paralyzed American thinking. He bemoaned declarations by Senators William Borah and Hiram Johnson on the supposed wisdom of keeping the US from helping to resolve European quarrels.[66] He regretted Congress's neutrality toward Spain as the republic staggered from blows dealt by Franco's rebels, backed by German and Italian combat units. He faulted Senators William McAdoo and Burton Wheeler, who pledged to keep US distance from the World Court while stoking popular skepticism with what remained of the League of Nations.[67] To FDR, Dodd railed: "So many men ... think absolute isolation a coming paradise."[68] An ostrich approach to foreign relations would produce devastation in Europe, yielding a world antipathetic to US security. He confided (1 February 1936) in his diary that ascendant pacifism spelt certain disaster: "The French and English peoples have become overwhelmingly pacifist and the Germans know this. Pacifism is the attitude of the United States ... but pacifism will mean a great war and the subordination of all Europe to Germany if the pacifist peoples do not act ... at this critical moment in their history."[69]

Dodd was a spent force well before he penned the above lines. His Foreign Service staff suffered him with quiet indignation. Wilhelmstrasse worthies, notably Neurath, snubbed him or made him wait for long periods before acknowledging him at prearranged appointments. FDR and the New Dealers, albeit unsettled by Nazi antics, were too distracted by the ongoing crises of the Great Depression to concentrate on him. And he dreamed of escaping Berlin to finish *The Old South*. Yet he stayed on. He did not want to appear a quitter; he was mesmerized by the stupendousness of German developments. He also believed that his continuing presence could somehow help put things right. In the meantime his physical health became shakier, his emotional equilibrium less sure. His judgment too by 1937 showed signs of slippage. That spring he gave to members of Congress written support of FDR's court-packing scheme. Critics responded by damning the meddling of a faraway ambassador on questions concerning the dignity of the Supreme Court and the delicate executive–judicial balance of power. He made matters worse when he claimed that a "near-billionaire" was plotting to cripple the New Deal while conspiring with Berlin and Rome to expand the fascist zone. When pressed by Senators Borah and Gerald Nye to divulge the name of this lout, Dodd hesitated. He doubtless had Hearst in mind. Unwillingness to identify anyone, though, caused pundits, as well as GOP partisans, to jeer anew. They called for the ambassador's resignation, much sought by other people for their own reasons.[70]

Hitler's Foreign Office notified Washington that Dodd was practically *persona non grata* after he, while on US furlough (August 1937), issued a critical statement about Berlin's hostility toward democracies.[71] Welles took advantage of the furor caused by Dodd's gaffe about the malevolent billionaire to sharpen doubts in the White House about the ambassador's overall fitness. William Bullitt, at the time an FDR darling and envoy in Paris, thought Washington could still establish a viable relationship with Berlin. He also wanted a type of Franco-German reconciliation, best hedge against a war from which – in his view – only communists would benefit. Consequently, he too lobbied to have Dodd replaced by someone more obviously committed to the restoration of European harmony; at the minimum a person was needed in Berlin who spoke with his Reich hosts. Symbolic of Dodd's waning star was the State Department's approval of attendance by Chargé d'Affaires Prentiss Gilbert to the September 1937 Nuremberg show (also visited for the first time by François-Poncet and Britain's recently appointed ambassador, Sir Nevile Henderson). With precious little ceremony, FDR relieved Dodd in December. This forced resignation bruised him but he blamed Welles, not the president.[72]

Upon return to the United States as a private citizen, Dodd worked to warn Americans about Germany. He surrendered all pretense of completing *The Old South*. Instead, he took a breathless speaking-tour in 1938 of eastern, midwestern, and southern cities. He met with the Chicago Council on Foreign Relations. He addressed audiences of church laity, activists troubled by Far Eastern or Spanish violence, university students. He rehearsed a litany of Nazi offenses: suppression of academic freedom, persecution of Jews, curtailment of Christian prerogatives, judicial travesties, war preparations. Germany, he reiterated time and again, was "the chief cause of the worst international dilemma in five hundred years."[73] To prevent a catastrophic war, he told his listeners, the United States had to cooperate immediately with Great Britain and France; only collective security and diplomatic hardihood would deter German aggression.[74]

Dodd's campaign acquired a near-frantic quality. He rushed to venues, often covering great distances by car. Almost seventy and physically unwell, he was not a good driver. He ate little. He slept fitfully. His sense of urgency, moreover, interacted devastatingly with personal sadness. His wife, who had been agitated in Germany and felt out of place, died of cardiac failure (28 May 1938). Disappointment also aggravated his sorrow; his son lost a bitterly contested bid to run as Democratic candidate from Virginia's 8th Congressional District in the 1938 election.[75] As for FDR and Hull, they kept a polite distance from Dodd. They inquired about his health. They offered condolences upon learning of his wife's death, but never endorsed his public utterances against isolationism. Hull told Dieckhoff that Dodd was addled, an embarrassment to the US quest for friendship with Germany, someone to be quietly disavowed.[76]

Dodd became careless of little things. He forgot to collect an honorarium that a Chicago audience intended for him after he spoke about the risk involved in US indifference to world affairs.[77] He also became inattentive. In a hurry and preoccupied while driving his car through a Virginia hamlet (5 December 1938), to address yet another assembly on the German question, he hit an African-American girl, four-year-old Gloria Grimes.[78]

Dodd did not stop. He drove away from the scene of accident, lest he were late to his engagement. His obliviousness to what he had done was dispelled when he was afterward charged with hit-and-run driving. He lost his license. His citizenship rights were temporarily revoked. He had to pay a fine ($250). He provided for the girl's medical expenses, plus an award to the family along with legal costs. Grimes survived her injuries.[79]

The penalties imposed upon Dodd could have been stiffer. In view of his age and absence of prior criminal offense, the courts dealt leniently with him. Would Virginia justice, one must also wonder, have been less forgiving were young Grimes white, the driver black? The accident, in any case, and publicity surrounding it ended Dodd's campaign to heighten public awareness of international questions. A frail man, he took refuge in Round Hill. There he died of pneumonia (9 February 1940) – to his friends a magnificent Cassandra, a pathetic old man to his critics.

Before Kristallnacht

Dodd had definite ideas about the kind of diplomat who should succeed him in Berlin. Ideally, he would be well versed in German history and exude a democratic spirit; millionaires, Foreign Service popinjays, and dullards should be refused. His list of unacceptables, that he submitted to FDR, featured two people mentioned by the press as candidates: Bullitt still in Paris, Ambassador Joseph Davies in Moscow. Dodd rejected both as self-satisfied socialites, who lacked the gravitas needed for Berlin tasks.

Dodd lobbied for James Shotwell, a Columbia University historian and Wilsonian devotee. He had for years urged US cooperation with the League of Nations and taken part in discussions leading to the 1928 Kellogg–Briand bar on war. A second best for Berlin, Dodd volunteered, would be Charles Merriam, a University of Chicago political scientist with the requisite commitment to progressive principles.[80]

To Dodd's disappointment, Roosevelt kept other counsel. He chose Hugh Wilson for the ambassadorship.[81] Unforeseen by anyone, it would last for less than a year, March to November 1938. Wilson, whose most recent assignment had been in Washington (serving as an assistant secretary of state), had put himself forward with Welles's and

Bullitt's endorsements.[82] A career Foreign Service officer, with experience in Europe, including a 1920 stint as counselor of Embassy Berlin, Wilson came from a prosperous Chicago business family. He was a 1906 Yale graduate. He voted Republican. He possessed a crushingly conventional personality. His appointment was calculated to reassure the Berlin embassy staff, which had for years endured the idiosyncrasies of Dodd and daughter.[83] Wilson's appointment too could be fairly read by Germans as signaling FDR's preference for better relations with Berlin, betokened by Wilson's decision – with administration acquiescence – to attend the September 1938 Nuremberg rites.[84] Previously, Neurath had reported to his masters that Wilson overflowed with good intentions and should be taken seriously, a view readily seconded by other German diplomats.[85] Joachim von Ribbentrop, who became foreign minister in early 1938, spoke well of Wilson and assured him that he enjoyed the regard of German officials. They were prone to view him as a "moderate," not someone to get excited about Berlin's Jewish policy, someone inclined to let Germans sort out their problems unencumbered by outside meddlers. Hitler, after momentary doubt, cordially welcomed Wilson and granted a wide-ranging interview.[86]

Instead of blocking the drift toward European hostilities, Dodd had by his foolishness contributed to the tensions that marked international life, so Wilson charged. Therefore, as he conceived his mission, he must salvage what he could for the peace cause. Should it miscarry, and were Europe swept by violence, then the United States should stay neutral and not lose its bearings as in 1917. Distance from Europe, plentiful resources, and abundant territory made America practically immune from Old World explosions, he felt. Besides, the United States did not bear moral responsibility for the unfolding of European affairs.[87] Victory in the World War had been a sham; the 1917 intervention should be read as a cautionary tale. He meditated in June 1938: "Twenty years ago we tried to save the world and now look at it. If we tried to save the world again it would be just as bad at the end of the conflict. The older I grow the deeper is my conviction that we have nothing to gain by entering a European conflict, and indeed have everything to lose."[88]

Wilson tried to improve the tone of German–US relations by congratulating Berlin officials on their achievements. He praised Hitler on Germany's eradication of twin problems: unemployment, galloping inflation. Wilson lauded the climbing rate of industrial and agricultural production. He noted with approval the brisker pace of foreign trade. He commented favorably upon the renewal of national esprit, in which he held the *Kraft durch Freude* (Strength Through Joy) program had made valuable contribution.[89] He committed to public print this admiration of Goebbels: "An interesting and stimulating conversationalist. Among the leading men of the Nazi Party there is none … so well able to expound the Nazi doctrine, or so competent to meet the foreigner upon his own ground."[90] In reports to FDR, Wilson likened Hitler to an artist with fine hands; he possessed an intuitive grasp of complex realities, "someone impossible to judge by customary standards." The ambassador also confessed to fondness for Goering, notwithstanding his obvious ruthlessness.[91] In October, Wilson hosted Charles Lindbergh at an embassy dinner, where Goering bestowed upon him the Service Cross of the Order of the German Eagle.[92]

On subjects Jewish, Wilson intimated to leading Nazis that Jews in the United States were also a nuisance. For example, he allowed, they wielded inordinate influence over the newspaper business, especially in the northeast. He emphasized that a majority of Americans did not want to be led by any religious minority into needless confrontation with Germany, which had made impressive strides on several crucial fronts.[93] He did suggest, though, to the Foreign Office's Ernst von Weizsäcker that Germany might enhance its image by involving itself in those works flowing from the July 1938 Evian conference (convened to find means of alleviating the hardship of Jews wishing to emigrate from the Third Reich). This idea was promptly rebuffed and, perhaps, a cause for hilarity within Nazi circles.[94] Regarding the stifling of dissent, the censorship apparatus, and burgeoning population of political prisoners, Wilson kept quiet when among his hosts. Unlike Dodd, he expressed not a modicum of reproof, perfectly in keeping with diplomatic convention: an ambassador does not pry into the domestic affairs of the sovereign state that suffers his presence. Wilson's only deviation from this course was his suggestion (summer 1938) to Nazi authorities that they treat Austria's Schuschnigg, languishing in solitary confinement, with more humanity than was their wont.[95]

Wilson's Berlin tenure coincided with two dramatic diplomatic events: the *Anschluss*, then Munich. Washington's role in these happenings was minor. In the case of *Anschluss*, the administration did not protest strenuously. The State Department, after brief debate, decided that the German–Austrian merger would last, and then liquid-ated the Vienna legation. The overwhelming response in Washington, as elsewhere, to the Munich deal was one of relief. Dreaded violence had been averted. Roosevelt's only contribution to resolving the Czech–German crisis was to circulate a reminder to European governments of their obligations under the Kellogg–Briand prohibitions on war. He also extolled for Hitler's benefit the virtues of nonviolent solution over the hazards of warfare, to which the Führer responded with a recital of Czech crimes against downtrodden Sudeten Germans. FDR subse-quently congratulated Britain's prime minister, Neville Chamberlain, for his purchase of peace: "Good Man."[96]

To Wilson's mind both the *Anschluss* and Munich boded peace-ful tidings into the deep future. Germans of every rank and political taste, the ambassador noted, were delighted with the Austrian annexation.[97] Absorption of the Sudetenland was eminently sensible too, he gushed. It completed Hitler's drive to unite all Germans under one authority, an ambition consistent with principles of national self-determination upheld in US tradition. A satisfied Germany seemed to Wilson to promise ultimate reconciliation with France, nicely advanced by Prime Minister Edouard Daladier and Hitler in their Munich communing. Wilson expected, consequently, to live the rest of his life "without seeing a first class war in this part of the world." As for Polish–German disagreement regarding Danzig and the corridor, he observed that the questions were negotiable, not so potentially explosive as those of the Sudetenland. He predicted an era of European serenity.[98]

The United States in these brightening circumstances should try to boost its trade/investments with Germany, including lifting barriers to the sale of helium, sought by Berlin for its zeppelins after the 1937 *Hindenburg* disaster. Americans should also cease their carping over alleged human rights violations in Germany, which needlessly compli-cated bilateral relations. "The continuous agitation of the Jewish ques-tion in Germany," Wilson jotted (June 1938) in his diary, "is going to keep alive the hatred in the United States ... I deplore the expression of hatred at home and the fact that it accomplishes no good."[99] Germany, he averred, had suffered hugely during the World War and in its aftermath. The Third Reich deserved patient understanding plus a fair chance to fulfill national destiny.[100]

Although intent on putting a rosy gloss on German develop-ments, Wilson was aware of problems, even as he tried not to dwell darkly upon them. The omnipresent police, he wrote to FDR, affected embassy life in unpleasant ways. They included placing Germans at risk who had the temerity to maintain social relations with US diplomats. Worse still, the spoliation and exodus of Jews placed a strain on Wilson's staff. It worked steadily, he reported, in conformity with the US immigration regime, to determine the suitability for visas of people who wanted asylum in the United States. The embassy had the duty, too, of conveying to Reich officials the texts of multiple US protests at Germany's anti-Semitic policies and then relaying Nazi rejoinders to Washington, the latter larded with wounded feeling or accompanied by reminders that the US record was hardly spotless, especially regarding African Americans.[101]

Wilson sent evidences to Washington of Nazi attempts to agitate among the German communities of South America and to undermine FDR's Good Neighbor policy, most notably in Argentina.[102] In cooperation with his military attaché, Lt. Colonel Truman Smith (relying upon Lindbergh's findings from inspection tours of German aviation facilities), Wilson told Washington of expansive Third Reich rearmament and the improving state of military preparedness. In reference to comparative air power, Wilson wrote FDR in July 1938: "The facts are that Germany, in the short time since throwing off the restrictions applicable to production of military aircraft, has produced an air arm second to none in numbers and *quality* of first line airplanes."[103] Yet Wilson maintained that a reasonable future could eventuate with benefit to Europeans and Americans alike, if all parties behaved with circumspection.[104]

Wilson's mission to rehabilitate Berlin–Washington relations unraveled with the pogroms of 9–10 November 1938, conducted in Germany-proper, Austria, and the Sudetenland: Kristallnacht. Goebbels portrayed it as the spontaneous uprising of popular wrath against Jewish criminality, revealed once more, said he, by the fatal shooting in Paris of a German diplomat by seventeen-year-old Herschel Grynszpan. More than 90 Jews were killed in Kristallnacht. Thousands more were beaten or imprisoned. Hundreds of synagogues were desecrated or damaged beyond repair. Jewish-owned shops, houses, and apartments also numbered among the vandalized properties. Penalty was added to this injury; authorities imposed a fine of one billion Reichsmarks upon German Jews to recompense the state for the Kristallnacht destruction and cleanup.[105]

Several governments – Great Britain, Netherlands, USSR – denounced the violence while expressing concern for the safety of their Jewish nationals in Third Reich cities. But only Roosevelt's government withdrew its ambassador, ostensibly for consultation.[106] Wilson left Germany on 16 November. He hoped, until resigning his ambassadorship (1 September 1939), to return to Germany to resume conciliatory diplomacy, notwithstanding personal disgust for the November events.[107] Alas, neither he nor any American returned as ambassador to the Nazi capital. Hitler likewise recalled Dieckhoff from Washington and never restored ambassadorial representation, despite Foreign Office apprehensions that its absence hurt Germany's cause among Americans.[108]

After Kristallnacht

The withdrawing of German and US ambassadors from their posts, albeit a serious step, did not equal the more drastic resort: a severance of Berlin–Washington relations. Such a move would have been injurious to US interests, State Department officers felt, denying them a listening post while hampering diplomacy in a period of rapidly unfolding crisis.[109] Still, without an ambassador the embassy operated with considerable disadvantages. It occupied a twilight zone between diplomatic normality and non-recognition, an untenable situation worsened by fogginess on whether or when ambassadorial representation would be restored. Under the best of circumstances political reportage and diplomatic routine were difficult in Germany, where secrecy reigned. Hitler, the organizing principle of political life, was an enigma, said Gilbert, chargé ad interim after Wilson's departure: "One cannot but be conscious of an underlying uncertainty in reporting from Berlin ... the possibility remains that what is reported is in reality far from the mark."[110] Naturally, as overall German–US relations continued to fray, embassy access to official Berlin diminished further. American diplomats found themselves increasingly isolated after the invasion of Poland, a condition that worsened as FDR's preference for Allied success became obvious after the summer of 1940 (the transfer of destroyers to the Royal Navy, increasing US naval cooperation with Britain, the March 1941 passage of the Lend-Lease bill).

Alexander Kirk, chargé during May 1939–October 1940, chafed under the quarantine that separated the colony of diplomats from society in Berlin.[111] Neither he nor Gilbert nor the embassy's last chargé, Leland Morris (October 1940–December 1941), was allowed – with an exception cited below – to meet with high-ranking German officials.[112] These US pariahs had to content themselves with perfunctory talks with Foreign Office functionaries. All ten US consulates – from Cologne to Dresden, Hamburg to Vienna – were closed in June 1941, thereby sealing the embassy's solitude.[113] In line with principles of reciprocity, German diplomats in Washington were treated with coolness; consulates were sent packing.

Embassy Berlin was involved just once, during the *Sitzkrieg* (phony war), with elevated diplomacy. The occasion, though, as it touched upon personnel was pro forma and underscored their aloneness. Sumner Welles visited the capitals of the belligerent countries in February–March 1940 to ascertain whether Washington might broker a peace.[114] This errand entailed a number of calls upon German leaders (1–6 March). None of the conversations was availing. They simply reinforced Welles in his dislike of the Nazis and their deeds. He thought Rudolf Hess a dolt, Goering a philistine, Ribbbentrop a stunted personality. Only Hitler appeared to Welles as a person of substance; the Führer's diction and manners were crisp. But he was unyielding on Germany's "just war" against the Allies and the Reich's need to organize central Europe's political and economic life. He also spoke heatedly on the justice to Germany of recovering its pre-World War colonies. Welles, in any case, brought Kirk along to each encounter with German bosses, none of whom he had previously met. Kirk contributed nothing substantive to the discussions but sat mutely. Hitler had probably wanted the embassy man excluded, but as a courtesy to Welles permitted Kirk to enter hallowed Nazi precincts.[115] His revulsion for their denizens was absolute. He urged FDR in mid-April, as German armies began offensives against Scandinavia and prepared to smash the Low Countries, to drop the pretense of normal relations with Germany and sunder every tie. Kirk became so disconsolate in May, when the United States refrained from military action on behalf of France, that he lost interest (briefly) in prolonging his own life.[116]

Though denied a role in diplomacy during the ambassadorial interregnum, the embassy kept busy by attending to other business. Washington's appetite for political reporting did not abate. Here, fair to say, the staff provided sound analyses, as illustrated in dispatches that tried to capture the shades of Berlin mood in the wake of

BARBAROSSA. "The immediate public reaction," wrote Morris to Hull, "to the invasion of the Soviet Union was one of almost shocked surprise since few Germans were able to believe that a campaign of such magnitude would be initiated in the east while the struggle with the British continued." Morris also commented as prospects of ever-lengthening warfare sank deeper into popular awareness: "While most Germans appear ... convinced of victory in the east within a reasonable time, bringing with it great economic, political and strategic benefits, misgivings are developing at the [commencement] of a Napoleonic enterprise."[117]

The embassy meanwhile assumed the burden of looking after French and British interests. Also American nationals in the Third Reich needed what protection US citizenship afforded and arrangement for departure from the war zone. Most poignantly, the embassy was besieged throughout 1939–1941 by tens of thousands of Jews who hoped to obtain coveted visas for emigration to the United States.

Queues of men and women formed daily outside the chancery. Inside, throngs of people pleaded for safety or hovered about the immigration section in hope of getting favor or glimpsing clues that not all effort was futile. Some of the diplomats were solicitous and tried, within the narrow parameters of US immigration laws, to be helpful. Notable in this was the Consul General in Berlin, Raymond Geist, who later received (1954) the Order of Merit from the West German government for his importuning Nazis for the sake of persons in danger of arrest.[118] Another helpful officer was Geist's assistant, William Russell. He pushed and annoyed his betters – he tempted Nazi reprisal – to win US passage for individuals and families. He had learned shortly after Germany's attack on Poland that Jews in that country had become the preferred targets of shooting by firing squads (*Einsatzgruppen*).[119]

Russell came to detest the Nazi government, but his hatred of it did not affect his feeling for everyday Germans. Rather, similar to Grew on the Japanese, Russell testified (in his 1941 memoir, *Berlin Embassy*) that Germany contained people with whom Americans in future years could enjoy cordial relations. He knew little (probably nothing) of such once and future heroes as Willy Brandt, Dietrich Bonhoeffer, Bishop von Galen, Anton Schmid, and Claus von Stauffenberg. Yet Russell sensed that their dissenting type existed. He appreciated, moreover, that many ordinary people cursed wartime rationing, hated the censorship while seeking relief in furtive listening to BBC broadcasts, and lived in hope of better days to come.[120] Until removed or felled by its own unworthiness, however, most Germans would go along with Hitler's regime. Besides, living as they did in a police state, they could not realistically mount overt opposition. Nevertheless, a majority of them, Russell posited, would put up with Hitler only for the duration of war. They would afterward endeavor to modify his excesses, perhaps getting rid of him altogether.[121]

Russell's assessment of Germany meshed with that of George Kennan who served in Embassy Berlin (as second secretary, then first secretary) during September 1939–December 1941. This veteran observer of central and east European affairs detected cracks within the Nazi edifice. The regime was riddled with factions and corruption, he held, and leaders of the major organizations – military services, labor front, foreign ministry, SS, propaganda, industries – worked independently of each other. When their jurisdictions or ambitions collided, the proconsuls quarreled until one or the other relented – or Hitler deigned to notice, then resolved the dispute. In other words, the Berlin boast of *Gleichschaltung* masked a type of anarchy. Kennan also believed that countless people kept an internal detachment from the regime's grandiose purpose. They were not seduced by rhetoric celebrating one folk united. He thought they would, should an opportunity arise, inflict retribution on Hitler and his crowd. Kennan respected those aristocrats whom he secretly met that plotted to dethrone Hitler, notably the Kreisauer Kreis's Graf Helmuth James von Moltke (whose record included cooperation with the young men and women of the *Weisse Rose*).[122] Until Moltke or other resistors triumphed, though, or until the Third Reich was militarily reduced, Kennan realized that Germany's future and that of Europe would be gruesome.[123]

***

After the declaration of German–US hostilities (11 December 1941), Kennan and colleagues were interned pending exchange for Third Reich diplomats detained in the United States. Repatriation of both groups took place in May 1942, the Americans embarking from Lisbon on the exchange ship *Drottningholm*. Until then their German counterparts were kept with other Axis representatives at the Greenbrier resort in White Sulphur Springs, West Virginia.[124]

The men and women of Embassy Berlin, augmented by US diplomats from additional European posts (plus magazine/newspaper reporters), spent their confinement at a formerly swanky hotel in the spa town of Bad Nauheim, not far from Frankfurt.[125] (Previous visitors to Bad Nauheim included FDR as a boy in the company of his parents, also Hearst who entertained Mussolini in 1931 and had pronounced him "a marvelous man.")

The Americans in Bad Nauheim deflected the tedium and tension with activities similar to those devised by Grew's captive outfit in Tokyo. Fitness and sports-oriented groups met (calisthenics, baseball). Study groups were established to examine diverse subjects (political history to foreign languages to the mysteries of biblical scriptures and philosophical texts) under the auspices of "Badheim University," organized by Philip Whitcomb of the Associated Press. The student assembly invented an irreverent motto and mythical traditions. The internees – whose number exceeded 130 – otherwise amused themselves with Christmas/Easter diversions or followed the columns of the *Bad Nauheim Pudding*, a newssheet produced by the journalists. Their writing featured parody, rumor, and whatever crumbs of information became available.

Despite querulousness related to mediocre food and inconveniences – dealt with by an exasperated Kennan, who assumed main responsibility for the detainees – morale was satisfactory at Bad Nauheim. A few romances bloomed.[126] Squabbling and gossip hovered only slightly below acceptable level. Just two people slipped over to the German side: Herbert Burgman (a senior clerk who had worked at the embassy since 1920), Robert Best (a newspaperman who reviled FDR).[127] Their defection was fair trade for the son of the German military attaché in Washington, Lt. General Friedrich von Boetticher. Before leaving US shores, he arranged for his psychologically ill son, residing in a Maryland asylum, to remain in America, lest upon return to Germany he was executed as a mental defective or *Lebensunwertes Leben* ("life unworthy of life").[128]

Stark questions confronted FDR's German policy in 1933–1941. First, how to contend with a regime that violated the normal decencies? It promoted not only euthanasia, applied even to the families of its leading military servants. Nazi table talk also, as Dodd experienced, refined upon the desirability of sterilizing black Americans plus the "absurdity" of letting African "animals," such as Jesse Owens (four gold medals), compete in the Berlin Olympics.[129] With tireless zeal, the Nazis tormented a religious minority – Jews comprising about one percent of Germany's 1933 population – and suppressed dissenting voices.[130] Prison camps, state-sanctioned homicides, and torture signified for most Americans – from Kristallnacht onward – the depth of Nazi malignancy. A second and, perhaps, greater concern for Americans involved Germany's seeking a revision of international politics through the instrument of intimidation, then aggressive war. German success would not only shrink the universe of parliamentary governments to which the United States was joined. German domination of Europe could also jeopardize US economic-military security in the Americas, especially if Nazis and Japanese militarists coordinated their moves.[131]

No more than in Washington, or among the broader public, did people in Embassy Berlin agree on how to cope with Hitler. The major division of viewpoint in the United States – "internationalists" versus "isolationists" – existed in microcosm in the embassy. Dodd had tried to disrupt what he saw as complacency about dangers radiating from Germany. As for Wilson's relative equanimity, it amounted to the public face of appeasement, showing a brave front as evidence mounted of German enmity toward all things American. Wilson's approach to Germany, in the final analysis, did not lessen Nazi antipathy for the United States or materially help those people who sought a nonviolent resolution to problems. German diplomats in Washington ridiculed the American mind, calling it "un-evolved." They thought Hull "chicken-hearted." Berlin publicists referred to Wilson's partner in the peace quest, Bullitt, as an obnoxious "half-Jew." The Führer pronounced this verdict: "America is in its whole intellectual and spiritual attitude a society dominated by Niggers and Jews."[132]

Berlin must have been unimpressed by periodic statements of US worry regarding anti-Jewish policies. True, FDR recalled Wilson after Kristallnacht. This move, however, could be interpreted as a temporary sop to Jewish activists in the Democratic party that would be put right after passions cooled. The authentic US attitude seemed manifest elsewhere: inactivity following the Evian conference as when Congress failed in 1939 to pass legislation (the Wagner–Rogers bill) to relax restrictions on the immigration of Jewish children from Germany. Ungenerous words also about American Jewry, spoken in confidence to German officialdom by Wilson at one time or another, must have helped allay Nazi anxiety about FDR's acting decisively. Joseph Kennedy, ambassador to Great Britain (1938–1940), must have been a comfort too. One month before Kristallnacht, he told a Reich diplomat that anti-Jewish feeling was rife in the United States; whole segments of the population sympathized with the German attitude toward Jewry.[133]

   More than two decades after the end of World War II, Kennan vented this feeling about the deliverance of a group of Jews who escaped to America. Their scheduled departure to the New World threatened at one point to delay (not cancel) the return of half the diplomats in Bad Nauheim to the United States:

> Individual Congressmen, anxious to please individual
> constituents, were interested in bringing these refugees to the
> United States, and this – although the refugees were not
> citizens – was more important than what happened to us.
> The [State] Department was obviously more concerned to
> relieve itself of congressional pressure than to worry about a
> group of its own employees ... whose fidelity to duty ... had
> caused them to fall into enemy hands.[134]

Kennan's complaint went beyond routine grousing. It hinted at the old canard about untoward Jewish influence, a view not atypical at the time in the Foreign Service.[135] Consider Ferdinand Mayer's explicitness. An intimate of Hugh Wilson, Mayer served in Embassy Berlin during the mid-1930s. He went on to head the US legation in Haiti, where he wrote the following to Wilson as German armies trounced France in June 1940:

> I am wondering whether International Jewry, which doubtless
> so largely influenced directly or indirectly your own
> withdrawal from Berlin, and has so dominated the
> Administration with regard to its attitude toward Germany,
> has begun now or will shortly begin to change its tune and
> subtly persuade the Administration to play ball with the
> Germans. That particular brand of Jew, in fact all Jews, have
> got to be on the winning side for that is how they make their
> money and maintain their influence. That being the case they
> are always on both sides and teeter toward the one which is the
> more dominant and therefore worthwhile at the moment.[136]

Kennan's words, to say nothing of those by Mayer, echoed the indifference (or worse) of many US officials to the plight of imperiled people.

The line between such sentiments as expressed by Kennedy or Wilson – or Dodd in his weaker moments – versus tacit approval of Germany's Jewish policy seemed fuzzy to the likes of Goebbels. Lackluster rescue efforts, dilatorily offset by FDR's 1944 establishing of the War Refugee Board, combined with evidences of bigotry gleaned in conversation with US envoys, encouraged Goebbels in this thought which he entered (December 1942) in his diary: "At bottom ... I believe the English and Americans are happy that we are exterminating the Jewish riff-raff."[137] As for the counterexamples of Geist and Russell, they were small fry in the US government apparatus. Easily ignored, they were of slighter consequence than even Dodd, defeated in Berlin and forlorn in America.

Whereas Grew in Tokyo had been charmed by traditional Japan, vestiges of which had survived modernization, Dodd recoiled from what he found in his once-beloved Germany. Nazi vulgarity repelled him as did the ubiquity of spies and informants. His democratic sermons and boycotting of Nazi pageantry did not endear him, nor did his attempts to place redundant Jewish-German professors in US universities. Rocky relations with his staff – aggravated by his frugality, dour countenance, roaming daughter – made Dodd's life at Hitler's court a misery. Nazis were certainly not the only people to criticize him. Yet he did have his fans. Albert Einstein was one. He praised Dodd's help to independent-minded scholars stranded in the Third Reich. He also applauded Dodd's post-ambassadorial preachments on the threat posed by Germany.[138] George Messersmith, maybe Dodd's only devoted officer in Berlin, paid his chief this tribute: he "saw through all the Nazi pretenses."[139] A more unexpected admirer was François-Poncet, who in Berlin had attacked Dodd (behind his back) for waging a private crusade against the Nazis. Years later, though, the Frenchman allowed that Dodd, albeit temperamentally too taut for a diplomatic job, had qualities to recommend: "an excellent man of strong character, fundamentally upright and true."[140]

Hugh Wilson was a self-conscious "realist." To him, deliberateness and caution were cardinal virtues, Dodd's version of "idealism" an invitation to dicey interventions abroad. This orientation meant for him that shifting power relations should be duly acknowledged and adjudicated by negotiations, Munich being exemplar, not resort to leveling violence as in 1914. This version of realism was not destined to prevail in post-1945 Anglo-American thought on international politics. Munich became synonymous with pusillanimity and a storing up of future troubles.

Wilson never repented of his attempts to recoup common ground between the United States and Germany. Yet once the two countries were pitted in war, he readily assumed another part. He joined William Donovan's Office of Strategic Services (OSS), where he rendered good service, even while remaining clear-eyed about the immensity of wartime destruction. To him it remained the sum of all avoidable evils.[141]

Seven decades after FDR withdrew ambassadorial representation from Germany, the US government opened (July 2008) a new embassy building in Berlin. This complex of offices and meeting rooms employs a staff substantially larger than the one circa 1938. The building itself is packed with modern technology that allows instantaneous communication with Washington or any place else. Marine guards and a host of anti-terrorist devices/barriers protect the embassy personnel and confidential affairs. The contrast between the present and older chancellery is striking. Yet FDR's people, if they could return, would recognize at least one thing: the setting. The new embassy occupies the same site as its late-1930s predecessor, the Blücher Palace.[142]

3 Left to right: Reichstag, Brandenburg Gate, US Embassy, in foreground Memorial to the Murdered Jews of Europe. March 2009.

The embassy now, as before, is within a brief walk from the Brandenburg Gate, from the Reichstag, from the Tiergarten. These venerable landmarks have been lovingly restored. They show few traces of the ruin that marked them in 1945 (*Jahr Null*). The nearby Unter den Linden has recovered much of its prewar elegance. It too would seem familiar to Roosevelt's diplomats. But one can only imagine how they would respond to the most startling changes in the embassy neighborhood. A huge monument, unveiled by Marshal Georgi Zhukov in November 1945, commemorates the Red Army's battle for Berlin during the closing violence of World War II. This monument is dominated by a colossal statue of a Soviet soldier and by two T-34 tanks, said to have participated in the fighting.

Across the street from the new embassy looms another monument, inaugurated May 2005. It is unapologetically abstract, designed by the architect Peter Eisenman. It occupies 4.7 acres. It is composed of 2,700 concrete gray slabs or stelae. It is dedicated to the "murdered Jews of Europe." Dodd had warned. Wilson had concentrated on other matters. Nowadays children play hide-and-seek among the slabs or rest upon them. The youngsters, needless to elaborate, are unaware of Degussa, a Düsseldorf-based chemicals enterprise that provided the anti-graffiti veneer which coats the stones – and had earlier produced Zyklon-B for use in the gas chambers.

Most adults wander quietly and respectfully, sometimes disoriented by the severe pattern, undulating ground, and varying size of the stelae. Only if one deliberately averts one's gaze upon entering or leaving the embassy can one miss the visitor groups or solitary walkers still trying to make sense of the Nazi blight.

3 NEW ROMAN EMPIRE

Italy in the 1930s–1940s did not strike most Americans as a formidable military power or one capable of overturning the international order. This ambition, were it achievable, might be realized by a German–Japanese combination, but that Italy could contribute to a drastic revision seemed improbable.

Movie audiences in 1940 laughed at the inanities of Benzini Napolini (Il Dig-a-Ditchy), Adenoid Hynkel's pal in Charlie Chaplin's lampoon of Hitler: *The Great Dictator.*[1] Italy remained the butt of humor, even after the July 1943 ousting of Mussolini and subsequent cooperation with Allied forces. The country's military deficiencies were targets of jest, raising the snide question of whether Italy helped or hindered its putative partners. The popular writer and comics illustrator, Bill Maudlin, reported in his *Up Front* this exchange between a GI and German soldier fighting near Venafro.

> *The American had a machine-gun position on top of a hill, and the kraut was a sniper, about fifty yards down the slope. They were well protected, and had been in those positions for many days. Both had cooties, both had trench foot, and each had an intense dislike for the other.*
>
> *An Italian division was supposed to move into the line near by. The Nazis, having had experience with the Italians when they were fighting on the German side, liked this new idea very much. The Americans, who had seen the Italians as German allies, were not cheered by the prospect.*

> *"How do you like your new ally?"* yelled the German to
> the American ...
> *"You kin have 'em back,"* said our guy, having come from
> a region where diplomacy bows to honesty.
> *"We don't want them,"* shouted Jerry, and he lobbed a
> grenade up the hill. It fell short ...
> *"Horse's ass!"* snorted the [GI].[2]

American dissenters from this strain of contempt did exist. Ezra Pound was one. A gifted poet, he was also eccentric and a Fascist apologist. He spewed anti-Jewish invective. He blasted Allied actions against Italy from 1940 onward. He loathed Churchill and FDR, whom he called slaves to "high kikery."[3] Pound advised US listeners in a July 1942 radio broadcast from Rome: "You ought not to be at war against Italy."[4] It and the charismatic Mussolini, Pound explained, were lifting the world from turpitude.

Rome's Fascists, by their own admission, were improving the human condition both at home and abroad. On the domestic front, after his Black Shirts swept into Rome (October 1922), Mussolini had established an estimable order. The nation was thereafter united, its power magnified, its merits multiplied. Manliness and undaunted modernity had supplanted hidebound parliamentarianism and antiquated morals. In international relations, Italy, heir to the glorious Roman empire, was spreading civilization's realm. This aim was supposedly advanced in May 1936 when Italian armies reached Addis Ababa, thereby subduing Abyssinia (Ethiopia) after less than a year of declared warfare.[5] This conquest, thrilling to a majority of Italians at the time, simultaneously avenged the 1896 debacle at Adowa and enlarged the domains of King Victor Emmanuel III, whose formal title thereafter proclaimed him Emperor of Abyssinia. Three years later Italian forces overran Albania, snuffing out that Balkan country's independence and forcing King Zog into British exile. Mussolini's ambitions, at their most extravagant, included additional African acquisitions (Sudan, Egypt, Kenya, British Somaliland, Tunisia), subjugation of Yugoslavia and Greece, concessions from France (Corsica, Nice), annexation of Palestine, control of the Suez Canal. These prospective gains would expunge the heartache of Caporetto (1917), to say nothing of the Great War settlement that "swindled" Italy of the spoils of victory.[6] Thus Italians would again master the Mediterranean zones while also commanding immense African space. By reason of its eminence, Mussolini's reincarnated Roman empire would become arbitrator of disputes among nations, the dispenser of Fascism's nobler versions of justice and bounty.[7]

Unfortunately for Mussolini, this grandeur could not be realized by Italian initiative alone. He came to comprehend, if grudgingly, that prudence trumped bold unilateralism. He would have to cooperate with the other dissatisfied state of Europe, Germany. The Pact of Steel (22 May 1939) gave symbol and substance to Italo-German cooperation. The trick for Mussolini was to derive benefit for Italy via the Third Reich – against the Anglo-French status quo powers – but not at the price of becoming Berlin's junior partner. In the event, he failed, finally existing only on Hitler's sufferance in 1943–1945 as head of the so-called Italian Social Republic, based in Salò. Inadequately equipped and overstretched Italian armies before then had been routed or destroyed, from North African battlefields to Stalingrad. The Duce's own end occurred in April 1945, when he and his mistress, Clara Petacci, were captured and executed by partisans, the corpses then displayed in Milan's Piazzale Loreto.

Two ideas dominated Roosevelt's pre-Pearl Harbor policy toward Mussolini. The first corresponded with the period before Italy joined Germany in belligerency against France and Britain, 10 June 1940. The aim here was to delay – to prevent, if possible – Italian intimacy with the Third Reich. Thereafter, US diplomacy sought to detach Italy from Germany, a goal undone when four days after Pearl Harbor, in solidarity with Hitler, Mussolini's government declared war upon America.

To have achieved his objectives, Roosevelt needed representation in Rome of highest caliber. This was not forthcoming. Breckinridge Long, assigned to Mussolini's court in 1933–1936, and his successor, William Phillips, 1936–1941, were well enough regarded by Washington to receive sympathetic hearing. They were poorly suited to the circumstances of emergent crisis, however. Long's reporting and outlook were especially faulty, presaging his censurableness as assistant secretary of state.

Mission to Mussolini

Long epitomized the category of diplomat that Dodd disparaged: self-aggrandizing, entitled. Not surprisingly, his Berlin communications to Long were few and perfunctory, some curt to the point of rudeness.

The ambassador in Rome responded in kind to, what was for him, an odd and unappealing schoolman.[8] That FDR's representatives in two key capitals should be on stiff terms ill served the administration and delayed the making of coherent policy toward the embryonic Axis.

Long was born of a patrician family, its roots stretching deep into American colonial history. He belonged to multimillion-dollar wealth, through which he obtained not only pampering and leisure but also, in Dodd's indictment, undue political access. Long evinced little interest in ideas or those types of scholarship that Dodd prized. Instead, Long breezed through Princeton University, class of 1904, where later (to his credit Dodd might have allowed) he earned an MA, having completed a thesis on the British Raj in India. He also wrote a treatise on the framers of the Constitution and their endeavors, published by Macmillan in 1925.[9] However gratifying these forays into advanced study, they did not divert him from his true vocations, practice of law in his native St. Louis (wherein he performed patchily) and pursuit of public office as an ardent Democrat. He meanwhile indulged his love of horses and racing. His stock of thoroughbreds – based at his second and preferred estate in Laurel, Maryland (Montpelier Manor) – as well as his own equestrian skill won him a fine reputation among sportsmen from Belmont to Saratoga.

Long's political career did not boast successes comparable to those he won at the racecourses. His run for the Missouri state assembly failed in 1908. His two attempts for the Senate (first in 1920, then 1922) also flopped. Nevertheless, as a donor to Democratic causes, he managed to retain party favor. His handsome contribution to Woodrow Wilson's 1916 reelection resulted in appointment as third assistant secretary of state in 1917. Long made even heftier financial donations to FDR's first presidential campaign. He worked effectively too as a floor manager at the suspenseful Chicago party convention (June 1932) that nominated the New York governor to head the Democratic ticket.[10]

The friendship of Long and Roosevelt dated to their time together in Wilson's administration, when the latter served as assistant secretary of the Navy. They shared a devotion to Wilsonian internationalism, most apparent in the case of Long by his helping to assemble the foreign policy plank for the 1916 Democratic convention, which contained favorable reference to a type of league of nations.[11] On the strength of personal bonds and Long's party loyalty, FDR wanted to grant suitable reward. He offered him several positions in 1933: assistant secretary of the Treasury, or assistant secretary of State (again), or a similar spot in the Attorney General's office. Long politely refused. The offer of Italy struck his fancy, however. Accepting with alacrity, he opined that this assignment would give him just the "opportunity to do a real man's job." Besides, the imagined glamour of an ambassadorship attracted his not inconsiderable vanity.[12]

In contrast to bilious Dodd, Long and his wife entered with pleasure into the whirl of balls and entertainment among Rome's diplomatic corps and social-political elect. The ambassador hosted lavish affairs at his sumptuous Villa Taverna, whose rent alone would have mortified Dodd. Long was smitten by the Italian aristocrats whom he met, so much more sophisticated than the horse-set or country club habitués that he knew in St. Louis and Maryland. He found his ambassadorial colleagues to be congenial. Among them were Germany's Ulrich von Hassell (eventually involved in plots to overthrow Hitler) and Britain's elegant Sir Eric Drummond. Although Long felt no affection for Jewish Americans, he got on well with their co-religionists in Italy, notably Mussolini's erstwhile mistress, the politically fluent Margherita Sarfatti.[13] (Her association with the Duce ended in 1935.) Roman ruins and antiquity further deepened his delight. He wandered wistfully through the Appian Way, Forum, and Coliseum. He allowed in romantic musing: "The atmosphere is surcharged with reminiscences of the past, with evidences of our civilization."[14] Long also immersed himself in Italy's equine world. He made himself familiar to local breeders. He assiduously followed their affairs, while taking time to monitor the foaling, training, and racing of his own creatures at Montpelier Manor.[15]

During the period of his diplomatic novitiate, Long relied heavily upon his Foreign Service officers. They tolerated his fumbling as he adjusted to unfamiliar procedures and gently instructed him in the norms of his new office. He requited by writing favorable fitness reviews. He praised the staff publicly and privately. When necessary, he also arrived promptly to rescue subordinates, as occurred in November 1933. The embassy's counselor, Alexander Kirk (later posted to Berlin as mentioned in chapter 2), got into a contretemps with Camilla Lippincott, widow of a former GOP senator from Rhode Island. She had said nasty things about FDR (his being unscrupulous, mendacious) at a dinner held by Kirk in his home and that included a British diplomat as guest. Kirk reprimanded Lippincott for speaking disrespectfully of the president in mixed company and while abroad. He told her to vacate the premises. He demanded that she cease all contacts with him. Kirk's attempts at apology the next day were rejected. Lippincott hissed that she would have him officially chastised through the intervention of State Department friends and removed from Rome. Long alerted Louis Howe at the White House about the fracas. No harm came to Kirk, who, incidentally, later served as the first US ambassador to post-Mussolini Italy. Long quipped that given the provocation, his officer had acted correctly: "My personal thought is the ruder the better under the circumstances."[16]

Long did push his staff hard during the first phase of Italo-Abyssinian war to provide timely analysis for Washington. The results were heartening from his viewpoint: "The Embassy is on a twenty-four-hour basis ... with no Saturday afternoons off and Sunday included in the work schedule."[17] Only in a few instances did he have to discipline anyone, as with Patrick Keelan, a civilian who worked in the office of the naval attaché. Keelan had gotten enmeshed in a potentially profitable but also shady scheme to deliver US-produced coal to Italy. Long was pleased to see him transferred from Rome in late 1933.[18] In an unrelated matter, Long had to dispatch the commercial attaché in 1935, as he too was immersed in dubious transactions.[19] Nor did Long hesitate to scold the military attaché, one Colonel Pillow, who produced skimpy reports concerning Italian preparedness.[20] Overall, Long proved an adequate manager. Nothing like the surliness that infected Dodd's Berlin mission polluted Embassy Rome.

The most obvious difference from Dodd in Germany was Long's pleasant interaction with his hosts. The ambassador's dealings with foreign office men at the Palazzo Chigi – Dino Grandi, Fulvio Suvich – were unfailingly civil. Long particularly liked Italo Balbo, an aviation pioneer and one of the more flamboyant Fascists, who exemplified the regime's passion for action. Balbo evidently reciprocated Long's feelings. He paid close attention to the ambassador and retinue during their 1935 fact-finding trip to Tripoli. Long came away impressed by Italian attempts to enhance the acreage and quality of arable land while introducing sundry improvements to local Arab economy.[21] He presented Balbo with the Distinguished Flying Cross after he and comrades flew a squadron of planes from Italy to the United States, an illustration to the ambassador's mind of Fascist courage and efficiency. Balbo's death during the war, mistakenly killed by his own men in 1940 over Libyan skies, saddened Long: "He had more mental and physical activity and virility than any other person I have known."[22]

Regarding Mussolini, Long was an admirer whose enthusiasm barely flickered during his embassy tour. The leader's lucidity and charm won the American. Even more important to him, the Duce possessed uncommon virtues: wisdom, vision, fortitude. In official reports and private missives, Long referred to him in superlatives: an "astounding character," "one of those remarkable people that comes over the horizon once in a long time," "eminently dignified."[23] Athleticism, violinist skills, and previous career in journalism only added to the man's aura. Long thought at times, when in Mussolini's company, that he was in the presence of a genius or Renaissance polymath.

That Mussolini had a brutal side never fazed Long. He did not fret about the dissolution in the 1920s of non-Fascist political parties or trade unions. He was not unduly troubled over murders, such as the 1924 killing of the Socialist party leader Giacomo Matteotti, or jailing of dissidents, or suppression of opposition newspapers. Long respected Mussolini's approach to the Church, codified in the 1929 Lateran treaties that reconciled the Vatican and Italian state. He also considered the Fascists a bulwark against communist malevolence, specifically a check to Soviet mischief in southeastern Europe. In the meantime, Mussolini, man of destiny, was the driving force behind Italy's transformation. Political fragmentation, poverty, and backwardness had given way to innovation and progress. The ambassador gave this testimony in September 1933:

> *Anyone who was in Italy before the War [as Long had been] and can recall the degenerate quality of Italian citizenship, the unkempt situation of the cities and of the towns, the moral and sanitary delinquencies, and who comes to Italy today and sees an entirely changed picture must realize that the [Fascist] system has worked wonders for Italy. But of course it is not all system. It is largely the spirit and enthusiasm and intelligent nervous expenditure of energy of the Head of the Government. He has made a million potential little Mussolinis in every corner of Italy. Their heads are up. Their eyes flash. They walk with a swing. They do their jobs. They study. Their minds work. And they are a changed people.*[24]

Long did not differ, then, from many of his American and British contemporaries in adulation of Mussolini. These numbered more than just quirky or disturbing personalities, such as Ezra Pound and Father Charles Coughlin. Among those who esteemed the Duce at one time or another were writers, labor organizers, scholars, and statesmen, only some of whom ever repented: Charles Beard, Austen Chamberlain, Winston Churchill, Samuel Gompers, William Randolph Hearst, George Santayana, George Bernard Shaw, Lincoln Steffens, Wallace Stevens, W. B. Yeats.[25] Two of Long's ambassadorial predecessors in Rome had also found Mussolini compelling: Richard Washburn Child (1921–1924), Henry Fletcher (1924–1929). The former helped in the writing of Mussolini's so-called autobiography, and, well after leaving the US diplomatic corps, broadcast the Duce's presumed virtues.[26] Even FDR could be moved to praise. He wrote to Long, after receiving a report of his first meeting with the Duce, that Mussolini was a person of obvious substance: "There seems no question but that he is really interested in what we are doing [in the New Deal] ... I am much interested and deeply impressed by what he has accomplished and by his evidenced honest purpose of restoring Italy and seeking to prevent general European trouble."[27]

Fortified by Roosevelt's respect for Mussolini, at least in the beginning, and anyway drawn to Italy's promise, Long plunged into a study of Fascist doctrine and practice. He was "intrigued." He called Italian Fascism "the most interesting experiment in political science which has evolved since [the US] Government was formed under the Constitution."[28] He decided that Fascism had much to offer to beleaguered people elsewhere – in Austria and Hungary, for instance. It might, if carefully shaped to US contours, also be useful to Americans as they struggled with the multiple hardships of prolonged Depression. By his reckoning, he told Washington officials, the New Deal with its regulatory provisions had commonalities with Italy's corporative structure, the National Recovery Administration being a case in point. In any event, he marveled, sloppy governance in Italy, signified by the discredited Chamber of Deputies, had been blotted out and replaced by "scientifically" organized institutions. Cooperation across classes and diverse enterprises – also between the state and citizenry – had eclipsed former rivalries to benefit collective life and enhance individual fulfillment while assuring unprecedented levels of orderliness.[29]

Roosevelt tolerated Long's discourse on the wonders of Fascism. He never chided the ambassador for suggesting that this Italian phenomenon, entwined with dictatorial machinery, had affinities with the New Deal or was pertinent to US circumstances. Of keener interest to FDR than the theoretical utility of Fascism were evaluations of Italy's international policy. Yet on this subject too Long tended to be starry-eyed. He failed to discern the aggressive opportunism that marked Mussolini's diplomacy, apparent to other observers well before Italy landed in Germany's camp. Rather, Long held that the Duce was an earnest peace-advocate, fully committed to the pacific resolution of international questions: "He is building up his influence as well as he can to be used in the interests of a peaceful Europe and to try and coordinate the industrial and commercial activities of European countries to bring an end to the panicky situation, to promote normal trade relations, and secure [stable] development."[30] Therefore, Long explained in 1933, Mussolini would never abandon Austria's independence to Germany, which would entail the added complication of bringing the Third Reich to abut northern Italy. He would use Italian suzerainty in Albania strictly as a defensive counter against Yugoslavia, itself abetted by France's hegemonic drive in the Balkans.[31] Most significantly, he would assume on critical occasions – and otherwise always behind the scenes – the role of peacemaker. He knew that another European war would cause unmitigated chaos from which lunging Bolshevism would benefit.[32] Thus Long hailed Mussolini as the hero of the 1933 Four Power Pact that upheld the League of Nations and the Kellogg–Briand censure of war.[33] The Duce, in Long's brief, also played the main part at Stresa, the April 1935 conference that confirmed Austrian integrity and the continuing relevance of the 1925 Locarno treaties (which emphasized the inviolability of borders in western Europe while providing for arbitration in the east).

As for purely bilateral Italo-US matters, Long believed that Mussolini and the foreign ministry, if not the embodiment of sweet reasonableness, were nonetheless eager to maintain a sound relationship. With modest results, Long tried to shield anti-Fascist Italian-born American citizens – conducting errands in the old country – from being jailed (or worse). He strove to clarify the protection owed to Italian-born Americans against having to comply with Rome's conscription laws. He worked patiently to increase volumes of trade, despite protectionist barriers in both countries and Italy's dilatoriness on payment of

Great War indebtedness. Still, none of these matters so distressed Long that he ever lost confidence. Irrespective of what might occur on the increasingly nervous European continent, Italo-US relations would remain decent. In Rome, after all, an exceptional person was in charge. Mussolini not only labored for the cause of nonviolence but also valued Italy's ethnic ties to the United States, historic destination for millions of emigrants who had found fresh starts and satisfaction.[34]

The war against Abyssinia that gave the lie to Mussolini as peace-champion did not much discompose Long. True, he admitted, his Fascist hosts had a pitiless side. The use of poison gas and dum-dum bullets against Abyssinians, contrary to international prohibitions then in place, were indefensible and Haile Selassie's pleas for aid from the League of Nations were moving. Long allowed: "Italy has not a leg to stand on, either moral or legal, in her invasion of [Abyssinia]."[35] Still, this assault upon a weak country did not obviate, in the ambassador's opinion, Fascism's many accomplishments or discredit the imperative of Europe's maintaining a version of stability. For that purpose, he insisted, Italy remained vital, well positioned still to play an affirmative role. In these circumstances, leniency toward Rome, not righteous US indignation, was indicated.

As the war progressed, Long tried to soften the severity of charges leveled against Italy by varied critics – ranging from Britain's young foreign minister, Anthony Eden, to African-American volunteers such as the legendary John Robinson ("the brown condor") who trekked to Abyssinia to fight.[36] Long told FDR that Mussolini had no alternative to declaring against Abyssinia after it refused to negotiate problems in good faith, outstandingly the disputed frontier (flashpoint at Ualual) running between Italian Somaliland and the African kingdom. Not to answer Abyssinian intransigence with stringency would have been tantamount to surrender, a humiliation that would have led to Mussolini's removal from office. What the Italian government wanted in Africa was perfectly explicable to Long: to redress the European imbalance of overseas possessions and status. In any event, he counseled FDR, Abyssinia fell far outside the US bailiwick and should not be allowed to distract the administration from attending to economic and social problems closer to home.[37]

Long taught that the London-led international protests against the invasion did not stem from pure morality or principled commitment to the sanctity of borders. He contended that Britain was mainly interested in defending and enlarging its African position, which placed the venerable empire at cross-purposes with upstart Italy. Its ambitions in Abyssinia ran counter to British commercial expansion into that country while raising questions in Whitehall about the long-term security of the Suez Canal and Royal Navy dominance of the Red Sea. Ultimately India was at stake, as were other possessions that lay east of Suez. From an objective standpoint, Long advised FDR, the self-seeking British and Italians were equivalent: "I can't get very excited about the moral standing of either contestant." Neither European claimant in this African clash of empires should presume on US sympathies, least of all the British who held millions of people in subjugation in defiance of democratic ideals.[38] Long suggested, therefore, that Washington observe impartiality and resist temptations to join the Anglo-French or other League powers as they toyed with imposing sanctions upon Italy, namely a contemplated oil boycott. He urged likewise that the United States in the event of an Italo-British war should stay aloof (in line with the 1935 Neutrality Act); it would likely trigger general European violence on the scale of 1914. At all costs, the United States, should not get sucked into such a conflagration or do anything that might spark it.[39]

Long was impressed by Mussolini's showing in Abyssinia, which before the war he predicted would be difficult in the extreme, and came to esteem Italy's "indomitable" armed forces. These could, he judged, should Rome so choose, disrupt the peace of Europe – Mussolini deploying at will a tough army, resourceful air force, and formidable navy which might actually bloody those of Great Britain were the issue ever forced: "Considering [the Italians'] strategic position, their concentrated organization, their modern equipment and their fanatic adherence to a leader who represents their national aspirations and their continuing economic existence, they cannot be easily dismissed even in conflict with the British fleet."[40]

Long held in spring 1936 that the totality of Italian victory argued in favor of Washington's admitting that Abyssinian sovereignty had ceased to exist, the country would thenceforth constitute an integral part of the Italian world. When FDR followed the Anglo-French powers in their retreat from taking strong measures against Italy, first signaled by the Hoare–Laval proposal to partition Abyssinia (December 1935), Long was pleased. The administration had, he congratulated himself, accepted his reasoning to avoid rash action, content to scold aggression but not apply unwarrantedly harsh or unworkable policies.[41] A sound precedent was thus in the making, said he. America's guarantee for future safety was one of isolation from the Old World's accumulating dilemmas: "I am for staying all the way out."[42]

Partly for reasons of health centered on an ulcerous condition that required surgery (done in June at the Mayo Clinic), Long left Rome in April 1936. Roosevelt, moreover, was eager to have him stateside to assist with the upcoming reelection campaign. Long, for his bit, was glad to be of service, health allowing. He also entertained high hopes for his successor in Rome, the outgoing undersecretary of state, William Phillips; he should be able to shift the weight of trade, formerly conducted by Italy with Britain, to the United States. Long's last item of ambassadorial advice to FDR was to reiterate an urgent point: recognize de jure Mussolini's absorption of Abyssinia and not fuss over the means used.[43]

After Abyssinia

A result of the Abyssinian imbroglio was to push the Italian and German governments closer together. Bruising caused by sparring over Austria faded. Lingering resentment in Berlin over Rome's 1915 desertion to the Allies dissipated. Hitler voiced not the slightest objection to Mussolini's Abyssinian adventure. In June 1936, Mussolini repaid the favor. He persuaded Austria's Schuschnigg to accept new levels of cooperation with the Third Reich, consummated by Berlin–Vienna agreement in July. Mussolini had meantime become disenchanted with London for having tried, albeit haphazardly, to block his destiny in Africa. And the British were turning by stages toward France as it contemplated Germany's impending next move against the Versailles structure. Just as these new alignments were taking hold in Europe, Phillips arrived in Italy to present credentials.

Phillips in Rome

He was among the most highly respected officers in the Foreign Service at the time of his Rome assignment, widely perceived to be on a level with his friend Joseph Grew. Like him, Phillips was descended from Boston Brahmins, in whose legacy counted the abolitionist Wendell

Phillips, as well as a clutch of luminaries connected to New England's public/commercial affairs. Independent wealth, marriage to Caroline Drayton of Astor family renown, and a web of social connections (including friendship with Franklin and Eleanor Roosevelt) formed the world of Phillips.[44] He inclined no more than Grew toward intellectual pursuits but preferred an outdoor life and was attentive to matters sartorial, earning him the sobriquet of the Beau Brummell of US diplomacy. Phlegmatic, ambitious to the extent allowed by decorum, Phillips was not one to challenge prevailing orthodoxy, not in any of its philosophical or political forms. He adhered to Talleyrand's injunction: "*Et surtout pas trop de zèle.*"[45] Listing to the starchy side, he was wholly dependable from the standpoint of the patrician class and Washington insiders, even if not elsewhere appreciated. New Dealer Raymond Moley called him a "stuffed shirt." Dodd dismissed Phillips as a specimen of undeserving privilege who ought to be reproved.[46]

As had Grew, Phillips benefited from early exposure to President Theodore Roosevelt. He took him on rambles in Washington's Rock Creek park, elevated him to membership in the "tennis cabinet," and advanced his diplomatic career.[47] Its highlights before Italy included assignments in pre-World War London, which helped solidify Phillips as an Anglophile. He was posted to China during the ministry of grave William Woodville Rockhill and was founding head of the State Department's Division of Far Eastern Affairs. Despite his Republican affiliation, Phillips served in Woodrow Wilson's State Department as third assistant secretary, working well with William Jennings Bryan, and imbibed heavily of the president's brand of internationalism. Phillips was promoted to first assistant secretary in January 1917 as reward for his multiple competences. Afterwards, he enjoyed a set of ministerial/ambassadorial appointments: the Netherlands (1920–1922), Belgium/Luxembourg (1924–1927), Canada (1927–1929). He worked too as undersecretary of state during Harding's administration. On the strength of friendship and donation to FDR's campaign coffers in 1932, the new president selected Phillips for a second term as undersecretary of state. As always before, Phillips, the "team" player par excellence, faithfully served.[48]

The reason for Phillips's resignation as undersecretary in 1936 remains obscure. Evidence suggests that he had become worn down by having to supervise the State Department's daily affairs.[49] Also Sumner Welles, more brilliant than Phillips, less deferential, and cozier with

FDR (and the First Lady), had been angling for the highest spot at State, still inconveniently occupied by Cordell Hull. The undersecretaryship was an acceptable second-best spot from Welles's perspective. The president, in any case, moved Phillips from his State Department slot, giving him Rome as consolation, luckily made vacant by Long. Albeit outwardly content to comply, FDR's reshuffling should have rankled Phillips. It may account for these barbs in his otherwise discreet memoirs: FDR was not wholly trustworthy; he lacked wisdom; the Hull–Welles feud, for which Roosevelt bore responsibility for not curbing, impaired the conduct of foreign policy.[50]

Phillips had two immediate tasks as ambassador. First, he had to reassure Rome that FDR's decision to withhold recognition of Italy's Abyssinian annexation, signaled by the envoy's being accredited only to the sovereign as King of Italy (omitting "Emperor of Abyssinia"), did not indicate antipathy for Mussolini's regime. The president, Phillips labored to persuade, was merely adhering to a universally applicable principle (Stimson Doctrine) insisted upon by the American public: not to legitimize territorial gains anywhere made by force. Italy, as such, was not being subject to special disapprobation. Phillips's second task was to secure a new Italo-US treaty of commerce–navigation–friendship upon the abrogation in 1937 of an obsolete one (dating to 1871). The proposed new treaty was never ratified. Although prettily dressed by Phillips, Washington's continuing non-recognition of Abyssinia's incorporation offended Italian *amour-propre*.

In his view, the treaty negotiations were misplayed and amounted to the squandering of a chance to stall Italy's drift toward Hitler. "Germany is the great danger in the world today," Phillips reflected in May 1938, "and I do not see the point of any action on our part which will tend to drive Italy and Germany into closer union."[51] Like Long, he wanted the United States to refrain from moral posturing and to acknowledge that novel facts, if unappetizing, obtained in Africa; to ignore them was perverse, incompatible with practical policy. It should have dictated trade with Italy as prophylactic against German domination of Rome's markets and diplomacy.[52]

Mussolini's new friendliness toward Germany, signaled by the Duce's trumpeting in October 1936 of a Rome–Berlin axis, strained the Rome–Washington connection. Phillips countered with attempts to cultivate the Fascist leadership – without trace of Dodd-like disdain for resident toughs – and impress upon it the idea that shared goals still bound Italy and the United States: preeminently, a common interest in European tranquility. Albeit less than Long, Phillips did admire the Duce and engaged him, occasionally applying copious flattery. The ambassador calculated that, if properly encouraged and lauded as savior-peacemaker, Mussolini would act to slow Hitler's war reflex.[53]

Phillips became well acquainted with Count Galeazzo Ciano, Mussolini's son-in-law and foreign minister as of 1936. At least for a while, Phillips hoped through him to prevent Rome from "dancing" to Berlin's "tune." This notion dovetailed with Ciano's wariness of the Germans, but was also undermined by his belief that the inward-looking United States was essentially irrelevant to Europe. Ciano's robotic obedience to the Duce, in any event, and penchant for parsimony with the truth perturbed the ambassador, most plainly in spring 1939 when the foreign minister claimed that Italy had no intention of quashing Albania.[54]

Phillips also tried to influence events via other people. Victor Emmanuel was one. Phillips came to view him as a disengaged oldster whose political horizon did not stretch past his desire to preserve the rickety monarchy: "a [pitiful] little man." The ambassador, alas, failed to grasp that the king was not enamored of things German and was bothered by Mussolini's confidence in the inevitability of Third Reich success. This skepticism, combined with Italy's botched post-Abyssinian military performances, led finally to the King's intervention in July 1943 to force Mussolini from power.[55] As for Pope Pius XII, installed in March 1939, Phillips could never directly approach him, not having been accredited to the Holy See, but appealed to FDR to appoint someone. That was done in 1939. The president made Myron Taylor – retired chief executive of US Steel, delegate to the Evian conference – his personal representative to the Vatican.[56] Taylor then had to confront the confounding passivity and political opaqueness of Pius, unwilling or unable to contain the rising swell of European disorders.

Phillips's reporting to FDR on the Italian side of these disorders was good of its kind. The Fascist empire, at the zenith of its power and popularity when Phillips reached Rome, then began to spin downward. He monitored this descent with particular attention to the lackluster record compiled by Italy's 75,000 "volunteers" in the Spanish civil war. Mussolini's contingents failed to duplicate their cheap glory in Abyssinia but suffered unexpectedly against Loyalist formations, as at Guadalajara in March 1937. At the same time, guerilla resistance in

Abyssinia flared, suppression of which required extensive pacification campaigns, as followed the assassination attempts on Viceroy General Rodolfo Graziani. Phillips accurately read the Spanish expedition and ongoing African involvement as constituting an impossible burden on men, materiel, and funding. He concluded that Italy – as Ciano intimated to him – would subsequently want to pursue nonviolent policies into the future, allowing the empire to develop properly while resolving its financial wobbliness. Suddenly a self-styled "satisfied power," Italy was neither ready nor willing to participate in pan-European violence, Phillips believed.[57] Mussolini's role as intermediary at the Munich conference seemed to validate this interpretation.

Hitler had plans of his own and was unwilling to let his Rome partner exercise a veto over them. Neither Mussolini nor Ciano was consulted about, or told much in advance of, Nazi initiatives. Both men were discomfited by Germany's swallowing of Austria in March 1938, which immediately raised the question of whether Third Reich ambitions might extend farther south to "protect" Austrians that inhabited the Italian Dolomites. The German seizure of Bohemia and Moravia in March 1939 also startled Rome, to say nothing of later rapprochement with Moscow or the war decision against Poland and its Anglo-French allies.

Phillips sensed rightly that Italian statecraft was embarrassed – indeed, angered – by these instances of Nazi unilateralism.[58] He emphasized to FDR that the commencement of German–Soviet hostilities against Poland in September 1939 confronted Mussolini with long-term existential problems: "Should the Allies succeed in overthrowing Nazism, Fascism is endangered ... should Germany win the war, Italy would become a vassal state ... should Communism enter the Balkans, there would be difficulty in keeping it out of Italy."[59]

Axis relations

As Phillips knew, Italy had been at risk of becoming a German lackey well before the eruption of 1939 hostilities. This was manifest in 1938, when Mussolini's government assumed its anti-Semitic stance. To begin with, Ciano made obvious to him that Italy was uninterested in associating itself with that year's Evian exercise. "It was in conflict not only with our line of action in international affairs, but with our political morality," the foreign minister stated.[60] Mussolini also rejected FDR's

4 William Phillips.

idea that the plateau region of Abyssinia be reserved for Germany's Jewish refugees seeking a non-European haven. More telling still, the government promulgated a series of anti-Jewish laws. Before then, Ciano had told the ambassador that Italy did not have a "Jewish problem." Jewish numbers were small, a mere 46,500 in a population of more than forty-two million; some Jews were actually enrolled on the membership lists of the Fascist party. The measures enacted in 1938–1939, nevertheless, called for the deporting of foreign-born Jews resident in Italy, barred Jews from holding public office or position in the professions, decreed the expulsion of Jews from universities, forbade "miscegenation," and confiscated varieties of Jewish property.[61]

Phillips perceived these discriminations as adopted to underscore alignment with Hitler, "to keep in [his] good graces." They were also indicative, he warned, of Rome's developing subordination, as German race experts in 1938 descended upon Italy to teach citizens about "blood defilement." Phillips, incidentally afflicted by a genteel species of anti-Semitism, took Ciano to task in discussions, saying that sanctions upon

Italian Jewry would limit the future of Washington–Rome cordiality as Jewish influence in the US press was not something with which to trifle. In keeping with lines promoted by Welles and Hull, Phillips also insisted upon the rights of American Jews in Italy – such as the art historian Bernard Berenson – to pursue their affairs in Italy without interference.[62] Phillips knew Berenson somewhat and admired his magnificent Villa I Tatti (Florence). Phillips advised him on how to protect his collection of masterworks and ensure his own safety. The ambassador was able eventually to involve Ciano in the wellbeing of Berenson, a precaution that led to his surviving the bitterest years.[63]

Eighty-five hundred Italian Jews perished in the Shoah, a number that would have been greater but for the half-hearted cooperation of ordinary Italians with Nazi policy.[64] They also proved to be less-than-stellar partners of Hitler in his war against the Allies, even when formally tied to the Third Reich, a point plain to Phillips; he called Mussolini's nation "the weak link in Germany's armor."[65]

He monitored with relish the accumulating tensions between the two Axis states in 1939–1941, for which purpose he relied upon hard evidence when available, otherwise upon speculation and collated gossip. All reinforced his notion that Hitler was annoyed by Mussolini's reluctance to declare against France and Britain until French defeat was imminent. Rumors reached Phillips in September 1940 that Ribbentrop had lectured Mussolini against invading the Greece of strongman Ioannis Metaxas; Berlin's leaders were thereafter livid that this guidance was ignored, resulting in Italian defeats/retreats in northwestern Greece and necessitating rescue (December) by German armies.[66] Italy's setbacks in Greece, Phillips knew, confirmed German unease about Fascist military prowess. At the same time, reports poured into the embassy of insults hurled between German and Italian soldiers in Greece. Spontaneous altercations occurred; both sides suffered casualties. Hatred between soldiers of the Axis was evidently greater than between Greeks and Italians or Germans and Greeks.[67] One high-ranking Wehrmacht officer apparently said while in Rome – so Phillips reported to Welles – that a war declaration upon Italy would hugely boost morale in Germany. This flimsy Italo-German combination could not possibly last, the ambassador predicted in September 1941.[68] The question, though, remained: when and under what conditions would the Berlin–Rome link crack?

Through no fault of his, Phillips could not hasten the demise of the Axis alliance or dissuade Mussolini from committing irrevocably to

Hitler's side. Phillips's role in Welles's two visits to Rome (late February, mid-March 1940) to determine chances for ending the war – perhaps with Italian help – was minor. The only breakthrough for the ambassador came in Mussolini's greeting him (while in Welles's company), something not done since February 1938, when the Duce, petulant over US criticisms of his regime, had decided to shun embassy officials. Welles himself, though struck by Ciano's distrust of Germany, concluded that Italy would inevitably, at the opportune moment, join Germany to hit the Anglo-French allies. Even before Welles left Rome for Washington, Hitler and Mussolini met at the Brenner Pass to coordinate future actions. These were not inhibited by FDR's subsequent offer of mediation or attempts to discourage Italy from attacking France.[69]

As the Allied front disintegrated in Belgium and France in May 1940, Phillips delivered emergency messages from FDR to Mussolini. These laced implicit warnings of Italian disaster, should the unprepared country go to war against Allied power, with pleas for forbearance, and promises to adjudicate fairly Rome's claims in the Mediterranean. None of these communications turned Mussolini. Instead, his army entered the French Savoy in June, a move that caused Phillips to grouse about deficiencies of national character: "To wait to strike until France was down and out was, to put it mildly, not chivalrous ... but then the Italians are not warriors or sportsmen so perhaps it is wrong to expect any such behavior from them."[70]

Wartime Rome

Mussolini's decisions in June 1940 deflated Phillips; the hour of diplomacy had passed, his mission was finished as Italy and Germany had merged into a single unit under Hitler's direction. He wanted to quit Rome as quickly as feasible. The absence of a US ambassador in Berlin reinforced Phillips's dejection, aggravated by bouts of bronchitis and pneumonia. "I am fully aware of my own uselessness here," he told Welles in July 1940.[71] Yet by cajoling and invocation of duty, FDR prevailed upon Phillips to stay in Rome. This he did until taking what he thought would be a routine furlough in 1941, scheduled to begin in October and terminate in December. In the event, he was in Massachusetts when the United States and Italy went to war. He thereupon resigned his ambassadorship.[72]

Phillips did yeoman service in Rome before this denouement. He concentrated attention in 1940 on taking responsibility for the interests of shuttered Allied missions: British, French, Dutch, Polish. He and his staff helped US passport holders to leave Italy, complicated evacuations that often meant getting people first to safety in Switzerland. At the same time, he had an embassy in his trust, administration of which naturally touched upon the usual run of human frailties, exacerbated by wartime emergency. Overall, though, he was satisfied with his subordinates. He had particular confidence in senior officers, such as George Wadsworth, who was serving as chargé d'affaires when Italy declared against America.[73] The embassy, meanwhile, had become a target of suspicion, spawned by US Lend-Lease aid to Britain (then extended to the USSR), and intensified by US–British naval coordination in 1941 against the Axis. The freezing of Italian assets in the United States in June 1941 was greeted in Rome as an act of de facto war. Consequently, fewer Italians maintained relations with the diplomats or their families. Police surveillance became more intrusive. Phillips's own interactions with Italian officialdom were correspondingly reduced, restricted primarily to Ciano. The ambassador was never disliked personally. Ciano thought him, quite accurately, both honest and a lover of Italy. But as FDR's envoy, he could not be trusted or courted, a condition underscored when Mussolini took umbrage on learning that Phillips's daughter, Beatrice, had earlier enlisted as an auxiliary with a French transport unit. The closing of US consulates in summer 1941 amounted to an amputation of vital links to larger Italy, adding measurably to the ambassador's felt futility.[74]

Despite formidable barriers to the gathering of information, Phillips's people managed to draw for Washington a vivid sketch of wartime Italy. Bleakness was the overall impression. The Greek disaster stirred anger against Mussolini and Ciano, the latter especially who as a "scape-goat" was safer to condemn than the exalted Duce. Italian losses to the British in Libya in January–February 1941 (Bardia, Tobruk, Benghazi) bewildered the population. The complete rout in November of Italian forces by the British in Abyssinia added to this sense of disorientation: the revived Roman empire was not supposed to crumble. Phillips, incidentally, offered Washington's good offices to help with the evacuation of Italian women and children from Abyssinia, an intercession that eventuated with a British guarantee to ensure repatriation and Ciano's gratitude. A "useful piece of diplomacy,"

Phillips then reported.[75] Italian participation in the German invasion of the USSR was, meanwhile, greeted with incredulity throughout the country. Anxiety grew apace, Phillips observed, when the stubborn Soviets chose not to surrender.[76]

Shortages in food and heating fuel added to the general apprehensiveness in 1941. British air-naval assaults at the time upon continental Italian cities (Genoa, Naples) and in Sicily also augured ill. Moreover, noted Phillips, the ever-expanding German presence in Italy (economic, military, Gestapo) was unpopular, when not actually despised. Italians of varied background and political stripes (Fascists too), he asserted, were "hanging their heads in shame" as Rome slipped subservient to the Third Reich.[77] The wide citizenry, he observed, had come to view the war as that of the regime, not theirs. Apathy abounded. Individuals withdrew internally from Fascist purposes, thought to be extravagant if not downright delusional: "This is 'Caesar's' war, to add to the map of Italy, and to glorify Caesar himself, while the people seem unconcerned and even indifferent to what is going on around them."[78] Mussolini at the time appeared unfocused and the object of creeping criticism – besotted by his latest amoret but unconcerned with Italy's welfare. "Although he is still nominally head of things," Phillips explained in a January 1941 briefing for Welles, "[Mussolini] is not in the picture as formerly. He seems never to be with his armies and only occasionally the press speaks of his visit to the wounded ... it is said that he spends a good deal of his time with his two mistresses, 'Mme. de Pompadour and her sister,' in the villa on the outskirts of Rome."[79]

That Mussolini was out of touch with feeling in his capital, that his prestige was plummeting as the number of Italian defeats rose, was bad enough. That he might blunder into new or worse misadventures was also a distinct possibility, at least to Phillips. He recorded on the Ides of March 1941: "Having failed so far in all his campaigns, if he took on the United States, the Italians would regard him as crazy."[80] Still, Mussolini, bewitched by German power in December 1941, pressing hard on Moscow and Leningrad, followed it into war against the United States – blind to the Allied preponderance of advantages (US industrial/ technological capacity, Soviet manpower, British tenacity). In his last interview with Ciano, October 1941, Phillips used blunt language. War against the US, he promised, would break Italy absolutely.[81]

Two months later, the foreign minister, stirred by Japanese exploits at Pearl Harbor, gave Wadsworth (Phillips being Stateside) notice to this effect: King Victor Emmanuel's government proudly considered Italy at war with the USA. Yet of the rally that then followed in Rome to celebrate this occasion, capped by Mussolini's oratorical bombast, Ciano wrote in his diary: "The demonstration . . . was not very enthusiastic. We must not forget that it was three o'clock in the afternoon, the people were hungry, and the day was quite cold."[82] Unease, then, flecked with moroseness marked Rome's decision for anti-US hostilities. Mussolini's arraying of his countrymen against Anglo–Soviet–US might, notwithstanding its reverses (which ran through mid-1942), count as one of the more colossal miscalculations in the catalogue of statecraft, a fact grasped by Ciano's subdued Roman crowd. This culminated in 1943 with Italy's defection under Marshal Pietro Badoglio to the Allies, which in turn precipitated German reprisals against its erstwhile partner.

***

Italian treatment of Wadsworth and his embassy in December 1941 was mild, mixed with apology for the inconvenience and, perhaps, dismay at being yoked to Germany in war against Americans. Until returned to the United States in late spring 1942 the diplomats (plus dependents) were housed in Rome hotels and enjoyed freedom of the city. Admittedly, police escorts for shopping errands were irritating. These nuisances also followed their charges to museums and church services. The diplomats too would have been happier to live without a curfew (11 p.m.) or rationed telephone use.[83] They escaped close confinement and that claustrophobia experienced by colleagues in Bad Nauheim and Tokyo, however. Baron Celesia, chief of the foreign ministry's Ufficio del Cerimoniale, and his underlings were by every account courteous (even when they forbade a proposed audience between the diplomats and Pius XII at the Vatican[84]). The Italians did, though, keep incommunicado the Reverend Dr. H. Gruber Woolf of St. Paul's American Church (Episcopal) in Rome. This friend of Phillips was charged with espionage and homosexual indiscretions but later permitted to return home with the diplomats.[85]

Two episodes, occurring shortly before the Americans departed from Rome, illustrated the atmosphere of overall leniency. In the first instance, a female relative of Prince Ascanio Colonna (Mussolini's envoy in Washington) invited a male acquaintance from the US embassy to an evening cocktail party at the home of friends. The young man, an unnamed junior officer, danced with her, was demonstrative, and suitably attentive until past the curfew. Rumors later raced about Rome that they were lovers heartsick at impeding separation. In any case, accompanied by an indulgent security detail, the American did not return to his hotel until the wee morning. The secret police subsequently went through a charade of making inquiries. Nobody on the Rome side seemed to care. The woman was not punished beyond pro forma reprimand and brief detention.[86] On a more solemn note: at one point, the military attaché, Colonel Norman Fiske, escaped notice from his minders long enough to pay respects at the tomb of Italy's Unknown Soldier, dedicated to the dead of 1915–1918. Mindful of Italians who might overhear and were sore about German haughtiness, he spoke these words: "I salute you as one who died in the last war – fighting as an ally."[87]

State Department officials, for their part, tried diligently to accommodate Italian diplomats stuck in America (supplying them with appropriate food, wine, reading material). Of their special needs, the most conspicuous sprang from distaste for their German comrades. At Colonna's request, the Italians concentrated at the Greenbrier resort were granted recreational space of their own. They were spared from having to exercise or mingle socially with the Germans, led by the imperious chargé d'affaires Hans Thomsen, who anyway preferred the company of Japanese internees. Nonetheless, bad feeling between the Italian and German groups became so thick that the former asked to be transferred elsewhere. Pleased to highlight anything that exposed cracks in the facade of Rome–Berlin unity, the State Department satisfied this request (March 1942). Colonna and colleagues spent the remainder of their confinement, co-terminous with Americans in Italy, at the stately Grove Park Inn in Ashville, North Carolina. There they enjoyed a more congenial company, detained Hungarian and Bulgarian nationals.[88]

Alert in Rome to comparable signs of Italian animosity toward Germany, Phillips perceived raw feeling across a broad social spectrum, high-ranking military officers and foreign ministry officials to plain folks. He felt not only that eventually the Berlin–Rome alliance must dissolve, but also that adroit US diplomacy could contribute to this end. Yet, however good an interpreter he was of German–Italian maladies, he was unsure of how to exploit them to Allied advantage. His suggestions to Washington on this matter were usually vague, not operationally helpful. A solid political reporter, he lacked the incisiveness to devise strategy or even a line of effective tactics. Had he been a soldier, he would have made a decent staff officer, but not a creative or inspiring commander. Phillips himself counted his Rome tenure an utter failure.[89]

Phillips's only hopefulness during the darkest period – after French capitulation and as Churchill tried to steady British spirits – rested upon an imagined European union of the future, from which demonic German dynamism had vanished. But here, too, Phillips only sensed the direction that political currents might take over the longer term. He was too diffident to suggest ways in which they could plausibly be channeled. He drifted instead upon a tide of shallow optimism:

> *Sometimes I wonder whether the gods who direct our destinies have not chosen, through sheer necessity, this ruthless method of uniting Europe when all other methods have failed. Our United States was formed by voluntary unions, but in Europe voluntary effort has been tried again and again and has failed. Probably Berlin will wield the big stick for many years, but ultimately Berlin's influence over Europe will collapse, leaving behind perhaps a framework around which a new and united Europe may be built.*[90]

Not until deep into 1941 did Phillips recognize the moral-political necessity of bringing US military force directly and immediately to bear upon European events. This meant that Lend-Lease aid was not enough to ensure British survival; nor was waiting for Mussolini to realize that he had picked the wrong side a useful stratagem.[91] During the subsequent years of US belligerency, Phillips, a late but committed convert to intervention, assumed a ready part. As head of the OSS in London, he worked as political advisor on General Eisenhower's headquarters staff. He served too as FDR's envoy in turbulent British India. He came away with decidedly anti-imperial views and provided analyses that buttressed the president as he tried to press Churchill toward decolonization.

As for Breckinridge Long: he also played a wartime role, but a lamentable one, foreshadowed by his Rome tenure. Contrary to Phillips, he had not shied away from entertaining large ideas on diplomatic strategy. In September 1935, he had, for example, proposed to Washington seniors and Mussolini a grand bargain aimed at ensuring the peace. This solution entailed letting Italy satisfy most of its demands in Abyssinia, allowing Germany to regain possession of former African colonies, and acknowledging Germany's right to rearm beyond Versailles strictures. Neither FDR nor Hull nor Mussolini paid these plans much heed. FDR shrugged. Hull was miffed at the presenting of an unauthorized but far-reaching scheme to a foreign head of state. The Duce, anyway, was intent on gaining all of Abyssinia.[92] Still, these 1935 suggestions indicated the unspoken assumptions of Long: wisdom and peace lay in a soft response to international transgressions. That he was also fascinated by Fascism has already been remarked.

This appeasement orientation touched Long's career as assistant secretary of state, 1940–1944. Long gave expression while in that position to anti-Semitism and nativism, surpassing in practical application anything attempted by most bigots of his generation. Jewish refugees seeking US safety, he maintained, included legions of connivers, social deviants, and Marxist revolutionaries, none of whom could be properly assimilated and whose presence must upset the nation's ethnic balance and overwhelm public welfare services. The Nazis, he also averred, would use the refugee stream to smuggle German agents and saboteurs into the United States.

Long managed to emplace an obstacle course of administrative procedures and devices whose purpose was to postpone or, better yet, prevent the granting of US visas to Jews in Nazi-conquered Europe. Consequently, tens of thousands of people who might have entered the United States were refused. He was, moreover, unhelpful to private philanthropic groups that sought to free Jewish or other hostages from German control and deliberately misled congressmen and journalists who inquired into the State Department's handling of immigration matters.[93]

By no means was Long alone responsible for preventing the admission of persecuted people into the United States. Nor can the overall ineffectiveness of US rescue of Jewry be attributed only to him. Military and civilian figures senior to him – ultimately FDR – bore main responsibility for US inactions. These were only partially countered by the War Refugee Board, whose work, however valorous, proved little and late. Still, Long stands out in the tale of FDR's ambassadors. He had not the least grasp in 1933–1936 of that reality captured by Italy's philosopher, Benedetto Croce: Fascism was a "moral illness."[94] Too easily, when later in Washington, protected by the routine and dignity of the bureaucratic office, Long helped thwart for many persecuted any alleviation of their plight.

Part II

Victims

4 MIDDLE KINGDOM

Japanese armed forces waged war against China with scant restraint. The fate of Nanjing was not singular. Summary execution of surrendered soldiers, massacre of civilians, use of chemical-germ weapons, indiscriminate bombing of cities, and rape claimed millions of victims in China during 1937–1945. By some accounting, nearly nineteen million Chinese, of whom the overwhelming majority was civilian, died from hostilities or related causes (famine). No number has been placed on the maimed, homeless, or displaced.

Chiang Kai-shek upheld what passed for national authority in China. He was an admixture of Confucian votary, Christian convert, military leader, demimonde habitué, modernizer, autocrat, and Guomindang (GMD) operator. He contended for control with communists centered in Yanan's fastness, provincial warlords, Tokyo's Manchurian satrapy (led by Puyi), and a Japanese puppet regime in China-proper (led by Wang Jingwei). Independence-minded ethnic minorities, notably Moslem Uyghurs in Xinjiang, grew restive with Han rule. Compounding these difficulties, the better units in Chiang's army were demolished during the early months of combat in defense of Shanghai and other cities lying westward along the Yangtze. Thereafter, Chiang fielded weak armies. They were directed by lethargic or corrupt officers who did not scruple to trade – even their Lend-Lease equipment – with the Japanese. They abused their commands of undernourished and ill-clad peasant conscripts. The inferior training organized by such officers was matched only by their spendthrift attitude toward the lives of their men. Thus did China – plaything of imperial states since the nineteenth

politically riven, constrained by economic and technological
rdness – face East Asia's preeminent power.

A strategy of attrition and trading space for time constituted
Chiang's only plausible expedient. It could produce little beyond survival, never anything like victory. Chinese territorial losses by late 1938
were massive. Japanese naval and land forces controlled China's coastline and littoral cities, were in charge of the North plain, and occupied
the middle and lower Yangtze valley. The country's most economically
important provinces belonged, in effect, to Tokyo.[1] Not until the
advent of Japan's war against the United States did Chiang glimpse
means of deliverance, a prospect clouded though by the rising influence
of the Chinese communist party (CCP).

To Roosevelt, when in expansive mood, China was a robust
democracy that valiantly resisted aggression. Led by a man of "great
vision," and defended by "heroic" soldiers, that ancient country FDR
told audiences – radio listeners to congressmen – would one day wield
economic wallop and assume a vital part in world affairs.[2] The president once confided to Admiral Lord Mountbatten that having five
hundred million well-disposed Chinese would be indispensable to the
West in future years.[3] Justice and a frank recognition of the flow of
events meant, then, that China should enjoy status, during and after the
war, comparable to that of the Anglo-Soviet–US powers. Provisions for
a China seat on the proposed UN Security Council (plus the November
1943 meeting with Chiang in Cairo) were symbol and substance of
FDR's preference, augmented by US renunciation (1943) of extraterritoriality and Congress's modification of the Chinese Exclusion Acts.[4]

The British government too renounced extraterritorial rights in
China but mainly to humor the Americans, who, from London's viewpoint, were annoyingly indifferent to Hong Kong's postwar fate and
GMD support of Gandhi's drive for Indian liberation. To Churchill the
new dispensation and China's ascension to the foremost Allied ranks
("Big Four") were expressions of FDR's romantic enthusiasm that
ignored reason. Even as Churchill recognized that the war might recon-
figure the East Asian balance of power – perhaps extinguishing the
French, Dutch, Japanese empires – nobody could convince him that
stricken China would help prop up any version of new order. The prime
minister, incidentally, did not deny all realism to Roosevelt but suspected
that his sponsorship of China was intended to win "a faggot vote" for
the United States in future attempts to dismember Britain's empire.[5]

Roosevelt was not immune to doubts about Chiang or his ability to contribute to the anti-Japanese effort and post-hostilities stability. FDR privately allowed that China had stalled in the eighteenth century.[6] His reservations, alas, were rarely communicated to British (or Soviet) leaders or shared with his own diplomats, omissions that contributed to the muddle that marked America's China policy. He continued instead to feed the public a line of exaggeration, positing Chiang as the incarnation of resistance to Japan.

Roosevelt employed three ambassadors: Nelson Johnson, Clarence Gauss, Patrick Hurley. Johnson was on hand from the July 1937 skirmish at the Marco Polo Bridge through full combat that by 1941 mired the Japanese in prolonged campaigns. Perversely, and contrary to Tokyo's calculations, Chiang failed to surrender. After hesitation, Johnson became a proponent of generous US aid to China. His successor, the capable but ignored Gauss, credentialed several months before Pearl Harbor, was skeptical of Chiang's democratic pretensions. The skullduggery of the secret police appalled him. He likened its leader, the unsavory Dai Li, and his agents to the Gestapo. Gauss, moreover, doubted that China added much to the Allied fight against Japan and could easily become a liability – the equivalent of Mussolini's Italy to Germany.[7] Despite these misgivings, Gauss did try to foster Sino-American cooperation consistent with FDR's aim: keep the China theater active, thereby diverting the resources and attention of Japanese soldiers (exceeding one million) south of the Great Wall, otherwise deployable against British-Commonwealth–US forces.[8]

The last of FDR's ambassadors, Hurley, was given two delicate tasks in 1944–1945 that would have taxed the most capable of diplomats, of which he was not one. First, he was to reinvigorate the flagging GMD by resolving the feud between Chiang and the senior US army officer in China, talented but abrasive General Joseph Stilwell.[9] Second, Hurley was supposed to coax communists and Nationalists into reconciliation so that they would cooperate meaningfully against Japan. He failed in both endeavors.[10]

Sino-Japanese War

Like Joseph Grew in Tokyo, Johnson was a carryover from the Hoover administration. Of modest background, many removes from the privileged world of Grew, and barely acquainted with FDR, Johnson nevertheless enjoyed the president's respect. He embodied continuity in a roiled part of the world; he was competent.

While Roosevelt breezily presumed expertise on China, based on his grandfather's business ventures in Canton, Johnson could credibly lay similar claim. His diplomatic apprenticeship began in 1907, when, after a year at college (George Washington University), he arrived in Beijing as a language student and translator for the US mission. Ebullient and purposeful, Johnson rose quickly among the Foreign Service's small corps of China hands. His postings included Harbin, Mukden, Chongqing, and Hankow, and he served as assessor to the Mixed Court in Shanghai. He was chosen to direct the State Department's Division of Far Eastern Affairs in 1925, by which time he had become steeped in Chinese history. After serving as assistant secretary of state (1927–1929), he was appointed minister to Chiang's newly designated capital in Nanjing, then made ambassador (1935) when the mission was elevated from legation to embassy. With the passing years he grew pudgy. His red hair thinned. A raconteur since youth, he became garrulous. Yet neither his essential seriousness nor his passion for all things Asian diminished.[11]

Years in China inclined Johnson sympathetically toward its people. He supported, from the 1920s onward, the abolition of extraterritoriality. He disliked the conceits nurtured in colonial-foreign settlements that lay near to teeming slums. He accepted on faith the idea that aggrieved China must one day arise rejuvenated. An amiable democrat, he got on well with all types: manual laborers, mandarins, Buddhist abbots, Guomindang activists.[12] He referred cheerfully to his "personal relationship" with Chiang, even though the Generalissimo's objection to social reforms disappointed him.[13] At no time was Johnson tempted to "go native," however. He never questioned the legitimacy of America's commercial–missionary–strategic interests. These, in turn, depended on the integrity of the Open Door, buttressed by the Nine Powers regime, and US gunboats. Japan's 1931 Manchurian-grab and southward seeping did concern Johnson. But as long as US enterprises were allowed to operate unmolested, he did not worry unduly. He reasoned that China might even profit from the orderliness and dynamism of Japanese-administered Manchuria; surely US businessmen in the area would also benefit from the resultant stability. He reasoned too that a Japanese presence in northern China and a prosperous Manchuria should dam the flow of Soviet influence in Asia, which unchecked would eventually disturb America's Far Eastern position.[14]

What confidence Johnson had placed in Japanese self-discipline and geopolitical usefulness vanished in 1937. Tokyo's swipe at China implied total US exclusion from the mainland, he concluded.[15] Emboldened by conquests and enriched by fresh acquisitions, Japan would pose a more tangible danger to the Philippines and America's Hawaiian possessions than the USSR (whose military services/political class were anyway dysfunctional if evidence from the ongoing purge trials was true). He welcomed FDR's call to "quarantine" aggressor states. He identified China's cause with America's, even as most of his compatriots – Grew too – were suckered by what Johnson called the "peace at any price boys." He advised the president in 1939: "We must lead the world out of the chaos in which it is now struggling ... Dictatorships such as that now controlling Japan understand force and will yield only to superior power ... The question is whether we are ready to fight for the ideals which we have hitherto held."[16]

His skepticism of whether China could muster effective resistance was relieved as Chiang's forces reassembled after Nanjing's capture. Johnson wrote FDR: "Japan lost the war when it failed to obtain a peace dictated on the basis of Japanese terms under the walls of Nanjing."[17] Tokyo, in other words, was enmeshed in a war that it could not finish, engaged by guerillas and regulars that, however ragged, stood a fair chance to drain their enemy's wealth and morale. The fighting spirit, Johnson claimed, transcended all divisions of region, class, and party. The GMD–CCP rapprochement especially, he thought in 1937, augured a national unity that could withstand any assault. Yet he allowed that nothing was certain; Japan might break the stalemate by sheer military weight or by resort to terror.[18]

Johnson did not directly witness the occupation of Nanjing. He did, though, experience the city's presurrender bombings, epitomizing for him an inhumanity for which the Japanese would ultimately pay. He wrote presciently in September 1937: "Some day the Japanese will regret their senseless bombing of towns for someone will subject them to a similar treatment and the world will be silent for they will have no court into which they can go with dirty hands."[19]

By State Department order, Johnson left Nanjing (late November) aboard the USS *Luzon* to follow Chiang's retreating government.

It evacuated first to Hankow, then (summer 1938) went farther inland to Chongqing.[20] Johnson nonetheless tracked events in Nanjing via a few officers left behind, headed by the embassy's reliable second secretary, George Atcheson. Both men knew of misdeeds committed by Japanese forces in Shanghai. The diplomats were also aware of attempts by non-Chinese residents – notably the French Jesuit, Father Robert Jacquinot – to organize safety zones for noncombatants. Approximately 300,000 civilians in Shanghai had found protection thanks to him. Thousands-upon-thousands of people in cities between Shanghai and Nanjing were likewise spared from the worst effects of Nationalist–Japanese combat.[21] On behalf of a Nanjing safety zone – devised by US teachers, doctors, and missionaries but led by an indefatigable German, John Rabe, of the Siemens company – Johnson kept in touch with Japanese officials: Ambassador Ariyoshi Akira in Shanghai, General Matsui Iwane of the Central China Area Army. Johnson entreated them to ensure the lives of Nanjing's civilians, entailing respect for the boundaries of the safety zone and permitting access to food, water, medicine.[22] In the event, 250,000 people were succored in Rabe's sanctuary as atavistic frenzy leapt about them.

Private and governmental American properties were also damaged or looted in Nanjing. The US flag was desecrated. Atcheson was threatened with bodily harm. A Japanese soldier slapped another diplomat, John Allison.[23] The USS *Panay* was sunk (see Chapter 1). Its survivors, including Atcheson, were subjected to additional attack from Japanese warplanes and land batteries. Johnson conveyed reports of these episodes to Secretary Hull, who then lodged complaints with Tokyo authorities. They in turn issued rebuttals, some apologies, and then types of compensation (substantial in the case of *Panay*). Johnson, though, remained unmoved. "Never again," he told Stanley Hornbeck in January 1938, "will a Japanese be able to hold his head high in pride when the story of Nanjing is told."[24]

Johnson's indignation did not abate in Chiang's improvised capital of Chongqing. A maze of narrow streets and dilapidated buildings, it clung to rugged cliffs, below which merged the untamed Yangtze and Jialing rivers. A miasmatic mist often shrouded the city. Waves of pestilence swept it. Refugees swamped it. Poverty and food shortages gripped it. The sewage-garbage swill that glazed city pavements in winter months turned to foul treacle by spring. Stifling summer heat and drenching humidity intensified the general desolation.[25] Only the city's brew of venality, political intrigue, speculation on whether Sir Archibald Clark Kerr (UK ambassador during 1937–1942) was cuckolded by his young wife, and tales of infidelity flooding from the Chiang household were sufficient to distract Johnson and colleagues from preoccupation with physical hardship, not ameliorated by their flimsy bungalows or makeshift offices.[26]

None of this unpleasantness surpassed what the city suffered during the bombing season, clear skies from April to August. Defended by a skeletal air force and antiquated anti-aircraft guns, Chongqing was a choice target for Japanese pilots. They bombed and strafed with impunity, leaving litters of victims – mostly children, women, elders – and smoky ruins. Johnson reported to Washington: "This thing that we are compelled to witness here in Chongqing is beyond all description in its brutality ... daily visits of a hundred or more bombers swinging back and forth over a city of helpless people who cower for hours in dug outs where many are overcome just by the bad air."[27] Scenes of suffering and his own fear of injury by bombs depleted Johnson's store of bonhomie. "It is awfully hard for a chap not to begin to feel sorry for himself," he confessed in June 1940, by which time he was petitioning superiors for release from Chongqing.[28]

Johnson believed that Japanese cruelty over the long-run, whether meted to Nanjing and Shanghai by ground troops or in Chongqing's aerial bombardment, would prove self-defeating. He predicted to Hull that wherever or whenever the Japanese weakened, the Chinese would strike mercilessly. Nothing like a new era of Asian solidarity or serenity, as advertised by Tokyo's propagandists, would take hold in China.[29] Guiltless people were at the mercy of vindictiveness:

> The Japanese armies have dealt terribly with the [captured] cities and areas. The populations have been terrorized and driven away. Thousands of the civilian population have been killed in cold blood. The soldiers have been allowed to rape freely the women of the occupied cities. The houses of the people have been looted systematically and contents carried off by the truck load to be exported to Japan ... Chinese factories have been systematically destroyed.[30]

Normally allergic to racialist slurs, Johnson could not contain himself. He sprinkled his conversation and correspondence with epithets, likening the Japanese soldiery to "unprincipled savages," the "hordes of Genghis Khan," a swarm of "little devils."

To ameliorate Chinese distress and discourage Chongqing from depending heavily on Soviet aid (a possibility until obviated by the April 1941 Moscow–Tokyo treaty), Johnson pressed Roosevelt to assist Chiang by varied means. These would help safeguard US interests in Asia until such time that Americans, if they awoke in time, took direct measures. In lockstep with Hornbeck, Johnson urged that the United States send materiel and warplanes to China. He supported the granting of credits to stabilize the faltering currency. He argued in favor of US training for Chinese pilots and the lifting of prohibitions on Americans willing to serve as volunteer airmen. (Claire Chennault's Flying Tigers first saw action in summer 1941.) He also lobbied the American Red Cross to supply relief via private subscriptions for medicines and surgical instruments.[31] None of this assistance would be squandered on a lost cause: "[The Chinese] are putting up a good fight ... they deserve help in their struggle with a mad man that knows no pity."[32]

The February 1941 arrival in Chongqing of Dr. Lauchlin Currie (New Deal economist) for talks with Chiang launched the start, if tardily from the ambassador's perspective, of a de facto Sino-US alliance and portended significant aid.[33] By the time Johnson left China – for posting as minister to Australia in summer 1941 – his government was sending supplies to Chiang and increasing the pressure on Japan to desist, which culminated in the oil embargo and freezing of assets. The spring 1941 schedule of Lend-Lease for China included railway and communications equipment, 4,000 trucks for military/commercial purposes, 5 million gallons of gasoline, 5,000 tons of diesel oil, heavy weapons, caterpillar tractors, and automobiles. This aid exceeded $40 million in value. More was promised, in which cause Currie was named Lend-Lease expediter for China (and designer of a secret plan whereby China-based US warplanes could bomb Japanese cities).[34] Johnson regretted only that this assistance was thin compared to the need, a view shared by Chiang who occasionally reprimanded him on the gap between Washington's supportive rhetoric and actual help.[35] Even the Red Cross had not collected the amount of medical stocks or China-designated funds originally envisioned by backers, including Roosevelt.

The fraying of China's social fabric was advanced by the time Johnson left Chongqing, a condition most apparent in the intermittent civil war that threatened to burst into full fury. Chiang's forces, on slender pretext, crushed the communist New Fourth Army in January 1941. The truce that had existed between Yanan and Chongqing thereupon ceased to exist in all but name.

Johnson had long thought that in the absence of Japan's invasion the Nationalists would have beaten their CCP rivals. Either way, he maintained that the United States should refrain from taking sides in the escalating civil conflict. It would be fought without quarter; solutions could not be dictated by outsiders.[36] The Japanese meanwhile showed no sign of altering their goal – quelling all Chinese opposition.

Johnson had yearned for US military intervention in East Asia well before December 1941. To him, despite the damages, the Pearl Harbor assault constituted, when it came, *the* welcome moment. He meditated shortly afterward in his Canberra chancellery:

> *The blow has fallen. It has been a shock to our pride.*
> *Perhaps it is the thing that our self-satisfied and complacent*
> *generation needed ... I hope that we will rise to the*
> *opportunity that it gives us to prove that we are not rotten*
> *within ... We cannot stop until Pearl Harbor has been*
> *expiated ... We cannot stop until we have eliminated Japan*
> *as a threat in the Pacific or elsewhere ... We now have*
> *something to live for that is worthwhile.[37]*

Muddling along

Gauss was as eager as Johnson for a viable Sino-American partnership. Like his predecessor, Gauss had witnessed wartime depredations aplenty in China, particularly as consul general in Shanghai (1937–1939), where he acquired among Japanese and Chinese a reputation as feisty defender of US rights.

The two ambassadors shared other traits. Gauss too was not to the manor born. He never attended college but graduated from a business high school in Washington, DC, where he had lived since birth (1887) and his father worked as a civil servant. The political sympathies of Gauss and Johnson were conservative, running toward the GOP, but neither was overtly partisan or inclined to vote.[38] Like

Johnson's China career, Gauss's had also begun before the World War. After working as a stenographer in a law firm and for the Invalid Pensions Committee of the House of Representatives, he joined the State Department as a clerk. His first assignment abroad (1907) was to the consulate in Shanghai. He climbed through the consular ranks in Tientsin, Shandong, Beijing, Amoy. Except for a 1935 stint in Paris, and rotations back to Washington, Gauss had never worked outside of China until designated US minister to Australia in 1940, which he left to swap places with a grateful Johnson. Like him, Gauss was admired in the State Department as a China expert, despite linguistic disability. Also like Johnson, the subordinates of Gauss thought him diligent. Among them were two China-born officers, John Paton Davies and John Service. They repeatedly testified to Gauss's perspicacity. Service, who shared Chongqing lodgings with Gauss in 1941–1942, was particularly glad of his attentiveness to staff and advice on private matters (as when Service, a married man, agonized over whether to divorce his wife to marry a Chinese actress, Val Chao).[39]

Despite points of overlap, Gauss was not just another version of Johnson. The latter lightly wore the stigma of a spotty education. Gauss was embarrassed by his lack of university training. He suffered from the hidden injuries of class, exacerbated by duty in the socially inferior consular service during the years before it merged (1924 Rogers Act) with the prestigious diplomatic corps into the Foreign Service. He chafed at snobbery or signs of slight. He did not indulge in small talk or light diversions. He lived only to work; he proudly authored the Foreign Service's manual on notary procedures. He was meticulous and private versus Johnson's spontaneity. He seems to have been desperate for intimacy, having strained the affections of wife and son. Gauss, though, had neither genius for friendship nor an easy grasp of people or social situations. Poor eyesight necessitated glasses with thick lenses, which did not flatter the angularity of his pallid face or relax his brooding expression. A cigar aficionado, he chomped twelve a day. He reeked of them.[40]

Chiang's confidants thought Gauss not only more odiferous than the usual Occidental but also *déclassé*. Far worse from their standpoint, he could not conceal his disdain for Chiang, whom he associated with the Shanghai underworld, thought grossly incompetent, and drawn to a variant of fascism.[41] Gauss at first inadvertently telegraphed his feelings (scowling, terseness), but later transmitted

5 Clarence Gauss crosses river to Chongqing to present credentials, 26 May 1941.

these with few traces of inhibition. Madame Chiang, whom the ambassador also could not abide, damned Gauss as unworthy successor to the genial Johnson. Even Madame Sun Yat-sen, widow of the Republic's founder and not a Chiang enthusiast, said acidly: "We should have somebody more important."[42]

At no time in Chongqing did Gauss enjoy solid support from his Washington masters. Roosevelt, Welles, and Hull treated him as little more than a placeholder. His chief recommendation had been his availability in early 1941, when practically no one in the diplomatic corps wanted billeting in China's battered capital.[43] Presumably, too, he had recovered in Australia from the trials of his last Shanghai assignment and was fit enough to resume strenuous service. Johnson alone expressed concern for the man upon learning of his Chongqing appointment: "I feel sorry for Gauss ... I have always had a very real respect for his mind."[44] Still, the main point stood: Gauss was bereft from the outset of patrons in Washington or even well-situated friends – as Johnson had in Hornbeck – and was left to fend for himself.

Gauss was minimally informed in late 1941 by the State Department of the ongoing Hull–Nomura discussions to produce a Japanese–US *modus vivendi*, a subject of keen interest to Chiang's government but on which the discomfited ambassador could shed no light. Later he was astonished when, without consultation, the State Department attached four of his second secretaries to Stilwell's staff: Davies, Service, Raymond Ludden, and the Japanese-language expert John Emmerson.[45]

Matters between Gauss and Washington were not helped by FDR's propensity to send dignitaries to supplement, if not supersede, ambassadors stationed abroad. Currie made a return call to China in July 1942. The GOP's Wendell Willkie arrived in Chongqing in October 1942 as part of his global goodwill tour, later memorialized in his *One World* (but chiefly remembered by locals for his amorous attentions to a receptive Madame Chiang).[46] Vice President Henry Wallace made a headline-grabbing visit in June 1944. These and other luminaries paid little attention to Gauss, or ignored him outright, as they conferred with Chiang or various in-theater Americans: Stilwell, Chennault, OSS agents, journalists, and naval intelligence officers under the enigmatic Commodore Milton Miles, who became entwined with Dai Li.

A finding of the Currie–Willkie–Wallace missions dwelt on Chiang's execrating of Gauss and Stilwell: they should be replaced forthwith by people acceptable to the Generalissimo.[47] Only Henry Stimson's and George Marshall's support of Stilwell prevented FDR from relieving him of his assignments (commanding general of US forces in the China–Burma–India theater, deputy supreme Allied commander in Southeast Asia, chief of staff to Chiang). As for Gauss, finding a replacement probably impressed the president as more bother than worthwhile. Besides, the State Department's Far Eastern Division had no complaint against him.[48] Gauss was allowed to stay on, tolerated but not endorsed, a shabby situation obvious to Chinese observers. Stilwell's continuing presence as the dominant American personality in East Asia, conferred upon him by the prestige of US arms and by his power to grant or withhold military aid, also diminished Gauss. The general, not the ambassador, was invited to consult with FDR and Chiang at the Cairo conference.

The storied dispute between Chiang and Stilwell, rooted in competing military strategies and personal antipathy, split China's American community. Chennault sided with Chiang. They preferred using air power – the 10th and 14th US Air-Forces – in which they had nearly mystical faith. These forces could ferry all needed civilian–military resources over "the Hump"; they would blast Japan to smithereens. Stilwell, instead, wanted to concentrate on the land war. He sought to use reinvigorated Chinese troops, whose training he supervised, along with American and British units to recover and hold ground. He deemed it critical to reopen the India–China supply road in Burma (shut by Japanese occupation in spring 1942). Chiang and Chennault countered that such a campaign would be prohibitively expensive. It would also distract from the checking of nearby dangers – Japanese armies in eastern China, Yanan's communists. Not until January 1945, after grueling battles and Stilwell's departure from China, was the land-corridor reestablished. By no means competent to judge between military plans, nor invited to do so, Gauss nevertheless gravitated toward Stilwell. Neither man had confidence in the GMD, nor hesitated to criticize its political-military defects, and looked hopefully to the day when party dissenters would dethrone Chiang. Yet Gauss and Stilwell hardly presented a united front. Touchy even in the best of circumstances, both men were jealous of their respective prerogatives in China, too wary to coordinate on sensitive matters. Consequently, each man sparred alone with Chongqing officialdom. Each had to solidify what alliances he could with Washington superiors, satisfactorily done in the case of Stilwell (until recalled in October 1944) but never in Gauss's.

Obstacles facing him aside, the ambassador managed an efficient embassy that monitored wide-ranging events and personalities. Gauss's officers became acquainted with such figures as Zhou Enlai, the urbane CCP delegate residing in Chongqing. Unfortunately, the staff's good analytical reporting, albeit read by cognoscenti (usually appreciative) in State's Far Eastern Division, seldom reached congressional audiences or the politically literate public. Rather, these analyses were buried by myths of Chiang's democratic commitment as retailed by the White House, GMD publicists, and publishers like Henry Luce (*Time*, *Life*, *Fortune*), and bolstered by Madame Chiang's celebrated 1943 appearance before Congress. Gauss in the meantime offered few consoling truths: Chiang would watch contentedly, almost passively, but give slight assistance to American and British forces as they mounted campaigns against Japanese armies.[49] As Gauss accurately predicted, the Guomindang would increasingly deal with other matters: maneuvering to geographical advantage for a postwar showdown with Mao, employing troops (approximately 400,000) to blockade Yanan, stockpiling Lend-Lease materiel, hoarding dollars. The GMD would also suppress warlords and sundry noncommunist parties. But Chiang's administration, Gauss reported, could be counted upon not to tangle directly with Japanese forces, a melancholy fact underscored by Tokyo's ICHIGO offensive (which in 1944 routed GMD armies, over-ran US airbases, and threatened Chongqing with capture).

Gauss advised against the issuance of anything that smacked of a blank check. Aid should be tied to Chiang's ability to use it well. Chongqing, moreover, should be held accountable for US dollars and materiel sent to it. Doubtful from the outset that such would be properly employed, Gauss recommended in December 1941 that a $10 million loan would suffice, not the $500 million requested by Chinese officialdom.[50] More, he said, might be sent if Chiang's armies resumed serious battle with Japan and the government took measures to calm rising popular discontent via equitable taxation, agrarian reform, and curtailment of the black market. He subsequently opposed other loans (in the $1 billion category) in 1943 and 1944, until Chiang demonstrated a whole-hearted commitment to helping the Americans (constructing airfields for use by long-range bombers and fighters, paving new roads to enhance military transportation and communi-cations, improving the quality and élan of army units). He alleged, consonant with Stilwell's complaints, that Chiang's administration actually impeded the war: "Confidential investigation ... has [indi-cated] extensive corruption, jealousies, delays and sabotage of honest effort."[51] As for periodic Guomindang threats to seek a separate peace, he dismissed them as crude attempts to acquire leverage over the United States without assuming reciprocal obligations. Warplanes, machinery, and moneys in abundance should not be shipped to China out of fear or on the back of a risible bluff. Gauss knew that Chiang knew that a separate peace with Japan would doom the Nationalists.

Although anxious about the communists' swelling strength, Gauss urged, along with Stilwell and Davies, that Washington establish diplomatic-military contact with Yanan and cooperate with its anti-Japanese operations. This goal was partially realized when Chiang, bowing to White House lobbying, agreed to let a military intelligence group – with Foreign Service component – enter the Marxist zone: the so-called Dixie Mission, emplaced in July 1944. Gauss also hoped that Washington would take steps to further GMD–CCP reconciliation, for which he volunteered his own good offices. He wagered that military–political coordination could develop, perhaps giving rise to a form of

Chinese unity that, however ephemeral in the long-run, should produce wartime dividends – shorter war, fewer US casualties. The State Department was encouraging of this initiative, but Chiang pronounced anathema on the communists, who he said served Kremlin goals, not those of China. Gauss's proposed "war council" and a convocation of all Chinese political parties consequently fizzled. By late summer 1944, the ambassador declared that suspicions between the GMD and CCP prevented any détente.[52] Rumors, meanwhile, of an anti-Chiang coup gained currency. Stilwell once confided in his diary (September 1944) that Chiang's countrymen should shoot the Generalissimo and his ministers ("dumb stooges"), an idea not at variance with what FDR once purportedly said to Stilwell and caused him briefly to plot: "If you can't get along with Chiang, and can't replace him, get rid of him once and for all ... put in someone you can manage."[53] Gauss himself would have welcomed a nonviolent removal of Chiang by any leadership, with or without US connivance, bent on vigorously prosecuting the war.

Irrespective of whether Chiang was prepared to yield his office, Gauss in summer 1944 was ready to surrender his. He had had enough. He had run out of ideas on how to prod the GMD out of its "cesspool" of inefficiency/corruption and into good governance. He was demoralized by what he took to be Chinese ingratitude for US efforts to contain Japan – first diplomatically in 1941, then militarily after Pearl Harbor. He resented the tendency of Chongqing ministries to blame every difficulty on the purported inadequacy of US aid programs. He was incensed by the Generalissimo, dictator of an undeveloped country but who grasped at "Big Four" pretensions and cynically parroted democratic slogans.[54]

Gauss's frustrations were heightened in early September. Hurley, one of FDR's itinerant troubleshooters, arrived in Chongqing on a mission to put the Sino-American house in proper order. A short time later, Gauss notified Washington of his intention to resign. He left Chongqing in mid-November 1944.

Gauss's departure was not inspired by mere pique. He had suffered physically, not just from China's hazards. An earlier affliction of the eyes had temporarily robbed him of their use; surgery plus recuperation had necessitated his taking lengthy medical furlough to the United States in 1943. Yet the risk to his sight remained, requiring additional treatment, which clinched his decision to resign.[55] After his medical crisis abated, Gauss hoped to serve in another State Department capacity, perhaps in Washington in the Far Eastern Division. But no niche was found. Roosevelt sent him a perfunctory note of thanks for duty rendered.[56] The Pacific–East Asian war consequently approached its awful climax without Gauss. He protested to the president in February 1945 but without avail: "It would seem that those having an intimate knowledge of foreign relations might be of continuing service to their country."[57] On this point, no doubt, FDR agreed but he trivialized Gauss's abilities; perplexing Chinese circumstances required an imagination honed by more than stenographic skills and notarial expertise. In the president's mind the contrast between Gauss and Hurley was striking: "I wish I had more men like Pat."[58]

Hurley and failure

Hurley was named ambassador two weeks after Gauss's exit, validating his campaign waged *sub rosa* for the post, and formalized his position. In selecting him, the president also completed his makeover of the co-directorship of US enterprises in China, begun with Stilwell's relief from authority in October.

Neither Hurley nor anyone else could have altered these stubborn facts: Chiang detested Stilwell, could not work with him, and, despite FDR's wish, would never place China's armies directly under his command. Hurley had participated – connived in a sense – in the recall decision when he told FDR: "My opinion is that if you sustain Stilwell ... you will lose Chiang Kai-shek and possibly you will China with him."[59]

A furious Stilwell was obliged to return to Washington. His China–Burma–India theater was divided. Lieutenant General Daniel Sultan took charge of India–Burma. Lieutenant General Albert Wedemeyer took command of US forces in China, without direct responsibility for China's armies but only to advise and assist.[60] After making these personnel changes, Roosevelt focused what remained of his declining energy and health elsewhere: Germany's impending collapse with the concomitant promise of Soviet help to defeat Japan; US naval and air assaults upon Japan's shriveling Pacific empire. China, not central to FDR's planning and subordinate to the Europe-first strategy, fell further in geopolitical importance. Yet the country was never seen as utterly inconsequential. Americans stationed there were still eager that the full heft of Sino-US power be brought to bear against Japan.

This resolve meant in Hurley's case, as earlier with the unsung Gauss, that every effort be galvanized to forge Chinese unity, particularly to mend the GMD–communist split.

Hurley brought some virtues to his China task. For one, he was no stranger to adversity. Born of Irish immigrants who settled on Choctaw land in Indian Territory (Lehigh, Oklahoma), his childhood was scarred by family tragedies and grinding poverty. A self-made man of Horatio Alger proportions, he had risen from chores in the Oklahoma coal pits to a multi-million dollar law practice in Tulsa. The Choctaw Nation was among his first clients. He later worked for the Sinclair oil company for which he negotiated a favorable deal with Mexico after Lazaro Cardenas's administration expropriated foreign-owned petroleum corporations. Chuffed to think of himself as a citizen-soldier (membership in the Oklahoma National Guard), Hurley also served as an army officer in Europe during the World War. He received a Silver Star for gallantry under fire.[61]

Public affairs consumed much of Hurley's postwar time. He became active in the Oklahoma GOP, although his wealth and standing never won him elected office. He made a sizable financial contribution in 1928 to Herbert Hoover's presidential campaign and stumped for the Republican ticket in Oklahoma. Hoover subsequently made him assistant secretary in the Department of War. Upon the death of Secretary James William Good (November 1929), Hurley assumed War's top job. During his incumbency he condemned Japan's Manchurian/Shanghai aggressions.[62]

Despite opposing the New Deal, Hurley's public-mindedness, not unalloyed with ambition, meant that he was amenable to aligning himself with FDR on national security questions.[63] As the world crisis intensified, FDR, eager to garner bipartisan support for his diplomacy, sought ways to employ GOP personages, exemplified by the enlisting in 1940 of Stimson for the War Department and Frank Knox for the Navy. Consistent with this approach, FDR made Hurley minister to New Zealand in 1942 and promoted him to flag rank in the army reserve – a major general by 1944. He had earlier organized, and helped lead, Allied supply ships to break the Japanese blockade of Bataan, a hapless but daring adventure lauded by General MacArthur. While on a 1942 fact-finding mission to the USSR, Hurley met with Stalin and toured the Stalingrad battle front. Roosevelt then sent Hurley to the Middle East in 1943. He reviewed

US prospects in oil-rich Iran, at the time under Soviet–British jurisdiction, and scrutinized the Anglo–Jewish–Arab snarl in Palestine
from a decidedly anti-Zionist angle. Hurley went later that year to
China to brief Chiang on the upcoming Cairo conference and deliver
the president's personal invitation. This record of service impressed –
at first – most Americans connected to China. One was Johnson.
From Canberra in December 1944, he conveyed his enthusiasm to
Atcheson, by then counselor of Embassy Chongqing: "Pat Hurley
will I am sure do a very good job. I am very fond of him, and
I know that he is capable."[64]

This assessment of Hurley was based on brief personal
acquaintance and sporty approval of his "can-do" reputation. Johnson
failed to fathom the vain imaginings that plagued the man. Nobody in
1944 could have guessed that the untoward effect of Hurley's time in
Chongqing would be felt into deeper years.

Ruddy, mustached, given to parading about in his beribboned
army uniform, Hurley, still handsome at sixty-one, cut a fine figure

6 Left to right: Generalissimo Chiang Kai-shek, FDR, Churchill, Madame Chiang.
Cairo 1943.

when he arrived in China. The contrast with dowdy Gauss was plain, of whom Hurley sniffed that he lacked bearing. Quite apart from supreme self-confidence and a cloying gregariousness that somehow meshed with FDR's effervescence, Hurley was an eccentric choice.[65] His suspiciousness ought to have disqualified him from running any wartime mission. He bullied subordinates. He censored. He allowed an atmosphere of intimidation to permeate the embassy.[66] His own antics verged on buffoonery.

In a rage he once pulled a pistol on Arthur Ringwalt, a level-headed embassy officer, for having sent material to Washington that contained unfavorable references to Chiang.[67] Hurley had to be prevented from fisticuffs with Wedemeyer's chief of staff, Major General Robert McClure, who, according to the ambassador, lacked patriotism and was frantic to provision Mao's armies with weapons. While sharing Wedemeyer's living quarters, Hurley ceased talking with his host for several days. The two men finally resolved matters in a flurry of apology and professions of friendship.[68] Wedemeyer nevertheless routinely sought to reassure Hurley to forestall misunderstandings, as on 10 July 1945: "Yesterday you stated that you loved me. I want you to know that your feeling for me is reciprocated fully. I feel as devoted to you as I would an older brother."[69] Determined to break Atcheson, Davies, Service, and others who held views at variance with his, or were less effusive in their affection for him than Wedemeyer, Hurley arranged their transfer from China. He replaced these people with men no more conversant in Chinese affairs than himself. Ellis Briggs, deputy chief of mission, was a Latin American specialist, who arrived in China with a "blank" mind (his adjective). Walter Robertson, an opinionated Virginia banker who basked in Hurley's friendship, possessed meager diplomatic experience.[70]

As for ambassadorial colleagues, one can only guess what Britain's Sir Horace Seymour (1942–1946) – mannerly product of Eton and Cambridge – thought of Hurley's emitting of Choctaw war whoops or his impromptu Indian dancing at social functions. The Dutch ambassador in Chongqing, A. H. J. Lovink, did record the following in 1945 for the benefit of his foreign minister:

Is it part of "modern" trends in diplomacy . . . to utter Indian war-cries in the most unexpected places and times, especially at official receptions or at dinner in my house?!! Choctaw calls might have sounded well on the plains of Oklahoma in the days of Buffalo Bill. And in diplomatic and Chinese official circles there is an appreciation for innovation. But Hurley's performance reduces everyone to laughter.[71]

Hurley's relations with US journalists in China were also poor, catastrophically so with Theodore White and Annalee Jacoby. Once when inebriated at a Sino-American banquet, Hurley confused Jacoby for his wife. In front of a flabbergasted assembly he cooed over her while reminiscing aloud about his wedding night. Jacoby thought the ambassador suffered symptoms of senility.[72] She and White wryly recorded his mispronunciation or incomprehension of Chinese names. He rendered Mao as "Moose Dung." Chiang became "Mr. Shek." White and Jacoby, along with colleagues (i.e. Harold Isaacs), lampooned Hurley as someone from Gilbert and Sullivan casting, "the very model of a modern major general." Their overall verdict was not unfair: "Most men who knew him well enough saw in him the tragedy of a mind groping desperately at problems beyond its scope."[73]

As for communists with whom Hurley came into contact, he initially puzzled them. On first meeting Mao and Zhou in November 1944 on Yanan's tarmac, Hurley let loose a shattering Choctaw yell. He then held forth in a disjointed monologue, the purpose of which, if any, was to draw parallels between rural life in Oklahoma and China. Colonel David Barrett, head of the Dixie Mission and a translator at the first Hurley–Mao encounter, recalled: "[The ambassador's] discourse was by no means connected to any readily discernible pattern of thought."[74] Mao later referred to Hurley as "the clown." Other endearments for him coined at Yanan included the "Big Wind." Toward the end of his China tour, Mao treated Hurley with epithets from the Marxist template: "imperialist," "reactionary," "exploiter."[75]

Chiang and the Guomindang elite had occasional reason to worry about Hurley. His major transgression occurred shortly after he arrived in China. He negotiated (10 November 1944) with Yanan terms of provisional agreement for GMD–CCP cooperation that were unacceptable to Chongqing. These upheld as axiomatic the principle of political equality between the GMD and all "anti-Japanese parties," including the CCP. Together they should organize a coalition government to revive the war, then plan for China's reconstruction. The Yanan proposal also allowed for integration of communist and Nationalist forces, but without explicitly recognizing Chiang as ultimate leader. Additionally, materiel obtained abroad (i.e. Lend-Lease) would be "equitably distributed" among all anti-Japanese combatants without reference to partisan affiliation, Marxist or other. Upon reading the Yanan outline, Foreign Minister T. V. Soong told Hurley that he had been sold a "bill of goods." Its acceptance, Chiang added, would lead to the collapse of rightly constituted authority and cripple China's war effort. So corrected, Hurley then acquiesced to the government's counterproposal – devoid of basis for approval by the CCP – in which the primacy of Chiang's regime was reaffirmed and the communists invited to place their military forces under Chongqing. Hurley also dutifully transmitted to CCP legates, principally Zhou, that only through Chiang's offices would US materiel be dispersed to parties other than the GMD.[76]

From the standpoint of his hosts, the ambassador's subsequent lapses were few. Maybe the GMD leaders were aware that he little esteemed the Chinese, no better in his reckoning than blacks, Mexicans, Jews, or other doubtful peoples.[77] His derogatory characterization to Henry Morgenthau about the Nationalists ("fascists," "thieves"), expressed in a moment's exasperation, would also, if known by the Generalissimo, have derailed GMD relations with Hurley.[78] Chiang and Soong too must have been as mystified as embassy officers when Hurley told them that he could coax the GMD and CCP into making common cause. After all, he taught, the differences between the two parties were no greater than those separating Democrats from Republicans. Besides, he knew how to mediate among rivals and to obtain a fair deal, witness his work in producing the Sinclair–Mexico accords.[79]

Hurley's oft-stated idea that the CCP was not composed of genuine Marxists or sponsored by Moscow was also unnerving to Chiang. He thought the ambassador naïve to believe declarations of disinterest by Stalin (expressed to Hurley while on visits to Moscow in 1943–1945) and then to describe the CCP as just a collection of "agrarian reformers."[80] Nor was Chiang pleased when Hurley delayed until 15 June 1945 to tell him about those agreements made at Yalta that conceded chunks of Chinese sovereignty to the USSR: commercial-railroad rights in Manchuria, naval use of Ports Arthur and Darien, continued Soviet hegemony in Outer Mongolia.[81] Chiang must have been irritated too by Hurley's occasional gestures toward the CCP. The ambassador helped engineer the appointment of a (token) communist to the Chinese delegation sent to approve the United Nations Charter in San Francisco in June 1945. Then in August, Hurley gave his personal guarantee of safety to Mao to visit Chongqing to explore means of averting full-blown civil war.

Overall, though, Hurley did not disappoint the Nationalists. He seemed a well-meaning novice whose missteps were forgivable and outweighed by his many evidences in support. He did not whine over restrictions on press freedom in China or object to the application of related strictures to US newsmen.[82] He did not reprove the GMD, as had Gauss, or scoff at Chiang, as had Stilwell (one of whose less offensive monikers for the Generalissimo was "the Peanut"). Instead, China and Chiang became synonymous in Hurley's mind: to back one required backing the other. Treating with any pretender to Chiang's place was impermissible. Hurley's attitude, which hardened into conviction by early 1945, meant that in any form of GMD–CCP cooperation Mao and company would have to swear fealty to Chongqing.[83] Consequently, Hurley's efforts to foster Chinese unity became increasingly desultory. Chiang disallowed political parity with the CCP. Mao would accept nothing less than equality; he meanwhile extended the scope of communist activity into areas once ravaged by the Japanese or abused by the privileged class. Still, Chiang believed that, with the United States, he would not only drive Japan from China but would also overcome the Marxist insurgents.[84]

From Chiang's standpoint, Hurley was educable and endowed with the right mental reflexes. He blocked his people from sending reports to Washington that were critical of the Nationalists. Those officers who did not comply were silenced or reassigned, as were those who thought that a working Yanan–US relationship would produce benefits (i.e. hastening the war's end, discouraging Mao from developing an exclusive reliance upon Moscow, and so sculpting the political landscape that Chiang would embrace reforms otherwise uncongenial to reactionaries in the GMD).[85] Hurley rejected such ideas, although he admitted that communist soldiers might usefully collaborate with the anticipated US invasion of the Japanese-occupied coastline. But until that day, he advised his superiors against sending weaponry to Yanan for ostensible use against Japanese forces. As Chiang emphasized, "You cannot arm my enemies!"[86]

Chiang also valued Hurley for his opposition to any re-imposition of British privilege in China (Hong Kong) or restoration to the Dutch and

French of their colonies in Southeast Asia (Indonesia, Indochina). Both men believed, as did Roosevelt, that Whitehall would have preferred to keep China weak and available for Western uses. In a tone similar to that taken by FDR with Churchill regarding India, Hurley told Seymour that the United States was not waging war to subvert the Atlantic Charter's principles or to rehabilitate European rule in Asia. At this admonition, Seymour took umbrage. He warned of unintended consequences and the eclipse of white power worldwide.[87] In effect, the FDR–Hurley notion of future free trade and an East Asian balance of power conducive to US security dovetailed with Chiang's wishes: the termination of European colonialism, a chance for China to regenerate.

Hurley's cozy relations with the intelligence–secret police outfit – SACO – run by Dai Li and Commodore Miles also gratified Chiang.[88] He had bridled when the Stilwell–Gauss duopoly asserted that SACO's practice of torturing and assassinating domestic enemies hurt the regime's reputation and wellbeing. Whereas Stilwell and Gauss had wanted to curb SACO, Hurley admired it. From it he learned in mid-January 1945 that Mao and Zhou had volunteered to visit Washington, a mischievous proposal, Hurley felt, that he quashed. He also preferred to use SACO's communications apparatus for the sending and receiving of confidential messages, thereby liberating himself from dependence on the embassy's presumptively unreliable signals office.[89] This situation also allowed Dai Li and Miles to monitor Washington–embassy cable traffic and track allegedly subversive diplomats, which information was shared with Hurley. He claimed later that the guilty parties (of which Service was supposedly ringleader), upon realizing that they had been exposed, had torched the evidences of their malfeasance on the night of 19–20 January 1945.

We intercepted letters [through Dai Li] ... The pro-Communists, the pro-Imperialists, and the anti-Americans were not slow in ascertaining the fact that I was reading and having the records read to me. As soon as this fact became apparent the Embassy was burned. The fire occurred about one o'clock in the night ... I was not advised of the fire until the next morning. I did, however, immediately institute an investigation. I found that the fire was an inside job ... This was intended to wipe out the evidence of the conspiracy to defeat the American policy and to overthrow our ally the

Republic of China, in favor of Communism. This went far toward the accomplishment of the purpose of the traitors and conspirators but it did not obliterate the facts which I had ascertained.[90]

Chiang never qualified his enthusiasm for Hurley, first expressed in October 1944: "General Hurley has my complete confidence."[91] His resignation on 26 November 1945, while on leave in Washington, disconcerted the Generalissimo, who by then was swept into the maelstrom of civil war. Yet he must have taken solace at the broadsides that Hurley leveled at their shared enemies, the Foreign Service officers who had criticized or made recommendations purportedly on behalf of Mao and Western imperialist masterminds. Hurley wrote in his resignation letter to Truman that this cabal, through tendrils that reached into the State Department, worked ceaselessly to undermine America's China policy:

The professional foreign service men sided with the Chinese Communist armed party and the imperialist bloc of nations whose policy it was to keep China divided against herself. Our professional diplomats continuously advised the Communists that my efforts in preventing the collapse of the National Government did not represent the policy of the United States. These same professionals openly advised the Communist armed party to decline unification of the Chinese Communist Army with the National Army unless the Chinese Communists were given control ... Throughout this period the chief opposition to the accomplishment of our mission came from the American career diplomats in the Embassy at [Chongqing] and in the Chinese and Far Eastern Divisions of the State Department ... [A] considerable section of our State Department is endeavoring to support Communism generally as well as specifically in China.[92]

Hurley reiterated these charges in public hearings convened in early December by the Senate Foreign Relations Committee, chaired by Tom Connally. Hurley bellowed the names of seven "disloyal" men: Atcheson, Davies, Emmerson, Fulton Freeman, Ringwalt, Service, John Carter Vincent.[93]

Connally's investigation sustained none of the charges brought by Hurley. He came to look ridiculous as he marshaled no credible evidence and as Secretary of State James Byrnes testified to the integrity of the defamed officers. Byrnes also refined upon the necessity of their being able to express themselves freely from the field, providing not only information but also candid opinion. Their criticisms of the GMD, he warranted, and willingness to seek cooperation with anyone willing to fight Japan did not equal endorsement of Chinese Marxism.[94] Byrnes, incidentally, did not bother to dignify Hurley's additional accusation concerning the Foreign Service as instrument of Anglo–French–Dutch imperialism. This misperception stemmed from an odd compound. As mentioned, Hurley shared FDR's distaste for European empires; he was an Anglophobe. What mental acuity he possessed was confounded as he equated Davies's crisp evaluation/warning of European states wanting to recover their colonies with the idea that Davies approved and schemed accordingly.[95]

The pyrotechnics that accompanied his resignation aside, Hurley had personal reasons to leave China after V-J Day. For one, his physical health was bad. He had endured splitting headaches in Chongqing, troubled eyesight, dental difficulties, and the disagreeable side effects of medications (such as sulfathiazole, an antibiotic used against infections both bacterial and malarial). He had been debilitated by "flu" on the night that his imaginary Foreign Service arsonists struck the chancery. He ran a fever on the day that he tendered his resignation. He admitted a few days later: "I came home sick [from China]. I am very tired."[96]

Despite his need of rest, Hurley was eager to relaunch his political career. Ideally, this would start with his election in 1946 to the Senate representing his adopted state of New Mexico. After that he might be picked to run on the second spot of the 1948 GOP presidential ticket.[97] Realization of such ambition necessitated prompt immersion in New Mexican matters and accounts for the manner of his resignation – not a private letter to Truman but an open one, followed by a spirited performance before congressmen and a capacity crowd in a conference room of the Senate office building. The good citizens of New Mexico would presumably be impressed by the drama of Hurley's continuing battle with demons, foreign and domestic.

Finally, Hurley realized that the Chinese civil war, exploding full-force by November and complicated by the presence of Soviet forces in Manchuria, was beyond his ability to contain. Better, therefore, to let

someone else try to mediate and take the blame for whatever disappoint-
ments ensued.[98] He was probably nervous about Truman's sending of
General Marshall to China. By his unique status, he might put matters
right, an achievement that would make Hurley appear small by comparison.[99] In the event, despite moments of promise, Marshall could not
parley an end to the civil war or save Chiang's weakening hold on power.
Eventually, in fact, anticommunist fundamentalists implicated Marshall
in "delivering" China to Stalinism. Yet Hurley gained little politically
from his own timely China exit. He did win the GOP nomination in
1946 for the New Mexico Senate seat but lost the election; he was
defeated again in two later Senate bids (1948 and 1952).[100]

***

Less than a decade after the Cairo conference, Roosevelt's hope that China
would prove a dependable partner to the United States lay in tatters.
Revolutionary China and Stalin's USSR entered in February 1950 into an
anti-Western pact. Admittedly not one destined to be brilliant or resilient, it
nevertheless constituted a setback for the United States. The Korean clash
between the "People's Volunteers" and US-led United Nations armies in
autumn of that year deepened the animosity between the former allies.
Indeed, the Korean bloodletting inaugurated twenty years of recriminations
and mistrust. Statesmen in Washington also justified intervention in Vietnam, at least in part, on the presumed need to prevent a hostile China from
encroaching on nations aligned with the West.

Why did America's China policy go wrong in the 1940s? Why
had Mao triumphed over an honored wartime ally, recipient of US
largesse? According to Dean Acheson and the compilers of the *China
White Paper*, issued by the State Department in 1949, the Guomindang
had been driven from power because of its ineptitude and profligacy
versus the fanaticism and discipline of the People's Liberation Army.
Americans, short of immense and unpredictable military intervention,
could not have rescued Chiang from himself or China from the CCP:

> *The ominous result of the civil war in China was beyond the
> control of the government of the United States. Nothing that
> this country did or could have done within the reasonable
> limits of its capabilities could have changed that result;
> nothing that was left undone by this country could have
> contributed to it. It was the product of internal Chinese
> forces which this country tried to influence but could not.[101]*

The *China White Paper* amounted to interlocking lies, countered Hurley from New Mexico and like-minded critics. The truth lay in this sordid detail: the peoples of China and the United States had been betrayed by a State Department infested with Marxist conspirators and their dupes. "The career diplomats in China," he avowed, "were opposed to the most important policies of our government and were opposed to the National Government of the Republic of China and in favor of giving control of China to the Chinese Armed Communists which they finally succeeded in doing after my resignation."[102]

Byrnes and Connally had discredited Hurley when he first conjured the specter of high-level betrayal. No harm had come in 1945 to China-based diplomats or their colleagues in the Far Eastern Division. Their exoneration bore insufficient protection during the later McCarthy phantasmagoria, however. Hurley had a long reach. Despite statements on their behalf by senior officials, including testimonials by Johnson and Gauss, the purges claimed Davies, Service, Vincent.[103] (A fatal airplane accident in August 1947 spared Atcheson from similar humiliation.) The dismissal of these and other officers, such as O. Edmund Clubb, devastated the ranks of China hands in the government's employ. In 1954, the year that John Foster Dulles fired Davies, only two officers from the war years remained in the Foreign Service. None of the victims had ever conspired against the United States – or even qualified as the coddled lightweights of William Dodd's screed – but were earnest men who had acquired their knowledge through conscientious study and experience in China. Their removal demoralized the Foreign Service and denied to future policymakers the benefit of consulting with a cadre of experts. Robert McNamara, after the Vietnam War, ascribed much of his sublime misjudgment in the 1960s to the absence of counsel on East Asia that a Davies or Service could have offered.[104]

Roosevelt never questioned Hurley's right to discipline underlings in Chongqing or considered the possibility that their interpretations had merit.[105] Truman too supported FDR's mercurial emissary to the end of his Chongqing tenure. The presidential preference was simple from Pearl Harbor onward: united China entailed Guomindang rule, a formula that relegated the CCP and other political parties to subordinate roles. Also in practice, despite Roosevelt's flashing impatience with Chiang, Goumindang primacy meant rule by the Generalissimo. On the vital points, then, Hurley and the White House shared a viewpoint from which Gauss, Stilwell, and other China hands deviated.

To the dissenters, Chiang's absolutism and GMD dominance were not sacrosanct. Both should be subject to reforms in the interest of national unity and the anti-Japanese war. By no means ought US victory over Japan be held hostage to the fortunes of any one Chinese party. Americans should retain freedom of action to pick their partners as war's shifting fortunes indicated and to qualify or amend alliances as needed. Davies put the case this way in January 1945. Much of Washington, he regretted, had become "attached to the fiction that only through Chiang Kai-shek can China in war and in peace realize its destiny ... It is difficult to escape the conclusion that we are ... the victims of the insularity and international political immaturity of our people and of the unwieldly processes of democracy. By our unwillingness and inability to engage in *realpolitik* ... we stand to lose that which we seek – the quickest possible defeat of Japan and a strong and independent China." [106]

That hyperbole about democratic China and Chiang's statecraft trumped the sound insight of Davies points to this liability. Washington officialdom was wont to superimpose its concepts and experience onto a profoundly alien civilization although none possessed an organic connection to China's culture, history, or contemporary institutions. Hurley's early belief that the CCP–GMD split was no greater than the difference between Democrats and Republicans was patent nonsense that blinded him to facts centered on the enmity between Mao and Chiang. This antagonism could not be wished away because Americans thought it impeded victory against Japan or was otherwise inconvenient. That Hurley raged against people – Davies, Service – who dared to suggest that reconciling the two political parties would be knotty only underscores his unfitness. He interpreted their caution in his typically bizarre way: the messengers were at fault.

Hurley, easy target of disparagement, was hardly alone among Americans whose unexamined assumptions about the proper ordering of life contributed to misperceptions of China and mutual incomprehension. Vice President Wallace, defender of the "common man," provoked an incident soon after he entered Chongqing. He refused to be drawn around in a rickshaw. The inhumanity offended him; no person of good conscience could use another as a beast of burden. To demonstrate solidarity with the drivers, he refused to climb aboard his designated rickshaw. He instead placed himself between the vehicle's shafts and commenced to pull. The rickshaw's driver and mates were amazed that this privileged American was stealing Chinese property and trying to seize local fares. Wallace had to be hurried away lest muttering drivers began a mêlée.[107] Even Service, a gifted interpreter of the Chinese scene, could lose perspective at times. His disgust for the Goumindang's waywardness inclined him to refine upon the asceticism and optimism exhibited at Mao's Yanan and to downplay its shortcomings. Something of his Oberlin idealism (class of 1931) and his father's YMCA background conditioned his view of the young revolutionaries, at the time unimaginably distant from the lunacy of their later devising (Great Leap Forward, Cultural Revolution) with numberless victims. "The general atmosphere in [Yanan]," Service reported in 1944, "can be compared to that of a rather small, sectarian college – or a religious summer conference."[108]

Roosevelt was among the most contradictory of Americans on the subject of China. At its grandest, his conception of the world order to come – pivoting on democratic capitalism, free trade, refurbished internationalism – allowed for a renewed China able to participate fully in world affairs. But when Chiang proved obstreperous, the president flirted with notions of removing him. Roosevelt also believed that Chinese troops were so inept that they had to operate under US command (Stilwell). Though Roosevelt was indisputably right about the deficiencies of Chiang and his armies, overthrowing another head of state or placing his military forces under US command were incompatible with any definition of China as member of the "Big Four" or future policeman of the global peace. Roosevelt's appointment of Hurley was yet another indication of the president's sloppy thought on wartime China. In the throes of a developing revolution, the country resembled no entrepôt familiar to FDR's grandfather or to the creditable ally drawn by Allied propagandists.

Johnson and Gauss in combination represented better wisdom. They were sober about China. They recognized that the country was too complicated to be a promising apprentice in the shop of American-style democracy. To the degree that the United States had economic and security interests in China, Washington should pay attention, but both ambassadors strove to keep US expectations at a moderate level. A competent fighting ally was obtainable and desirable; expectations of anything more were delusional. Hence Johnson's pre-Pearl Harbor support of Lend-Lease aid. Hence advocacy by Gauss of reforms to enhance China's political solidity and his receptivity to making common cause with the CCP against Japan. In short, Americans should deal strictly with the material at hand. They should maintain a cool detachment from the swirl of China's internal politics beyond their ability to shape. Meddling in the affairs of weak nations was easy, Johnson liked to say, but extrication was an altogether different proposition: "An intervener never gets out."[109]

The level of human suffering in China during 1937–1945 constituted time outside of normal time. Yet even here FDR's first two ambassadors played a useful part. Circumstances did not allow Johnson to stay in Nanjing in 1937. His role in mitigating the wickedness of what occurred will always and rightly be remembered as less than that of Jacquinot (in Shanghai), Rabe, and Wilhelmina Vautrin, the American dean of Nanjing's Ginling College for women who protected her students from Japanese assailants.[110] Still, from a distance Johnson tried to help by reminding Japanese authorities of their humanitarian obligation and assumed a useful liaison between them and the leaders of the safety zone. Those of his subordinates who stayed in the city also acquitted themselves well. That they never doubted his rectitude or eagerness to oblige counts in his favor too.

A member of the Nazi party, Rabe also had confidence in his leader, albeit misplaced. Rabe wrote in his diary as the crescendo of the Nanjing crisis rose: "The Führer won't leave me in the lurch."[111] Rabe upon return to Germany was scorned for making a fuss over the Nanjing "incident" and casting aspersions on Germany's co-sponsor of the anti-Comintern crusade.

Meanwhile in Shanghai, Gauss, then still consul general, and his staff plied their trade. It encompassed a brisk business in granting more US visas to Jewish refugees – whose improbable flights from Europe had landed them in China – than Washington stipulated. This consulate, like Geist's in Berlin, did not neglect the duty to rescue but bent US immigration protocols to serve the moral law.

5 FRANCE AGONISTES

Unlike prostrate China, France of the late 1930s enjoyed unequivocal status as one of the great powers. Expert opinion on military matters held that the French army, steeped in traditions of Napoleonic glory, and latterly confirmed by steadfastness (at the Marne, Verdun, Somme), was the world's finest. In contrast with Chiang's enervated forces and doubtful officer corps, France's confident soldiers were led by Great War heroes, not least of whom were Generals Maurice Gustave Gamelin and Maxime Weygand. The system of modern fortresses and barriers, running along French frontiers from Switzerland to Belgium, was of unexcelled design. This promised national safety at a casualty rate far below the numbing totals of 1914–1918, 4.5 to 5 million killed or wounded.[1] Premised on the superiority of defense over offense, a lesson learned on the Western Front, the impregnable Maginot Line demonstrated France's inventiveness in military engineering, a species of genius dating to Marshal Vauban. The navy too was a formidable war machine, its ships, crews, and bases having benefited from attention lavished on them by Admiral Jean-François Darlan.[2] Admittedly, France's air units might properly have numbered more bombers and fighters. Yet the high quality of French warplanes, arguably superior to anything manufactured in Germany, was generally thought to compensate for purported deficiencies in quantity. France, so responsible analysts testified, was guarded by men endowed with élan; they had at their disposal an arsenal bristling with armaments of the latest type and best caliber.

Virtually all Frenchmen, foreign observers too, including many in Berlin, were astonished in May–June 1940 by the rapidity of German victory, ratified on 22 June with the signing of an armistice in Com-piègne. Two days later Mussolini also imposed a victor's peace that entailed territorial changes to Italy's advantage. Marc Bloch, medieval-ist and reserve army officer, lamented: "We have just suffered such a defeat as no one would have believed possible."[3] The novelist Irène Némirovsky wrote anxiously about the sudden birth of a disjointed world.[4] Simone de Beauvoir, social theorist, noted this physiognomy in her newly occupied Paris: "Victory was written across every German face, while every French face proclaimed defeat aloud."[5]

Humiliation generated a Vesuvius of explanations and alibis by Frenchmen, across the political spectrum, to account for the collapse of the nation's proud arms. Bloch faulted the army high command as incompetent. Brigadier General Charles de Gaulle emphasized the inertness of Allied forces during Hitler's invasion of Poland. Energetic actions against Germany should have weighed heavily upon an overex-tended and preoccupied Wehrmacht, he claimed. He had earlier warned (January 1940), as Gamelin and other commanders shuffled trance-like through the *drôle de guerre*, that inaction was tantamount to submission.[6]

Conservatives charged that a pernicious French communist party compounded the blunder of missed opportunities. Supposedly, the communists, in cooperation with Hitler's Soviet accomplices, had committed acts of sabotage and intrigued with Germany. These critics also blamed the US ambassador, William Bullitt, for allegedly manipu-lating an unprepared France into fighting while making false promises that America would join against Germany.[7]

A few writers focused their postmortems on public panic, evidenced in roads clogged with civilians (six to eight million) fleeing southwards, a congestion that blocked efficient routing of materiel and hampered army maneuvering.[8] Other observers concentrated on the "perfidiousness" of allies, such as King Leopold III, who abruptly withdrew Belgium from hostilities in late May. Churchill became a favorite target of deprecation as Anglophobia swept the populace: while offering far-fetched plans for an Anglo-French union, and spouting oaths that France honor its pledge not to enter into a separate peace, he had shamefully withheld RAF units at the crucial moment, when the air battle might yet have taken favorable turns. The escape from Dunkirk of the BEF, which in its haste abandoned all equipment, had the added effect of banishing from French affections – at least for a time – any residual warmth for the "feckless" Britons. Even worse than their faithlessness was their treachery; in July French warships were seized in London-controlled ports or sunk while peacefully anchored elsewhere (1,300 French sailors died at Mers-el-Kebir).[9] Thereupon the government, reconstituted in the spa town of Vichy and headed by octogenarian Marshal Henri-Philippe Pétain, severed relations with Great Britain. That country, he growled, would fight Germany only "until the last available drop of French blood."[10] He hopefully anticipated British defeat; he later expressed satisfaction with the Anglo-Canadian fiasco at Dieppe (August 1942).[11]

A stark question confronted the Vichy regime, technically in charge of a rump France (*zone libre*) and still responsible for a far-flung overseas empire. To what degree would Pétain's regime have to cooperate with the Germans? They had, as dignified by the armistice agreement, established themselves in Paris. They had imposed an indemnity and required Frenchmen to pay the costs of Wehrmacht occupation. Germans controlled two-thirds of metropolitan France (including the entire Atlantic coastline), had reclaimed Alsace-Lorraine, and held in captivity roughly two million French POWs. Nearly 900,000 French laborers ("volunteers") were eventually sent to Germany to work in factories and farms. Waning British power, meanwhile, seemed on the brink of disaster as comprehensive as that suffered in France. In these circumstances, then, Vichy might properly acknowledge new realities and adapt as gracefully as possible to Nazi domination of Europe.

Regarding domestic matters, the Vichy preference was not in doubt. Pétain's cabinet sought, from installment (16 June) onward, to implement an authoritarian transformation that would return France to its original virtues, undermined since 1789. This restoration would be accomplished by disciplining those furies loosed by generations of irresponsible democrats. Freemasons, shifty parliamentarians, socialists, trade unionists, left-leaning educators, Roma, Jews, and other enemies of decorum and order would have to surrender that pride of place which they had promiscuously enjoyed under the lax Third Republic. They would perforce adjust to profounder principles. *Liberté, égalite, fraternité* and attendant cant would yield to authentic French notions, nurtured in centuries of Catholic piety, attachment to the soil, and respect for race. Pétain's *Révolution Nationale*, vindication of traditionalists and anti-Dreyfusards, exalted wholesome truth – its distillation in slogan being *travail, famille, patrie*.

The Vichy axioms never won majority support within France (on neither side of the 1940 demarcation line), or within the empire, nor among survivors located abroad, especially not within that eclectic group of London exiles who sheltered symbolically under the Cross of Lorraine and clustered around de Gaulle. Over BBC radio he broadcast (18 June) defiance of Vichy capitulation, one of the sins for which he was sentenced to death in absentia by Petain's courts: "The flame of French resistance must not and shall not die."[12] De Gaulle's struggles thereafter multiplied. He had to contend not only against Vichy's growing compliance with Berlin, but also with non-Vichy claimants to future rule (i.e. communist elements in the *maquis*) and against Anglo–Soviet–US contempt for France. This last, he worried, could induce untoward events leading to forfeiture of the empire, from Africa to Indochina to the Americas.

The struggle between Vichy and de Gaulle and other pretenders amounted to a slow-motion civil war (summer 1940 to V-E Day and beyond). Set against a background of mounting scarcity, it featured rivals whose philosophical orientations and attitudes toward German ambition were wholly irreconcilable.[13] Concurrent with the Allied–Axis war, provoked by it, but also distinct from it, this civil convulsion had long been foreshadowed. Auguries had included political wobbliness; twenty-four administrations had formed during 1933–1940. Gathering instability allowed right-wing Parisian rioters in February 1934 to cause the fall of Edouard Daladier's center-left government. On Bastille Day 1935 Colonel François de la Rocque's anti-republican Croix de Feu, one of many rightist leagues that had arisen, strutted down the Champs-Elysées. Denunciations of that "subtle Talmudist," Léon Blum, and his Popular Front government (1936–1937) created a permissive atmosphere that had allowed physical battery on his person by thugs of Action Française's *camelots du roi*. Verbal attacks on Jewry by such intellectuals as Louis-Ferdinand Céline, a literary genius possessed of measureless hatred, did not abate but increased. Reputable writers, Robert Brasillach and Pierre Drieu la Rochelle, likewise contributed generous measures of vitriol against "decadence" and "parasitic" Jews who sucked France's vigor. The culmination of right-wing audacity occurred during 1940–1944, when Vichy authorities purged the civil service, executed dissenters, organized show trials (enthusiastically but not effectively at Riom in February–April 1942) of Third Republic leaders, and aided the German murder of 75,000 Jews (native and foreign-born).[14]

Vichy did not instigate all of the fratricidal violence. Blood flowed when de Gaulle's Free French took the initiative (with the British) against Pétain's garrisons in Dakar (September 1940) and Syria–Lebanon (June–July 1941). As *La Libération* burst forward in summer 1944 fighting between *maquis* and Vichy's *milice* produced tens of thousands of victims on both sides, plus political assassinations, as in the case of Philippe Henriot (Vichy minister of information) and Georges Mandel (unflinching *belliciste* and Third Republic statesman). Summary justice and incipient anarchy threatened to plunge France into a free-for-all. An OSS reporter stated in late July: "The situation of the country recalls the worst epochs of the Middle Ages. The country lives in fear – fear of German reprisals, fear of occupation by the *maquis*, fear of vengeance of the *milice*."[15] Some among the newly freed in 1944–1945 satisfied their hunger for retribution by meting primitive justice to women (*collabos horizontales*) suspected of consorting with the enemy. Public revilement (shaved heads, whippings) followed quasi-judicial rituals. The authors of these punishments aimed to remove the Vichy stain while, subconsciously one suspects, expatiating the sin of men who had failed to protect their homeland. Albert Camus, editor of *Combat* and resistance fighter par excellence, recoiled from the "odious" excess of the *épurations* (purges).[16]

The main goal of FDR and Bullitt in 1940, as French rout turned into surrender, had been twofold: to discourage Frenchmen from developing an exclusive orientation centered on the Third Reich; to prevent French naval and military resources from falling into German (or Italian) hands. American anxiety, shared by Churchill, was that Hitler's acquisition of French warships and ports/bases (Martinique to Dakar to North Africa to the eastern Mediterranean) could decisively tilt the Anglo-German naval war in Berlin's favor. A result would be to compromise New World security, ensured over generations by the Royal Navy. When Americans in December 1941 formally joined Britons against Germany, this mix of considerations in Roosevelt's thinking – and that of Bullitt's successor in France, Ambassador William Leahy – gained still greater saliency. Thereafter, as plans progressed for the British and American landings in North Africa (TORCH – 8 November 1942), Washington officials sought even more assiduously to maintain decent relations with Pétain, despite his government's cooperation with varieties of Nazi policy. The alternative, so the prevailing line held, would encourage Vichy's armies (in Morocco, Tunisia, Algeria) to resist British and American forces or otherwise hinder their campaigns against Erwin Rommel's Afrika Korps. To save the lives of Allied soldiers and for the sake of military expediency, Roosevelt, Hull, and Leahy – plus most embassy officers in Vichy – were willing to make what, they conceded, was a desperate bargain. Phrased in less charitable language, the "Vichy gamble" entailed suspension of principles (enshrined in the Four Freedoms, Atlantic Charter), but – in the event – did little to inhibit Vichy criminality or cooperation with Berlin.

An immediate effect of the North African campaign was the termination of Vichy–Washington relations, closely linked to FDR's search for another French partner. The president rebuffed de Gaulle, who since 1940 had tirelessly promoted his own candidacy. Roosevelt fired to Churchill in June 1943 "that there is no possibility of our working with de Gaulle ... we must divorce ourselves from [him]."[17] The Free French head proved tenacious of life, however. He outwitted his rivals. He wore down his detractors. He left American and British leaders no alternative but to deal with him. The daunting task of mending damages fell to Jefferson Caffery, the first US envoy to de Gaulle's relaunched France.

Defeat

Bullitt had served as ambassador in Paris for more than three years before German soldiers paraded (14 June 1940) through the Place de l'Etoile and the Arc de Triomphe. Not yet fifty, he had already achieved an enviable record of public service with exploits that verged on the swashbuckling. Scion of a prominent Philadelphia family – blending Huguenots and colonial-era Yankees with Jewish German arrivals (on his mother's side) of later vintage – he first distinguished himself at Yale, where he graduated Phi Beta Kappa in 1912. Following terms in law school, as a newspaperman (with the *Philadelphia Public Ledger*), and as an assistant secretary of the State Department, he had in 1919 embarked for Moscow on a hazy venture, putatively commissioned by Woodrow Wilson: to determine whether and by what means the West and Lenin's Russia, in the grip of civil war, could establish common ground. Wilson's repudiation of Bullitt's tentative accord with the Bolsheviks led the young man to break with the president, whom he previously idolized, and to testify against him in Senate hearings on the Versailles treaty and later in public prints (most damnably in a psychological biography of Wilson, embossed by Sigmund Freud's imprimatur[18]).

Bullitt subsequently joined the migration of bohemians and voluptuaries – "lost generation" – that settled in post-World War Paris, which city commanded his abiding fondness (and where he died in 1967). He dabbled in the writing of fiction, producing one novel, *It's Not Done*.[19] He exercised his considerable journalistic talents. He became enamored of psychoanalysis, at the time still an infant science whose Vienna proponents he esteemed.[20] He tried his luck for a second time at marriage, disastrously with the adventuresome Louise Bryant, widow of the revolutionary John Reed. Bullitt also monitored events in the USSR. He was thrilled by what he understood to be its strides toward modernization and equality. He worked for a sympathetic understanding between the proletarian republic and capitalist America. Upon the establishment of Soviet–US relations in 1933, Roosevelt – drawn to Bullitt's ebullience, susceptible to his flattery, grateful for his contribution to Democratic coffers – chose him as representative to Moscow. After brief satisfactions in Stalin's capital, the ambassador was overcome by the pitilessness of Soviet life. Omnipresent police surveillance, judicial travesties visited upon leading personalities, and the dissemination of falsehoods horrified Bullitt. He lost what confidence he once entertained for the Soviet experiment. He converted to anti-communism that deepened over the decades. In fullest bloom, it reduced him to near-hysteria on the subjects of Marxism, the USSR, and apologists for Stalin, to which group Bullitt assigned (during the Cold War) a "bamboozled" FDR.[21]

Bullitt and the French

Abundantly glad, Bullitt had left Moscow in May 1936. He got needed relief later that year, when Roosevelt posted him to Paris. There a handful of extreme rightists grumbled. They claimed that this "agent of Jewish finance," who also worked on behalf of Soviet conspiracies, wanted to entangle France in gratuitous war against the Third Reich.[22]

The capital's enlightened classes, by contrast, embraced Bullitt as one of their own: witty, cosmopolitan, culturally *au courant*. His intuitive grasp of social situations and individuals also helped – admittedly a rare gift, though qualified in Bullitt's case by his holding the world to high standards while insisting upon special understanding for himself. As he had since childhood, he spoke French with assurance. He was a connoisseur of fine wines; he kept an ample stock at his plush abode on the grounds of the Château de Chantilly.[23] A gourmet, he possessed a peerless kitchen staff whose chefs were coveted by the culinary illuminati (some of whom and cabinet ministers were Bullitt's mirthful dinner guests on 9 May 1940, the eve of Germany's western blitzkrieg).[24]

Above all, Bullitt was appreciated – here the French judgment was exaggerated, perhaps skewed by Bullitt's own self-advertising – as one who knew Roosevelt intimately and enjoyed his unconditional confidence. Blum, Daladier, Paul Reynaud, and other members of the political elite established warm relations with Bullitt, a love feast of sorts that led Secretary of the Interior Harold Ickes to muse: "Bullitt practically sleeps with the French cabinet." Parisian punditry claimed that he held a de facto ministerial position without portfolio. In a more serious vein, Daladier once said of FDR's envoy: "[He] is as much a Frenchman as the most patriotic Frenchman among us ... the most faithful and most helpful of friends." The Minister of Air, Guy La Chambre, averred that he and Bullitt empathized from the day they met, as if brothers.[25]

The main passion shared by Bullitt and his hosts centered on French security. He had originally thought that this could be achieved by Franco-German rapprochement, a cause that he expected (noted in Chapter 2) to advance in cooperation with Hugh Wilson in Berlin. To this end, Bullitt not only lobbied for the dismissal of William Dodd, whom he thought unforgivably gloomy, and promoted the appointment of Wilson. But Bullitt also encouraged French and German interlocutors to seek mutually advantageous resolution of problems. His conversations were wide-ranging with Hermann Goering, who spoke gaily about the brightening prospects of a Franco-German alliance (implicitly aimed at Britain) while prattling about Hitler's peaceful ambitions.[26]

For the sake of Paris–Berlin reconciliation, Bullitt favored letting Germany take the economic lead in central Europe and the Balkans. He also hoped adjudication could be devised favorable to the claims of Sudeten Germans, thereby granting France a face-saving way out of its pledge to Czechoslovak integrity. Other measures too – restoring to Germany its former African holdings – should be adopted as corrective to the punitive Versailles treaty, which Bullitt judged "one of the stupidest documents ever penned by the hand of man."[27] In exchange for these accommodations, France would obtain peace into the future and, with Germany functioning as satisfied partner, could lead Europe into new vistas of tranquility and prosperity. The alternative dismayed Bullitt. Should another European war occur, he predicted, the USSR and its communist affiliates would organize the dazed survivors along Stalinist lines. Western civilization would slip into a protracted era of moral and political ruin, unknown since the Dark Ages.[28]

Inclined to blame "inadequate" Czech statesmanship for not making worthwhile concessions, Bullitt hailed the Munich averting of pan-European warfare.[29] The trespassing in mid-March 1939, though, of German forces upon Bohemia–Moravia turned him away from the presumptive virtues of appeasement. He, thereafter, saw in Hitler not just an excitable politician but someone bent on boundless German aggrandizement.[30] Against it, Bullitt urged Frenchmen to coordinate closely with the British to contain Hitler, ideally via firm diplomacy but by violence if necessary. Even the USSR, he cautiously advised at one point, might be recruited to check Germany.[31]

Like most observers, Bullitt thought in the event of a showdown that French forces would perform as well as in 1914–1918 and, with British assistance, again stop the Germans.[32] His estimate was based on personal inspections of Maginot fortifications and weaponry, corroborated by reports from the embassy's military and naval attachés, and reinforced by upbeat presentations to him by Paris's defense officials.[33] As for the French nation in arms, he taught that a second *union sacrée* would emerge, which, as in 1914, would bind political antagonists and disparate social constituencies into single purpose. He reported to Washington in 1939 immediately after the German attack on Poland: "The entire population of France is facing war with a resolute courage that is beyond praise."[34] He told FDR in October: "We are expecting the bombs to begin falling … in about a week; but nobody either here [Paris] or anywhere else in France is disturbed by the prospect."[35]

Intimations of difficulty did occasionally flit across Bullitt's awareness, enough to spoil – only for moments – his roseate picture of French prowess. He was irked that Parisian statesmen failed to take seriously his repeated warnings: contra 1917, the United States would not directly intervene in another European war.[36] And he winced at evidences of French anxiety, as in spring 1939 when Premier Daladier offered Washington cash ($300 million), and French islands in the New World/Pacific, as partial payment on France's multi-billion dollar World War debts. Daladier mistakenly hoped that this gesture would satisfy the 1934 Johnson Act, which forbade transactions with any government in default of its obligations to the United States, and make France eligible for financing in case of war.[37] Other members of the French political class exhibited nervousness too; the pessimism of Georges Bonnet (variously ambassador to Washington, foreign minister, finance minister, justice minister) irritated Bullitt.[38]

Occasional expressions of defeatism by the foreign ministry's secretary general, Alexis Leger, also annoyed Bullitt. A dispirited Leger allowed (30 September 1939) that the USSR would shortly join Germany (and Italy) in war upon France. "The game is lost," he confided to Bullitt. "France stands alone against three dictatorships. Great Britain is not ready. The United States has not even changed the Neutrality Act … The Germans know that at this minute with Russian and Italian support they can crush the French Army."[39] Traces of demoralization also infected high military levels. With a shudder, General Edouard Requin – commander of formations expected to breach the Siegfried Line – once told Bullitt that France could not again fight Germany and achieve anything like authentic victory. The losses would be prohibitive.[40]

Bullitt did assimilate the deepening French worry focused on allegedly superior German air power, a supposition Charles Lindbergh perpetuated to audiences at Chantilly confabs. When unleashed, the Luftwaffe could reduce all cities within reach to heaps of wreckage. Recovery would be impossible, even if France managed to prevail over Germany. La Chambre predicted that Allied insufficiency in pursuit planes would mean that German-inflicted destruction in Paris should surpass imagination.[41] Bullitt later attributed Allied passivity during September 1939–May 1940 to the hope that the Germans would reciprocate by sparing the great British and French cities aerial bombardment. Not until spring of 1942, he guessed, would Allied air forces be sufficiently self-assured and equipped to mount major offensives.[42]

Though bothered by French display of "bad nerves," Bullitt never dwelt on dreary scenarios. The French needed bolstering during their hours of doubt, he felt, but they would see the crisis through to a successful end. In these circumstances, serious but hardly hopeless, FDR's government should throw its moral weight behind the British and French governments. Notwithstanding neutrality legislation, or the objection of officers like General "Hap" Arnold to selling advanced warplanes, Roosevelt should also covertly fill whatever Allied deficits existed in quantity and quality of hardware. In tandem with direct French appeals to Washington – and the dispatching by Paris of Jean Monnet as purchasing agent in the United States – Bullitt pressed the White House to deliver the needed machines and munitions. These Bullitt–French actions were not without impact, as FDR allowed the purchase by January 1939 of 555 warplanes. Of these only 200 fighter planes had arrived in France by September 1939, however. Just 137 wholly assembled US bombers were available to France on 10 May 1940. Daladier had hoped that before that year ended the British and French air forces would have obtained from Washington 10,000 planes, a number that he – plus Bullitt – should have known exceeded US production schedules.[43]

Not until the battle of France began to unravel in May did Bullitt drop his relative equanimity. He lectured State Department seniors that no matter how removed Americans hoped to remain from Europe, Germany's defeat of France would jeopardize their security. The United States, sooner or later, would be carried into hostilities; better to join them immediately than to wait events whose outcome must deny America useful partners.[44]

Bullitt urged FDR to take measures, even if Congress denied the danger and refrained from declaring war. First, the president should arrange to sell surplus warships to Peru for quick resale to France. Second, the commander-in-chief ought to dispatch elements of the Atlantic fleet to make courtesy calls in Mediterranean ports, thereby discouraging Italy from attacking France or its North African possessions. Third, Roosevelt should offer Pope Pius XII asylum in the United States, where residency and threatened excommunication of the Duce might further impress Mussolini. Most importantly, the president, as Reynaud (premier as of 21 March 1940) pleaded in early June, should hurry the delivery to France of swarms of warplanes and volunteers to pilot them.[45] That substantial quantities of such things did not exist in

7 In center William C. Bullitt, upon presentation of credentials, 13 October 1936.

America in May–June 1940 – that isolationist congressmen would have created a furor as the administration moved the country toward intervention – were facts of life that Bullitt did not care to recognize. He was, in any case, astounded by FDR's hesitancy as the supreme emergency arrived and so told him: "At this moment words are not enough. Indeed unaccompanied by acts they are rather sickening." In high dudgeon, Bullitt borrowed these words from Daladier and flung them at Roosevelt: "It [is] sad that civilization in the world should fall because a great nation with a great President could simply talk."[46]

Bullitt–FDR Relations

Bullitt's May–June scolding eroded Roosevelt's forbearance. This was clear when (31 May 1940) the president upbraided his ambassador for advancing "fantasies" about the availability of Atlantic fleet ships for Mediterranean maneuvers.[47] Under the best of circumstances, Roosevelt seldom invited criticism from his diplomats. Bullitt's querulousness made him wary; he never forgot, along with other Democrats of his generation, that Bullitt had turned spectacularly on Woodrow Wilson.

Policy toward France, FDR may have thought, could provoke another of Bullitt's public tantrums and disavowal of a sitting president.

The FDR–Bullitt friendship did not end until well after the battle of France and, in any case, was not decisively affected by it. Roosevelt exiled Bullitt from presidential favor after he retailed (from 1941 onward) stories in the oval office concerning Sumner Welles's homosexual indiscretions (including boozy propositions in 1940 of African-American porters on the presidential train). The motive for this tattling stemmed from the Bullitt–Welles struggle for presidential attention and Bullitt's conviction that the dimming of his Washington fortunes resulted from his rival's pouring calumny into FDR's ear. Bullitt's attempt to recover fading luster, and defaming one of the few persons whom FDR genuinely respected, produced presidential rebuke, then enmity.[48]

In its glory days the relationship between Bullitt and FDR, more important to the former than the latter, rested on unexceptional bits of compatibility. Both men, in each other's company, affected bonhomie and jocularity, often puerile. When opportunity arose, they could become loquacious. With avuncular approval (possibly veiling jealousy) FDR followed Bullitt's romancing of Marguerite "Missy" LeHand, the president's prized personal secretary. The couple were actually dining with Roosevelt at the White House when (February 1940) he collapsed from a mild heart attack.[49] The ever-solicitous Bullitt, never precisely fawning but purposeful, reinforced these intimacies with other attentiveness. He sent foreign stamps to the White House philatelist. Bullitt squired assorted presidential relatives around Paris, including one FDR cousin, Elsie Hooper, of notable girth. Her waddling sparked an exchange of presidential–ambassadorial snickers. Nor did Bullitt hesitate to indulge his boss's delight in prurient matters, as when he observed of Reynaud's and Daladier's dueling mistresses: "Poison injected in the horizontal position is particularly venomous."[50]

Concerning State Department machinery, Bullitt certainly shared the president's misgivings, a point about which he often – with glee – reminded FDR. Bullitt's indictment of the typical Foreign Service officer included this 1938 coarseness, laced with jabs against Welles: "The upper brackets of the Foreign Service contain many morons, fairies, and neurotics."[51] Assuming that FDR got the fairy-Welles hint, he chose to overlook it, just as he later ignored Bullitt's mischievous recounting of Welles's peace mission to Paris in March 1940 (in which the undersecretary, in Bullitt's version of events, preached the greatness of Mussolini and German invincibility).[52] Still, FDR did ask for Bullitt's opinion on individuals and their suitability for promotion or posting. On this subject, Bullitt was frequently caustic. When asked about Clarence Gauss, for example, Bullitt fired that he was an intellectually dull "Baptist veterinarian," "totally incompetent," not exportable: "Anyone less qualified to get along with foreigners of any sort or, indeed, Americans outside the Monkey Trial Bible belt, I do not know."[53]

Such appraisals, Bullitt could contend, were based on his own experiences as an embassy chief. He had discovered multiple faults with his Moscow staff, George Kennan being an exception. The same was true in Paris. Except for the embassy's senior officer, Robert Murphy, and Bullitt's aide-de-camp, Carmel Offie, the ambassador thought (shades of Dodd in Berlin) his subordinates pampered and indolent.[54] Of the vice consul in Marseille, Hiram Bingham (whose father had served both as senator from Connecticut and governor), Bullitt derided him as the "feeble" offspring of a line once distinguished but since lapsed into lassitude.[55]

Bullitt was not only wrong about the conscientious Gauss, but also misjudged Bingham, who possessed uncommon mettle. Dissenters, Jews, intellectuals, artists, and other people at risk of Vichy–German capture benefited from Bingham's rescue work (explained in subsequent pages). On other matters too Bullitt erred. One egregious instance occurred when, in late August 1939, he uncritically accepted a report by French army intelligence that claimed a hundred or so Jewish-German refugees in France were working for Hitler's spymasters. Bullitt made not the slightest effort to corroborate these charges, this at a moment when 15,000 foreign-born Jews had already enlisted in the armed services to fight for France.[56] He evinced no curiosity about the duress that might have induced individuals – those with relatives still in Germany, for instance – to accept such assignments. Certainly, he knew nothing about that ruse employed by Admiral Wilhelm Canaris, the anti-Hitler head of the *Abwehr* (German military intelligence): as part of an effort to help Jews, Canaris provided some with token training as *Abwehr* "agents" and had them sent abroad – France, among other places, being a way station to safety.[57]

Rather then probe or wonder about the anomaly of Jews in Nazi service, Bullitt made this recommendation to FDR that, as it percolated through Washington, strengthened the inflexibility of Breck-inridge Long and immigration skeptics in the FBI and Congress: "I believe that you should instruct our counter-espionage services of all sorts to keep an especially vigilant eye on the Jewish refugees from Germany."[58] The president, in fact, did not need encouragement to inspect the refugee stream for suspicious characters. His preference in 1939 was to let it dissipate before it hit US shores, in which connection he had uttered not a word of support for the proposed Wagner–Rogers bill. Had Congress adopted it, twenty thousand Jewish children (under age fourteen) from the Third Reich would have gained US admission. Perhaps, he and other guardians of public safety surmised, the children's chaperones would include malefactors intent on sabotage. As French armies gave way in May 1940, Roosevelt – in a "fireside chat" – warned listeners against spies who operated under innocent guise.[59]

Less consequential, but controversial at the time and damaging to Bullitt's relations with FDR, was the ambassador's decision in June 1940 to stay in Paris. Ordinarily, the US representative, like the envoy from any country that enjoyed relations with France, would have stayed with the government as it evacuated the capital (10 June) and sought safety in other precincts: Tours, Bordeaux, Clermont-Ferrand, finally to Vichy (whose chief recommendation was its abundance of hotels that could accommodate government ministries[60]). Consistent with normal practice, Nelson Johnson had followed Chiang's government out of Nanjing in 1937. Anthony Biddle in 1939 had fled Warsaw with Polish officials for French sanctuary. Laurence Steinhardt in 1941 would, obedient to Soviet instruction, quit Moscow and take to Kuibyshev. That Bullitt failed to do likewise angered the State Department. Hull interpreted his staying in Paris as a dereliction of duty.[61] As for FDR, he read the behavior of Bullitt as another instance of his undependability, not one in whom to repose future trust.

Bullitt gave varied reasons for delaying in Paris. He invoked three of his predecessors as precedent: Gouverneur Morris who remained in Paris during the revolutionary upheavals of 1792–1794, Elihu Washburne who weathered the siege and Commune of 1870–1871, Myron Herrick who stayed in the capital as German armies pressed upon it in 1914. These worthies, Bullitt testified, had reinforced French morale during times of acute danger. He could do no less.[62] He also feared that vengeful communists would use the occasion of national humbling to seize the capital, like the communards of 1871, and kill the better classes before German soldiers occupied the city. He thought, at least claimed, that his presence in Paris would inhibit such atrocities – or should revolution anyway erupt that he could check its worst effects. To defend the embassy and help maintain municipal order, he asked the State Department to send him a dozen Thompson submachine guns with ammunition.[63] Finally, Bullitt apparently felt that he might ease the tensions bound to arise as German soldiers entered Paris; he would act as de facto mayor and deliver the city intact to its new authorities. As for maintaining US contacts with the French government, he appointed Biddle (still beside his Poles in France) as deputy ambassador to go whither it went.

The presence of Bullitt in Paris during the June happenings bore mixed results, none as grand as he predicted but not useless. On the one hand, his continued residency did not appreciably bolster popular morale. De Gaulle actually concluded that his staying in Paris, while the government withdrew, indicated that FDR had lost interest in France.[64] So, too, nothing like a communist rebellion developed for Bullitt to repel – just how he would have done so must remain a matter of pure conjecture. For their part, the Germans, in a manner that gave no immediate cause for alarm, calmly took possession of Paris (earlier declared by Weygand an "open city," a designation for which Bullitt had worked lest the capital suffered Rotterdam's May fate). In the meantime, in Bullitt's favor, he and staff members secured the embassy chancellery; they disposed of its confidential archives. He also performed a service to the redoubtable René Pleven (an early de Gaulle supporter) by arranging the evacuation from Brittany to safety of his wife and children before the Germans arrived.[65] Bullitt, quite creditably, flooded Washington with appeals, urging that the Red Cross deliver medical supplies to the millions of Frenchmen displaced by war. Possibly stung by uneasy conscience, and disinclined to overestimate the mental qualities of insouciant Biddle, Bullitt also dispatched senior embassy officers led by H. Freeman Matthews – seasoned European hand – to steady the deputy ambassador in dealing with Reynaud.[66]

Critics in June 1940, and later, insinuated that Bullitt's motive for staying behind was not so gallantly minded as the would-be savior of Paris held. Was he, some asked, such as Ickes, indulging a proclivity for heroic stunts?[67] Was Bullitt hoping for quick repatriation to America to assume a cabinet position (head of War or Navy) for which he had been badgering FDR since 1939? If so, Bullitt could more easily be plucked from Paris than were he on the run in provincial zones (or were he stranded in North Africa with remnants of the French government).[68] Was he, some intimated, protecting an unnamed lover, maybe a man? Irrespective of the answer to these questions, the absence of Bullitt's counsel to the flying French cabinet, as it deliberated on whether to continue the war, was a serious matter. Matthews, who witnessed the baleful influence of Reynaud's defeatist mistress – Comtesse Hélène de Portes – on the premier's willingness to wage war from North Africa, and watched as parliamentarians voted the Third Republic out of existence, gave this critique:

> *Whether any human being could have succeeded in generating enough courage and energy in the crumbling morale of the French authorities ... to keep up the fight and to give their fleet to the British or send it overseas, I do not know. There was one man who, with his enjoyment of their confidence and his dynamic personality, might at one or two critical moments have succeeded in giving the necessary push to swing the scales. That man was Ambassador Bullitt. In spite of all arguments of his associates in the Embassy that the one time the French Government would need his advice and encouragement most would be in the dark days after its departure from Paris, he chose to remain at the capital on the quixotic theory that an ambassador should not run away from his post. From the tenth of June he was consequently helpless to do anything. Certainly the last person in the world to succeed in the task was the nice, genial, playboy ambassador selected for the job ... the effort to keep [Biddle] on the proper track – or any track at all – was not the least of my problems.*[69]

Bullitt and retinue finally decamped from Paris on 30 June (leaving behind a skeleton crew at the embassy, not totally abandoned until January 1942) to rendezvous with the government.[70] By the time he reached it, Reynaud was out of power and diehards, like Daladier and Mandel, were trying to reach Africa in the hope of still prosecuting the war. Pétain had, meanwhile, been selected as head of state. The marshal's supporting cast at that hour consisted of Pierre Laval (vice premier), Paul Baudouin (foreign ministry), Weygand (national defense), Darlan (navy), Raphael Alibert (justice), Adrien Marquet (interior), and Henri Lémery (colonies). Gaston Henry-Haye, previously mayor of Versailles, was named ambassador to Washington, where he arrived in August. Eventually forty governments established formal ties to Vichy; several, including the Soviet and Japanese, maintained full-fledged embassies in Pétain's capital.[71] This diplomatic enclave, de Gaulle later griped, dignified a toady regime and "cool[ed] the ardor of those personalities whose first impulse might have driven them toward the Cross of Lorraine."[72]

Bullitt formed a favorable impression of Pétain. Along with French votaries of the marshal's cult – that ranged from ecclesiastical leaders to Left Bank nonconformists (briefly André Gide) to housewives to manual workers – Bullitt admired him for his World War services: "hero of Verdun." He also shared Pétain's view about the British as deceitful. He declared the old warrior "straightforward," determined to redeem French honor.[73]

Bullitt was gratified that a portion of French gold had been shipped out of the country for safekeeping in the United States, in which transfer he had assumed a useful role. His chief concern, like that of Washington officialdom, pivoted on whether the government would deliver the surviving French fleet – two-thirds of which had escaped British interception – to the German navy.[74] Any transfer to Germany of French ports and military bases in North Africa and the Middle East would also enhance German advantage. He felt that Pétain would, true to his and Darlan's repeated assurances, resist German demands for these French naval/military assets.[75] Yet Bullitt also doubted that Vichy, if abandoned and scorned by the English-speaking powers, could counter German importunities (seemingly confirmed or, at least, foreshadowed in October 1940 by the Hitler–Pétain meeting in Montoire). Therefore, Bullitt urged, in step with what became doctrine in Washington, that the United States do everything possible to dislodge Vichy from Berlin's orbit and fortify Pétain against those of his ministers – notably Laval – who wanted closer association with Hitler. Later, Bullitt refined these ideas in missives to FDR: the US must stiffen Pétain; woo French North Africa from Vichy and organize an anti-German government (perhaps in Algiers); support the Free French war against Hitler. "It is not beyond the wit of man to do all [these] without breaking relations with Vichy," Bullitt stated in 1941.[76]

Contrary to orders that he tarry in Vichy to embolden opposition to the armistice's severer provisions, Bullitt on 10 July left France via Madrid/Lisbon.[77] Once back in Washington to brief FDR, he pronounced this verdict on the French: "The simple people of the country are as fine as they have ever been."[78] The ambassador then traveled the country to argue the case for military readiness (plus conscription), aid to the British empire, and the necessity of making immediate effort against Germany.[79]

While isolationists excoriated him, Bullitt waited for a cabinet appointment (which he evidently believed FDR had promised in early 1940) commensurate with his aptitude and worth. None came. Not only did FDR withhold all ministerial portfolios, but also in November Bullitt learned indirectly – without White House consultation or observance of protocol – of the impending appointment of Leahy as ambassador to Vichy.[80] This move underscored the president's cumulative displeasure with Bullitt. Only grudgingly did the White House later offer him secondary assignments, a few of which he accepted: more speaking tours to support national preparedness, fact-finding expeditions to the Middle East and Equatorial Africa, special assistant to secretary of the Navy.

Impatient for greater action and at a loose end, Bullitt ran for mayor of Philadelphia in 1943. He lost the election in a landslide. Personal salvation did not materialize until spring 1944. With de Gaulle's blessing, he joined the Free French army (with the rank of major, lowly for an ex-ambassador). As a staff officer under General Jean de Lattre de Tassigny, Bullitt entered liberated Paris in late August 1944. He made his way to the forlorn embassy on the Place de la Concorde. From the chancellery's balcony, he delivered celebratory words, applauded by a Parisian crowd that, in the confusion, apparently misidentified him as de Gaulle.[81]

Vichy

Roosevelt's preference in autumn 1940 was to substitute General John ("Black Jack") Pershing for Bullitt. Outspoken advocate of aid to the Allies, Pershing held promise as an ambassador. Pétain should have endorsed the appointment of this former companion-in-arms, who had served faithfully during 1917–1918. Their implicit trust in each other could only have produced bonuses for Washington. Pershing, alas, was too old (b. 1860) for any such assignment, his health too precarious.[82]

Unlike Pershing, Leahy was not personally acquainted with Pétain. Yet the marshal, FDR rightly predicted, would be taken by Leahy's service record, which included a stint as Chief of Naval Operations, January 1937–August 1939. Leahy's selection, moreover, signaled America's ongoing interest in the disposition of the French fleet. After Laval's mid-December toppling by members of Pétain's inner circle (likely with the marshal's cooperation) and temporary house arrest, Leahy's appointment seemed serendipitous; he should prove a good fit with Darlan, the new number-two man in Vichy. Presumably, the camaraderie of seafarers would play to Leahy's benefit.

Roosevelt's relations with Leahy dated to Great War days and were cemented by shared devotion to ships and sea lore. Leahy's duties at one time included captaining of a dispatch boat, the USS *Dolphin*, upon which Assistant Secretary of the Navy Roosevelt had cruised along coastal waterways. Following the admiral's retirement (August 1939), FDR named Leahy governor of Puerto Rico; his tenure (September 1939–November 1940) mixed equal parts of conservatism with heavy-handed paternalism. Then came the French diplomatic assignment for which he had neither background nor aptitude, his linguistic talents and knowledge of the country being rudimentary.[83]

Unlike Bullitt, Leahy was not a murky personality. He was not impulsive. Insubordination was beyond his fathoming. He wore his prejudices without adornment or apology. He disliked Jews, was cool toward African Americans, and dismissed anyone who, by his reckoning, lacked strength of character or the fortitude to live strenuously.[84] He was a process man whose intellectual inelasticity disallowed novel ideas. He reflexively opposed internationally pretentious organizations such as the League of Nations (or later the UN), of whose purported merits he sought to disabuse FDR.[85] Leahy most assuredly did not flatter or presume. Unsentimental and prudish, he could not have conceived of signing letters to Roosevelt – as had Bullitt – with "love." To the president, a person whose good-natured volubility hid unplumbed depths of reserve, Leahy constituted a version of merciful peace after Bullitt. At no time did FDR wonder whether Leahy would interpret his Vichy mission in an idiosyncratic fashion. He would insofar as possible carry out instructions to the letter: win the confidence of Pétain, foster Vichy's goodwill toward the United States, restrain Franco-German collaboration against beleaguered Britain, press the French to keep their ships and colonies from Hitler's grasp.[86]

In the wee hours of 6 January 1941 Leahy and his wife, Louise, reached snow-piled Vichy. There shortages of heating fuel and food had begun to degrade the wellbeing of the population. Its number, much increased above the peacetime average, hovered around 130,000.[87] Like Chiang's Chongqing, Vichy, hitherto famous for its medicinal waters, was an ongoing exercise in making do. This meant, in the case of Americans, hostelry-housing and placing the ambassadorial office in the rooms of a former medical practice. Home to the fashionably infirm, of whom some in search of "cure" still crept around crablike, Vichy combined wartime dreariness with vestigial gaudiness, all clinging incongruously to the city's casinos, villas, and music halls. The stoical Leahys in this unlikely billet set to work with whatever passed for France's sovereign government, ensconced in the Hotel du Parc, favored destination for wealthier health aficionados.[88]

The admiral ran his embassy like a ship's skipper, attentive to detail and "hands on."[89] He respected his Bullitt-inherited subordinates, senior of whom were Murphy and Matthews (the former rarely in residence but detailed by FDR to North Africa to cultivate Weygand, then Vichy's high commissioner for Morocco, Tunisia, Algeria). They were assisted by younger men, including Douglas MacArthur II (nephew of the army general) and a handful of military–naval attachés, among whom was Lieutenant Commander Thomas Cassady, in reality an OSS agent. Having supped with Vichy officialdom, and lived in isolation little disturbed by outside news, these people had – by the time of Leahy's arrival – come to share much of Pétain's viewpoint. Thus Matthews accepted the marshal's explanation of the 1940 defeat, supposedly rooted in Third Republic effeminacy, the diffusion of socialist principles, and irresponsible schoolmen who taught unpatriotic history.[90] Matthews had no doubt of the need for a conservative-led rehabilitation of the nation. He evinced little qualm about the circumstances leading to the detention in July 1940 of 40,000 Jews in the unoccupied zone. He dismissed the tough-minded Mandel, arrested by Pétain's government in June, as nothing but "a cold blooded Jew."[91] Matthews expressed only perfunctory disapproval of Vichy's anti-Jewish decrees (July and October 1940) that rescinded the citizenship of recently naturalized Jews and forbade Jewish employment in the officer corps, news media, and upper echelons of the civil service.[92] He did, though, place much confidence in the officer corps of the regular army, not an obvious conclusion given the ineptness of senior ranks in May–June. Taking Pétain as guide, Matthews particularly deplored the presumption to legitimacy of de Gaulle's London congregation. He judged it "a poisonous crowd of Jews, emigrés, crooks."[93]

Habituated to relying upon careful staff work in the navy, Leahy, as a newcomer to diplomacy, looked to his Foreign Service men for insights about Vichy and de Gaulle. The admiral quickly developed sympathy for Pétain's work of resuscitating France. He thought, at least initially, that the marshal's chances were fair for deflecting the siren call of advisors who urged cooperation with Germany to secure France a respectable place in the Nazi order.[94] From the outset, Leahy – much like Matthews – was fond of Pétain, thought him scrupulous, and never held his lapses into mental fatigue against him. Leahy sought, within the limited means available, to buttress the marshal against flapping would-be successors – notably Darlan and Laval, the latter of whom Petain once professed to loathe. In sorrow, not contempt, the ambassador admitted that Pétain was an overwhelmed geriatric, preyed upon by manipulators who tended to dominate him.[95] At the time of his 1945 arrest and trial, Leahy gave this support: "I held your personal friendship and your devotion to the welfare of the French people in very high regard."[96]

About de Gaulle, Leahy harbored reservations in 1941, which he never shed. Essentially, he felt, de Gaulle lacked all semblance of democratic mandate; he was a self-appointed leader who commanded negligible military or other assets. Besides, and more disturbing, his confederates, per the Matthews critique, represented the least desirable social elements, many of whom needed no pretext to terrorize Christian society. They could contribute little to the Allied cause; irrespective of the war's ultimate outcome, they offered nothing affirmative for future France. Of his clandestine talks with Free French operatives and *maquis* fighters, Leahy reported to FDR in July 1941: "The radical de Gaullists whom I have met do not seem to have the stability, intelligence, and popular standing in their communities that should be necessary to success in their announced purpose."[97] Not until 1945 did Leahy slightly modify this evaluation of the Free French, by which time also Pétain had tumbled in the admiral's estimation.[98]

Leahy deployed various means, of which the most important were related to relief, to keep the Vichy administration from sliding irrevocably onto the German side. He helped ease the way for the transfer – despite objections by the American Board of Economic Warfare and British naval blockaders – of modest amounts of US foodstuffs/medicine (plus fuel for agricultural machinery) to civilian populations in the unoccupied zone and French North Africa. Little of this aid, contra the fears of critics, made its way by confiscation or third-party trade into German possession. At some level, impossible to pinpoint, this assistance nurtured sympathetic feeling for the United States among vulnerable peoples while strengthening Vichy claims to being national protector, worthy of Washington's notice.[99] Moreover, of vital importance to Embassy Vichy, this US largesse gave cover to Murphy and his dozen "consular agents" scattered in North Africa. Under the guise of supervising aid distribution and promoting commerce, they (along with OSS operatives) conducted reconnaissance and other covert activities preparatory to the TORCH landings.[100]

Leahy cultivated what anti-German officials he could find at Vichy. They were, worth stressing, by no means synonymous with the factionalized resistance movement or friendly to de Gaulle. Some were well-placed functionaries in the Foreign Office and in army or navy intelligence; they were willing via the embassy to funnel what militarily useful information they could to Washington.[101] While he kept marked distance from militant collaborationists, like Laval, Leahy did court fence-sitters, like Darlan, a consummate opportunist who altered his position with the changing fortunes of war.[102] Leahy preached the inevitability of Allied victory – first in British form, later in Anglo-Soviet partnership, finally in Anglo–Soviet–US combination – over the Axis powers. To this message he affixed suggestions, increasingly unsubtle as the TORCH date advanced, that French statecraft ought to plan accordingly. If France in the meantime veered abruptly in Germany's direction then, he let it be known, Washington would cut connections with Vichy, thereby depriving it of a crucial counter to Berlin's pull. Unchecked, it would – as Leahy knew that Pétain understood in his lucid moments – propel France and its empire into political extinction.

From several sides, the FDR–Leahy policy of engagement with Vichy faced challenges that became more acute after the December

1941 German–US declarations of war. First, the concentration of French POWs in Germany, augmented by labor levies for work in the Third Reich (*Service du travail obligatoire*), and a fervent desire not to justify Berlin's imposing new indemnities or other punishment, inhibited Pétain from seeking – or appearing to seek – intimacy with Washington. In the event, as Leahy's tenure unfolded, Vichy succumbed increasingly to German pressures and threats (i.e. invasion of the unoccupied zone). These resulted in significant concessions: stepped-up tempo of agricultural deliveries to Germany, even as French civilians went hungry; the lending to German purposes of air, rail, and port facilities in Syria (stipulated in the May 1941 Paris Protocols), followed by Vichy's defense (unsuccessful) of them against Free French attack in June–July 1941); the November 1941 removal from his Algiers office of Weygand (too cozy with Murphy and intent on building North Africa against Axis incursions); the February 1942 deliveries via the Tunisian naval base at Bizerte by French merchant ships of supplies to Axis troops in Libya.[103]

Leahy's mission to Pétain had also to cope with German authorities and diplomats stationed in Paris. The likes of self-styled Francophile Ambassador Otto Abetz hoped to dampen Vichy–Washington conciliation.[104] To this end, they inspired the Paris press to air an anti-US campaign. It demonized Leahy – as greedy Jew, agent provocateur, warmonger.[105] He and Roosevelt were also accused of plotting to annex African/New World portions of the French empire to the US imperium.

Making matters more fraught for the embassy, de Gaulle took actions that embarrassed Leahy's professions of friendship for Pétain. An instance of this was the December 1941 conquest by Free French naval forces of the Vichy-administered islands of St. Pierre and Miquelon (near the Newfoundland coast). The assumption in Pétain's cabinet was that such an invasion, then plebiscite to validate it, would not have occurred but for US cooperation and anyway contravened earlier Washington–Vichy pledges to honor the status quo of French realty in the Americas. Hull's condemnation of the Free French acts (taken without consultation of Washington, London, or Ottawa) and subsequent demilitarization of the islands and declarations on their neutrality did not placate Pétain or Darlan. They worried that Hitler would use the episode as a pretext to seize French territories in North Africa, where, under the cover of visiting Axis armistice commissioners,

scouting was underway. Leahy, his ambassadorship already complicated by Washington's decision (November 1941) to make de Gaulle's
movement eligible for Lend-Lease assistance, felt that the contradictions of US policy rendered his job untenable. Consequently, FDR had
to reassure him (February 1942) of fundamental geopolitical calculations and the need for his staying in Vichy: "Not only is our presence
in France and North Africa the last bridgehead to Europe but it likewise helps to hold the Iberian Peninsula in line."[106] Still, a short time
later – in yet another move that alarmed Vichy and rattled Leahy's
position – Washington formally recognized de Gaulle's control of
French Equatorial Africa.[107]

The extension of Lend-Lease to the Free French, and recognition of de Gaulle's primacy in key African territories, helped to soothe
irritation in America over policy toward France. Prominent commentators – Walter Lippmann, Reinhold Niebhur, Dorothy Thompson,
Edward R. Murrow – complained that the State Department propiti-
ated Vichy but shunned the true spirit of fighting France, personified by
de Gaulle. The intemperance of Hull over the St. Pierre and Miquelon
expedition, in particular, raised questions for critics about the secretary's
judgment and generated calls for his resignation. Ambassador Henry-
Haye, meantime, had become a target of revilement in Washington. Not
saved by Murphy's public reference to him as "my friend", he was
accused by journalists of abetting Axis saboteurs.[108] Naturally, none of
this commotion calmed Leahy but only stirred his feeling that so-called
liberals (his language) were undermining sound diplomacy that, should it
succeed, would hasten the war's end. To pleaders who asked that he
protest the restrictions imposed by Pétain's government upon Jews in
France (foreign, naturalized, native), an impatient Leahy responded that
he could do nothing affirmative. Only Jewish citizens of the United States
fell within the embassy's protective purview – such as Gertrude Stein and
Alice B. Toklas, who rejected suggestions from the consul at Lyon to leave
France.[109]

Meddlesome do-gooders (again Leahy's epithet) who made their
way to France also vexed the ambassador.[110] Their aim to help people in
distress was laudable, he admitted, but he felt that the presence of these
self-designated humanitarians complicated his job. Laura Corrigan for
one, a wealthy widow who sought to ameliorate the plight of malnour-
ished French families, got on Leahy's nerves. He mustered considerable
self-discipline to suffer civilly her presence in Vichy.[111]

The most problematic Americans in France, from Leahy's standpoint, were those involved in facilitating the flight of people wanted by German–Vichy authority. They included escapees from the Third Reich and its empire: socialists, communists, Jews, sundry undesirables. By the terms of the 1940 armistice, French officials were obligated to cooperate in the apprehension of these runaways – according to Article 19 "to surrender upon demand" anyone so designated by Berlin.[112] Subverting this mandate were rescue projects sponsored by the Unitarian Service Committee (USC), YMCA, Quakers, and – most spectacularly – the New York-based Emergency Rescue Committee (ERC), formally charged with saving scholars and artists. The ERC's principal agent in France was Varian Fry, who reached Marseille in August 1940. Aided by a handful of people in the unoccupied zone (periodically cooperating with members of other groups, conspicuously the USC's Charles Joy, and Martha and Waitstill Sharp), Fry managed in thirteen months from his Marseille quarters to spirit via Spain, Portugal, and North Africa roughly two thousand "protégés" out of France to the New World.[113]

He could not help everyone in need, such as the writer and painter Max Jacob, who eventually perished (1944) at the Drancy camp (Paris) while awaiting deportation. Nor did everyone that Fry reached survive, among whom the critical theorist Walter Benjamin. He ended in September 1940 as a suicide (morphine pills) in Port-Bou, Spain.[114] Among the lucky rescued were such luminaries as Hannah Arendt (political philosopher), André Breton (surrealist writer), Marc Chagall (artist), Marcel Duchamp (dadaist/surrealist artist), Max Ernst (abstract expressionist), Lion Feuchtwanger (novelist), Hans Habe (journalist), Jacques Hadamard (mathematical physicist), Erich Itor-Hahn (composer), Claude Lévi-Strauss (anthropologist), Jacques Lipchitz (sculptor), André Masson (surrealist painter), Otto Meyerhof (Nobel laureate in medicine), Max Ophuls (film director), Hertha Pauli (actress/writer), Anna Seghers (novelist), Victor Serge (writer), Franz Werfel (novelist/playwright).

To effect the escape of these people, along with their dependents, Fry and his associates resorted to bribery (border guards, policemen, municipal officials), forged passports and visas, hid fugitives, blackmailed or bluffed when expedient, haggled with black-marketeers, and in other ways circumvented the laws and norms of Vichy France. In so doing, Leahy felt, the Fry band not only risked arrest but also undercut Vichy–Washington relations while discomfiting resident diplomats. Consequently, with the blessing of State Department seniors, the embassy tacitly worked with Vichy to hobble Fry's enterprise.[115] Even Eleanor Roosevelt, an ERC booster, became persuaded that the forced cessation of Fry's work – by State Department refusal to renew his passport, followed by his expulsion from France in September 1941 – served the imperatives of US policy. "He will have to come home," the First Lady testified, "because he has done things which the government does not feel it can stand behind."[116] Even after the repatriation of Fry, his colleagues nonetheless managed to continue, despite ever-steeper hurdles, and – until the German intrusion into the unoccupied zone – routed several hundred more people out of Pétain–Hitler reach.[117]

Once back in the United States, Fry tried via a series of essays to raise popular awareness on the predicament of refugees. His most hard-hitting article appeared in a December 1942 volume of the *New Republic* – "The Massacre of the Jews: The Most Appalling Mass Murder in Human History." Much later, Fry became a subject of interest to J. Edgar Hoover's FBI. He had after all – as Leahy, Matthews, plus Long had fretted – consorted with pariahs and foreign-born characters who held unorthodox ideas.[118]

During his time abroad, Fry had sought to enlist people at the embassy and the consulates (Marseille, Nice, Lyon) in the ERC cause. Bullitt and Welles, evidently, had led him to believe, just before his leaving for France, that Leahy's team could be counted on to provide assistance. Only gradually, with mounting bitterness, did Fry realize that the diplomats – from the ambassador downward – were opposed.[119] Leahy ignored his requests to meet and refused to acknowledge Fry the one time when circumstances (shared train ride to Barcelona on the occasion of Fry's ejection from France) forced the two men together.[120] Matthews dodged all conferences proposed by Fry and was otherwise unhelpful.[121] MacArthur II, who did talk with Fry briefly at the embassy, told him coolly that the embassy could do nothing on his behalf. The senior consul in Marseille, Hugh Fullerton, also ducked Fry's appeals for support.[122] The consuls in Lyon and Algiers were similarly unavailing.[123] From Clark Husted, vice-consul in Lyon, Fry was instructed that efforts to get unaccompanied "alien minors," as the children of Ludwig Coperman (a Jewish-German member of Fry's staff), into the United States were unwelcome, especially if the children were orphans or likely to become so:

There is no law prohibiting the entrance of children into the United States unaccompanied by their parents, but there is a law which says that all persons going to the United States must be able to prove conclusively that they are not likely to become a public charge. It is extremely difficult, as you will understand, for minor children to meet this requirement when the persons other than their parents to whom they are destined have small resources and have perhaps furthermore never seen the children, know nothing about them other than that they are related by blood. It is a grave responsibility for an almost total stranger to give, sight unseen, a guarantee that he will care for these children for an indefinite period of time. At the present time if families become separated and something should happen to the persons guaranteeing the children in the United States, the parents would have no way of extending their aid to the children and it is not certain indeed that the parents will ever be able to emigrate to the United States because of the war, because of the race of the parents in many cases which threatens them with the concentration camp ...[124]

The sole exception to this wall of legalism and implacability was the vice consul in Marseille, Hiram Bingham and his assistant (the unlikely named Myles Standish). Even before making Fry's acquaintance, Bingham had involved himself with organizations committed to helping people-at-risk. Martha Sharp and her USC board of supervisors informed Hull, and through him Long and Fullerton, that Bingham in Marseille was superb – praise that amounted, in the circumstances, to a kiss of death.[125] Fry too thought him excellent as he procured a plentitude of US visas for the ERC. Bingham also used his villa as hideaway for Feuchtwanger, after organizing his escape from Vichy detention, and temporarily housed the son (Golo) and brother (Heinrich) of Thomas Mann. With Fry, Bingham convinced a skeptical Chagall of the wisdom of seeking US shelter. Bingham, moreover, at his own initiative and without the consent of his supervisor (Fullerton) toured five Vichy transit camps, where tens of thousands of adults and children had been interned; they ranged from Spanish republican resisters against Francisco Franco, to German dissenters, to stateless Jewish fugitives. Bingham forwarded his findings on the camps – detailing substandard shelters, rampaging diseases, meager food rations – to Washington. This reportage, had it come to the attention of Pétain, could only have created additional awkwardness between the marshal and Leahy.

Luckily from the ambassador's standpoint, the State Department yanked Bingham out of Marseille on the grounds that he skirted immigration procedures and lent himself to groups that operated outside the US government and evaded the laws of a country with which Washington enjoyed correct relations. Bingham was transferred in May 1941 for brief posting to Lisbon, then sent to Buenos Aires. There he produced competent reporting on Nazis circulating freely in Argentina, but otherwise languished until the end of the war, ignored by his trouble-averse superiors.[126] Passed over for promotion, he resigned from the Foreign Service in 1945, his solace being that he had done the Lord's work in France. "All men are born equal in the sight of God," he professed, and deserve to share "in the abundance which God in his goodness has placed upon this earth for all equally to enjoy." Bingham nevertheless remained distraught over the humanitarian problem in France and the paltriness of intervention. "Nothing has ever been done which could not have been done better," he declared.[127] Bingham's replacement in Marseille shared none of this introspection or quasi-theological orientation but was made of flintier stuff. Fry described the new man as imperious and untutored, unable to distinguish social democrats from Stalinists. Still worse, he commanded a position from which to cause harm: "[He] seemed to delight in ... refusing as many visas as he possibly could. He was also very weak on modern European history, but very strong on defending America against refugees he regarded as radicals."[128]

In the months following Bingham's removal, changes occurred at diplomatic grades well above the Marseille consulate. Matthews was slotted in November to London, where he assumed tasks related to TORCH planning, becoming General Eisenhower's political policy advisor.[129] Matthews's place in Vichy was filled by S. Pinkney Tuck. He belonged to that category of Foreign Service officer ridiculed by Dodd and parodied by satirists. Tuck had attended fancy Swiss boarding schools. He frittered time as bon vivant at Dartmouth College, class of 1913. In 1936 he wed an heiress, Katherine Whitney Demme Douglas, one of whose philanthropic donations in 1937 was to FDR's rehabilitation center in Warm Springs. Tuck played polo. He affected British locution. He dressed nattily. He held membership in exclusive social clubs, and so forth.[130] There was more to Tuck's moral and intellectual fiber than inverted snobbery permitted, however.

Opposite to Matthews, Tuck kept an open mind about de Gaulle. Nor did Tuck reflexively dismiss as repugnant or futile the anti-German communist resistance, "the best organized outfit in France" he opined in August 1942. He was also lucid about the nature of Vichy and of German rule in France.[131] He particularly admired Blum, not least for his making "monkeys" out of the Riom judges. Still, Tuck initially had inclined, along Matthews–Leahy lines, to emphasize Pétain's virtues. And he taught that Laval's mid-April return to governmental preeminence, at Darlan's cost but at Ribbentrop–Abetz insistence, need not kill a workable Washington–Vichy understanding. Of Laval, he felt that Americans should better deal with him than wish for his downfall, as people even worse than he waited in the wings. Tuck had in mind far-rightists Jacques Doriot and Marcel Déat, both of whom wanted France to declare openly with Germany against the Americans and British: "As long as [Laval] does not attempt to traffic in those questions which are of military importance to us – the Fleet and the North African bases – we might deal more advantageously with a government headed by this sly but able fellow."[132]

Tuck's assaying of the relative inoffensiveness of Laval notwithstanding, it was precisely his return to primacy that triggered FDR's recall of Leahy for "consultation." But for his wife's unexpected death (21 April 1942), Leahy would have immediately set sail for the United States.[133] Coincidentally, when time came, he obtained the same passage from Lisbon on the *Drottningholm* – landing at Jersey City on 1 June – that ferried Kennan and other Bad Nauheim internees.

Leahy never went back to Vichy. He was reactivated to naval duty in which capacity he served as FDR's senior military advisor and chaired the Joint Chiefs of Staff. In his absence, Tuck headed Embassy Vichy – chargé d'affaires ad interim – and so remained until the November severing of French–US connections.

Tuck continued the policy of cultivating Pétain, an increasingly unrewarding proposition as he retreated deeper into mental torpor and the control of courtiers, especially Laval, who concealed nothing of his Axis bias or hatred of America's Anglo-Soviet allies.[134] Tuck, for his part, sought consolation where he could.

He believed that honest Frenchmen were counting the days until they could exact a "thorough reckoning" upon their oppressors.[135] He was gratified by repeated utterances from Laval and Pétain: Vichy wanted good relations with the United States and would not allow Germany to acquire French warships. On the strength of these assurances, and as the TORCH date advanced, Tuck probed deeper. He asked Pétain to clarify Vichy's attitude should US forces enter French North African territory pursuant to operations against Rommel. To such queries, Pétain answered that France would resist all outside powers, including the United States, which occupied any African province. Neither this rebuff nor other discouragements, though, caused Tuck to despair or suggest that America's Vichy diplomacy be amended.

Germany's French policy meantime became draconian. Arrests and reprisals in the occupied zone soared. In Paris and elsewhere hostages, sometime numbering as many as fifty, were executed for every German soldier killed by underground resisters. The crackdown on Jews intensified. Thousands were assembled in July at Drancy, then shipped abroad, ending at Auschwitz. One report sent (August) to Embassy Vichy contained this summary of eyewitness accounts of the July roundup (*la rafle*), incarceration, and transport of "foreign" Jews (first defined as non-Aryans who had entered the country after 1 January 1936, but later set back to 1931, then to 1927):

> Some 15,000 women and children have so far been taken, plus about 3,000 men. The small proportion of men is accounted for by the fact that they have been previously taken or had fled.
>
> As they were rounded up they were centralized in the circus of the Vélodrome d' hiver, where as many as 8,000 were assembled for as long as 7 days under most adverse conditions – no bedding or other facilities other than straw to sleep on and inadequate sanitary provisions.
>
> Children over two years of age, and up to about 12, are taken from the parents and placed in separate camps.
>
> The parents are taken from the camps and herded into freight cars – 42 to each car – and sent to an unknown destination ... They are locked in the cars for the duration of the voyage ... They are accompanied by children of age 13

*and above. Girls and boys of 15 and 16 picked up are sent
along without their parents ...*

*When picked up these people had no time to prepare their
affairs or to carry with them the necessary toilette articles.
Everything is taken from them down to personal items
including wedding rings. Also little items that might be used
in any way as weapons, such as needles, mirrors, etc.*

*All the work of rounding-up has been done by French
police. The Germans appear only in the background in
civilian dress watching the proceedings ...*

*At the freight cars the German authorities take over and
their treatment becomes worse ... [For example] a French
Red Cross worker attempted to pass a jug of water to those
in one of the wagons. This was jerked from her hands by a
German officer and thrown away with the remark "What
are you trying to do for these dogs?"*[136]

Abetz's prodding, and Laval's willingness, caused thousands of "foreign"
Jews, Roma, and other "troublemakers" to be similarly sent from
unoccupied France into German hands.[137] Irrefutable evidence on the
fate awaiting the train passengers reached Tuck. It shook him, as did
Nazi euphemisms ("resettlement") and other attempted deception. He
meanwhile learned from consulates in southern France and churchmen
(Catholic and Protestants) of nearby doings, such as assaults on Jews
and synagogues in Marseille and Nice by the *Service d'Ordre Légion-
naire*. He was comparably disturbed by what he learned of rising rates
of suicide among inmates in Vichy's squalid internment camps. The
collecting of Jewish children particularly shocked him, as did their
separation from parents selected for what was advertised as labor in
Polish Galicia.[138] There, so Vichy police officials were told by Gestapo
spokesmen, a Jewish state would be organized – all Jews to live in one
place, the rest of Europe freed from their malevolence.[139]

Few of Vichy's ordinary policemen in summer 1942 were gullible enough to think that Nazi plans for Jewry were anything other
than heinous. Some men tried (in Paris too) not to cooperate in the
roundups and warned would-be victims of impending raids.[140] On
these matters, a few police officials surreptitiously contacted Tuck. As
for children obliged to stay in Vichy France as their parents were sent
away, Tuck told Hull: "As it appears to be the intention of the Nazi

authorities that [the] deported parents should not survive the treatment they are now undergoing many of these children may already be considered orphans."[141] Of the evacuations themselves, Tuck gave the State Department this assessment in early September:

> *The inhuman manner in which these deportations are*
> *effected is beyond belief. Pregnant women, women and men*
> *over the age of sixty, sick people, are herded together into*
> *cattle cars and sent East to unknown destinations.*
> *The condition of the children thus separated from their*
> *parents ... is lamentable. From the ages of 2 to 15 they have*
> *been sent to concentration camps at Pithiviers, Drancy, and*
> *Beaune-la-Rollande in the occupied zone, and their fate*
> *remains uncertain. A report has reached me, which I have*
> *been unable to verify, that a number of Jewish girl scouts*
> *attending a camp bordering on the demarcation line have*
> *been rounded up and are destined for brothels in Poland.*[142]

In consultation with US relief agencies, Tuck in September–October undertook negotiations with Laval and René Bousquet, *Secrétaire-général à la police*, to obtain the release from France of Jewish children (estimates ran from five to eight thousand) who were living in detention or hostels without parental supervision. The youngsters would then be delivered – in batches of five hundred to one thousand – to child welfare institutions in the United States and then, it was hoped, to welcoming families. The negotiations nearly came a cropper on Vichy sensitivities. Laval and Bousquet did not want the orphans' arrival in America to spark another round of press criticism of Vichy, or be used for anti-German propaganda, or play into the hands of Free French publicists. On these points Tuck was able, with State Department backing (in the person of Welles, behind whom stood Eleanor Roosevelt), to offer a package of guarantees. Matters thus resolved, Vichy authorized the transfer of five thousand children to US custody.[143] Tuck had, in effect, achieved an agreement, albeit fragile and vulnerable to contingencies, worthy of Fry–Bingham. He had done so without alienating Vichy, or disrupting TORCH, or discombobulating Hull, who remained morbidly uneasy about Nazi recruitment of Jews for espionage.[144]

The schedule of military operations, alas, undid Tuck's work. The North African landings – if secretly pleasing to Pétain – caused

Vichy to terminate relations with Washington. Arrangements concerning the children were not implemented. Consequently, the youngsters had to stay in France and fend for themselves however they could as German forces, accompanied by SS and Gestapo hunters, drove into the Vichy zone on 11 November.[145] Their prey included forty-four Jewish children (ages four to seventeen) snatched from an orphanage in Izieu, not far from where Stein and Toklas lived in anxious seclusion.[146]

After TORCH

Full-fledged French–US relations were restored in late 1944. Embassy Paris reopened to the public on 1 December. A few weeks later, Jefferson Caffery presented his credentials to de Gaulle while Washington received Henri Bonnet. Momentous events had intervened between these Paris–Washington ceremonies and Tuck's parting interview, 8 November 1942, with Pétain.

Vichy policemen, upon the Algerian–Moroccan invasion, had placed US diplomats – with dependents, journalists, Red Cross workers – in Lourdes on 11 November. The universal assumption was that their detention in the shrine city would be brief. They should be promptly exchanged for Henry-Haye and his colleagues who had been taken into custody in Hershey, Pennsylvania. Not until March 1944, however, were US personnel repatriated, marking a period of captivity for Tuck and his 130 companions (including his wife) that far outstripped that experienced by colleagues posted to Axis capitals in December 1941.

Questions regarding the eligibility for exchange of captured members of the German–Italian armistice commissions delegated to North Africa snarled the repatriation negotiations conducted through Swiss intermediaries. Complicating matters further, only a handful of the 150 French nationals in Hershey wanted to return home. Most preferred to associate themselves with de Gaulle or align themselves with whatever else might evolve into an anti-Vichy regime in North Africa. A unit of SS guards, meantime, transferred (mid-January 1943) the American detainees from Lourdes to Baden Baden, a resort town in the hills of the western Black Forest.[147] French employees – none enjoying diplomatic immunity – of the US embassy and consulates fared less well. They were subjected to Gestapo/Vichy police investigation. Some were imprisoned, as was the cherished factotum at Lyon, Marguerite Sandoz, who died in 1945 at the Ravensbruck camp for women.[148] Others suffered combinations of torture and forced labor.

Like earlier diplomats in Axis keeping, boredom, uncertainty, and close quarters afflicted the Baden Baden company. To combat the ill effects, the inmates – inspired by Bad Nauheim and Tokyo ventures – organized sports clubs, skits, chess tournaments, and a "university" with instruction ranging from foreign languages to history to economics. Radio broadcasts featuring "Lord Haw Haw," German and French newspapers and magazines, and lending books also helped. Cheerier moments, internees later reported, occurred as fleets of Allied bombers thundered overhead on their way to strike German targets. The sound of distant bombs could be heard at Baden Baden, whiffs of acrid smoke detected, and the orange glow of burning buildings seen.[149]

The Gestapo interrogation of Cassady constituted the most harrowing moment for the captives. His OSS affiliation and contact with French partisans – to devise escape routes for downed Allied airmen – had come to the attention of German intelligence. He was savagely beaten. He would have suffered worse but for Swiss objections.[150] Naturally, Cassady's mistreatment deepened anxiety among the Americans, their nerves anyway stretched as exchange-negotiations stalled, leaving people to wonder whether their stamina would hold. Tuck expressed their collective relief when, upon finally reaching US shores, he remarked: "After 15 months of detention we now are able to appreciate the full value of the word *freedom*."[151] For his part, after several weeks of recuperation, Tuck was appointed envoy to Egypt (which post he held until resigning in protest in May 1948 over Harry Truman's "precipitate" recognition of Israel).

The only diplomat not to join the exchange ship, *Gripsholm*, embarking from Lisbon on 6 March was Walter Orebaugh, a vice consul in Nice (briefly in Monte Carlo). He had been captured by Italian troops at the same time that Americans elsewhere were collected by Vichy police. He then managed to flee his captors. He subsequently linked with Italian partisans. He fought German soldiers and fascist militias, and gathered military and political intelligence for Allied armies in their Italian campaigns. This service won him the Medal of Freedom, the highest decoration that can be bestowed upon a civilian.[152]

While Orebaugh budded into a "striped pants" guerilla and his colleagues bided at Baden Baden, Pétain's regime completed its transmogrification. Whatever semblance of autonomy Vichy once enjoyed vanished after November 1942. Berlin's writ swept aside every rickety barrier erected by the marshal against Nazi rapacity. The only exception to this state of affairs was the scuttling of French warships by their crews on 27 November. This was done just before Axis units could seize them; it set Vichy sailors in brief but earnest combat against German air/military forces in Toulon, where the bulk of warships had long been anchored. The Germans captured just one destroyer intact. The French systematically wrecked all other ships, including the heavy cruiser *Strasbourg*.[153] Darlan trumpeted this Toulon action as vindication of his and France's good name. On this basis, he expected Allied support of his claim to lead the country, a role – he explained in a radio broadcast from Algiers on 1 December – that Pétain could not play in overrun Vichy.

Underway before the Toulon drama, the British and American landings in North Africa met short-lived resistance by Vichy armies (but after hundreds of Allied soldiers had been killed along with many more French[154]). Most French units then turned – in compliance with Darlan's orders – to join the English-speaking invaders against Rommel. Despite intelligence snafus, confusion among field commanders, uncertainty about the utility of newly acquired French cobelligerents, and setbacks (Kasserine Pass), North Africa was cleared of German and Italian forces by mid-May. Throughout this period of November 1942–May 1943, London and Washington grappled with questions related to competing French factions and on whom to attach Anglo-American favor, FDR's preference being for anyone but de Gaulle.[155]

Roosevelt's feeling against de Gaulle sprang from diverse sources. Leahy's embassy had argued that de Gaulle was an "apprentice" dictator. Once assigned to Washington with the Joint Chiefs, Leahy continued to sound the tocsin: De Gaulle was devoid of virtue. He was saturated with self-righteousness. He was surrounded by congenital misfits and leftist adventurers, none of whom possessed loyalty to France. In the months just before D-Day, Leahy advised that Pétain – not de Gaulle – was the best bet to rally popular French support behind the British and American armies after they stormed Normandy.[156] Various French exiles in Washington harbored comparable misgivings about de Gaulle, among them Alexis Leger, who insisted that the general and his "gang" were unsuited to govern. They presumed to represent France, Leger complained, but had never been tested by popular referendum; they were no more than one element in the political caldron bubbling with factions and rival agendas.[157]

Not only was de Gaulle politically suspect from the FDR–Leahy perspective, but he also lacked military acumen. According to this line, the Free French had botched the Dakar expedition because of their failure to prepare useful intelligence regarding the allegiances and preparedness of opposing forces. Dakar's Vichy garrison proved able and willing to counter de Gaulle (and accompanying British naval contingents), for which mishap Washington blamed him. Breaches in Free French security in London, and de Gaulle's broadcast as the expedition neared Dakar, were counted against him as additional illustrations of incompetence, unforgotten by US war planners. The inability of his coterie to maintain secrecy was later cited as reason for FDR's not telling de Gaulle about TORCH. It was presented as a fait accompli, which inclined him to assume the worst about Anglo-US motives.[158] Were the Anglo-Saxon powers, he wondered, about to slice off sections of France's North African empire for their own? (Similarly, de Gaulle suspected the UK of having designs on Syria and Lebanon and on Vichy-administered Madagascar; in this second instance the British excluded him from the island's 1942 invasion.)

Given de Gaulle's defects as defined by Washington, and the withering of ties to Vichy, the problem for FDR turned on finding an alternative French leader. Roosevelt had been once willing to deal with Weygand. Discreet pre-TORCH inquiries were made of him, via Leahy and MacArthur II, on whether he might leave his retirement in southern France and return to North Africa to head Frenchmen in coordination with the Allies. This idea met with disappointment. Weygand replied that he could take such action only if Pétain, to whom he had sworn fealty, so commanded, which was unlikely.

The Americans next sought to use in TORCH the dashing General Henri Honoré Giraud, commander of the Seventh Army in 1940 and a 1942 escapee from Germany's Königstein prison. In the event, his part in the Casablanca–Oran–Algiers operations was trivial, signaled by comic-opera mistiming and fumbles. As fast became apparent, he also lacked prestige among North Africa's Vichy military governors, having never been one of Pétain's own. Into this political vacuum Darlan famously stepped. At the time of the North African landings, he was in Algiers for private reasons (to visit his naval officer son, Alain, recently stricken by polio). Britons and Americans capitalized on his unexpected presence in North Africa. They exploited his resentment over Laval's superseding him in Vichy, which subject Murphy and Major General Mark Clark (of Eisenhower's staff) refined upon in secret meetings with Darlan. The Americans promised to work with him in exchange for his ordering local Vichy commanders to cease firing upon the Allied attackers. Once done, Eisenhower recognized Darlan on 13 November as head of the civil government in North Africa, his Vichy malignancy expunged by fiat. This constituted a startling reversal of fortunes for a man who until then was simultaneously outflanked by competitors (Laval) and reviled by Americans and Britons as a French Quisling.[159]

Darlan might have emerged as the first leader of post-Pétain France, save for an assassin's bullets, fired by a Royalist (Bonnier de la Chapelle) on Christmas Eve 1942 in circumstances still shrouded by mystery. Giraud, in any case, then became French high commissioner in North Africa, in which office he was slow to undo Vichy institutions – thus the continuance into Spring 1943 of internment camps whose inmates included Spanish republicans and some Gaullists – and imposed sanctions against Algerian Jewry (abrogation of the 1870 Crémieux decree).[160]

The Casablanca conference, 14–24 January 1943, primarily remembered for the announcement on unconditional surrender policy, allowed the "shot-gun marriage" of Giraud and de Gaulle, over which awkward nuptials FDR and Churchill presided. The prickly Brigadier de Gaulle and the self-regarding General Giraud (4 stars) then entered into tentative cooperation, crystallized in June in their co-presidency of the *Comité français de libération nationale* (CFLN). This arrangement did not last. Giraud, although the object of FDR's favors, was outfoxed by de Gaulle and in November lost his spot in the CFLN. Murphy's verdict on Giraud was not wrong: "Politically ... he was quite innocent."[161] Even his military role was scaled back and he, then being a non-factor in Fighting French affairs, retired from the army in April 1944. Thus the field fell to de Gaulle, who alone among Frenchmen could credibly claim to direct a movement that had become a quasi government-in-exile. By early 1944, he had more than half a million French and colonial soldiers under his command and held the loyalty – if not exactly absolute – of *maquis* units in German-occupied

France.[162] De Gaulle also retained British patronage, though subject to Churchill's fits of distemper and threats of disavowal.

After delaying as long as feasible, and having failed to find an alternative, FDR recognized (October 1944) the de Gaulle-controlled CFLN as France's provisional government, well after the British and Soviets had conferred this dignity. Before this recognition was granted, though, de Gaulle had (to the ire of FDR and Churchill) in June nearly refused his endorsement of the D-Day operations, about which he had been barely consulted on the military or political and administrative aspects.[163] A few weeks later he and FDR met in Washington, but the meetings, albeit outwardly cordial, did little to thaw the accumulated frost between host and guest. The formal recognition that de Gaulle craved had been withheld, as had increases in materiel that he hoped to obtain for Free French armies.[164] In his 25 August radio address, broadcast from Paris, he declared that Frenchmen alone were responsible for the liberation of their capital, which statement he qualified by pro forma mention of the Allies but without reference to their Normandy deeds. Thus glowering suspicion continued to mar relations between Washington and de Gaulle, underscoring the validity of this observation made (summer 1944) by Elmer Davis, director of FDR's Office of War Information: "Americans are dying on French soil for the liberation of France; American arms have equipped the French armies; America has guaranteed that Frenchmen will choose their own government. Yet there never was a time when Frenchmen who have free access to news were as hostile to America as they are today."[165]

Caffery and de Gaulle

Caffery conceived of his mission as one to cauterize festering French–US wounds before they created problems even graver than that identified by Davis. This would, if successful, preserve Allied military and diplomatic cooperation for the remainder of warfare and encourage European repairment.

The first career Foreign Service officer appointed envoy to Paris, Caffery contrasted sharply with Bullitt and Leahy. He was not so verbal as the former (he suffered from a mild speech impediment) or so impetuous. Caffery was precise, dry, and prone to self-effacement, though punctilious about the trappings of ambassadorial office. Contra

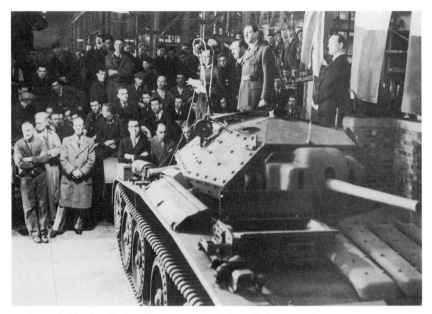

8 General Charles de Gaulle inspects British tank factory, circa 1940.

Bullitt, his tastes ran toward the ascetic. His marriage at fifty produced neither domestic rapture nor children but was companionable. Unlike Leahy, Caffery esteemed the diplomatic vocation and was an experienced practitioner with a reputation for pragmatism. His record of yeoman service, mostly compiled in Latin America, dated to 1911, when he left his native Louisiana (where in Lafayette he had been reared in comfort and Cajun legends). Also contra Leahy, he was a contemplative. A convert in middle age to Roman Catholicism, Caffery read Aristotle for recreation along with treatises on theology and Patristics. In 1944 he befriended the Papal nuncio and doyen of the Paris Diplomatic Corps, Archbishop Angelo Roncalli, destined to become the innovative Pope John XXIII.[166] Caffery's most important pre-Paris ambassadorial posting was to Brazil in 1937–1944. There he helped press, with threats of US boycotts of Brazilian coffee imports, the government of Getulio Vargas to forsake its Axis infatuation and join (August 1942) the Allies.[167]

Though Caffery's appointment to Paris triggered arch words among commentators – that he was not eminent – it was, by White House lights, perfectly defensible. He was untainted by that diplomacy which had emphasized working relations with Vichy at the expense of sympathetic understanding of Free France.[168] Caffery did share much of the State Department's skepticism about de Gaulle, however. While conceding that he was capable of reconstructing a robust France, Caffery labeled him "a sour puss."[169] As for de Gaulle, his treatment of the ambassador from 1944 onward was correct, but never approached the intimacy achieved by Bullitt with Daladier/Reynaud or had any of the melancholy rapport that tinged Leahy–Pétain interactions. The concerns that concentrated the attention of de Gaulle and Caffery were three: maintenance of the wartime coalition; the fate of Paris's overseas empire; the nature of postwar French society and economy in which connection local communists and their Soviet ties constituted an added layer of complexity.

Regarding coalition diplomacy, the question that most directly involved Caffery sprang from the Yalta summit, 4–11 February 1945. De Gaulle believed that France, by right of return to belligerency against Germany, deserved a place at Yalta, a view not shared by Roosevelt or (to slightly lesser degree) his fellow conferees, Stalin and Churchill. Their decision not to invite French representation infuriated the general, who belittled the conference as a hollow exercise in new world ordering. In pique, and contrary to White House expectation, he rejected FDR's proposal to rendezvous in Algiers after the Yalta meetings.[170]

This snubbing of the president galled US officialdom, not least Caffery. He did, incidentally, join FDR at Algiers for a debriefing on Yalta, where decisions favorable to France were made: allowing the country an occupation zone in post-hostilities Germany and a place as permanent member with veto power in the prospective UN Security Council. De Gaulle's foul humor meanwhile was widely reported in France, where some people cringed at his "ingratitude" and others wondered about his emotional equilibrium.[171] Caffery suggested that Roosevelt henceforth assume an aloof stance toward de Gaulle, but not do anything – such as reducing humanitarian aid to France – that might upset serenity of mind in Paris or so agitate popular feeling that military operations would suffer: "While perfectly willing to call de Gaulle all the names in the devil's calendar, I would like to say that it is essential for us, with so many troops at the front, to have order maintained in France ... we must not let lack of food and other things reach a point where the population might create difficulties for our lines of supply."[172] Caffery advised the president in March, that he consider making a visit to Paris in the Spring, an idea undone by Roosevelt's death on 12 April.[173] Caffery actually learned from de Gaulle's own lips about FDR's passing, for which the Frenchman expressed genuine regret.[174]

Caffery's labors to preserve Franco-US cooperation during post-Yalta warfare did not make a notable splash. He played a second-ary, if helpful, part in defusing that potentially sticky situation when (late April) senior American officers tried to get units of de Lattre's French First Army to abandon their position in Stuttgart, a city assigned – by prior agreement – to occupation by the US Seventh Army. At one point, Eisenhower wanted to force the issue by withholding further materiel from the French for the duration of war. Luckily for the sake of Allied unity, other counsel prevailed, including that conveyed by Caffery to Paris. He also reasoned with de Gaulle in April–June as Truman urged the French army to cease actions in north-western Italy (Val d'Aosta) that were manifestly annexationist. De Gaulle did back down – under a shower of White House threats about terminating transfers of military equipment and financing – but not before letting Caffery know that Americans were meddling in a matter that was not their business.[175]

As to the fate of the French empire, Caffery was an interested observer but not immersed in the more pertinent Washington–Paris discussions. He did share the dismay felt by Truman and Churchill when, in May–June 1945, de Gaulle's air, naval, and land forces sought to squelch the renewed Syrian–Lebanese bids for independence. Damascus was shelled, civilians killed. Caffery urged moderation to de Gaulle and Foreign Minister Georges Bidault. But the violence did not abate until Churchill prepared to deploy British troops to impose peace. Regarding Indochina, whereas FDR had opposed France's return to supremacy, Caffery was prone to side with de Gaulle. Caffery did meet in 1946 with Ho Chi Minh, Paris-based Marxist nationalist, and thought him poised and intellectually attractive. The ambassador did not, though, support Ho's request that the United States help Vietnam gain independence. By 1947, in fact, Caffery was convinced of the desir-ability of France's re-conquest of Indochina, the alternative being, in his view, the spread of Soviet-sponsored dictatorships in Southeast Asia and a weakening – possibly fatal – of liberal-minded parties in France.[176]

The subject that most engaged Caffery centered on the quality of French economic and political renewal. The extent of disruption caused by national defeat, German looting, and wartime privation may have been difficult for him and his staff to gauge fully. Nevertheless, they were sobered by the problem, its scale suggested by these statistics: the human cost included 600,000 war-related deaths, mostly civilian (among them were Némirovsky, deported to Auschwitz in 1942, and Bloch, executed by a German firing squad in 1944). Roughly 5 million people (12.5 per cent of the population) were displaced in 1940 onward, many to Germany or farther east. One-fourth of the nation's buildings had been destroyed. The merchant marine had fallen to a third of its pre-war size. Coal production was off by 40 per cent of pre-war amounts. Industrial production had plummeted to less than 30 per cent. Grain harvests in 1945 were half of previous levels. Public indebtedness had skyrocketed. Salaries were depressed while the cost of living had tripled. Inventories of cement, locomotives, and trucks had shrunk by crippling orders of magnitude. Food stocks were depleted, owing to German requisitioning, with caloric intake in 1944 around 900 calories per day. Although the French food crisis did not equal the starvation that stalked the Netherlands or eastern Europe, food rationing stayed in place for years after 1945.[177] Caffery noted in February 1946, soon after de Gaulle retired from executive office, that shortages – above all of food and coal – and "malaise" blanketed France. The pace of recovery seemed depressingly slow: "The average man is still cold, hungry, unable to buy what he needs and frustrated by the feeling that not enough progress has been made."[178]

Caffery early adhered to the idea – later a tenet of faith in Washington – that were the French economy not revived and social conditions allowed to deteriorate, local communists, enjoying vast prestige in post-liberation France, would exploit the situation. They could easily form a government by conventional electoral means or coup d'état. Either way, a French communist administration would, he predicted, align itself with the USSR and antagonize the Americans and British. To avert this, he lobbied after V-E Day for transfusions of aid (Lend-Lease surplus, grants, loans) to France. He later became an avid booster of the Marshall Plan and worked with its supervisors and Parisian recipients.[179]

Caffery was also attentive to the psychic side of France's regeneration. He keenly followed the 1945 return from Sigmaringen castle of

Vichy's castaways, who had fled their country – or were forcibly removed in the case of Pétain – as Allied armies reclaimed it. These included Laval, tried by a drumhead court and executed in October. As for Pétain, after trial, he was sentenced to death, but this was commuted (by de Gaulle) and he suffered life imprisonment on the Ile d'Yeu, where he died in 1951 at ninety-five. Caffery meanwhile took satisfaction in the return to France of works of art – twenty thousand pieces had been hauled to Germany. (Hundreds of paintings, the work of "decadent" artists, had been burned in the Louvre's courtyard.) And he tried to check instances of misconduct toward women by GIs, curb their condescension toward civilians, limit the casual requisitioning of French property, and counter widespread reports (exaggerated) of American leniency toward German POWs.[180]

Like two of his intimates, Breckinridge Long and H. Freeman Matthews, Caffery was not gifted with balms of empathy or liberal spiritedness.[181] He managed to apply some relief where needed, however. He spoke movingly to France's Jewish and gentile survivors of Nazi persecution. He hosted a determinedly cheerful Hanukkah party in 1947 for more than two thousand Jewish orphans and distributed presents donated by American children.[182]

Did memory of these postwar gestures stir MacArthur II, employed in Caffery's Paris embassy as earlier under Leahy, and cause him in pensive mood to confess (1987) this collective failure? "We were under very formal training and instructions at that time [circa 1940–1942] about the requirements that were [exacted] of people who were applicants for visas. But in retrospect, we were perhaps too strict."[183] And yet, as MacArthur also knew, rules could be adjusted on behalf of personal favorites or Embassy pets, particularly if titled. To Matthews in 1962, Baron Jean de Lustrac (then residing in Norfolk, Virginia) delivered this effusive testimonial: "You gave me a letter asking the American authorities to welcome me. So in October [1940], when I went to Marseille, for a visa to U.S. there was a line of thousands of Jews waiting at the American Consulate, since several days. With your letter, I was received first of all by [officials] who gave me a visa immediately!"[184]

***

As a third secretary in Embassy Vichy, MacArthur bore no responsibility for the design of US immigration policy or visa regulations. Their making and enforcement rested with individuals on Capitol Hill, along

State Department corridors, in the White House. Congress chose not to loosen restrictive 1924 legislation governing immigration or to amend quotas in favor of people at risk. Hull's chief State Department assistants were anyway not eager to have all quotas filled; some ambassadors in the field, including the only two of Jewish faith or antecedents, namely Bullitt and Laurence Steinhardt (reviewed in Chapter 7), harbored doubts about persons trying to reach the United States. On the ship that bore him back to America in May 1942, Leahy wondered how many of the non-English-speaking passengers were worthy, though they carried valid papers.[185] As for Roosevelt, not until 22 January 1944 did he allow establishment of the War Refugee Board. It managed to save 200,000 Jews and 20,000 other people, a commendable effort but overwhelmed by the emergency's enormity.[186] The president himself had been slow to understand, indicated by comments he made during the Casablanca conference to General Auguste Nogues, previously Vichy's senior man in Morocco. Roosevelt observed that a surfeit of Jews in North Africa occupied major business and professional slots (law, medicine, scholarship) just as their coreligionists had in Germany, where "understandable complaints" by citizens had been leveled and acted upon against a disproportionate presence.[187]

Against this discouraging backdrop, the efforts of Fry and Bingham shone brightly. Their work went unrecognized by US officialdom for decades, however. Not until February 1996 in a tree-planting ceremony at Yad Vashem to honor Fry did Secretary of State Warren Christopher acknowledge his resourcefulness. To this praise, Christopher added: "Regretfully during his lifetime, his heroic actions never received the support they deserved from the United States government, including, I also regret to say, the State Department."[188] (Thirty years earlier, the French made Fry a Chevalier de la Légion d'Honneur for his rescue work.) The intrepidity of Bingham was saluted in Washington only in the twenty-first century. Secretary of State Colin Powell and the American Foreign Service Association posthumously conferred (June 2002) upon him the "Constructive Dissent" award. The citation read: "His actions violated the State Department anti-refugee policy... [and showed] his willingness to put humanity before his career."[189] In 2006 the US Postal Service issued a commemorative stamp series that featured six "Distinguished American Diplomats," of whom Bingham was one.[190]

Coincidentally, another of the diplomats memorialized in the 2006 stamp series was Robert Murphy. He had won promotions and decorations (Distinguished Service Medal, Croix de Guerre) in his lifetime surpassing any known by Bingham. A celebrated mastermind of TORCH, Murphy's post-1942 life included two ambassadorships (Belgium, Japan), appointment as undersecretary of state for political affairs, anointment as Career Ambassador. Yet Murphy did have detractors among Britons and Americans, and most Free French. They never forgave his being chummy with reactionaries (Marcel Peyrouton of Vichy's Interior Ministry and industrialist Jacques Lemaigre Dubreuil) and were skeptical of the stratagem that required his playing friendly to Darlan. Endorsement of Giraud's revocation of Crémieux, and postwar affidavit on behalf of Weygand as US ally, also fed suspicions that Murphy preferred "pro-Nazi Frenchmen."[191] The success of the "Vichy gamble" came at the expense, so critics charged, of those ideals for which the United States supposedly fought. Lippmann claimed that Murphy radically "misjudged the situation." Supreme Court Justice Felix Frankfurter labeled him "grottier than the grotties."[192] De Gaulle dripped this sarcasm in his memoirs: "Long familiar with the best society [Murphy] apparently rather inclined to believe that France consisted of the people he dined with."[193] To these disparagements one can add that a collateral effect of TORCH was the scotching of Tuck's orphans initiative, not to mention the intensified danger that befell all Jews as German armies crossed the demarcation line. Critics have also cited careless words by Murphy about North African Jews, for being less than fulsomely grateful and too impatient with the pace by which Vichy restrictions were suspended.[194]

Even if all faults ascribed to Murphy were true, they would not clinch the argument against him or cancel the test of other – affirmative – results. TORCH proved, for the first time, that US soldiers could give a fair account of themselves against the Wehrmacht, a morale lift for London and Washington and instructive for those Kremlin men who wondered about making a separate peace with Berlin. In conjunction with British success at second El Alamein (23 October–4 November 1942) TORCH also ensured the destruction of Axis power in the North Africa–Near East theatre. This achievement preserved the Suez Canal and related shipping lanes for the Americans and British, who also acquired a springboard for their 1943 invasions of Sicily/Italy. The defeat of Rommel meant too that the Jewish communities in North Africa and British Palestine would not be abandoned to German mercies.[195] Finally, a North Africa securely in Allied hands was prerequisite to any invasion of southern France, successfully undertaken by Anglo–US–Free French armies in August 1944.

The appearance of Allied armies in northern and southern France in 1944 expunged whatever residual legitimacy clung to the Pétain–Laval government during its post-TORCH twilight. Not only was the fiction of Vichy autonomy finally exploded as cabinet ministers and hangers-on were bundled off to German asylum to constitute Fernand de Brinon's wretched *Délégation gouvernementale française pour la défense des intérêts nationaux*. But also the full scale of Vichy sham was divulged. German-caused destruction in 1940–1944 belied Vichy apologists, who had condemned Gaullists for "running away" in contradistinction with their stalwart selves.[196] Collaboration had not protected France from German expropriations or reprisals, nor elevated the country to a privileged position in the Nazi order. Collaboration could not guarantee the survival of Paris that was on Hitler's order, except for the disobedience of General Dietrich von Choltitz, to experience demolition in the Warsaw fashion. Other French places did suffer in Lidice-like manner, such as Oradour-sur-Glane, where SS soldiers on 10 June 1944 massacred the inhabitants (640 men, women, children) and set the buildings ablaze.[197] If not comparable in scale to that visited on peoples in eastern Europe, the misery inflicted upon France was stunning in an absolute sense.

Defeat and Vichy have long harried Western memory. To Hannah Arendt the problems of 1940 and Vichy usurpation were attributable to a dearth of confident democrats. "What made France fall," this ERC "protégée" judged, "was the fact that she had no more Dreyfusards, no one who believed that democracy and freedom, equality and justice could any longer be defended or realized under the republic."[198] Even after a democratic ascendancy was established, first in the unsure Fourth Republic, then in the steadier Fifth Republic, an inconvenient past kept making its presence felt in France. Affiliation with Vichy smudged the reputation of so respectable a figure as François Mitterrand. Maurice Papon, a Pétain functionary in Bordeaux and responsible for the roundup of sixteen hundred Jews, served (1958–1967) as police prefect for Paris, then as budget minister for President Valéry Giscard d'Estaing. Not until 1998 was Papon convicted and sentenced to prison for crimes against humanity; only three years earlier President Jacques Chirac conceded – unlike Mitterrand who had refused – Vichy responsibility for mass arrests of French Jews. The national railway (SNCF) apologized in November 2010 for its role in Jewish deportations – clearing the way for the SNCF to bid for contracts to build high-speed rail projects in California and Florida, where legislators had blocked eligibility until admissions of responsibility were issued.

Against the moral bog of Vichy stood the unbending, arrogant, ruthless, impossible – but also magnificent – de Gaulle. Jean-Paul Sartre, an equivocal and self-exonerating resistant, once declared: "I do not believe in God, but if in [a] plebiscite I had the duty of choosing between Him and [de Gaulle], I would vote for God: he is more modest."[199] Even Raymond Aron, writer and de facto editor of the Free French newspaper *La France libre*, thought the general unbecomingly ambitious and autocratic.[200] Yet in his absence the French narrative of World War Two would be dismal, an elaboration on Bloch's pronouncement that endless years must pass before the blot of defeat could be erased.[201] Against all odds, contrary to reasonable calculation, and in face of national ignominy, de Gaulle swore that June 1940 was only an episode, not the whole story, and France would rise resplendent, the dictatress of her fate: "France is a world power. She knows it and will act so that others may know it."[202]

Nothing in de Gaulle's organizational skill, bravado, and eloquence, nor the myth he manufactured of a nation unbowed, could secure France against decline, signaled – not caused – by June 1940. Virtually every part of the empire broke away during his postwar career, at times sparking national crisis: the 1954 surrender at Dien Bien Phu, the Algerian struggle for independence. The 1956 Suez debacle confirmed French weakness and dependence on Washington – not nullified by de Gaulle's boycott of observances in Normandy commemorating the twentieth anniversary of D-Day or by France's 1966 disassociation from the NATO command structure. Only as part of a uniting Europe, ironically in partnership with Germany, as de Gaulle came to comprehend, would France begin to recover any of that standing which pre-1940 Parisians and Bullitt had accepted as a matter of course.

Part III

Victors

6 BRITANNIA

Having fielded arms on land and sea and in the air against Axis might, the British Empire figured prominently in 1945 among Allied victors. The cost to Britain had been immense, however. The empire was declining, as shown by all major indices in 1945. The House of Commons in October extended wartime emergency power for five years to Clement Attlee's Labour government. The economic crisis, sparked by the spending of reserves on wartime expenditures, could not otherwise have been surmounted. In December the United States granted an emergency loan of $3.75 billion to Britain to stave off bankruptcy, supplemented by a Canadian loan of $1.25 billion. Two years later, India, jewel of the empire, acquired independence. Two hundred years of British rule on the subcontinent thus ended and set in train future imperial departures from the Middle East, Africa, East Asia.

Great Britain's most trying year in the war stretched between the collapse of France and Hitler's 1941 assault on the USSR. Unaided by effectual allies, British forces during that time could not reduce Germany's dominant position in Europe. Luftwaffe bombers plastered British cities. Submarines and surface raiders nearly strangled the country's maritime lifeline to the wider world. Berlin's military planners studied ways to conquer and occupy the isles. American navy destroyers – swapped in September 1940 for ninety-nine year leases on British bases in the New World – helped only slightly to alleviate pressure on the United Kingdom. Of the fifty pledged warships, all of World War vintage, London had taken possession of only nine by the end of 1940. Lend-Lease did ultimately provide tangible aid to the British Empire, valued between $21 and $25 billion.[1] Yet the question stood in 1941: Would enough Lend-Lease supplies arrive in time? As for the German invasion of Soviet Russia, London's military and civilian leaders perceived a respite, but most felt that the Red Army must crumble. Hitler's fury subsequently would be redirected against Britons. Thus they were obliged to live in continuing suspense of a German cross-Channel invasion and waged mainly rearguard operations.[2]

Two decades after Britain's fight, President John Kennedy, in tribute to Churchill's oratorical virtuosity, said of the prime minister: "In the dark days and darker nights when England stood alone – and most men save Englishmen despaired of England's life – he mobilized the English language and sent it into battle. The incandescent quality of his words illuminated the courage of his countrymen."[3] Notable among people during the critical moment who thought that Britain would succumb, and that the islanders lacked requisite fortitude, was the president's father: Joseph Patrick Kennedy, ambassador to the Court of St. James's, 1938–1940.

He doubted from the war's outset that combined Anglo-French arms would be enough to stop Germany. Following France's removal from hostilities, he predicted that Britain would suffer outright defeat or accept Hitler's terms while eking out a circumscribed autonomy on German sufferance. Good sense in these circumstances meant the following for Kennedy: Americans should maintain distance from the weakening British, extend only moderate aid, and build naval and military levels to deter Axis aggression against the New World. (The US army in 1939–1940 ranked nineteenth in size, smaller than that fielded by Holland.[4]) If deterrence failed, the United States needed sufficient force to defeat any conceivable German–Japanese–Italian incursion into the Americas. "It may not be convenient," he advised FDR in late September 1939, "for us to face a world without a strong British Empire. But whatever we do or don't do, we shall have to face it. Neither we nor any other Power can re-create what has disappeared, and the leadership of the English-speaking world will, willy-nilly, be ours. Certainly it is going to be a hard, difficult and dangerous world in which to live, and the United States will only be able to thrive in it by pulling itself together as a nation and being ready and prepared to protect its own vital interests." All of which, by Kennedy's estimation, lay in the western hemisphere.[5]

These ideas, expressed in public as well as confidentially, made the ambassador unpopular in Churchill's London. His words also ran against the grain of Roosevelt's thought. After the French capitulation, FDR viewed Britain as indispensable to the Atlantic flank of US security and resolved that the United Kingdom must not collapse. Prudence led him, though, to endorse Churchill's worst-case contingency steps: shipping gold and foreign exchange/security reserves to Canada in summer 1940, devising plans to wage guerilla warfare after a German occupation, preparing to transfer Royal Navy ships to New World ports.[6]

Roosevelt replaced Kennedy in early 1941 with an envoy of more congenial outlook, John Gilbert Winant. From then to war's end, he helped to stabilize Anglo-US relations. He salved many of those irritations that plague even the sturdiest alliance. To countless Britons, high and low, he also symbolized US commitment to their safety. Labour party's Ernest Bevin, a wartime minister in Churchill's coalition cabinet, explained in 1946: "It's a vivid recollection to us to see [Winant] walking round the streets during an air raid witnessing how London took it ... he shared our sorrows ... he gave one a feeling of optimism."[7]

Appeasement

Traditionally the most coveted ambassadorial posting in the White House gift has been assignment to London. Presidents before FDR and since have awarded it to party donors or luminaries. Until Kennedy's appointment, the position had been the preserve of Protestant Anglo-Saxons. It was coextensive with social prestige and American aristocracy. Among Kennedy's predecessors were these, five of whom eventually became chief executive: John Adams, Rufus King, James Monroe, John Quincy Adams, Albert Gallatin, Martin Van Buren, Edward Everett, George Bancroft, James Buchanan, George Dallas, Charles Francis Adams, James Russell Lowell, Robert T. Lincoln, Joseph Choate, Whitelaw Reid, Frank Kellogg, Andrew Mellon.

To even the score for slights inflicted upon him by Boston bluebloods and eager for preferment, Kennedy contrived – with aid from the president's son, James, and columnist Arthur Krock – to obtain Embassy London once vacancy arose. It did so in November

1937, when deathly ill Ambassador Robert Bingham returned to the United States.[8] Except for the status involved, and pleasure at being the first Irish Catholic to represent Washington in London, diplomacy hardly interested Kennedy. Nor did he possess an affinity for it. He was brash, profane, self-absorbed. He was too untutored to grasp the complexities that layered European life in the late 1930s. A self-made multi-millionaire – fortunes amassed in real estate, finance, shipbuilding, Hollywood, liquor sales – he questioned his own qualifications for the ambassadorship. He wrote to FDR on receiving Senate approval: "I don't know what kind of a diplomat I shall be, probably rotten."[9] Had he his druthers, Kennedy would have taken the Treasury portfolio, unluckily held by a rival, Henry Morgenthau.

The president had doubts about the appropriateness of Kennedy for London. They stemmed from his philandering and the antipathy of New Deal true-believers, who perceived him as an overly ambitious tycoon. They charged that he had a well-earned reputation for pushing multifarious business schemes to the legal limit. Surely, the former "bootlegger" was too indiscreet for diplomacy's subtlety, too unvarnished for His Majesty's court. Roosevelt therefore tried to cure Kennedy of his British fixation, offering to place him in charge of the Commerce Department. This cabinet slot should be fair recompense for his financial and other aid to FDR's election campaigns (1932, 1936), plus an expression of gratitude for his shrewd chairing of the Securities and Exchange Commission (1934–1935) and directing the Maritime Commission (1937–1938).[10]

Kennedy held fast. The president, unwilling to alienate a generous supporter, one whose religion and ethnicity also connected him to core elements of the New Deal assemblage, relented. He made FDR's decision easier when he intimated that he desired only a brief tour in London before returning to America with his family at last enrolled in the *Social Register*. Anyway, the notion of setting a gum-chewing rascal upon Whitehall prigs and Mayfair fops amused Roosevelt. "A great joke, the greatest joke in the world," he chortled.[11] Insofar as FDR was bothered by rumors – well-founded – of Kennedy's criticizing New Deal innovations, the idea of sending the man abroad had added appeal. "Kennedy is too dangerous to have around here," the president told Morgenthau.[12]

To son-in-law John Boettiger, Roosevelt shared this assessment of Kennedy: "thoroughly selfish."[13] Such a person had to be watched.

He required reminders too of who was boss and could make or break him, and the careers of his sons, if he proved awkward or disloyal. Hence the hazing that occurred in the Oval Office one autumn day in 1937, when Roosevelt summoned Kennedy to review his diplomatic prospects. After a round of verbal jousting, in which each man encouraged the other to cease his extramarital liaisons, the president told Kennedy to drop his trousers. Stunned by the request but at the mercy of his ambition, he complied. The president, who rarely referred to his polio-stricken legs, then made a show of examining Kennedy's lower limbs. Pronouncing him hopelessly bowlegged, Roosevelt warned that he would cut a silly figure upon presentation in the knee breeches and silk stockings prescribed by Buckingham palace protocol. Kennedy answered that he could get an exemption, if by so doing Roosevelt would hire him. In the event, Kennedy did win British permission to wear striped pants and cutaway coat upon being introduced (8 March 1938) to King George VI. Kennedy later told newsmen that his attire indicated independence of mind, contra previous ingratiating ambassadors, such as Walter Hines Page (who, said critics, was so duped by the British that he stupidly supported US intervention on the Allied side in 1917).[14] What FDR made of this account or what Kennedy privately thought about the president's teasing remain matters of guesswork. Surely, Kennedy would have agreed with Averell Harriman's observation, made in another context, that Roosevelt "always enjoyed other people's discomfort."[15]

The ambassador arrived in Britain amid German–Austrian tension, subsequently dispelled by the mid-March *Anschluss*. As the British–American response to this event was muted, and no emergency arose between the English-speaking powers and Berlin, he was able to slide unimpeded into diplomatic routines and entertainments. He read them as markers of the social distance that he had traversed since childhood on Boston's mean streets (the supreme validation taking place in Rome in March 1939, when he represented Roosevelt at the coronation of Pope Pius XII). Kennedy and his wife, Rose, were weekend guests at Windsor castle. Their nine photogenic children were fussed over by journalists. The ambassador's golfing prowess was praised when, days after arriving in London, he made a hole-in-one at Stoke Poges. His decision in April to suspend the embassy's presenting of American debutantes to the royal court, except for those resident in Britain (which loophole allowed his eligible daughters), was cited by the press as evidence of his penchant for novelty over musty rites. Roosevelt must have been surprised by the Kennedy–British love feast. London's stuffier class stifled misgivings about the president's Irish parvenu, at least for the time being. When Randolph Churchill did harrumph in the *Evening Standard* that Kennedy's wearing of trousers at the Buckingham reception left the American indistinguishable from the lesser rank of waiters, FDR gave advice and this turn of the screw: "When you feel that British accent creeping up on you and your trousers riding up to the knee, take the first steamer home for a couple of weeks holiday."[16]

Kennedy became heavily subscribed by what he called the "top side people." They included the Virginia-born Nancy Lady Astor, mistress of Cliveden, and her husband, the bigoted Viscount Waldorf Astor. The so-called Cliveden set – intent upon Britain's avoiding another war with Germany – also numbered Lord Lothian, Lord Londonderry, Geoffrey Dawson (editor of the London *Times*), Lord Robert Henry Brand, and Lord Halifax. Lady Astor and her circle dazzled Kennedy; he once told her that he would follow wherever she beckoned.[17] He soon settled into a frenetic life laced with rewards. When not attending receptions, dashing off missives from his chancellery in Grosvenor Square, or promoting Anglo-US trade, he pursued private hobbies: frolicsome paramours, early-morning horseback rides through London's Hyde Park.

Of the government ministers whom Kennedy knew, none became closer than Neville Chamberlain, whom he thought swell.[18] Their mutual regard sprang from success in business. They shared a fear of social and political disorders and abhorred communism. Above all, they were proponents of appeasement, which term in the late 1930s did not possess the pejorative connotations later associated with it. Instead, for both men, the idea denoted magnanimity plus a proven way to reduce international tensions. It centered on great powers making timely concessions to discontented ones that might otherwise press their grievances to the point of war. This orientation, as applied to the Third Reich, meant that Hitler's territorial claims compatible with principles of national self-determination should be satisfied (for instance, Austrian–German union). Germany's eastward expansion and organization of the lesser European economies also made sense in this context, as had the earlier suspension of punitive Versailles provisions, namely those stipulating large reparations. A satisfied Germany, according to this logic, would become habituated to seeking diplomatic solutions to knotty questions. German leaders would not provoke another war, certain to spawn chaos from which only Moscow and its Comintern instrument could profit. Chamberlain likened Germany after the *Anschluss* to a gorged boa constrictor that required considerable time to digest its food before getting restless again. Admittedly, the prime minister said to Kennedy, Hitler was uncouth. Yet one could conduct business with him.[19]

Kennedy believed that a pentagonal power scheme was arising. One day this would supplant the discredited League of Nations and conduce to perpetual peace. In this framework the United States would exercise New World leadership. A Franco-British bloc, nourished by overseas colonies, would guide western Europe. A German system would operate in central and southeastern Europe. Moscow's Bolsheviks could manage their sprawling Eurasian zone in whatever way they thought best. Japan, with China as junior partner, should organize East Asia. These five pillars of power, each legitimate and responsible by its own lights, would under-gird world commerce.[20] Before this new order obtained coherence, the powers privileged by the 1919 peace settlement, Britain especially, had to advance European concord. For Kennedy, these considerations dictated sensitivity to justifiable German aims. He therefore stinted nothing in his support of Chamberlain during the 1938 German–Czechoslovak impasse.

Kennedy met with Chamberlain several times during the weeks before the Munich denouement. The former's purpose, apart from staying abreast of evolving British thought, was to strengthen London's dedication to a peaceful solution. These Kennedy–Chamberlain meetings went beyond anything that Roosevelt or Hull approved. Neither one, despite determination to keep the United States uninvolved, wanted the British or French to abandon Czechoslovakia entirely to Germany. Kennedy, in any case, persisted in keeping Chamberlain true to the appeasement faith. Kennedy's confidence here barely wavered and both men believed, albeit in error, that the Luftwaffe was superior to anything that the British and French could deploy.[21] Charles Lindbergh, a Kennedy darling, had conveyed this evaluation to the ambassador (21 September) that quickly made its way to upper British echelons: "German air strength is greater than that of all other European countries combined ... Germany now has the means of destroying London, Paris, and [Prague] if she wishes to do so."[22]

Kennedy took the precaution of sending his younger children to Ireland as the Czechoslovak question sizzled. He also asked British authorities to make gas masks available to American youngsters in London (adult-size masks issued by the US army being too big for snug fitting).[23] He claimed much credit at the time for calming Chamberlain's cabinet during the Munich tension, thereby saving the peace of Europe, and, he later insinuated, allowing the United Kingdom more time to prepare for a showdown with Germany. Incidentally, by a twist of fate, Kennedy and Jan Masaryk, Prague's minister to Britain, shared a cab after attending the session of Parliament (28 September) in which Chamberlain announced to delirious galleries the convening on the morrow of the four-power Munich summit. Masaryk allowed to Kennedy: "I hope this does not mean they are going to cut us up and sell us out."[24]

Events after Czechoslovakia's dismemberment swept Kennedy along, no more able than anyone else to predict their course or withstand them. Kennedy did bestir himself briefly on behalf of Jews who had fled the Third Reich. He conversed with Halifax, Chamberlain, and Colonial Secretary Malcolm MacDonald in late 1938 on what might plausibly be done to help, from which emerged the "Kennedy Plan." It amounted to little more than gab concerning the location of suitable land for refugees (in Africa or South America), transport to new sites, and provision for means of survival. After making a few lofty-sounding public statements, likely with an eye to the upcoming election season in which he thought himself a possible presidential contender, Kennedy dropped the matter. He chose not to cooperate with George Rublee, FDR's post-Evian appointee in London, charged with expediting the exodus of Jews from Germany and their resettlement. They were anyway, in the opinion of Kennedy, deserving of the scorn in which Berlin held them.[25]

Regarding the Spanish civil war's finale, he reproved the Loyalists as atheists radiating a Soviet hue. He was an ardent supporter of ongoing US neutrality and arms embargo. He helped secure British aid to rescue twenty-eight Sacred Heart nuns driven to flee Barcelona. "The Jews from Germany and Austria are not the only refugees in the world," he confided to his diary in July 1938.[26]

Kennedy did endorse Chamberlain's efforts to bolster British arms in 1939 via conscription and naval–military outlays. Though miffed at being kept out of the planning, he also appreciated that the June visit of King George to America signaled FDR's concern for British wellbeing – not an idle gesture after the disappearance of Bohemia–Moravia into the Nazi empire, then the announcement of the Berlin–Rome Pact.[27] Moreover, at FDR's urging, Kennedy testified before Congress in January 1939 on the desirability of increased defense appropriation. He did so with this proviso, however. The United States should be prepared for any emergency that might arise in the Americas, but must keep out of European warfare.

Kennedy believed – not entirely wrongly – that the Paris and London governments wanted in August–September 1939 to escape their pledges to uphold Polish independence. Further, he favored such extrication, justifying it as a purchase of time to close the Allied–German military gap. Poland should, he stated, be pressed by its guarantors to accommodate German demands regarding Danzig and placement of the corridor. These, along with other frontier adjustments, were worth the price of peace.[28]

The commencement of Anglo-French hostilities against Germany left Kennedy aghast. "It's the end of the world," he sputtered over the transatlantic line to FDR, "the end of everything."[29] He hoped that Roosevelt would take upon himself the role of mediator before hostilities flared out of control, not an idea well received in Washington, where preference bent toward an Allied check on Germany.[30]

War

The burnish that once gleamed upon Kennedy's mission had faded before September 1939. Critics of the government, both Labour and Tory, disliked the ambassador's appeasement zest and coziness with Chamberlain. They were first alerted to what they saw as the defects of Kennedy, when, in his maiden London speech (18 March 1938 to the Pilgrims Society), he announced that the United States would never again casually intervene in a European conflict as it had in 1917; only if US security were directly jeopardized would Congress declare war. British propagandists should not expect a repetition of their Great War experience – fulsome reception in America, unreserved support from Embassy London. He told US friends shortly afterward: "I have not as yet been taken into the British camp ... it was imperative ... to tell our British cousins that they must not get into a mess counting on us to bail them out."[31]

A few weeks after the Munich conference, as anti-Chamberlain voices became bolder, Kennedy sprang to the prime minister's defense. At their annual Trafalgar Day dinner, he declared to members of the Navy League that the democracies and Axis powers should endeavor to find common ground. Differences in philosophy or political organization ought not to divide them: "We have to live together in the same world whether we like or not."[32] His forecasts in subsequent months concerning German victory over Britain in any conceivable war – near or distant – provoked paroxysms of anger and rebuttal from Francis-Williams of the *Daily Herald* and parliamentarians, prominently Churchill.[33]

Kennedy's standing had also tumbled in official Washington and among pundits. Lippmann declared the ambassador maladroit. Editorial opinion in the *New Republic* in June 1939, suggesting that he be replaced, cited his reflexive support of Franco-British appeasement and nonsensical words to acquaintances about Jews running US foreign policy.[34] Certainly Roosevelt did not care for the tenor of his talk, to say nothing of Kennedy's public addresses that contradicted the

9 Joseph P. Kennedy.

"Quarantine" idea. Even when Kennedy's formal remarks were reviewed in advance of their delivery by State Department officers, and extreme passages amended, the ambassador's main themes obtruded; these implicated FDR in a more distinctly isolationist position than he countenanced. Furthermore, Kennedy's comportment and self-promotion bothered Roosevelt, a feeling fanned into indignation by cabinet secretaries Ickes and Morgenthau. They worried aloud that Kennedy was building a base of support independent of FDR, from which to launch a 1940 march on the White House. Compounding matters, the ambassador employed his own publicist – Harold Hinton, formerly of the *New York Times* – in the embassy. Kennedy also maintained a private mailing list of readers privy to his musings on British ways, US politics, and European affairs. The list of readers included Bernard Baruch, William Randolph Hearst, various senators, a batch of anti-administration editors, and sundry officials, but not the president. His suspicions deepened when he learned that he was excluded from this select readership of Kennedy – an astonishingly slick man, FDR concluded.[35]

The crescendo of anti-Kennedy feeling peaked in wartime. To British figures of the Churchill ilk, Kennedy became virtually persona non grata. He enraged them when he suggested during the battle of France that the United States would be wasting its substance by delivering materiel to Anglo-French field commanders. They were bound to lose, said Kennedy, and valuable equipment would wind up in German hands, perhaps to be used in future years against the New World.[36] The United States, he told Churchill to his face, should not be left "holding the bag for a war in which the Allies expect to be beaten."[37]

After the Dunkirk retreat, Kennedy held that the sooner Britain sued for peace, the better for civilization. If not, he told journalists, the Germans would shatter London with bombs, then take the country, a feat that could be completed by mid-August 1940. King George, who took exception to this prediction, tried to put matters straight for the diplomat: "The British mind is made up."[38]

Comments by Kennedy in 1940 about the moral equivalence of the Axis and Allies, and the inevitable demise of parliamentary institutions, fired feeling to greater heat. Harold Nicolson, then an MP, lumped him in the same category with would-be collaborators, such as Sir Oswald Mosley, head of the British Union of Fascists. Harold Laski of the London School of Economics, and one-time tutor of Kennedy's two older sons (Joseph, Jr., John), berated the ambassador in public prints for discounting British grit: "We shall emerge, no doubt from this conflict scarred and crippled; at least, as victory comes we shall emerge from it as free men."[39] Even Chamberlain's affection for Kennedy dipped. His decision during the blitz to evacuate his London premises in favor of a countryside estate (St. Leonard's) elicited charges of cowardice from "top side people" to cockney hearties. Churchill could not bear the man. After becoming prime minister on 10 May 1940, he tried to ignore him and fumed that Kennedy encapsulated every known species of cravenness. Churchill meantime pursued direct links with the White House, and relied upon the British embassy in Washington (led by Lothian from August 1939 to December 1940, then Halifax to 1946) for assessments of American mood and trends. Still, this circumvention of Kennedy did not dispel the prime minister's anxiety – that US voters would elevate him to the presidency in 1940 or that he would, by other office or means, exert decisive influence in an isolationist direction after FDR finished his second, and presumably last, term. The ambassador was placed under electronic surveillance. The Foreign Office kept tabs on his nattering. It instructed Whitehall departments not to share important information with the "dirty" Irishman. To the besieged British, in effect, his lack of solidarity constituted double-crossing.[40]

This feeling against Kennedy fed anti-American sentiment, already stoked by resentment over continuing US refusal to join with Britain against the Axis. An October 1940 opinion poll indicated that only 27 percent of Britons regarded the United States with favor. Understandably, Americans living in London were upset by this and they, not least journalists and embassy personnel, thought the ambassador reprehensible.[41] Edward R. Murrow of CBS, whose radio broadcasts to America ("This is London") riveted audiences with UK tales, could not stomach the ambassador's jeremiads.[42] Nor could James Reston of the New York Times, who sniped that Kennedy "couldn't keep his mouth shut or his pants on."[43] The embassy's military attaché, Colonel Raymond Lee, judged him guilty of desertion by quitting London for countryside safety.[44] The embassy's senior Foreign Service officer, fastidious Herschel Johnson, earlier discomfited by the ambassador's gaucheness, was undone by what he judged to be Kennedy's hysteria; the boss also had no intellectual depth but was blind to the implications for New World security of German victories in Europe.

The Tyler Kent episode was a manifestation of the demoralization that Kennedy allowed to creep into his chancellery. This disgruntled code clerk had acquired a collection of fifteen hundred classified documents exchanged between the British and US governments. These papers revealed, among other things, that Churchill and FDR were in secret communication with each other (from September 1939 onward), before Churchill had even become first minister.[45] A devout isolationist, Kent hoped that these purloined documents in the right hands – members of the America First Committee, GOP partisans, congressional foes of aid to Britain – would lead to FDR's impeachment, scuttle Anglo-US cooperation, and aid London-based German intelligence. His arrest by MI5 agents on 20 May 1940 ended his shenanigans. (Mosley was taken into custody a few days later as part of the detention of presumptive Fifth Columnists.) But Kent's capture and incarceration did nothing to enhance the Foreign Office's trust in the embassy. It continued to rile Churchill, who deemed it the repository of intrigue and unreliability. A dumbfounded Kennedy did waive Kent's diplomatic immunity upon learning the facts, but too late to recoup anything of his own London standing.[46]

Kennedy's career suffered, then, on all fronts. His relations with Churchill's government and members of London's American community were toxic. As he held views contrary to FDR on the wisdom of Anglo-US collaboration, Kennedy had to live in isolation from the conduct of foreign policy; the president permitted him no role in the cash-and-carry decision or talks on the destroyers–bases deal.[47]

Apart from being barred from Anglo-US negotiations, and seen as a security risk, Kennedy was eclipsed in London by visiting Washington personages assigned to gauge British needs. Hypersensitive in ordinary times, he was maddened by the spate of visitations – unnecessary, he snorted, as he was perfectly able to provide Roosevelt with impartial assessments of wartime Britain.[48] The peripatetic Welles on his March 1940 peace quest did pay Kennedy the compliment of bringing him along on visits: to 10 Downing Street, the Foreign Office, Churchill (lubricated and wreathed in cigar smoke), David Lloyd George (garrulous and admiring of Hitler), and Buckingham Palace. But the ambassador played a secondary part throughout, tolerated for the sake of propriety, not substance.[49] Other visitors proved less solicitous than Welles. They dispensed with any pretence of consulting with Kennedy. William Donovan in July 1940 spared no time on the ambassador and gave a rosier report to Washington on UK resiliency than Kennedy would have admitted.[50] Generous American aid was warranted, said Donovan, and it would enhance New World safety. Similar recommendations along his lines came from US military and naval officers: General George Strong, Admiral Robert Ghormley. Avoiding Kennedy, they consulted (July–August 1940) with their British counterparts and the embassy's service attachés.[51] These, plus other high-profile delegations, confirmed his marginalization. Sick with self-pity, he complained that his job amounted to nothing more than that of a glorified clerk. He wanted to go home and so informed Hull.[52]

Roosevelt was in no hurry for Kennedy to return to America, once telling the First Lady that he never again wanted to see "that son of a bitch."[53] The president believed, as the 1940 election season advanced, that the envoy could complicate matters: embracing the GOP side, headed by Wendell Willkie, and inspire millions of Catholics and Irish Americans to stampede away from Democratic Washington.[54] The aim, as it evolved in White House council, was to keep Kennedy away from US shores for as long as possible, ideally until after the election was decided. Then he could be withdrawn from London and the vacancy filled by someone sound.

The uncooperative ambassador, adept at securing lengthy furloughs to home, managed to land another in late October. Speculation in Democratic conclaves pivoted on whether he would condemn Roosevelt as a reckless interventionist or support Willkie (more internationally inclined, in fact, than the mainstream GOP). In the event, Roosevelt flattered, fawned over, and cajoled Kennedy in a meeting at the White House, following which he announced on behalf of FDR's unprecedented third term. He told a national radio audience, just days before the election, that FDR was the man for peace. He would not let anyone inveigle the United States into a senseless war.[55]

What Kennedy got out of this endorsement is still unclear. Perhaps he won a type of quid pro quo in which FDR promised to aid him, or his sons, in later bids for elected office. His post-election resignation from the diplomatic corps was, anyway, accepted forthwith.

Only days after the balloting, in an interview with Louis Lyons of the *Boston Globe*, Kennedy rehearsed new prophecies of British surrender and the death of US liberty. He said much the same to Breckinridge Long at the time, adding that Hitler would define the future. Americans should, therefore, seek economic – and perhaps other – cooperation with Germany.[56]

Few people in Whitehall regretted not seeing Kennedy again. Hope reigned there that William Donovan would arrive as next ambassador.[57]

Alliance

Kennedy was an easy act to follow. Nearly anyone would have been preferable to him, who had in his final British months lingered sullenly. Roosevelt, facing a grimmer world than when he lightheartedly set him upon London, was not about to lumber Anglo-US ties with another dubious appointee. Donovan would probably have compiled a respectable record as ambassador, a proposition untested as he was swept into OSS adventures.

Like Donovan, John Winant was a Republican, and as such another instance (Stimson, Knox, Hurley) of FDR's buttressing of wartime bipartisanship. In addition to rival party affiliations, the differences between Kennedy and Winant were striking. The former, a conservative businessman, was recruited by the New Deal to help assuage the doubts of corporate America. Winant, by contrast, was a progressive. His theoretical and practical orientation actually placed him close to the Henry Wallace-wing of the Democratic party. Roosevelt once referred to him as "Utopian John."[58]

Whereas Kennedy had scrambled to escape his Irish-Boston liability, obsessively acquiring wealth and acceptance, Winant's pre-London life had been unexceptional. Bashful son of a New York businessman (real estate), Winant prepped at St. Paul's School in Concord, New Hampshire. After flunking as an undergraduate at Princeton University, he returned to St. Paul's to teach history. He eventually assumed the duties of assistant rector. A shambling and introverted man, he did not excel as instructor. His halting speech and fidgetiness aggravated matters. Only devotion to his students – and flair for lessons on Abraham Lincoln – prevented his young charges from insurrection. He joined the army during the World War, paying his own way to France. He served as a pilot with reconnaissance air squadrons, rising to the rank of captain.[59] He drifted back to St. Paul's in 1919, then joyless marriage to a socially striving wife,

Constance Rivington Russell. She liked light recreations and resented her husband's interest in public affairs.[60]

Despite his atrocious speechifying – mumbling, inaudibility, syntactical mangling – Winant first won election in 1916 to the New Hampshire state legislature while still on the St. Paul's faculty. He was returned to the state legislature (senate and house) following his war-time service. He was thrice elected governor of New Hampshire, serving two-year terms (1925–26, 1931–32, 1933–34). While in office he pushed a series of programs to alleviate the hardship of unemployed laborers and destitute farmers, aptly dubbed by observers as the Little New Deal. He also supported a minimum wage, advocated a reduction of the work week (to 48 hours) for women and children, promoted regulatory reform of banks, championed civil rights for African Americans, and favored the abolition of capital punishment. He surfaced as a possible presidential candidate in 1936, briefly winning attention by GOP kingpins. Winant's commitment to social-political reforms had meanwhile won Roosevelt's attention, then appointments: first to chairmanship of the Social Security Board, finally to the directorship in 1939 of the International Labor Organization in Geneva. In this second job, Winant, though a disorganized and temperamental manager, established good relations with trade unionists from around the world, including Bevin, and was acknowledged as one whose feelings gravitated toward the "common man."[61]

Winant's 1941 assignment to London made sense in that Roosevelt did not want to identify his administration closely with the domestic policies or electoral fortunes of Britain's Tories. Winant would, naturally, conduct himself properly with the Conservative leadership but could also be counted upon to cultivate relations with the government's Labour ministers. A more equitable postwar Britain, implicitly promised even before the 1942 Beveridge Report, argued for support from New Deal America.[62] True to this spirit, Winant pleased Labour constituencies in his expressions of hope for a future expunged of class and economic injustices:

> *There was something fundamentally wrong in the prewar days when, on one side, workers were standing idle, and on the other side, people were underfed, badly housed, short of clothes, and children were stinted on education and deprived of their heritage of good health and happiness ...*

When war is done, the drive for tanks must become a drive
for houses. The drive for food to prevent the enemy from
starving us must become a drive for food to satisfy the needs
of all people in all countries. The drive for physical fitness in
the forces must become a drive for bringing death and
sickness rates in the whole population down to the lowest
possible level. The drive for manpower in war must become
a drive for employment to make freedom from want a
living reality.[63]

Article five of the Atlantic Charter, pledging Anglo-US cooperation to improve international labor standards and social security, gratified Winant. His later monitoring of public opinion meant that he was less surprised than most outsiders when voters turned the Conservatives out of office in July 1945. Upon his departure from the Court of St. James's in 1946, the British Trades Union Congress bestowed its Gold Badge upon him, a decoration never before conferred upon an ambassador.[64]

Britons responded nicely to Winant, who for years had excoriated Nazi Berlin.[65] Upon his arriving in Britain, 1 March 1941, and in a break with tradition, King George greeted him at the Windsor train station. Winant's first public utterance was electrifying, transmitted throughout the anxious kingdom: "I am very glad to be here. There is no place I would rather be at this time than in England."[66] Thereafter popular feeling rushed to contrast him with Kennedy's inveterate skepticism. By many accounts, women particularly liked him for his shaggy good looks – "like a sensitive protective collie," wrote one reporter for the *Daily Mail*.[67] Nicolson, himself a former diplomat, was won by Winant: "one of the most charming men that I have ever met."[68] Intellectuals sought his company while forgiving his forensic clumsiness, notably the socialist Laski but also the historian R. H. Tawney, the economist John Maynard Keynes, the reformer Sir William Beveridge, and writer H. G. Wells. Winant was also lionized for his bravery, demonstrable in his darting through rubble-strewn London streets with embassy officers to help blitz victims or douse fires caused by incendiary bombs.[69]

Only the Foreign Office harbored reservations. T. North Whitehead observed that Winant struggled hard to find the right words. Lacking the art of repose, he was "not a restful companion." Under-Secretary R. A. Butler, originally acquainted with him in

Geneva, considered his a "mystifying" personality and doubted that, as an untrained diplomat, he would provide Washington with "scientific appreciations."[70] Foreign Minister Anthony Eden approved of Winant from the outset, however, and respected his "instinct" for disentangling intricate questions. The two men worked closely together. They dispensed with formality and eschewed – to the regret of later historians – memoranda in favor of private conversation. They also became companionable, to the point of sharing garden chores at Eden's home in Sussex. The torment of fathers with military sons in peril proved a deep-felt bond. (Eden's Simon was killed in Burma. Winant's John, pilot of a B-17 Flying Fortress downed over Germany, was taken prisoner.) Churchill too felt warmth for Winant. He frequented Downing Street and visited Chequers, present at the latter when the BBC flashed its Pearl Harbor bulletin.[71]

London-based Americans were drawn to Winant, an attraction reinforced by relief at being rid of Kennedy. Murrow befriended the new ambassador. Colonel Lee thought him an able, if high-strung, person who deserved his subordinates' loyalty. The embassy's Foreign Service staff respected him, even though he drove his people hard.[72] He was still more relentless on himself, according to witnesses. He once confessed in a low moment: "I have no life."[73] His indifference to his own safety during air raids – often avoiding even rudimentary shelter – struck acquaintances as weird, almost a death-wish. He never thought, in any case, to leave London for the countryside but maintained a simple apartment near the embassy office that sustained damages.[74]

Winant's "finest hour" corresponded with his days in Britain before the United States declared war on Germany. His main contribution resided less in the realm of practical business than in the psychological effect of his presence. He intended to reassure Britons – irrespective of caste, party, region – of US solidarity with them, that Washington would do everything, to the limit of what churning public opinion could allow, to ensure British security. He toured (often with Churchill) Bristol, Cardiff, Coventry, Swansea, and other cities to inspect Luftwaffe handiwork. He offered condolences. He listened to homeless people in makeshift hostels. He visited hospitals. He walked through smashed factories and smoldering docksides. He promised aid, confirmed by climbing levels of Lend-Lease comfort. He spoke passionately of a future free of Nazi terror. He also established sufficiently good relations by mid-1942 with Deputy Prime Minister Attlee to be of use as he sought to quell restive coal miners whose work stoppages threatened to disorder industry. Winant told a delegation of strikers in northern England:

> *You, who suffered so deeply in the long depression years, know that we must move on a great social offensive if we are to win the war completely. Anti-Fascism is not a short-term military job. It was bred in poverty and unemployment. To crush Fascism at its roots, we must crush depression democracy. We must solemnly resolve that in our future order we will not tolerate the economic evils which breed poverty and war.*[75]

The miners responded with unfeigned praise for Winant. They returned to work, subsequently receiving boosts in salary and London's gratitude. He also took time to participate in varied goodwill activities. He chaired the "science and human needs" section of the British Association for the Advancement of Science that met (September 1941) in London. He encouraged the development of American studies programs in British curricula, from elementary schools to universities.[76]

The ambassador's reports to Roosevelt in 1941 stressed several themes. On the affirmative side, the British were plucky. They were competent in waging island defense. They mounted effective, albeit limited, offensive operations. All of these factors supported the continuance of U.S. aid and high-level naval–military consultations. Winant commended the skill of British soldiers, sailors, airmen, laborers, plus London's emergency services. He also praised the quality of British women, as imbued with endurance – as ready to sacrifice – as their men folk, both on the home front and in foreign billets. Meanwhile, he made certain that reports on the British experience, from the treatment of phosphorus wounds to radar advances to warplane design, were sent to relevant US agencies, resulting in benefits to national preparedness.[77]

Still, in the absence of US intervention, Winant felt that Britain would be bled, then obliged to cease hostilities on unfavorable terms. German chances, in other words, kept rising for however long Americans dawdled, even after the distraction of Berlin's declaring against the USSR. On these subjects an animated Churchill frequently discoursed to him, becoming visibly impatient after the Placentia Bay conference failed to result in a US war declaration in August 1941. The ambassador, requiring no persuasion, repeatedly warned compatriots: "It will be a tragedy if we do not get into the war."[78] Earlier he had pressed FDR – with Churchill's blessing – to expand (April) the US defense line in the Atlantic to 26 degrees west and dispatch (July) US soldiers to Iceland, thereby allowing the redeployments of thinly stretched British naval–military units.[79]

Ironically, given the eagerness of Winant for American intervention, his role in Anglo-US relations became less central after December 1941. Even earlier his importance had been overshadowed: first, by the arrival in London of Harriman (mid-March) as Lend-Lease "expediter" with rank of minister, then by Harry Hopkins (July) as FDR's special emissary to Churchill to review the supplies situation. Hopkins, in charge of all Lend-Lease beneficence, stayed only briefly in Britain before leaving for Moscow to confer with Stalin about Soviet materiel needs. The harm done to Winant's prestige was correspondingly minor. Hopkins anyway was solicitous of the ambassador and spoke considerately of him to British officialdom. Harriman also had not intended to compromise Winant's standing, despite privately scoffing at what he viewed as the ambassador's overwrought idealism. But by the nature of his mission, not to mention his aplomb, Harriman became a favorite of Churchill's. He was also rightly seen by cabinet ministers as one who – like Hopkins – enjoyed FDR's particular confidence. Not deliberately but inexorably, Harriman came to eclipse Winant in Whitehall's corridors during 1941–1943. Strain developed, notwithstanding efforts by both men (more pronounced on Winant's side) to contain it. Their staffs were affected by uncertainty over lines of jurisdiction and wound up fighting a gratuitous battle for publicity and reputation.[80]

Winant felt by summer 1943 that his position had been usurped. He complained to Hopkins that, according to a whispering campaign, either he or Harriman would be assigned to head the embassy. In pique, Winant declared: "An ambassador cannot be an effective representative in London unless he is better informed and given more support than I am receiving." As for the Foreign Office's seniors, they sympathized with the perturbed ambassador. They were not, though, about to question or interfere with US arrangements.[81] Winant's frustration was not helped by Churchill's and Roosevelt's wont to dispose directly of the items on the Anglo-US agenda, doing so with little ambassadorial or other consultation.[82]

Winant soldiered on. Albeit outside Churchill–Roosevelt exclusiveness, and hounded by a nagging sense of inadequacy, he did contribute to Allied cooperation. He found the right tone and words to buck up Churchill in 1942 as setbacks accumulated. Britain's Singapore fortress surrendered to a numerically inferior Japanese force (February). Burma fell (May). The Afrika Korps captured Torbruk plus 30,000 British soldiers (June). The House of Commons threatened to censure the prime minister (July). Amidst this bleakness, Churchill told FDR: "Everybody is inspired by [Winant]."[83]

This widespread regard produced benefits for the United States. Winant obtained Parliament's approval (not without complaint from members) to giving US military authorities jurisdiction over GIs charged with committing criminal acts anywhere in the United Kingdom. Winant's personal capital helped to mollify Churchill's uneasy ministers about the deployment of African-American servicemen in Britain: roughly 100,000. His prestige worked to advantage when he defended Washington in November 1942 over the Darlan deal, an acceptable expedient, he argued, to reduce casualties. His decent relations with senior British officers – specifically Field Marshal Bernard Montgomery – fostered trust between them and US commanders, notably General Dwight Eisenhower and Admiral Harold Stark, both of whom regularly conferred with Winant. He was instrumental in summer 1944 in getting British concurrence in the rescue of thousands of Hungarian Jews from German hands and transfer to safety via neutral and Allied territories. He meantime led a bustling embassy that conducted business with twenty-two different UK ministries. It functioned as the nucleus of an ever-proliferating number of US agencies of varying status with their personnel sometimes seconded to the ambassador's staff. These were concentrated on Lend-Lease, refugee relocation, scientific/atomic researches, OSS schemes, and OVERLORD planning.[84]

Winant's links to the American home front were comparably broad. He informed newspaper/magazine/radio audiences that Britons were waging their war without whine. "The most moving thing in England today," he wrote for readers of the *Atlantic* in May 1942, "is its unity of purpose."[85] His interactions with ordinary US servicemen stationed in Britain were pleasant. He also encouraged them to adopt a respectful attitude toward their counterparts. Their lower pay and poorer rations, he taught, should not be objects of contempt but taken as a measure of sacrifices coolly borne.[86] He intervened when possible to mend injured feelings or resolve misunderstanding when such occurred between Britons and Americans, typically involving lapses in etiquette or correct demeanor as interpreted by one side or the other. "It is only the caring people who get hurt," he brooded.[87] On a brighter note, he hosted congressional delegations and American celebrities in London, most famously Eleanor Roosevelt. She thought his a luminescent personality. When the time came, he led the US delegation at the memorial service for FDR held at St. Paul's Cathedral, 17 April 1945. There he read from scriptures. He escorted and sought to reassure a distraught Churchill.[88]

European Advisory Commission

Winant offered little advice to Washington or London on the military side of life, leaving that to the expertise of the Combined Chiefs. He did, though, enthusiastically endorse daylight bombing of German targets.[89] Otherwise, he looked forward to the prosecution of Nazi leaders responsible for atrocities and stuck closely to political matters related to the Grand Alliance and Germany's future.

Winant was involved in helping British negotiators as they finalized their May 1942 treaty of alliance with the USSR, in effect getting the Soviets to back off – at least for a while – from claims to the Baltic republics and eastern Poland.[90] Respecting overall Anglo-US relations with Stalin, Winant argued for intensive cooperation and hoped that the partnership would last into the postwar era. To this end, he urged prompt establishment of a second front in western Europe to relieve the heavily taxed Red Army. He advised that the 1943 Italian surrender not be solely an Anglo-US affair but the Kremlin should be informed and a party to the event; this consideration ought to produce reciprocal benefit for London/Washington in eastern Europe when the Red Army accepted German surrenders and assumed local responsibility. He made a special point of staying on friendly terms with the Soviet envoys in London: first, the sophisticated Ivan Maisky, then wooden Feodor Gousev. The idea of sending Hopkins to visit Moscow in 1941, incidentally, originated with Winant and Maisky.[91]

Winant attended only one of the Big Three meetings: Tehran, 27 November–1 December 1943. There he met with the young shah,

10 John Gilbert Winant.

Mohammad Reza Pahlavi. On the eve of conference, Winant also briefed General George Marshall and Admiral Ernest King on British thoughts concerning a range of questions: the possibility (slight) of Turkey's joining the Allies, the bombing campaign against German cities, OVERLORD's timing.[92] Winant was not, though, involved in the main Tehran conversations about the pending invasion of western Europe, or Soviet pledges to join against Japan after Germany's defeat, or Polish questions. He later conferred with FDR in Egypt after the Yalta conference and expressed concern that the Grand Alliance might fracture over problems related to post-hostilities Germany, a topic then under review by the European Advisory Commission (EAC).[93]

    The EAC's charge, mandated by the 1943 foreign ministers' conference in Moscow, was to anticipate the Third Reich's surrender and devise methods and machinery to effect post-hostilities order. The EAC met in London's Lancaster House from mid-January 1944 to August 1945. The able Sir William Strang headed the British delegation, Gousev the Soviet. Winant led the American group. It numbered

George Kennan (until detailed to Moscow in spring 1944), Brigadier Generals Cornelius Wickersham and Vincent Meyer, and Professor Philip Mosely. A French delegation, headed by René Massigli, joined the EAC deliberations in November 1944.

The commission recommended the separation of Austria from Germany, plus the partition of each into three zones of occupation, each governed by one of the conquering powers (amended by agreement at Yalta to provide for French control zones). Berlin and Vienna were likewise to be split and administered. An Allied Control Council was also proposed for Germany – similar ones for Austria and Italy – that should act consensually (originally applied to the UK, USSR, and USA but then revised to include France). The EAC sought also to refine guidelines for Germany's "unconditional surrender."

Postwar criticisms of the EAC focused on its vagueness concerning the duration and nature of occupation in Germany. This imprecision yielded varying Allied policies (i.e. on reparations, denazification) and two antagonistic Germanies, each with rival Cold War patrons. Divided Berlin also congealed into two entities to become a Cold War flashpoint.[94]

Unlike Strang, Winant did not live long enough after the war to have to defend the EAC, but he suffered monumentally at the time from his role in the work.[95] Neither FDR nor Hull nor their successors (Truman, Stettinius, Brynes) provided guidance or evinced strong interest in the EAC negotiations, a third-tier operation according to Roosevelt.[96] Winant came to think that future Anglo–Soviet–US relations would be undermined by FDR's indifference to the commission's enterprise. Making matters worse, the War Department, in the person of Assistant Secretary John McCloy, had ideas of its own on the proper organization of Germany, not wholly compatible with long-term inter-Allied coordination.[97] The War Department preferred a maximum retention of flexibility, prerogative, and initiative by military officers in the US zones.[98] Uncertainty about whether the punitive "Morgenthau plan" was taken seriously by the White House contributed to the US delegation's hesitancy of manner. Winant, for one, thought this proposal grotesque and unworkable. The Soviets, meantime, proved alternately obstinate or unresponsive.

The American delegation was hardly a model of unity or finesse. Winant's administrative ineptitude came crashing to the fore. Periodically overwhelmed or ill-prepared, he made a sorry contrast with the methodical British. Kennan, whom he judged "invaluable," was lost to Embassy Moscow. Mosely held some views uncomfortably close to the War Department's; he was dismayed by Winant's unwillingness to secure guaranteed Anglo-US access routes to Berlin. The US group floundered. Execution of Winant's last important wartime task, in short, was botchy from start to finish.[99]

***

Three discrete stages marked Anglo-US relations in 1938–1945. The first coincided with the close of what W. H. Auden called "this low dishonest decade." While tilting toward the Allies, Roosevelt adopted a policy of neutrality from the Munich summit to France's defeat. The United States was technically not a belligerent in the second stage, June 1940 to December 1941. Nevertheless the administration pursued a policy toward Britain of benevolent neutrality, underscored by Lend-Lease and undeclared naval warfare against Germany. The third stage, from Pearl Harbor onward, was one of firm alliance. Difficulty dogged Anglo-US relations throughout each of these periods, as shown by the vicissitudes of ambassadorial careers in London. Kennedy proved an irritant, then a liability. Winant's tenure was also marked by friction, despite indubitable Anglo-US "teamwork." The crux of the matter lay with the waning of British power and surging American might, realities that fit awkwardly in Churchill's consoling mythology rooted in a "special relationship."[100]

Like FDR who needled Churchill on British rule in India, Winant never hesitated to take aim against imperialism. He enjoyed pronouncing on the imminent demise of colonialism. He insisted to British interlocutors that the maintenance of their empire aroused Americans (who, nevertheless, without compunction, and insensible to their own unreflecting hegemonic purpose, took over Caribbean bits of the receding empire in compensation for fifty old ships). He expostulated with a gathering at the Royal Empire Society in July 1942, just as Gandhi was preparing to launch his Quit India campaign: "We [Americans] have [little] in common with your colonial empire. A careful survey of public opinion in the United States show[s] there [is] a greater divergence of viewpoint on British colonial policy than on any other subject that divide[s] us."[101] In line with Irish-American feeling, from Boston to San Francisco, Winant pressed FDR's preference upon Churchill regarding Northern Ireland; the six provinces should be exempt from conscription.

In another display of tension in the "special relationship," an abashed Winant delivered (November 1944) to Churchill a proposal on arranging future international civil aviation routes that baldly advantaged the United States over Britain. Bundled with it were hints that London's rejection would trigger reductions of Lend-Lease aid. Churchill's private secretary, John Colville, labeled the idea "pure blackmail."[102] Still, it was not allowed to disrupt cordiality with Winant. Like his digs against empire or his Northern Ireland meddling or his defense of Eisenhower–Darlan accords, the civil aviation idea did not count against him. His unusual standing insulated him from the bile and barbs that had rained upon his predecessor.[103]

However much Kennedy merited dismissal, he had satisfactorily performed the secondary duties of his office. He was diligent in securing passage homeward for Americans wanting to repatriate in autumn 1939. With his son, John, he sought to assist the three hundred American survivors of SS *Athenia*, torpedoed off Ireland's coast by a U-boat on 3 September 1939. To his credit, Kennedy properly deployed his reportorial staff, whose members wrote sensibly on the psychological impact of German bombings, hardship in asphyxiating underground shelters, and on the condition of continental escapees in need of sanctuary.[104] That he chose to interpret such accounts narrowly or with less empathy than Winant is, of course, another manner. In fairness to Kennedy, he also meant to run an efficient embassy in trying circumstances.[105] This goal, needless to elaborate, was undercut by the chariness with which his underlings regarded him, a situation exacerbated by the Tyler Kent affair.

The failure of Kennedy resided in his inability to comprehend the big picture. He was hardly alone in this deficiency – witness such brother ambassadors as Hugh Wilson or Breckinridge Long or anti-interventionist Senators Robert Taft, Gerald Nye, Burton Wheeler, and Hiram Johnson. Yet the point stands that Kennedy was too ready to give Berlin benefit of the doubt. He was too eager to compromise, too prone to underrate the depth of anti-Nazi feeling in Europe, too blind to what was ultimately at stake.[106] The following truths, as developed by Reinhold Niebuhr in testimony to the Senate Foreign Relations Committee (January 1941), were simply lost upon Kennedy.

Beyond the problem of our national interest is the larger problem of the very quality of our civilization, with its historic liberties and standards of justice, which the Nazis are sworn to destroy. No nation can be unmindful of its

*obligations to a civilization of which it is a part, even though
no nation is able to think of these obligations in terms
disassociated from its national interest. If we should define
the present struggle in Europe as merely a clash between
rival imperialisms, it would merely mean that a strange
combination of cynicism and abstract idealism had so
corrupted the common sense moral insights of a people that
we could no longer distinguish between right and wrong.
History never presents us with choices of pure good against
pure evil. But the Nazis have achieved something which is so
close to the very negation of justice that if we cannot
recognize it and react to it with a decent sense of moral
indignation, we would prove ourselves incapable of
preserving the heritage of western culture.*[107]

Kennedy after his London tour remained steadfastly opposed to US intervention in the war. The Roosevelts and Niebuhrs appalled him. He spoke publicly in varied venues on the folly of foreign entanglement. He issued warnings against the snares hidden in Lend-Lease. He met with Hollywood producers and Hearst to explore ways to thwart US belligerency. He was tempted but declined to accept the chairmanship of the America First Committee, thinking that he would be more effective if he operated outside of its framework.[108]

Once Congress did declare war, Kennedy hoped to rejoin FDR's government. Nothing was found for him in Washington, however. New Dealers still disparaged him. Roosevelt once suggested that, given the chance, Kennedy would try to erect a fascist regime in the United States. A few doubtful offers were shuffled his way: to reorganize national shipyards, or better coordinate the system of railway transportation, or help with the planning of new civil defense facilities. Kennedy refused these jobs as unworthy.[109] Consequently, he had to watch events unfold without him. Not until many years later did he glimpse his place in American memory: patriarch of a political dynasty. Yet even in that moment of satisfaction he could not entirely escape his London past. Tyler Kent, by the early 1960s a health foods aficionado in southern Texas and purveyor of white supremacist publications, brought suit against Kennedy, alleging defamation and conspiring to bring about World War Two.

Kennedy's oft-expressed fears of global conflagration were premised on his children and the risks they would face. He commented in 1935: "I don't want them to be killed in a foreign war."[110] Searing images from 1914–1918 also unsettled him. Yet his forebodings did not prevent him in 1941 from pulling strings – through his former naval attaché in London, Captain Alan Kirk – to obtain naval commissions for his two service-eligible sons.[111] Kennedy was disconsolate in August 1944, when his namesake, an aviator, was killed while on secret mission against German targets on the Belgian coast. His second son, skipper of PT-109, was a year earlier injured and almost died in the south Pacific. The ambassador's daughter, Kathleen, lost her British husband, Lord Hartington (heir of the Duke of Devonshire), in European action. Nothing in later life compensated Kennedy for these catastrophes. They only confirmed him in his conviction that the United States must renounce international activism. He opposed the Truman–Acheson containment policy; he counseled that the United States withdraw from Korea and Berlin.[112]

Whereas the war embittered Kennedy, the London experience of Winant fortified his confidence in liberal internationalism. He had not only looked hopefully toward postwar Anglo-US collaboration with the Soviet Union, but also urged that modalities be devised to harness atomic science to benefit all nations. He was, consequently, upset by Churchill's 1946 "iron curtain" gloominess and rising Moscow–Washington acrimony. Not without ambition, he hoped to win appointment as secretary general of the United Nations, from which post he might further the peace cause. Such an appointment, though, was never realistically in the offing. Roosevelt had toyed with the idea of making Winant his vice-presidential running mate in 1944 and briefly considered him for a cabinet post, perhaps head of State (after Cordell Hull) or Labor (if vacated by Frances Perkins).[113] Bypassed by FDR, Winant stood no chance of favor from Truman. He preferred sterner diplomats over "Utopian John," whose intellectual reflexes seemed suspiciously like those of Henry Wallace.[114] Hence Truman's 1946 appointment of Harriman, who had no illusions about the emergent East–West dispute, to the Court of St. James's.

Like William Dodd whom he admired as prophetic, Winant died soon after his ambassadorship.[115] Both had been exhausted by their diplomatic tasks and spooked by blackening premonitions. Dodd succumbed to the infirmities of old age. Nervous fatigue encased

Winant. Outbursts of uncontrollable rage shook him, directed – most uncharacteristically – at his subordinates. All of this misfortune was compounded by bursitis, drinking problems, continuing unhappiness in marriage (aggravated by extramarital tugs), and financial distress with indebtedness around $750,000 by 1947.[116] He spoke with confidants about the purported wisdom of suicide.

Winant tried to find constructive release as US representative to the United Nations Economic and Social Council, an assignment from which he resigned in despondency as Cold War quarrels drowned the agency's usefulness. He served as chair of the Fourteenth Annual Brotherhood Week in 1947, then wrote his wartime memoirs, finishing one of two projected volumes.[117] But nothing calmed him. His personality unraveled in self-recriminations and despair. He ended his life with a pistol shot to the right temple on 3 November 1947 in his New Hampshire house. He was, as a few observers noted at the time, a casualty of the war and of the poisoned peace that followed.[118]

Winant had received numerous British tributes plus honorary degrees from universities, among them Oxford and Cambridge in autumn 1945. King George awarded him the Order of Merit in 1947 in a ceremony at Buckingham Palace.[119] His most handsome recognition, he might have judged, was given posthumously and meant to perpetuate his memory. Winant House was opened in London on 5 July 1951. British and American benefactors established it – a dozen apartments of varying size – for impecunious elders and young couples. The housing stock in London at the time was woefully low, not recovered from the destruction wreaked by German bombers or V-1 and V-2 rockets. Families in need of accommodation on the waiting list of the London County Council numbered 207,000 – of which more than 60,000 constituted emergency cases.[120]

Ten years before the doors of Winant House were officially opened, nearly to the day, the ambassador had visited a shelter, Abingdon House, for homeless men in the desolate area of London's bombed dockland. He had conversed with the residents. He had taken tea with them. He had inspected their quarters and played games. The shyness of these men, their inarticulateness and emotional opaqueness – Winant's own traits – did not prevent them from cheering when time came for leave-taking.[121] The impression made at Abingdon and places like it stamped him. He had never faltered in his "faith," as he phrased it to FDR, "in the common people of England."[122]

7 GREAT PATRIOTIC WAR

Winant probably never knew of the existence of Anna Akhmatova or anything of that eminent poet's *Requiem*, wherein she chronicled the calamities of Soviet life during Stalinism. But he doubtless would have admired her resolve, even as her ordeals – censure, persecution, execution of loved ones – lay radically beyond his experience or ken. He would have appreciated too her wartime verse, written not in the official stentorian style to praise Red Army prowess and Stalinist statecraft. She celebrated a subtler heroism: "Through the bombardment is heard the voice of a child." As German armies invaded and Nazi zealots sought to expunge all monuments of Russian civilization, she vowed this determination to defend the country's literary and ethical tradition:

> And we will preserve you, Russian speech,
> Mighty Russian word!
> We will transmit you to our grandchildren
> Free and pure and rescued from captivity
> Forever![1]

Viewed from the perspective of her dingy Leningrad flat, immediate postwar life must have struck Akhmatova as fraught with uncertainties and dangers as it did to Winant. In her case, she was subjected to yet another blast of vilification after her two meetings (November 1945, January 1946) with British diplomat and scholar Isaiah Berlin. The Central Committee of the Communist Party declared her guilty of "eroticism, mysticism, and political indifference." Andrei Zhdanov, arbiter of Soviet good taste, condemned her in 1946 as "half-nun, half harlot."[2] Her Leningrad, meanwhile, whose tribulations she had commemorated, became site to massive efforts of restoration. Innumerable buildings had been damaged past repair during the siege, September 1941 to January 1944. Transportation and communication infrastructure was mangled. Water works and electrical power were smashed. Hundreds of thousands of Leningraders – a million noncombatants – had died from starvation, exposure, or shelling.[3] Of them, Akhmatova had written:

> Everyone down on your knees!
> A crimson light pours!
> And the Leningraders come through the smoke
> in even rows –
> The living and the dead: for glory never dies.[4]

The desolation that Axis forces inflicted upon Soviet cities and countryside has few rivals in the annals of warfare. German armies and partners – Finnish, Hungarian, Italian, Romanian – were on a crusade, as Hitler conceived it, to eradicate communism and secure for future generations of Third Reich colonists that *Lebensraum* improperly occupied by "noxious microbes," of whom Russians and Jews were most conspicuous.[5] Tender feelings in this context should not be squandered on the three million-plus Red Army POWs destined to perish in German camps or the annihilation of more than two million Soviet Jews.[6] Between twenty-five and twenty-seven million Soviet civilians and soldiers were killed during 1941–1945, a total of fatality that exceeded even China's while dwarfing that suffered by all European/ North American belligerents combined.

Stalin's disregard in March–June 1941 of intelligence reports warning of German invasion, dismissed as false or provocative, helped deliver unprepared Soviet military formations to destruction in the first months of warfare. By late November the Wehrmacht had captured Kiev and the Ukrainian granary while advancing to the outskirts of Moscow and Leningrad. Lest the capital fall, the government had earlier vacated (October) most of its offices; they were relocated hundreds of miles eastward to the squalid city of Kuibyshev on the Volga. Foreign embassies followed, including the American, led by Laurence

Steinhardt, residing in Moscow since conclusion of the Soviet–German nonaggression pact (23 August 1939).

Moscow's cooperation with Berlin in 1939–1941, although fated to end in near-catastrophe for the USSR, entailed benefits, not least of which was a purchase of time. This respite allowed the military high command to begin to recuperate from the purge of previous years, evidenced in the 1939 success of General (later Marshal) Georgi Zhukov against Japanese forces during Mongolia–Manchukuo border combat. While trade with Germany flourished, featuring Soviet raw materials (oil, metals) and foodstuffs for Third Reich credits and finance, Stalin extended the USSR's sphere of influence westward. He thereby enlarged the buffer zone between the communist heartland and cresting German power. Great chunks of Poland fell to Soviet assault, as did substantial bits of Finland and Romania. The Baltic states – Lithuania, Latvia, Estonia – were seized outright by the USSR. From a humanitarian standpoint, the results were grim. Arrests, rigged elections, evictions, and terror marked these Soviet occupations. In the Polish case, 1.5 million people were uprooted and deported to the USSR (typically to central Asia or Siberia), where many died in abysmal circumstances. Stalin ordered the shooting in March–April 1940 of 22,000 Polish army officers (regulars and reservists from the learned classes) plus others taken captive by the Red Army. Most were executed in Katyn forest, near Smolensk (others in Belarus, the Ukraine, or Russia proper). Their wives and children were sent to Kazakhstan.[7]

Stalin and his foreign minister, Vyacheslav Molotov, were eager in August 1939–June 1941 to deepen their cooperative relations with Germany, to the extent of joining the Tripartite Pact if practicable.[8] That this stratagem ended abruptly, that the first military defeats were numbing, suggested to Steinhardt this scenario: either Stalin's regime would collapse before December 1941 or a remnant of it would retreat eastward beyond the Urals to rule over a trifling state. Either way, he was convinced by mid-November, when he quit his post, that Hitler's empire was on the brink of obtaining victory and boundless Soviet provinces. In vocabulary hardly different from that used by Churchill to denounce Joseph Kennedy, Soviet leaders castigated Steinhardt for faint-heartedness.

Roosevelt replaced Steinhardt in February 1942 with a retired naval officer, Admiral William Standley. He witnessed during his diplomatic tenure the dramatic reversal of fortune in Soviet–German fighting. Despite Stalin's ineptness in June 1941, Red forces absorbed, then blunted, the German attack, weighed down by overextension and wanton cruelty which forfeited the initial goodwill felt by hundreds of thousands of Ukrainians and Balts (even some Russians) for their Wehrmacht "liberators." Field Marshal Friedrich Paulus surrendered his Sixth Army at Stalingrad on 2 February 1943. Months later (July–August) the tank battle at Kursk confirmed the irreversibility of ebbing German strength and portended the immensity of Soviet triumph, which before running its course inflicted 75 percent of all casualties suffered by Germany with commensurate damage to Axis artillery, warplanes, and logistics.[9] An American strategic survey in summer 1943 observed: "Russia occupies a dominant position and is the decisive factor looking toward the defeat of the Axis in Europe."[10] According to later estimates, as US and British armies stormed ashore on Normandy beaches in June 1944, 60 German divisions were stationed in France and the Low Countries. At that same moment 199 German divisions, augmented by 50 satellite divisions, were committed to the eastern front.[11]

The USSR's military achievements were fueled in part by Lend-Lease aid that before war's end provided 17,000,000 tons of food, military supplies, and machinery.[12] A major part of Standley's portfolio was to ensure the smooth transfer of this assistance to the USSR via the portals of Murmansk, Archangel, the Persian Gulf, Vladivostok, and the Alaskan–Siberian airway. The admiral obliged, within the limits of his understanding, nettlesome Soviet bureaucrats and shifting contingencies. Yet his growing qualms about the reliability of the Stalinist regime abraded his confidence in this mission and damaged his standing among Kremlin leaders. FDR came by mid-1943 to judge him unusable for diplomacy.

The halcyon period of Soviet–US cooperation coincided with the ambassadorship of Averell Harriman. He capitalized on the goodwill occasioned by these episodes: Stalin's promise, first expressed to Hull at the 1943 Foreign Ministers' conference in Moscow, to join the fight against Japan after German surrender; Roosevelt–Stalin meetings at Tehran; Soviet cheering of the OVERLORD landings; jointly issued Allied statements at Yalta that reiterated mutual goodwill and pledged varieties of postwar cooperation.

Despite his efforts, Harriman never dispelled the pall of wariness that hung over Soviet–US collaboration, manifest even during days of rapid Allied military advance. Imperceptibly at first, almost against his will, he gradually changed into one of the early Cold Warriors. He warned FDR, then Truman, against Soviet policy in Europe antithetical to US interests.[13]

Nonaggression Pact to BARBAROSSA

Fourteen months elapsed between the departure (11 June 1938) from Moscow of Ambassador Joseph Davies, who had sought mightily to accommodate Stalin's regime, and the arrival of Steinhardt (11 August 1939). Embassy Moscow during this interim was competently run by its Foreign Service staff, headed by a succession of chargés d'affaires, the last before Steinhardt's advent being Stuart Grummon. The ablest among Grummon's officers was Charles Bohlen, who from May 1939 monitored Hitler's courting of Soviet officials and the dilatoriness of British and French suitors.

Bohlen's investigations were aided by contact with an anti-Nazi diplomat attached to the German embassy, Hans von Herwarth.[14] Bohlen kept the State Department abreast of fast-paced German–Soviet negotiations with the result that official Washington was less startled than other capitals by the Ribbentrop–Molotov treaty.[15] Before its signing, Roosevelt warned Stalin via Steinhardt – and Ambassador Constantine Oumansky in Washington – of the hazards likely to arise from it versus the desirability of an Anglo–French–Soviet accord.[16] Stalin's rejection of this advice reflected the new course then being adopted by Berlin and Moscow, which simultaneously nullified the anti-Comintern pact while invalidating the Left's popular front strategy. The Ribbentrop–Molotov deal divided eastern Europe into clearly delineated Soviet and German spheres of influence, the main quarry being Poland, split between the two predator states.

In the ensuing time, before Hitler turned on the Soviet Union, Steinhardt evaluated the resilience of Berlin–Moscow cooperation with reference to Stalin's response to German victories, particularly the defeat of France. He sought also to ensure the safety of US citizens in the Soviet zone of Poland (in Finland and the Baltic republics too) while doing something to placate the Polish diaspora, eager to assist persons in areas of Red Army control.

Steinhardt brought estimable qualities to his Moscow mission. He possessed an analytical mind, honed by years of corporate legal practice in his native New York. An indefatigable worker, he did not take shortcuts. An unvarnished realist, his thinking was unencumbered by sentimentality or the seductiveness of utopian projects, such as establishing a proletarian paradise on earth, on which subject he was withering.[17] His urbanity and self-containment, shading at times into inapproachability, were leavened by a dry sense of humor, at times self-deprecating. Of an assimilated Jewish family, and married to an Episcopalian, his religious outlook was ecumenical (though he retained into later years a youthful interest in Zionism). Yet, as he readily admitted, he also possessed traits that marred his human relationships. He could be abrasive. In common with other descendents of Jewish-German families who settled in pre-Civil War America, he was uncomfortable around east European Jews of later arrival; he did not want to be associated in the public mind with them or their exotic costumes and strange habits. His legal-business persnicketiness lent itself to sanctimoniousness that disallowed sympathy for acquaintances on Wall Street victimized by the Depression or toiling folk struggling against foreclosure and insolvency.[18] Thin-skinned, he found insult when none was meant. His vanity and political ambitions – centered on winning the New York gubernatorial office – were apparent in exaggerated competitiveness with other ambassadors, particularly Joseph Kennedy and William Bullitt.

Steinhardt, well launched on a diplomatic career before Moscow, had no intention of ever returning to what he considered the humdrum of legal practice. His overseas adventures had begun in 1933, when FDR named him minister to Sweden, reward for sizable contributions to and early support of Roosevelt's candidacy. Steinhardt acquitted himself well in Stockholm. Among his accomplishments, he helped negotiate a lauded Swedish–US trade agreement. Roosevelt then elevated him to the rank of ambassador in 1937 with an appointment to Peru. In that office he bolstered hemispheric solidarity against Axis trespass. He played reliable understudy to Secretary Hull in December 1938 at the Eighth Pan-American Conference, convened in Lima. Steinhardt arrived in the USSR confident that he enjoyed broad support in the administration. He was persuaded too that his prior diplomacy would win him approval among fellow ambassadors and Foreign Service subordinates. The latter, whom he came to respect, included his "most loyal" Bohlen, who for a year served under him in Moscow.[19]

Steinhardt, in fact, was not FDR's preferred choice for Moscow. Rights of earlier refusal had gone to a New York banker, Sidney Weinberg. Only thanks to Hull's lobbying did FDR pick Steinhardt for the USSR.[20] Nor did the local diplomatic corps rate him as highly as he did himself. The British ambassador, Sir Stafford Cripps, a leading Labour figure who occasionally tussled with Steinhardt, thought him "a typical bumptious U.S.A. business-lawyer type."[21] Cripps was delighted when Washington withdrew him. Foreign Service officers in Moscow were also more equivocal than Steinhardt, who flattered himself as quickly accepted by this company, ever realized.[22] In the case of Bohlen, Steinhardt's feelings went unrequited. Bohlen thought Steinhardt an amateur diplomat – unschooled, egocentric, pushy.[23] As for the Soviets, their impressions were unfavorable, close in spirit to the Jew-baiting German press that reviled him. Oumansky, for one, referred to Steinhardt as "a wealthy bourgeoisie Jew ... permeated with the foul smell of Zionism."[24]

Of the above criticism, Bohlen's was the most serious. It was not wholly fair, however. It reflected the proverbial resentment of career diplomats for political appointees. It also smacked of the unselfconscious anti-Semitism that permeated the Foreign Service, into which even so unbigoted a man as Bohlen could lapse. Steinhardt's failure to win him over may also have been related to the ambassador's initial unwillingness to credit the Herwarth channel, maintained at risk to the German and potentially compromising of Bohlen. Steinhardt in mid-August was not yet persuaded by – or perhaps not aware of – the intelligence gotten from Herwarth, as implied in the ambassador's prediction to Washington: the Soviets, although leaning toward the Franco-British side, were not about to enter into far-ranging agreements with anyone but would retain freedom of maneuver for an indeterminate time.[25] Steinhardt did quickly amend this faulty forecast and came to value the remarkable qualities of Herwarth, but evidently too late to impress Bohlen. As for Washington, it praised the ambassador's last-minute confirmation of impending German–Soviet agreement plus his revelations concerning the "secret protocol" that consigned eastern Poland, Latvia, Estonia, and Bessarabia (to which Lithuania was later added) to the Soviets. Here too was another possible strand of Bohlen's discontent: Welles and Hull congratulated Steinhardt but either did not know the specifics of Bohlen's tie with Herwarth or, for other reasons, chose not to mention it in dispatches.[26]

In common with State Department students of the USSR, Bohlen was impatient with US officials in Moscow who were unread in Soviet history and sealed off from society by barriers of language. Case in point was Joseph Davies, whose abject ignorance – by Bohlen's account – was larded with fantasies of Soviet–US convergence.[27] Steinhardt, though, did not occupy anything like the same category in which Bohlen placed Davies. Albeit not at home in Russian, Steinhardt had mastered two foreign tongues (French, German) and never doubted the importance of precision in language or the need for translating expertise. Moreover, indicative of his seriousness, he immersed himself for weeks prior to Moscow in the embassy's reports dating to the 1933 establishment of Soviet–US relations. He consulted with former diplomats posted in Moscow and with government specialists on the USSR, notably Loy Henderson, at the time with the State Department's European division. Steinhardt also interviewed journalists and Soviet representatives in Washington, including the belittling Oumansky. Steinhardt even developed a body of precepts to guide his actions with Kremlin leaders. It eschewed Davies's version of jolly intimacy while stressing the principle of reciprocity.[28]

Steinhardt's dedication to correct quid pro quo was tested immediately upon his reaching Moscow. Dr. Walter Nelson, embassy physician, was scheduled in late summer 1939 to return to the United States. In the spirit of courtesies granted to Soviet officials exiting Washington, the embassy asked that customs agents dispense with their usual rigorous inspection. Might a milder one, more likely to preserve the integrity of his sterilized instruments and other delicate medical paraphernalia, be conducted at Nelson's apartment? The Soviet authorities balked, against which Steinhardt retaliated. With an assist from Henderson, he persuaded Hull to stop passage through the Panama Canal of the Soviet steamer *Kim* (for purported irregularities concerning the ship's bill of health). The Soviets responded by easing the departure of the inconvenienced doctor; the *Kim* was then speeded along its way. This Soviet relenting validated to Steinhardt's satisfaction the practice, as well as principle, of linkage.[29] He resorted to this tactic again in trying to acquire *laissez-passer* for a number of consular officers whose entry into Soviet territory had been blocked in 1939; he prevented the issuance of equivalent documentation to Soviet officials until the Americans got theirs. Roosevelt buoyed him with this endorsement: "We should match every Soviet annoyance by a similar annoyance against them."[30]

Presidential irritation with Soviet violations of diplomatic convention stemmed from a deeper dismay, centered on Stalin's cooperation with Hitler. It counted not only the partitioning of Poland, but also threatened to compromise US rights as a neutral to conduct peaceful commerce unmolested. A crisis arose in October 1939 around the merchantman *City of Flint* bound for Great Britain. The warship *Deutschland* intercepted this vessel, declaring that a portion of its cargo was contraband. A prize crew thereupon sailed the *City of Flint* to Murmansk, where the American sailors were then confined. Embassy officers were not permitted to interview the captain or men; their medical and other needs went unaddressed, despite Steinhardt's protests. Not until later in the year, as the simmering Soviet–Finnish crisis erupted full-blown, with potentially serious ramifications for Moscow–Washington relations, was the *City of Flint* released from Murmansk detention.[31]

During the *City of Flint* affair, the embassy's main focus rested on Soviet aggression against Poland, then Finland. In the Polish instance, Steinhardt, inundated with requests for news concerning the wellbeing of persons in Soviet-occupied land, was nearly at a loss to provide information or deliver aid. The essential problem was that Soviet authorities would not allow US observers, neither diplomats nor journalists, into Poland (lest they stumbled upon evidence of atrocities). American requests to enter the territory were denied on "technical" grounds: want of appropriate visas or unavailability of transport or booking excess. The embassy's inability to get reliable information on Polish conditions was modified slightly when in late December the Soviets finally permitted one of Steinhardt's officers, Angus Ward, to visit Lvov to assist local Americans. He subsequently reported scenes of chaos, aggravated by police crackdown (but he missed clues of mass deportations).

Against his better self, Steinhardt chafed under the load of petitions to aid individual Poles or their families. He could not readily forgive Polish anti-Semitism in the 1920s and 30s, connected to the teachings of the chauvinistic Endecja party or actions approved by some Catholic prelates and political leaders (boycott of Jewish businesses, exclusion from civil service, revival of the hoary blood libel, physical assaults). As he reviewed pleas emanating from Poles in west European sanctuary, he wondered: "Were the situation reversed, just what [would] the Polish aristocracy have done for *me*?"[32] In the event, circumstances in Moscow's Polish mandate – martial law and administrative perfidy – conspired against his extending help, except in a handful of cases. Incidentally, Steinhardt also had little luck in resolving Jewish emergencies. He proved ineffective in learning the whereabouts of Professor Moses Schorr, a renowned scholar and chief rabbi of Warsaw; after incarceration in Moscow's Lubyanka prison, Schorr was sent to a labor camp in Uzbekistan, where he died in July 1941.[33]

Overall, the attitude of Steinhardt on humanitarian matters was pinched. He opposed the admission into the United States of large numbers of east Europeans, irrespective of their gentile or Jewish identities. He held that mischief-makers – in the employ of Moscow or Berlin – would smuggle themselves into the United States via the refugee intake. He was emphatic on this subject in his communications to Assistant Secretary of State Breckinridge Long, who naturally welcomed Steinhardt's support against proponents of liberalizing the immigration laws.[34] One of Steinhardt's missives (8 May 1941) contained this:

> I am of the opinion that when there is even the remote
> possibility of a conflict between humanitarianism and the
> welfare of the United States that the former must give way to
> the latter. I feel strongly that when our country is facing
> perhaps the greatest crisis in its history, its security from
> foreign machinations is of a great deal more importance
> than the entry of this, that, or the other immigrant, no
> matter how good a case he or she can make out on
> humanitarian grounds. In my opinion some of the
> sponsoring organizations and many of the individuals
> associated with them have been derelict in their duty as
> American citizens to admit so-called refugees and even to
> vouch for them without assuming a commensurate
> responsibility, and in ninety-nine cases out of one hundred
> knowing nothing about the activities of these so-called
> refugees after they have been admitted to the United
> States … I am convinced that there are some among them
> [refugees] who will engage in activities inimical to our
> institutions and that willingly or unwillingly some of them
> will serve the interests of foreign powers after their arrival in
> the United States … Some of the most dangerous potential

saboteurs have been admitted to the United States during the past eighteen months as refugees under the guise of humanitarianism ... [They represent] not only a menace to our institutions, freedom, and democratic way of life, but to our very national existence as long as the present war continues.[35]

Steinhardt's embassy concentrated in the expanding Soviet zone on trying to safeguard US nationals and their property (which entailed recovering the Warsaw possessions of Anthony Biddle). Yet Steinhardt was capable of making decent gestures, as when he deliberately risked Kremlin wrath in October 1939. To show solidarity with Poland, he attended a farewell party for Warsaw's envoy to Moscow, Waclaw Grzbowski, expelled on the grounds that his country had ceased to exist.[36] Still, not until later in the war, while heading Embassy Ankara, did Steinhardt revise his attitude toward people trying to reach safety in the United States or third countries. Before then he was chillingly bureaucratic. He was also wrong about the main facts touching on the fate of east European Jews, a people who anyway disconcerted him. He surmised in October that the German acquisition of Polish provinces with large Jewish populations would necessitate Berlin's relaxing of racialist policies. Militant anti-Semitism would perforce yield to the logic of responsible administration: "I understand there is already some modification."[37]

In that same October 1939 Steinhardt thought that problems between little Finland and the USSR would be resolved by measures short of war. Stalin's requests of the Helsinki government to negotiate territorial adjustments near Leningrad – plus use of Finnish islands and ports – were accompanied by offers of compensation with pledges to respect Finland's independence. Soviet economic vulnerabilities, Steinhardt ventured, meant that the Kremlin had no choice but to proceed cautiously.[38] Once the Winter War (November 1939–March 1940) commenced, he did offer, with Washington's urging, to mediate an armistice, which initiative Molotov rejected.[39]

Apart from exposing the Red Army's defects to German observation, the Finnish war injured Soviet standing beyond that already connected to the Polish annexations. Member states of the League of Nations expelled (14 December 1939) the USSR from their society. Britain's Chamberlain and France's Daladier pronounced openly for

Finland, their parliaments ready to deploy naval and military forces in its defense. Even as the conflict approached its March climax, Steinhardt was predicting an Anglo-French war against the Soviets.[40] At the time, Roosevelt, asserting that Stalin's tyranny was as absolute as any in the world, declaimed that US sympathy was overwhelmingly with the Finns. He also imposed a "moral embargo" to discourage US manufacturers of warplanes and aeronautical equipment from exporting to the USSR.[41] Condemnation, meanwhile, sprang from newspaper editorials, burst from the pens of pundits, and poured down from Capitol Hill. All emphasized Moscow's treachery, contrasted it with Helsinki's rectitude (earlier demonstrated by singular repayment of Great War debts to US creditors), and deplored the lopsidedness of contest between Soviet Goliath and Finnish David. The gravitational pull of sympathy toward Finland was so strong that some figures, former president Herbert Hoover among them, argued that Roosevelt should cut US relations with Moscow.

As had Hugh Wilson after Kristallnacht, Steinhardt countered that maintenance of an embassy in a given country did not denote approval of its domestic or foreign policies. Indeed, the Soviet bombing of Helsinki horrified him, so much so that he recommended that Washington supply the Finns with arms. He nevertheless objected to the closing of diplomatic missions. Their functioning, he contended, was strictly a matter of utility, their reportage alone ensured a better-informed foreign policy than otherwise possible. To suspend recognition or reduce an embassy merely deprived Washington of an asset. Hull and FDR concurred. They also believed, or at least prayed, that the Soviet–German alliance would not thrive into the deep future. American patience should yield dividends – a cracked alliance and Moscow's eventual adherence to the anti-German cause. Hull afterwards explained: "We had to be careful not to push [the USSR] in the other direction."[42]

Even as Steinhardt's preference won out for keeping channels of communication open, the Winter War continued to roil Soviet–US relations. Sumner Welles, who employed Steinhardt as main messenger of State Department displeasure, decried Moscow's refusal to permit establishment of a consulate in Vladivostok. Both men accused the Soviets, with ample justification, of unwillingness to expedite the removal of US passport holders from strife-torn eastern Europe. Steinhardt also complained to Molotov about the sundry inadequacies of living accommodations and office space allocated to US diplomats in Moscow. The Narkomindel (Commissariat of Foreign Affairs) responded with its own recital of grievances. It objected to the "iniquitous" moral embargo, discriminatory banking practices leveled against Amtorg (New York-based Soviet trading corporation), and obstructions to the chartering of merchant ships to carry exports to the USSR.[43]

At first haltingly, but then steadily, the intensity of recriminations dropped. This improvement, shy of full-scale rapprochement, owed much to the tectonic shift caused by Germany's defeat of French armies. Suddenly, Kremlin leaders faced new facts. Whereas the European continent had recently boasted three great land powers, France's surrender collapsed the balance of forces; henceforth, Soviet security would depend more than ever on the unpredictability of Hitler and his "goodwill." As for the Americans, like the British, they were more eager than ever to nudge the Soviets away from Germany and looked for signs of Berlin–Moscow tension. Welles held a series of talks (August 1940–April 1941) in Washington with Oumansky to resolve miscellaneous (mostly economic) problems that had undermined Soviet–US mutuality. None was disposed perfectly from a US standpoint, but the holding of these conversations encouraged civility. They could, in the best of all possible outcomes, weaken Soviet attachment to the German alliance, which White House wisdom assumed to be increasingly brittle. The administration suspended its moral embargo of the USSR in January 1941.[44]

Contrarily, Steinhardt doubted that the British and/or Americans could do anything that would encourage a German–Soviet decoupling. He felt that Washington's *démarche* rested on risible optimism that ignored the degree to which Soviet interests had advanced via cooperation with the Third Reich. He cited in his brief the extent of Soviet land grabs to which Hitler acquiesced, cheerfully by all accounts. Steinhardt was impressed too by the briskness of Soviet–German trade. The security regime that smothered Embassy Moscow also contributed to his skepticism. The ubiquity of informants, enforced isolation from normal society, plus arrests of the embassy's Soviet employees (translators, typists, research assistants), reinforced Steinhardt in this view: Stalin was unalterably hostile.[45] The Soviet Union was practically at war with the English-speaking democracies. The comrades were intent on consolidating the advantage attained through the German connection and wanted to seize new opportunities "on a frankly imperialist basis" should they arise. Above all, in Steinhardt's estimation, Stalin was intent upon avoiding war with Germany, to which end he would grant nearly any concession.[46]

This difference in attitude toward Moscow between Steinhardt and the White House only widened. He argued in March 1941, as evidences of invasion became irrefutable, that Washington should not bother to warn the Kremlin. Even as Germany's ambassador in Moscow, Count Friedrich Werner von der Schulenburg (martyred in 1944 for his part in the July attempt against Hitler), sought to alert his hosts of mounting danger, Steinhardt counseled caution:

> The cynical reaction of the Soviet Government to approaches of this character would lead it to regard [this] gesture as neither sincere nor independent ... Furthermore, should the Soviet Government have no advice of its own tending to confirm our information regarding German attack, and especially should developments fail to confirm the information, our action would thereafter be regarded by the Soviets as having been merely an attempt to drive a wedge between the Soviet Union and Germany, at British instigation.[47]

In the event, Welles explained to Oumansky the findings of US intelligence regarding BARBAROSSA, whereupon the envoy turned pale. Yet Stalin chose not to believe, an inexplicable stubbornness that paved the way for his mental indisposition on first learning of the German onslaught.[48] A slightly more composed but equally confounded Molotov asked Schulenburg at the critical moment in June: "What have we done to deserve this?"[49]

The doubts entertained by Steinhardt about the likelihood of a German–Soviet clash did finally dissipate in April 1941, the turning point for him being Hitler's invasion of Yugoslavia, begun the day after Belgrade's representatives concluded a treaty of friendship with the USSR.[50] That same month, discarding previous qualms, he told the Narkomindel's S. A. Lozovsky that all verifiable evidence pointed to a German offensive.[51] Tipped off later by an informant in Schulenburg's embassy of the launch time for BARBAROSSA, Steinhardt sent his wife and daughter to Stockholm before Hitler's armies crossed Soviet frontiers. Earlier, in anticipation of emergency, he had leased a dacha, located twenty miles northeast of Moscow (Tarasovka). He transformed the house and grounds into a well-stocked haven (tents, stoves, blankets, food, fuel) for use by US personnel. Incidentally, the Moscow chancellery and ambassadorial residence – fabled Spaso House – did sit short distances from the Kremlin and other government sites, each an irresistible target for German aviators. Steinhardt predicted heavy loss of life in and around Moscow's US precincts. Nor did he think that more than a few weeks would elapse before Wehrmacht units captured the city.[52]

The haste with which the embassy staff repaired to its rural refuge on 22 June 1941 caused a stir among Soviet officials. Steinhardt was derided as "coward." Cripps too felt that his colleague's rush from Moscow was unmanly.[53] The Americans, in fact, did shortly return to the capital, where they dutifully resumed workaday routines (to which were added the devising of plans to evacuate embassy archives and ciphers). Most military opinion in Washington held, meanwhile, as did the embassy's army attaché, Major Ivan Yeaton, that Soviet forces would capitulate in a matter of months. Just days before the German assault began, General Marshall received a report from military intelligence that underlined the point: "Germany can rapidly defeat Russia, overthrow the Stalin regime, and seize her western provinces. It is also possible that she could totally destroy the Russian Army before the end of 1941, thereby securing to herself European Russia and those parts of Siberia west of Lake Baikal."[54]

Not all expert opinion, or what passed for it, supposed that Soviet power was on the brink of extinction. Cripps and Joseph Davies, the latter of whom FDR highly regarded, believed the Red Army would show to considerable advantage; German success in 1941 was by no means a foregone conclusion.[55] Steinhardt, though he wished the Red Army might bleed the Germans and wage guerilla combat after the surrender of main cities, remained in step with mainstream military and diplomatic opinion: Soviet defeat was impending. It would be comprehensive.[56] This attitude naturally placed him in an awkward position with the Narkomindel. It wanted, no less than Stalin, to impress the Americans and British with Soviet staying power and to acquire prompt aid. As had Kennedy in London, so Steinhardt worried that materiel sent to the USSR would fall to German capture, then be turned against what remained of Allied power. He expressed this anxiety not only in cables to Washington, but also directly to Harry Hopkins (late July) and to the Lord Beaverbrook–Averell Harriman commission (late September) when they visited Moscow to assess Soviet prospects.

The observations of Hopkins–Beaverbrook–Harriman buttressed FDR and Churchill in this thinking. First, the USSR, irrespective of whether it ultimately prevailed against the Wehrmacht, stood a chance to reduce German power – perhaps by margins substantial enough to ensure British survival and, by extension, that of the north Atlantic community on whose integrity US safety depended. Second, because the Soviets were fighting not only their war but also "objectively" helping the Anglo-US cause, they deserved whatever London and Washington could give, from military equipment to food and medical supplies. Give without stint became the mantra, in Hull's phrase "all aid to the hilt."[57] FDR declared the Soviet Union eligible for Lend-Lease help on 7 November.[58]

Against the prevailing new trend, Steinhardt still insisted that the probabilities of Soviet survival were slim. Most aid to the country, however skillfully used by its recipients, would fall into Axis hands. He also urged that the Soviets be obliged to take tangible steps in return for whatever Lend-Lease bounty they received. He had in mind unexceptional but potentially helpful actions, such as the Kremlin's letting his military attachés visit frontline Soviet positions and freeing the embassy from the envelope of police scrutiny. To ask nothing of the USSR, he said, while sending varieties of aid, would reinforce Stalin's contempt for the West and might eventuate in conditions permitting a renewed Soviet deal with Germany.

Stalin in his meeting with Hopkins, later with Harriman, roundly criticized Steinhardt. Subsequently, both special emissaries – who, anyway, tended to ignore Steinhardt – told FDR that the ambassador should be replaced, on which subject the president had no doubts and, indeed, had already made up his mind.[59] He needed a man in tune with the idea that assistance to the USSR served vital US interests, regardless of Soviet orneriness or past misbehavior: "Of course we are going to give all the aid we possibly can to Russia."[60]

Unsurprisingly, Steinhardt, dissenting from the White House line, played a minor role in Soviet–US relations during his last months abroad. Aggravating matters further, he loathed his quarters in Kuibyshev, where he and all foreign diplomats were obliged to huddle (even as Stalin and Molotov tempted fate by remaining in Moscow). He resented Kuibyshev's isolation, dearth of amenities, and myriad nuisances. He threatened, after plumbing mishaps spoilt his cramped "suite," to visit revenge on Andrei Vyshinsky, Molotov's chief lieutenant and senior Narkomindel officer in residence. "You call Vyshinsky," an exasperated ambassador once ordered the embassy operator, "and tell him if my toilet isn't working in one hour, I'm going up there and use his."[61]

Chagrined by exclusion from talks between Stalin and visitors (Hopkins, Harriman), entombed in Kuibyshev, and opposed to unconditional aid, Steinhardt was glad in November when instructions arrived: return to Washington, consult with the president.[62] After completing a perilous thirteen-day trip, followed by anxiety when he expected chastisement for his Soviet performance, Steinhardt learned this news. His services were still wanted.[63] In January 1942 he was appointed ambassador to Turkey. There his self-discipline and drive were harnessed to added purpose, to erase from Roosevelt's mind whatever doubts had arisen about his diplomatic fitness.

Steinhardt's subsequent Turkish contributions were two. First, he parried, with Lend-Lease provisions and Britain's Sir Hughe Knatchbull-Hugessen, the efforts by Ambassador Franz von Papen to align Ankara with Berlin. Second, via contacts in President Ismet Inonu's office, Steinhardt helped Zionist organizations and the War Refugee Board's Ira Hirschmann to deliver (by land and Black Sea) thousands of Jews from the German-dominated Balkans to Palestine.[64] Three years after accusing US immigration policy of being riddled with misconceived "humanitarianism," a somber Steinhardt in Ankara declared (11 November 1944): "All that we have been able to do has been to rescue a pitifully small number [of people] from [Nazi] clutches."[65] This turnabout constituted a remarkable conversion on Steinhardt's part. It was compatible with, but not simply explained by, his New York gubernatorial ambitions (unrealized) and desire to reassure Jewish voters, among whom rumors had flown concerning his 1941 solidarity with Long.[66]

Fragile alliance

In the weeks after Steinhardt left Soviet territory, the war's scope expanded to include direct US involvement: Pearl Harbor, the German and American declarations against each other. Equally significant,

Hitler's offensive against the USSR stalled. The early onset of a severe winter played havoc, as did the quality of Red Army resistance, far exceeding the expectation of skeptics. Amid these events Roosevelt selected a new ambassador. His mission would be twofold – encourage the bloodied USSR against making a separate peace with Germany along the lines of the 1918 Brest-Litovsk treaty, and facilitate the delivery of sufficient aid to the Soviets that would enable them to continue the war.[67]

Major General James Burns was Roosevelt's choice for envoy. Recently detailed to the Beaverbrook–Harriman mission, he had liked what he saw of Moscow defenses and planning. His value to Hopkins's Lend-Lease administration, slated to become its executive director, was so great that FDR was prevailed upon to rescind his original offer of ambassadorship. Burns stayed in Washington. Roosevelt next approached Joseph Davies for an encore mission to the USSR, where feeling for him ran high. He refused, citing health problems and doctor's orders, objections doubtless reinforced by the disagreeable prospect of residing in typhus-ridden Kuibyshev. Harriman too ducked FDR's offer of ambassadorship; he emphasized the importance and demands of his Lend-Lease job in London. Into his artfully worded rejection he suggested that Standley, another veteran of the Beaverbrook–Harriman expedition (charged with reviewing Moscow's naval requirements), would do nicely among the fighting Soviets.[68]

Roosevelt had good reason to trust Standley. They had been acquainted since the World War, when Standley was posted at Annapolis and had opportunities to meet with the Navy's assistant secretary. Thereafter, although hardly intimates, they remained on pleasant terms, rooted in shared devotion to naval readiness and FDR's respect for Standley's judgment on security questions. As newly installed president, Roosevelt promoted Standley to Chief of Naval Operations (CNO), which office he held until retiring in 1937. (William Leahy was Standley's immediate successor as CNO.) He continued to follow the course of international events, despite the distraction of various civilian pursuits (i.e. director of foreign participation in the 1939 New York's World's fair, consultant for the Electric Boat Company in Connecticut). He was a pre-Pearl Harbor proponent of US intervention in the European war and alliance with Britain. He tracked dangers emanating from Japan. He welcomed the emergence in June 1941 of an

Anglo-Soviet combination against Germany. He taught that the USSR should receive plentiful US aid. Two additional qualities of Standley recommended him. First, as a naval man, he was sure to understand the complexity of transporting US supplies, mostly by sea, to the Soviet Union. Second, habituated to life in a clearly defined command structure, he was unlikely to copy Steinhardt's example of second-questioning FDR's Soviet policy.[69]

Plain-spoken, physically spry, and mentally alert, Standley was sixty-nine at the time that he accepted ambassadorial duty.[70] No novice to foreign affairs or Washington's rough-and-tumble ways, he had served on the US delegation to the 1935–1936 London Naval Disarmament Conference. While CNO he had often functioned as acting secretary of Navy (owing to the precarious health and absences of Secretary Claude Swanson). Returned to the active duty navy list in February 1941, Standley had also worked with the Planning Board of the Office of Production Management and later played a part on the Roberts Commission, charged with probing the multifarious facts related to the Pearl Harbor attack.

Standley's Soviet background was limited. A native of the rugged coast of northern California, he had in his youth known Russians, who lived near his Ukiah ranch and Fort Ross (southernmost point of nineteenth-century czarist penetration in North America). He liked them: "Those California Russians were good neighbors, always ready to help you with money or labor if you were in trouble."[71] Later, as a junior naval officer, he landed in Vladivostok, where he witnessed (1899) Russian participation in suppression of the Boxer Rebellion. He felt fortified in 1942 with these few but vivid experiences; he was eager to do whatever possible to enhance Soviet–US cooperation.[72] His time in the USSR, alas, was a study in frustration. It left him everlastingly disillusioned with that country and with Roosevelt's foreign policy.

Not until a couple of weeks after his arrival in the USSR did Standley meet Stalin (23 April 1942), in the admiral's view an unconscionable delay, contrary to considerations due to the personal representative of the US president. Worse still, the tone and substance of the meeting were disappointing. Standley took offense at Stalin's saying that the US navy was incapable of operating well against German submarines. Stalin also seemed little moved by Standley's conveying of what the ambassador thought was a novel notion from FDR, namely, that he and the Soviet premier ought soon to meet – perhaps off Alaskan shores – to review strategic matters.[73] Unbeknownst to Standley, the White House, in fact, had earlier floated this proposal. Molotov would soon be on his way to Washington to examine the idea's feasibility along with other confidential matters (i.e. projected timing of US and British landings on the continent) about which nobody in the administration had told Standley. Not for the last time, Standley later sighed, did he find himself placed outside the main circles of information and confidence.

According to the ambassador's account, the mood of this first meeting lightened only when the subject turned to the job of crushing Hitler's armies (which by Berlin's own confidential estimation on 1 March 1942 had cost 1.5 million soldiers): "I said that if at any time I might be of use in helping him [Stalin] kill Germans, I wished he would let me know. He replied that the Russians were killing many, many Germans at the front, that the poor Germans had received orders that they must not retreat or give way an inch and the result was that they were killing them like pigs."[74]

Standley made little headway in the months that followed this conversation with Stalin. Problems piled high, but their resolution seemed to Standley lost in the maw of an unresponsive Soviet bureaucracy.[75] His own attention and time were fragmented between conferences with second-tier apparatchiks in Kuibyshev (where the diplomatic corps remained until its 1943 return to Moscow) and Stalin, who held continuous court in the capital. Standley grew irate over what were to him incomprehensible rebuffs. The Soviets, to his consternation, interned American plane crews (from the 1942 Doolittle raid onward) forced to make emergency landings in eastern Siberia after bombing Japanese targets. He understood the Kremlin's desire to avoid provoking Tokyo by taking measures that were, or could reasonably be construed to be, contrary to Soviet neutrality in the Japanese–US war. But he was dumbstruck by the obstacles emplaced by Soviet officials that delayed or, in instances, prevented embassy officers from visiting the airmen to check on their condition. Surely, he told Molotov, Americans, as producers of Lend-Lease aid and partners against Germany, deserved better. Might the Soviets arrange, Standley suggested, to let some airmen "escape" from the USSR via Iran (eventually allowed in cases). Comparably upsetting to him, Soviet intelligence withheld data from his naval attachés that it acquired about the placement of Japanese warships in the north Pacific.[76]

On other matters too, even petty ones, the Soviets struck Standley as arbitrary or unforgiving. He never accepted the NKVD escort that trailed his every move as being compatible with Allied solidarity. Officials withheld exit papers from Soviet wives of Americans (diplomats, servicemen, journalists). A Dr. Lang, naval physician attached to the embassy, was repeatedly blocked from visiting local hospitals or conducting investigations into the areas of his medical specialty (fevers, bacteriology). Prohibitions were placed on US broadcasting of propaganda aimed at audiences in the Third Reich.[77] The establishment of American weather stations, potentially useful to U.S. pilots ferrying cargo over the Alaska–Siberia route, was forbidden; a survey party was prevented from examining the USSR's eastern provinces to determine safest air routes. The Soviets were also stingy in sharing their knowledge of German tactics and weaponry with embassy military and naval attachés. Nor did the Soviets ever, to Standley's satisfaction, look after those Allied sailors in distress (wounded, penniless, disoriented) in Murmansk who had braved U-boat wolf packs and turbulent seas to deliver Lend-Lease relief.[78] For several months in 1942–1943, Anglo-US convoys to northern Soviet ports were decreased or entirely suspended as the Germans sank record-breaking levels of tonnage. To Standley's disquiet, the Narkomindel attributed these reductions to the work of sinister forces in Washington bent on the USSR's ruin, with intimations that the admiral necessarily played a sly part. Stalin himself took liberties with the ambassador's dignity, asking on one occasion whether Standley was afraid to quit Kuibyshev for Moscow.[79]

The Soviets were at their most obstreperous on the subject of Poland, with whose government – in London exile – they had grudgingly reestablished relations in July 1941. Stalin later edified the world when he announced that Wladyslaw Sikorski, the Polish prime minister, happily cooperated with Nazi puppet-masters.[80] Molotov opined to Standley that trouble was always afoot where Poles were concerned.[81] The ambassador objected to this preposterousness while at the same time he tried to coax Soviet leaders into allowing tens of thousands of Polish soldiers (and their dependents) to leave the USSR for flight via Iran into Egypt. There they could join with other Polish forces, already assembled under General Wladyslaw Anders, for renewed action against Germany (most famously at Monte Cassino). The actual departure of some Polish fighters (and families) for these purposes was eased by the ambassador's persistent efforts. Standley also urged the Soviets to treat humanely those remaining

Poles, ranging from orphans to combat veterans, scattered from eastern-most Siberia to cells in Lubyanka.

He refrained from going beyond certain limits, however. In keeping with FDR's wish, Standley did not pry into the Katyn allegations in Spring 1943. Neither he nor the president was inclined to dignify Goebbels's charges that German soldiers had discovered the remains of Polish officers slain in Soviet captivity – and were disinclined to question Kremlin protests of innocence, in whose midst an indignant Stalin again severed relations with Polish authorities. Rather, Standley urged Stalin and Molotov to find means of reconciling with the London Poles, at the time demanding that the International Red Cross employ forensic specialists to determine the truth about Katyn's dead.[82]

Standley also went on record to this effect. Too great a fuss about matters Polish would corrode Anglo-US ties to the Soviet Union, the only Ally in 1943 that was inflicting substantial damage on Germany. Polish problems in this context constituted a secondary matter. The US and British governments, he suggested, should press Sikorski to make changes in his cabinet; members notable for their antipathy toward the USSR should be dropped in favor of persons better disposed toward the Kremlin. Furthermore, the Americans and British were in danger of aligning themselves too closely with Sikorski's insistence that the Soviet–Polish frontier be reestablished along the prewar line. The Stalinist leadership, Standley averred, would surely want in coming years to guarantee the USSR's exposed western frontier with buffer territory; the English-speaking powers ought not to delay or prevent such a Polish concession.[83]

Secretary Hull disliked this version of realpolitik and the implied admission of Anglo-US dependence on Soviet power. He told the ambassador: "The Soviet Government would, in all probability, not consider a changed Polish Cabinet as favorable to the Soviet Union unless it would be prepared ... to acquiesce in Soviet claims to Eastern Poland ... We feel that we cannot concur with your suggestion that our proposals are based too strongly on the Polish desiderata."[84] The USSR, he went on to tell Standley, had to be brought around to a settlement based on justice and equity.

Doubtless Standley could have lived without Hull's preachment. It was mild, though, compared to the other nonsense, as he perceived it, that normally emanated from Washington. He especially disliked the White House's penchant for sending high-profile emissaries to meet with Stalin and Molotov. Standley felt he was made to look the chump, unworthy to be trusted with top-secret matters. His dyspepsia quickened with each visitation by dignitaries. The list included Harriman with Churchill (August 1942) to explain postponement of the second front, globe-trotting Wendell Willkie (September 1942), and Joseph Davies (May 1943), dispatched to deliver FDR's latest request to meet with Stalin. None of these visitors, Standley brooded, paid him proper deference while the hoopla surrounding them reduced his prestige. They rarely shared anything of what they discovered in conclave with Stalin.[85] Standley subsequently let loose in his 1955 published memoirs. He portrayed Harriman as arrogant and obsequious, Willkie as buffoon, Davies as oily self-promoter.[86]

Standley did not defer all vengeful gratification until 1955, as illustrated in the Davies case. Rather, in 1943, Standley conspired with Moscow-based US journalists (Quentin Reynolds, Eddy Gilmore, Bill Downes) to embarrass the self-styled Soviet expert in a press conference with tough questions. These centered on the Kremlin's press censorship and reluctance to share intelligence with local Americans. A testy Davies responded to the reporters' interrogatory with an injunction against defaming an ally, thereby aiding German propagandists eager to pounce on evidences of Soviet–US rift. Pandemonium then broke out. Insulted newsmen and Davies volleyed charges of irresponsibility and disloyalty. Standley, who thoroughly enjoyed the spectacle, expressed this disingenuous concern to Washington superiors: "A protracted and exceedingly bitter controversy on the subject of Soviet cooperation ensued between the members of the press on one side and Davies on the other in which I fear unconsidered remarks were made and tempers almost lost."[87] He could not help wondering, he innocently added, about the wisdom of sending visitors to the USSR who held dogmatic views.[88]

Standley could have derived only slight comfort from the Davies donnybrook. This stubborn fact remained. Celebrity visitors overshadowed him and, inadvertently or not, subverted his office. Case in point, the Soviets told Davies during his stay that the Comintern would be dissolved. Later, he casually let the ambassador know.[89]

Divisions within the official American community in the USSR were even more detrimental to Standley's authority than Davies et al. Tangled lines of jurisdiction and vague accountability surpassed that found in London (Winant versus Harriman) and nearly equaled the

muddle in China, where US soldiers, diplomats, and intelligence operatives squabbled with resultant advantage to indigenous parties. The
problem in the Soviet instance hinged on the administrative separate-
ness of the local Lend-Lease operation from that of Standley's mission.
The former, under Brigadier General Philip Faymonville, took its cues
from Washington's Office of Lend-Lease Administration (OLLA), and,
though willing to cooperate when necessary with the embassy, never
felt answerable to it. Faymonville was his own law.

Complying with OLLA outlook, Faymonville meant to funnel
aid to the Soviets without hitch or inhibition. Thus they had no need to
work with Standley on such matters as timing of aid shipments, their
contents, or distribution of materiel. Resolution of these questions lay
directly with Faymonville, who, having never quit Moscow for Kuibyshev, enjoyed proximity to Kremlin leaders. Most significant, he was
unwilling to require reciprocal favors for Soviet-bound assistance, as
the embassy would have liked. Standley and his attachés, notably
Brigadier General Joseph Michela, felt stymied as the Red Army shared
little of its knowledge obtained in battle, intelligence that they should
have received were Faymonville not in the way. The animosity between
Michela and the Lend-Lease representative became fierce, with the
former convinced that Faymonville was a communist stooge or victim
of blackmail for homosexuality. Once to his face, Standley called
Faymonville a traitor to the United States. Meanwhile, from a Soviet
standpoint, Faymonville continued to function as the alternative and
preferred ambassador, despite an intervention (half-hearted) by FDR to
curtail his autonomy. Eventually treated as a pariah at the embassy,
Faymonville emerged a beneficent hero to the Soviets. When General
Burns visited Moscow (April–May 1943) on Lend-Lease duty, he conferred at length with Faymonville but had little to do with Standley or
his people. The ambassador, boiling with anger over an untenable
situation, wanted to tender his immediate resignation.[90]

Albeit normally self-contained, the former CNO in Kuibyshev–
Moscow drifted anxiously on what were for him uncharted diplomatic seas.
At no time was his loss of compass more apparent than on 8 March 1943, a
moment of interlude between his unwanted VIPs. Without mentioning
Soviet suffering, but alive to the difficulties surrounding Lend-Lease and
the cost paid by convoy crews and taxpayers, he complained to journalists
about the Kremlin's dearth of public thanks for US assistance. His gripe was
instantly communicated throughout the USSR and abroad:

> *Ever since I have been in the Soviet Union I have been*
> *carefully looking for recognition in the Russian press of the*
> *fact that the Russians are getting material aid from the*
> *United States . . . I have thus far failed to find any real*
> *acknowledgement in the press of this fact.*
>
> *There is no question that the American public knows that*
> *relief and other supplies are coming to the Soviet Union.*
> *However, the Russian people apparently do not realize this.*
> *It is not fair to mislead the American people who are giving*
> *millions of dollars and think that they are aiding the Russian*
> *people when at the same time the Russian people do not*
> *realize that this aid is coming from the American people.*
> *The American people are doing this out of friendship for*
> *the Russian people but the Russian people are not aware of*
> *this fact.*[91]

The reasons for this outburst remain unclear. At least two explanations are plausible. First, as Standley tried to persuade Washington, he may have been so fed up with the "ingratitude" of Soviet leaders that he had to clear the air.[92] Along this line, he had in mind the publicized remarks by Stalin in October 1942 to Henry Cassidy of the Associated Press. These omitted mention of Lend-Lease while containing invidious comparison between Anglo-US contributions of "little effect" versus Soviet hammer blows against Germany. Stalin stressed similar themes in words that he delivered to the Red Army in February 1943.[93] Second, as Standley later contended, he may have meant by his venting of spleen to provoke timely Soviet acknowledgements. These would permit Congress to surmount the hesitation of some members – such as Senators Hugh Butler, Richard Russell – and approve the Lend-Lease Extension Act (which did pass on 11 March 1943).[94]

The Soviet rebuttal to Standley was furious, if slightly tempered by admission that Lend-Lease had its uses. One citizen was quoted as saying: "We've lost millions of people, and they want us to crawl on our knees because they send us spam. And has the 'warmhearted' Congress ever done anything that wasn't in its interests? Don't tell me that Lend-lease is *charity*!"[95] As for Britons and Americans, a handful applauded Standley, but did so only in private. The overwhelming response was one of disapproval as Leningrad still starved, as swathes of Soviet territory remained under Axis occupation. Widespread denunciations of "callous"

Standley preceded calls for his dismissal.[96] Welles, Davies, Hopkins, Burns, and Senator Tom Connally urged that the tactless diplomat be replaced. Puzzled by Standley's unauthorized utterance, Roosevelt wasted no time in trying to identify a successor.[97] Upon recruiting one, he accepted Standley's resignation in the later summer.

Contrary to what critics charged, Standley was not oblivious to Soviet sacrifices. His treks to parts of the USSR included visits to orphanages. The boys and girls and their watchful minders stirred him: "a lump came into my throat."[98] He respected the dedication of women as they worked in farm fields, factories, and on the front lines.[99] He visited wounded Stalingrad. He admired the hardiness of its defenders – living testimonials of "courage and unflinching tenacity," he reported.[100] Upon returning to the United States, to enter into duties on the planning board of the OSS, he enumerated the Red Army's virtues to audiences (civic clubs, fraternal orders, church assemblies).[101] He invariably reminded them of the price paid in human lives and treasure: "Years of war effort . . . [have] demanded from the Russian people untold suffering and hardship, sacrifices unconceivable to us here."[102]

Harriman

Roosevelt still hoped in 1943 that Davies could be persuaded to accept another turn in Moscow. Davies again refused, citing as before medical reasons and the creeping aches of age (b. 1876). Evidence suggests that the president also briefly considered Hopkins and Winant. If so, the first was ruled out because of his indispensability in Washington (plus physical frailty). The sensibility of the second disqualified his keeping company with Stalin.[103] With Hull's encouragement, FDR did pursue the USSR idea with Harriman.[104] This time he agreed, though not without regret about leaving colorful London and friends (among whom the alluring Pamela Churchill) for Moscow and NKVD oppressiveness. Gloomier still, he would no longer occupy a spot near the Churchill–FDR *pas de deux* whose choreography at times closely involved him.[105]

Embassy

Harriman sensed the importance of the Soviet mission at the moment of his appointment, 7 October 1943. Allied victory in

Europe was a foregone conclusion, but its timing and terms were yet to be determined, matters in which an ambassador at Moscow could conceivably play a significant part. So too detailed questions related to Soviet entry into the fight against Japan and the contours of postwar order remained unanswered, again matters in which an attentive American should have a say. To Harriman, then, the assignment would test his mettle, perhaps serving as vehicle for future preferment. He told Standley, content to be done with Moscow, that "those Russians" are "only human." Come what may, "Stalin can be handled." The old man judged his successor a portrait in bravado.[106]

From the standpoint of Soviet ideology, Harriman was not just a creature endowed with surplus confidence. He was a thing more significant, as suggested by his earlier errands to Moscow and the company he kept (with Beaverbrook in 1941, with Churchill in 1942). He exemplified the category of US ruling class, the tycoon who controls governmental–social–military levers. He was born into wealth, son of the railroad baron Edward Henry Harriman. To this original fortune, the younger Harriman avidly added. His capitalist empire included not only railway holdings, but also investments in aviation, shipbuilding, steel manufacturing, utilities, banks, petroleum production, and glamorous resorts (Sun Valley in Idaho). This empire even reached into the USSR, where in the 1920s he ran an extensive, albeit unsuccessful, manganese-mining operation in the Caucasus (Georgia). One of the wealthiest men in America, he was by definition a broker of prestige and politics. In dealing with him, the Kremlin was directly in touch with authentic power, not mediated by a shyster lawyer or a cranky navy man past his prime. Thus Harriman's posting to Moscow confirmed for Leninist-Stalinist theoreticians the fact that America's ruling caste at last regarded the proletarian republic with appropriate seriousness. Years after the war Nikita Khrushchev explained to Harriman: "We like to do business with you, for you are the master and not the lackey."[107]

To Roosevelt, Harriman was not quite so grand as Soviet theory held, but the president certainly prized him as conscientious advisor. Acquainted since childhood, connected by school ties (Groton), and sharing a passion for distinction, the two men used each other to mutual advantage. Harriman's endorsement of New Deal projects had helped alleviate the apprehensions of businessmen that

11 Left to right: translator, Churchill, W. Averell Harriman, Stalin and
Molotov. Moscow 1942.

socialism would overcome America. This "tame millionaire" also performed his New Deal chores with manifest efficiency. He had served in
the National Recovery Administration, for three years chaired the
Business Advisory Council in the Department of Commerce, and occupied a seat on the Office of Production Management. FDR and Hopkins sought his economic expertise. With each new position of trust
thrust upon him, Harriman's appetite grew for more.[108]

While in London with Lend-Lease, Harriman studied the
medium of political power. He observed Winant's travails (indeed, contributed to them). He grew accustomed to skillful manipulations by such
masters of the art as Churchill. Based on this education, Harriman drew
lessons for his Moscow ambassadorship. These bore on the risks of
scattered responsibility. He resolved that US officialdom in the USSR
must function as a unity. Under his authority, it might allow, but would
not suffer in the deflated Steinhardt–Standley manner, visiting Washington personages to conduct business with Stalin.

With backing from FDR, Harriman oversaw personnel changes
and clarified lines of authority, much in the spirit of Hurley in Chongqing
but to better effect. Harriman ended the Faymonville–Michela feud by
having both officers reassigned out of the USSR. Their functions were

combined under a single command, headed by Major General John Deane, formerly American secretary to the Combined Chiefs of Staff and thenceforth accountable directly to the ambassador. The two men shared a common mentality – pragmatic, decisive – that anchored the most effective of FDR's wartime embassies. (Deane's military mission included Brigadier General Hoyt Vandenberg for the Army Division, Commodore C. E. Olsen for the Navy Division, and Brigadier General Sidney P. Spalding for the Supply Division.[109]) Harriman also insisted that one of the Foreign Service's Soviet experts be detailed to Moscow. He originally wanted Bohlen, who did serve briefly in the embassy before being claimed as FDR's Russian-language translator for the Tehran conference. In June 1944 Harriman succeeded in obtaining George Kennan, gratefully liberated from the European Advisory Commission's deliberations. Harriman, whose wife remained in the United States, entrusted the embassy's social side to his young daughter, Kathleen (b. 1917), who also took part in the publishing of *Amerika* magazine (intended to educate Soviet readers about the United States). Her skills as hostess, previously demonstrated at her father's side in London, and management of Spaso House won respect from the diplomatic corps. Approving members contrasted her conduct with Martha Dodd's Berlin improprieties, the retelling and embellishment of which had already become lore. The ambassador's personal assistant of long standing, Robert Meiklejohn, coordinated the business side of the embassy and kept track of Harriman's crowded calendar, which featured lengthy sessions each week with the Foreign Service/military staffs.[110]

Harriman's presence, and the changes he made, lifted the embassy out of the doldrums that pervaded it during the Standley era. John Melby, who worked under both ambassadors in Moscow, noted in October 1943: "The new regime here is distinctly more on the big-shot side of life. The conversation is all Winston this, Tony [Eden] that, and Franklin the other. In one sense it rather seems that the White House has moved into the Embassy."[111]

Unlike the more affable Standley, Harriman was not an easy boss. He could be brusque or dismissive. He had a short temper. He pushed himself hard, putting in days of eighteen or twenty hours. He expected the same of his subordinates, who under Standley had grown used to a slower pace. The intellectual reflexes of Harriman pressed toward the achievement of measurable results. He did not allow playfulness of ideas or historical speculations to divert his attention, concentrated solely on winning the war and framing a peace in accordance with FDR's designs.

Albeit later professing to admire Harriman, Bohlen harbored doubts in 1943 about his quality of analytical mind.[112] Kennan in his 1967 memoirs handsomely praised Harriman ("remarkable man") and in the postwar years they remained friendly. But even in these memoirs a countercurrent is discernible, based on Harriman's failure to consult more closely, or take more seriously than he did, the bigger Soviet reality as depicted by Kennan: "He was often peremptory ... He had a way of riding roughshod over unsolicited suggestions."[113] On occasion Harriman had Kennan rewrite his reports when they veered in "too abstract" a direction for the government to act upon. "If sent to Washington, they'd think we'd lost our perspective," Harriman later reminisced.[114]

Kennan's literary-mindedness and yearning after an elusive Russian past could only have struck Harriman as irrelevant, if not slightly self-indulgent. What, one wonders, would he have thought had he read Kennan's diary entry, written after a brief visit to post-siege Leningrad? In a spirit akin to that of Akhmatova (whom he did not meet), Kennan recorded: "I know that in this city, where I have never lived, there has nevertheless – by some strange quirk of fate – a previous life, perhaps? – been deposited a portion of my own capacity to feel and to love, a portion – in other words – of my own life."[115] Yet, as de facto tutor to the ambassador, Kennan did exert an influence on Harriman, hastening him toward greater skepticism of the Kremlin and its willingness to coordinate closely with the West into the future.[116]

Limited cooperation

Roosevelt's 1943 instructions to Harriman emphasized the importance of cultivating cordial relations with Stalin. These might entail internationalization of the trans-Iranian railway – thus guaranteeing the Soviets a warm-water port on the Persian Gulf – and postwar aid to the USSR. Could the Soviets in exchange, FDR asked, refrain from making unilateral territorial demands on the Poles and Balts and instead let local peoples determine by plebiscite the extent of Moscow's proposed boundary adjustments? The president later expressed (May 1944) to Harriman the hope that Stalin might be induced to "give the Poles a break."[117]

Cooperation with the Soviets, Harriman discovered, proved difficult but hardly impossible. As earlier, US aircrews forced to make emergency landings in Soviet territory after bombing Japanese targets were interned; to his satisfaction, the men were allowed – more easily than before – to "escape." The Soviets were increasingly responsive to requests that he and Deane made about German military tactics, weapons systems, and orders of battle. Soviet intelligence officers also became more forthcoming about the East Asian war. They shared data on Japanese morale, naval deployments, and political–diplomatic developments in Tokyo. Once Stalin himself confided to Harriman that Japanese confidence, per reports by the Soviet embassy in Tokyo, was weakening in tandem with US air campaigns and Pacific successes.

Harriman was pleased when, after difficult haggling, the Kremlin agreed to modalities of OSS–NKVD collaboration. These permitted, among other things, for agents of each organization to operate freely on the national territory of the other. This plan, alas, was derailed in March 1944, when J. Edgar Hoover raised objections about letting communist operatives roam at will in the United States, never a good idea but especially not during an election year. Harriman and Deane protested the decision, but in vain.[118]

The most ambitious Soviet–American venture during Harriman's tenure pivoted on shuttle operations conducted by elements of the US Army Air Force (USAAF): the Fifteenth Air Force based in Italy, the Eighth Air Force based in Great Britain. Beginning on 2 June 1944, squadrons of heavy bombers from these units fell upon Third Reich targets and then proceeded to Ukrainian airfields. There the crews rested. They were debriefed. Their planes were refueled and reloaded for renewed attacks on Germany and Nazi-controlled territories in Poland, Hungary, and Romania – against oil refineries, Wehrmacht encampments, factories, harbor facilities. Code-named FRANTIC, these operations depended not only on US pilots and planes, but also upon stockpiled munitions and American ground crews assigned to the Ukrainian airfields of Poltava, Mirgorod, Piryatin. Twelve hundred USAAF personnel were put on station there (with headquarters located at Poltava). Soviet laborers built the three airfields. Red Army soldiers maintained them and assumed responsibility for security.

Logistical problems, linguistic barriers, rivalry between US and local servicemen for Soviet women, and command-control questions were knotty. Misunderstandings repeatedly surfaced, bruised feelings too. Still, FRANTIC had the potential to hurt Germany, met with success at first, and seemed a promising precedent for future campaigns against Japan to be launched from eastern Siberia.[119] Kathleen Harriman captured the exhilaration felt by Soviets and Americans, after watching with her father the landing of US planes (Fifteenth Air Force), fresh from pounding Third Reich sites:

> We were driving out to the field when the first bombers appeared as specks off in the horizon – it looked like thousands then suddenly the first squadron was overhead with its welcome roar. Jesus but it was exciting ... Ave[rell] said he didn't think he'd ever been so thrilled by anything ... It was certainly a wonderful day and I don't imagine I'll forget it for a long, long time. Most of all the Russians were impressed by our bombers being in formation after a long bombing mission ... and they appreciated the skill of our pilots – the skill of our bombardiers too after they saw the photos of the damage done to the targets ... All in all the shuttle bombing has made a great impression on them and it's certainly a big step forward to proving that god damn it we all can do a job of work together.[120]

Contrary to the expectation of Harriman and Deane, who had worked hard to win Stalin's approval of FRANTIC, the program came apart soon after its start. The difficulty stemmed from the Soviet inability to detect or intercept a Luftwaffe raid (night of 21–22 June 1944) against the Poltava field. Neither Soviet fighter planes nor anti-aircraft batteries proved effective. Destruction on the ground was substantial. Forty-seven Flying Fortresses were irretrievably damaged; nineteen others required costly repair. Munitions, fuel, and oil were lost in what Americans at Poltava dubbed "the other Pearl Harbor." The next night the Luftwaffe hit Mirgorod, where Soviet air defenses again showed themselves inadequate. Gasoline and ammunition depots were obliterated.[121]

Soviet and US military officers traded recriminations. Harriman and Stalin did issue public statements meant to smooth the friction and otherwise tried to downplay the crisis in confidence.[122] All the same, American enthusiasm fell sharply, albeit modest shuttle bombing continued through late autumn 1944. Thereupon the USAAF withdrew what few resources were still slated for FRANTIC and strategic air operations launched from the east ceased (though the last Americans did not leave Poltava until after V-E Day).[123] Plans for Soviet-based shuttle bombing campaigns in the Far East were also allowed to languish. Neither Stalin nor Molotov had ever relished the idea.[124] The US capture of Pacific islands within bombing radius of the Japanese homeland preempted the need for Siberian airfields, while Harriman, Deane, and Washington read FRANTIC as a melancholy tale.

Poland

Matters not directly associated with the aerial war also undermined FRANTIC. On 1 August General Tadeusz Bor-Komorowski ordered his underground *Armia Krajowa* (AK), linked with Polish leaders in London, to expel the German occupation from Warsaw. He planned to coordinate with nearby Soviet forces, under Marshal Konstantin Rokossovsky, that had been advancing westward; they were poised only miles away on the eastern bank of the Vistula river, whence their artillery and warplanes had been attacking German positions. The AK fighters secured two-thirds of Warsaw within forty-eight hours and prepared to join Soviet forces to destroy whatever Germans remained in the capital, then press further against the Wehrmacht.

Rokossovsky's army did not liaise with the AK or mount any operations in support of it. The Soviets stood still. Their artillery fell silent. Their planes ceased to strafe German positions. This pause was necessary, Stalin claimed at the time and later, to consolidate recently won possessions while replenishing spent supplies. Then the refreshed army would resume its offensive.

The German counterattack against the AK left Warsaw a charnel house. More than 200,000 civilians died; more than 15,000 AK fighters were killed.[125] The Germans systematically razed the city block by block. Remnants of the AK surrendered on 5 October, thus ending the military base of the London Poles. Their prime minister, Stanislaw Mikolajczyk, meanwhile met (early August) in Moscow with figures from the Soviet-sponsored Committee of National Liberation (Lublin Poles): Edward Osobka-Morawski, Boleslaw Bierut, Marshal Rola-Zymierski, Wanda Wassiliewska, Andrzej Witos. The prime minister, desperate for Soviet relief of Warsaw, was obliged to reserve a majority of cabinet seats in the postwar Polish government for the Lublin group.

He was also pressed to accept territorial adjustments to Soviet advantage (the so-called Curzon line), redolent of the 1939 Ribbentrop–Molotov partitioning.

Only after the AK's vanquishing did Rokossovsky's army enter Warsaw, 17 January 1945. Before then Stalin blocked Anglo-US aid from reaching the city. He forbade the RAF or USAAF to use Soviet airfields as part of operations to parachute medicines and weapons to the AK; no plane launched from Great Britain, Italy, or elsewhere and destined for Warsaw could operate in Soviet skies. To justify this decision, Stalin mentioned the difficulty of ensuring the safety of RAF and US airmen, for which purpose the specter of the German surprise at Poltava was conjured. Stalin also traduced the Home Army as incompetent and its London chiefs as rash; they alone were responsible for having brought disaster upon Warsaw, not the valiant Red Army, which agency alone would bring about Poland's liberation.[126]

Not until mid-September, when the AK–German struggle had virtually ceased, did the Kremlin permit American and British planes to use Soviet fields as part of a belated effort to help Warsaw. Too little and too late, most of the parachuted supplies fell into zones that had since been retaken by German soldiers.

Responses by London and Washington to Soviet idleness mixed incredulity with outrage. Churchill's cabinet protested to the Soviet foreign ministry: "Our people cannot understand why no material help has been sent from the outside to the Poles in Warsaw."[127] Roosevelt's appeal to Stalin stressed the urgency of aid, which produced a thinly veiled reminder of Soviet intentions to join the war against Japan and more disparagement of the "criminals" who had led the Warsawites into ludicrous battle.[128]

Horror dominated the feeling in Embassy Moscow. Kennan felt that Lend-Lease deliveries to the USSR should have been suspended until or unless Kremlin leaders took action on behalf of the AK, at the minimum cooperating with RAF and USAAF relief efforts.[129] Harriman's beseeching of Kremlin leaders met alternately with evasion and defiance. The impact on the ambassador of Soviet contrariety was profound. Before the Warsaw events, he tended to criticize the London Poles as shrill anti-Moscow aristocrats, heaving with reactionary sentiments (exemplified by General Kazimierz Sosnkowski, chief of the armed forces and unabashed Russophobe). "I am so out of sympathy with the Polish Government in London," Harriman had told American correspondents in Moscow. To the Lublin group, he had given benefit of the doubt: "My impression is they are sincere earnest patriots."[130] Harriman, moreover, had swallowed his private doubt about the quality of evidence to accept the Soviet version of Katyn: the Germans had perpetrated the murders.[131] Warsaw stripped him of all illusions, however. He still went along with the Washington idea that the Americans and British had to maintain a working relationship with the Soviets to reduce the cost of finishing the war against Germany and (later) Japan. But as Warsaw illustrated beyond refutation, the Western allies also had to recognize that the USSR was a ruthless partner – that postwar collaboration would prove chimerical and responsible statesmen should prepare accordingly.[132] As Warsaw burned, he told Hopkins that the time had come for Washington to "make clear what we expect of [Kremlin men] as the price of our good will. Unless we take issue with the present policy there is every indication that the Soviet Union will become a world bully."[133]

The destruction of Warsaw in 1944 was one in a set of indignations suffered by Poland during the war. Others included the German massacre in April–May 1943 of what remained of Warsaw's Jewish ghetto (once inhabited by 360,000 souls), previously subjected to starvation, diseases, and deportations to Treblinka. The ghetto's remaining population (60,000), led by the redoubtable Mordechaj Anielewicz and his lightly armed Jewish Fighting Organization, waged a pitiable battle against German preponderance (tanks, artillery, heavy machine guns). Their plight was aggravated by disinterest among many Polish gentiles, anyway distracted by concurrent Katyn reports, and Allied dithering (highlighted by the Anglo-US Bermuda conference in April that failed to fashion any genuine plan to rescue Jewry).[134] Roughly 14,000 Jews died in the ghetto resistance. Most of the rest were taken to labor or extermination camps. Small numbers managed to escape, sometimes with aid from the AK and the communist People's Guard. Survivors lived long enough to fight again in Warsaw during the 1944 uprising.[135]

Heinrich Himmler's murder archipelago constituted the profoundest offense visited on wartime Poland. This encompassed not only Treblinka but also the equally dark islands of Auschwitz, Belzec, Chelmno, Majdanek, Sobibor. Embassy Moscow followed the reports issued by the Red Army as it reached these places in its march toward Germany.[136] Harriman had earlier sent to Washington graphic accounts of the Third Reich's war on Soviet Jewry, notably the shooting of hundreds of thousands of Ukrainian Jews (including the Babi Yar slaughter).[137] Still, nothing fully prepared him for the discoveries made in Poland, where countless Slavs, Roma, west Europeans, and others died beside Hitler's "filthy" Jews. In late August 1944, a group of Moscow-based US journalists, including hardnosed Bill Lawrence of the *New York Times*, had gone to Lublin to interview Osobka-Morawski. The correspondents then toured Majdanek, lying on the city's southeastern edge. They later met with Harriman, whose daughter Kathleen wrote this account:

> *Estimates of victims ... include some twenty-two nationalities. Bill Lawrence compared the camp to an American production line – the victims for a particular day were first completely unclothed, made to wash in a shower with 72 water spigots, then moved on down the passageway to gas chambers where they were killed. After that the bodies were inspected for gold fillings and some x-rayed if they were suspected to have swallowed capsules with information. In the nearby field, three small blast furnaces were used to cremate the bodies, the ashes removed to fertilize the surrounding country. The correspondents then were taken to huge warehouses, one containing nothing but shoes, old discarded shoes, considered not worth shipment back to Germany, all of every size and shape. The estimated numbers ran into hundreds of thousands. From there they saw warehouses where the clothes of the victims had been sorted while waiting shipment back to Germany. Articles were carefully categorized and stacked. Women's corsets, nail files, shaving brushes, suits, etc., on down to one room which contained nothing but children's toys and games ... Bill Lawrence, the biggest skeptic among correspondents here on any horror story he sees, told us about this with tears in his eyes.[138]*

Ambassador Harriman learned that even during the last stage of German rule in Poland Jews were routinely killed. The surviving inhabitants of the Lodz ghetto, numbering between 60,000 and 80,000 people, were shipped to Auschwitz in September 1944. In the remaining months of 1944 and into the new year, his embassy also filed reports of pogroms in post-Nazi Poland – stoked by still unsatiated anti-Semitic indigenes – including Lublin, once a seat of rabbinical learning.[139]

Uncertain victory

Red Army units did not liberate Auschwitz, largest of the murder camps, until 27 January 1945. Soviet military governors by that time controlled most of Poland. Across its ravaged tracts, US and UK soldiers, sprung from German stalags (in Poland, Romania, eastern Prussia), sought to reach Polish transit centers, as in Lublin. Thence the former POWs, numbering about 25,000, were to be removed to Soviet ports (Odessa) for shipment to American and British destinations. Harriman, Deane, and their senior British colleague in Moscow, Ambassador Archibald Clark Kerr (of Chongqing yore), had earlier struck agreements with Soviet army officers, reiterated at Yalta: Red forces would provide American and British returnees with necessities – medical aid, transportation, shelter. In practice, little along these lines was forthcoming. Numerous GIs who made the eastward trek – by walking, hitchhiking, boxcar – reported tales to embassy officers that belied Soviet pledges to help. Red Army comrades neglected the GIs. Thieves preyed upon them. Inclement weather and the inhospitality of life in war-torn zones demoralized them. Harriman informed FDR and spoke to Stalin. The latter fired countercharges alleging that former Soviet POWs, unluckily "freed" by US and British forces in western Europe, faced heartless persecution by their "emancipators" and were bivouacked in foul quarters.[140]

    Stalin's mendacity concerning the fate of Soviet POWs in American and British keeping helped prepare the way – vaguely foreseen at first by Harriman but then with clarity – for the enforced repatriation in 1945–1947 of hundreds of thousands of Soviet soldiers (maybe two million).[141] Some had collaborated with their German captors and served in the anti-Soviet "Russian Liberation Army," commanded by General Andrei Vlasov. That army was composed of men who were anti-communist or wanted simply to avoid the horrors normally meted out to Soviet captives in German confinement.[142] Men wholly innocent of any cooperation with the German army guessed – correctly in the event – that upon return to the USSR they would be disdained, suspected of cowardice or betrayal, and would pay the price: execution or penal servitude in Siberia. The British and US governments, in any case, were eager to do whatever was necessary to get their men back, did not want to jeopardize impending Soviet help against Japan, and, at least in the mind of Roosevelt, looked toward a constructive post-hostilities relationship with Moscow.[143]

The US and British veterans of German stalags did eventually make passage home, but only after enduring a version of Soviet abandonment that left Harriman and Deane livid. Few traces remained by early spring 1945 of what had once passed for their confidence in the USSR.[144]

As a consequence of military operations against Germany, Russian power extended farther into Europe than at any time since Czar Alexander paraded his army through Paris at the end of the Napoleonic wars, a point refined upon by Stalin and Harriman in July 1945 at Potsdam.[145] Well before this conference, Harriman had gone along with FDR's hopefulness centered on the idea that Soviet forces would vacate European provinces after German defeat. Consistent with this thinking, he had told Churchill in October 1944, as the prime minister met with Stalin in Moscow, that Washington could not endorse the formula concocted by the two chieftains to divide the Balkans into Soviet and Anglo-US spheres (by which, according to first draft, the USSR would get 90 percent influence in Romania, 10 percent in Greece, 50 percent in Yugoslavia, 50 percent in Hungary, 75 percent in Bulgaria).[146] Harriman even allowed himself at the Yalta meetings to take seriously, at some psychological level impossible to pinpoint, the Declaration on Liberated Europe, whose text on national self-determination and free elections indicated the return of Soviet armies to eastern borders.

Harriman understood that FDR at Yalta was constrained. He could do little but extract promises from Stalin that he would respect promises to promote democracy and allow national self-determination in eastern Europe. If he chose, though, to define such language in ways contrary to Anglo-US understanding, FDR would have to acquiesce. His alternative seemed packed with risks: forfeiting Red Army contributions against Japan, losing Soviet diplomatic support for a solution to the German question, and jeopardizing international peacemaking machinery (the United Nations Organization). Harriman believed that Poland, in particular, was a lost cause. He regretted that FDR never publicly acknowledged, neither before nor after Yalta, that the Poles must adopt a policy inoffensive to Moscow. In the event, despite the cosmetic of cooperation with a few admissible London exiles and attempts by Harriman in talks with Molotov to ensure political diversity, the Lublin Poles established a new regime (recognized by Washington in July 1945) in the Soviet image. They did so on the bayonets of the Red Army and, with NKVD aid, proceeded to run the country according to Stalinist dictate. It mandated a communized buffer zone lodged between the USSR and Western menaces. The most outstanding of these in Kremlin imagination linked a revitalized Germany with Anglo-US power, for which evidence Stalin could cite UNTHINKABLE. This contingency plan, devised by London strategists in May-June 1945 at the behest of Churchill, was premised on the idea that British–American–German forces could launch a winning offensive to drive the Red Army from Poland.[147]

Whether Harriman learned of UNTHINKABLE at the time of its brief Whitehall vetting is unknown. He certainly did share Churchill's disgust at Soviet behavior in Red Army-occupied lands. There, as Embassy Moscow was reporting, people beholden to Stalin were installed in sensitive posts, the rape rate exploded, plundering rose, and innocents were arrested or made to disappear (Raoul Wallenberg in Budapest).[148] With due alarm in 1945, Harriman tried to prod Washington into adopting a firmer line toward the USSR. To the president (FDR, then Truman), Stimson, Forrestal, and influential journalists (including an unconvinced Walter Lippmann), Harriman argued thus: the Kremlin would establish exclusive writ wherever its military and police powers touched, allowing neither for the feeling of local peoples nor for the liberal preferences espoused by American and British statesmen.[149] A week before FDR's death (12 April 1945), he cabled Washington: "We must clearly recognize that the Soviet program is the establishment of totalitarianism, ending personal liberty and democracy as we know and respect it." In his first White House meeting with Truman, the ambassador recommended that measures be immediately devised against a "barbarian invasion" of the West.[150]

Yet at no time did Harriman embrace the assumptions underlying UNTHINKABLE. He argued that Soviet assertiveness could be checked by measures short of war, that the United States could play successfully upon a middle ground between appeasement

of the USSR and bellicosity. In sum, the USSR and its ideology constituted a challenge to the United States, but not an imminent threat;
that country was yet too poor, too weakened by the recent war to pose
a military danger to the Anglo-American world.[151]

Albeit gratified that Truman inclined toward a steelier attitude
toward Moscow than had FDR, Harriman was displeased by the new
president's verbal lashing of Molotov (23 April 1945). It famously
injured the cosseted commissar: "I have never been talked to like that
in my life."[152] Harriman helped persuade Truman to countermand his
order issued right after V-E Day that abruptly terminated Lend-Lease
aid to the USSR. Harriman later prevailed upon Truman to send
Hopkins to Moscow, where he tried hard (25 May-7 June 1945) but
unsuccessfully to fix the unraveling Soviet–US alliance. Over the longer
term, Harriman hoped that US grants and loans earmarked for Soviet
reconstruction projects would nudge Kremlin leaders in moderate foreign policy directions.[153]

Harriman spent his last months in Moscow, from which
he hoped to retire soon after V-J Day but had to stay past, trying
to maintain a modicum of Soviet–US cooperation. This entailed ceremonial duties of which some were delicate. On one occasion, in
mid-August, he dedicated a new hospital (stocked with US medical
equipment) in Smolensk. He intoned the wartime heroism of Smolensk's citizens. He spoke reverentially of the "friendship" between
Americans and Russians. He whispered not a word about his doubts
or the deepening controversies connected to nearby Katyn.[154] He was
comparably tactful on other, more immediate, matters. Crisply but
without rancor, he made plain to Stalin that Soviet forces could not
share occupation duties in Japan with General MacArthur's command
(notwithstanding the Red Army's rout in August of Japanese forces
in Manchukuo).[155] The Soviets finally conceded this point at the
December 1945 conference of Allied foreign ministers (Bevin, Byrnes,
Molotov) in Moscow. Harriman, meanwhile, tried to ensure a product-
ive meeting of these ministers via personal appeals (and consultation/
visit with Stalin at Sochi during one of his rare Black Sea holidays).[156]
Through no fault of Harriman's, though, the actual proceedings of the
Moscow confab did not close the widening gap between the Soviet
the Anglo-US blocs. Elections and representative governments, as con-
ceived by Bevin and Byrnes, were disallowed in Soviet-dominated
Balkan states.[157]

When Harriman left Moscow (January 1946), he was most impressed by two phenomena. First, Kremlin leaders were shaken by the incinerations of Hiroshima and Nagasaki, were nervous about US monopoly of the atomic bomb, and would try quickly to develop similar weaponry.[158] Second, he thought that Stalin's hold on power was not absolute; much of it seemed to have shifted toward the great man's lieutenants, specifically Molotov and Lavrenti Beria.[159] Should such men acquire majority control, they would adopt an even sterner policy toward the West. Harriman felt that Stalin, however enigmatic, was decidedly less inclined to take actions disruptive of ties with Washington. Three decades after his ambassadorship, Harriman admitted to a continuing ambivalence toward the Generalissimo, whom he characterized as a bundle of contradictions. He was not only a tyrant who had sent millions of his countrymen to violent death or incarceration. He also possessed rare intelligence. He could flash "human sensitivity." He was a shrewd war leader and diplomatic mastermind: "I must confess that for me Stalin remains the most inscrutable and contradictory character I have known – and leave the final judgment to history."[160]

***

Few celebrations in Allied cities after German surrender rivaled for enormity or feeling that held in Moscow on 9 May 1945. Nearly two million people descended upon Red Square, festooned with patriotic bunting and displaying German trophies.

Tens of thousands of revelers, not guided by party dictation but spontaneous and energized, milled beside the British and US embassies on Mokhovaya street and poured roars of approval upon the diplomatic and military staffs. A British general and several US officials were swept into a sea of well-wishers, who tossed them hands-over-heads ("like a cork on water," said Deane) from the chancellery steps to the crowd's distant reaches. In the absence of Harriman that day, Kennan addressed the demonstration: "Congratulations on the day of victory. All honor to the Soviet allies." Muscovites that evening were treated to a spectacular fireworks display.[161]

This euphoria, needless to elaborate, did not last. The war's cumulative sorrows were beyond the balms offered by party or state to console. Florid speeches, military bands/parades, cannonades, and newsreel depictions of Politburo grandees atop Lenin's mausoleum created a din in summer 1945. These could not restore to health the millions of people maimed or forever missing nor recompense the destitute and homeless. Against officialdom's blare, Akhmatova sought a quieter solitude to memorialize the numberless sufferers:

> And not with a glance, not with an allusion,
> Not with a reproach, not with a word,
> > But with a bow down to the ground
> > In a green field
> > Will I pray.[162]

The enthusiasm of US and Soviet soldiers who met on the Elbe river in late April, and the optimism of conferees from fifty countries who gathered (April–June) in San Francisco to ratify a constitution for the United Nations, also proved ephemeral. A different and flintier sort of international system was dawning, heralded in 1946 by Stalin's "two worlds" speech (9 February), Kennan's "long telegram" (22 February), and Churchill's "iron curtain" warning (5 March).[163]

London, Berlin, Tokyo, and Paris were no longer the cockpits of power. The emergent Washington–Moscow order swept all else to the margins. It was not – contra the Four Freedoms and Atlantic Charter – intended as a peace system, nor a justice system, and most assuredly not a mercy system.

The new order took root in the shambles of the interwar regime devised at Paris in 1919, just as that had supplanted the 1815 Vienna arrangement (with subsequent amendments) that had survived for a century. The postwar order, destined to last to 1989–1991 (demolition of the Berlin Wall, implosion of the USSR), would be defined by bipolarity, self-regulation, distinctive spheres of influence, and rival ideologies that buttressed political legitimacy in the respective blocs while fostering social and intellectual conformity therein. These properties allowed for a basic stability. Within it the major antagonists never came to direct blows, preferring instead that relative safety derived from proxy combat. Washington's and Moscow's monitoring, moreover, of the diplomatic–military equilibrium prevented its dissolution by ongoing threats: competition in the periphery (i.e. the "Third World"), propaganda struggle, arms races. The resultant proximate peace was, as with any power system, imperfect from the standpoint of idealists or people living in vulnerable zones (Eastern Europe, Korea, Southeast Asia). Yet this order, however pocked with brutality and alarms (1962 missile crisis), proved more resilient than the one born in 1919 and in certain respects was preferable to that of post-1991, with its peculiar scourges: rampant ethnic strife, religious fanaticisms, failed states, audacious terrorists, protracted neocolonial wars (Afghanistan, Iraq). The great powers spun a set of rules in the postwar era by which they usually abided. Lesser states occupied reasonably defined niches in political–economic blocs. Even the weakest – allowing for exceptions like Cuba or South Vietnam – were left with room for maneuver to play the main rivals against each other, reaping benefits from both, per the nonaligned movement's stratagem.[164]

Overall, the post-World War Two order was not without virtues: predictability, continuity, keeping a lid on tribalism (not least in the Balkans). Still, unhealed wounds from the Second World War lingered for decades. Some touched upon the performance of Embassy Moscow in 1939–1945, most outstandingly in connection with Katyn and the Shoah.

Not until 1990, during the twilight of Soviet power, did the Kremlin – in the person of Mikhail Gorbachev – admit responsibility for the Katyn executions. His admission, albeit aimed at advancing Soviet–Polish reconciliation, had the unintended effect of underscoring the embassy's willful gullibility in 1944. Harriman and his staff chose to accept a fabrication concocted to hide murder, doing so for reasons of expedient diplomacy but in defiance of truth.[165]

The FRANTIC enterprise involved bombing raids against oil refineries and I.G. Farben facilities in the Auschwitz districts. No action, though, was taken to strike the camp's gas chambers, crematoria, or feeder railways, despite their susceptibility to aerial assault. Neither Harriman nor Deane questioned the War Department's decision in summer 1944 that ruled out such attacks as "impracticable" and costly diversion from defeating the Axis. The idea evidently never occurred to the ambassador or general to make suggestions – along lines then being argued by Henry Morgenthau and Jewish/Christian activists – whose implementation would have hampered Auschwitz's operations.[166] Thus interacted sins of omission with narrow imagination, foreshadowed by Steinhardt to Breckinridge Long in 1941: exceptionable measures of rescue should not be undertaken for refugees, presumed unworthy until proven otherwise.

As for the emerging Cold War world, FDR's ambassadors in Moscow/Kuibyshev got an early taste. They disliked the surveillance of residences and offices, where excavations unearthed congeries of listening devices. Attempts at entrapment were usually clumsy. Crude insinuations, attaching even to such unlikely candidates as Kathleen Harriman, and intrusive police accompaniments were resented by the diplomats.[167] This apparatus of spying-intimidation was nothing new in the Russian political universe (uninvited attentions had irked Westerners before the Bolshevik revolution) but felt exceptionally galling at a moment when Soviets and Americans were joined in struggle against Germany. Kennan put the matter tartly to a Soviet acquaintance in July 1944:

> *We are supposed to be Allies, and you continue to treat us individually as spies ... Do you seriously believe that our Government would give you this tremendous support [Lend-Lease] and then instruct its diplomats to engage in all sorts of dirty little intrigues? ... You can continue to act on the theory that the world is your enemy. You can continue to send out one generation after another of embittered and insulted diplomats from your little college of diplomacy. But you must be prepared to accept the results of this policy, to accept the repercussions of the resentment and sense of grievance which it inevitably spreads.[168]*

Of FDR's wartime ambassadors to the USSR, Standley departed the most incensed. His ire festered for years. He advised President Eisenhower in 1957 to end diplomatic and other ties with Moscow. Standley had earlier lent himself to rightwing causes in California. He alleged in 1948 that communists exercised a baleful influence on the public school curriculum taught in his city of retirement, San Diego. He contended that Truman's administration was leading Americans toward twin disasters: socialism and dictatorship. He seems even to have entertained the idea that FDR was of Jewish ancestry, which supposed fact accounted for the communist–Jewish–internationalist drift in postwar U.S. life.[169] Steinhardt, by contrast, was never so dispirited, mainly because he never expected much in the first place. Not from a European world intent on exterminating warfare. Not from self-styled Soviet revolutionaries whose purported concern for the wretched of the earth veiled homicidal compulsions. Not from the Kremlin's masters to whom diplomatic niceties were anathema: "They have absolutely no standards of ethics or conduct, excepting a hatred for all foreigners, particularly diplomats."[170] As if to corroborate, Stalin once said in jest but revealingly all the same: "Bring the machine guns. Let's liquidate the diplomats."[171]

Harriman allowed himself less indignation than his two predecessors, doing so for overarching reasons in line with Roosevelt–Hopkins thinking: Soviet participation in the war against Japan was wanted at the earliest moment possible, a view not revised until summer 1945 as Tokyo's surrender became imminent. Harriman also enjoyed greater entrée to Soviet leaders than did Steinhardt or Standley. It permitted him occasional confidences from Stalin. The most candid of these was that the Soviet peoples were steeped still in traditional religious–nationalist outlook. Looking askance at scientific materialism, they fought Hitler to preserve their ancient birthright, not for any version of Kremlin–Marxist comradeship: "for their homeland, not for us."[172]

Harriman drew heavily on his Soviet experience in the decades after World War Two, when he served as foreign policy advisor to Presidents Truman, Kennedy, and Johnson (as well as championing Democratic party causes, governing New York for a term, bidding for the 1952 and 1956 presidential nominations). Harriman never thought that the Cold War would necessarily conclude in nuclear exchanges. He retained the diplomat's faith that a way could be wended between the choices of total war versus abject retreat. Above all, he felt that the USSR, where the disasters of war were unforgotten, would go to considerable lengths to avoid confrontation with the militarily superior United States. The ambassador, who died only a few years before the USSR dissolved, pleaded for recognition of shared humanity, tested but not obviated in the twentieth-century experience. Akhmatova could not have improved upon the aged diplomat when he said plaintively in 1976: "The Soviet leaders also want peace with the United States ... They, too, have children, grandchildren, and great-grandchildren whom they love as much as we love ours."[173]

8 CONCLUSIONS: US DIPLOMACY AND WAR

Roosevelt left behind a sparse paper trail, discouraging to biographers and diplomatic historians alike. No private diary or self-revealing letters written during his presidential years reside in the public domain, a result being that the mind and intentions of FDR remain hazy. Consequently, one is obliged to judge the quality of his statecraft by reference – at least in part – to the people that he appointed to high office, not only cabinet secretaries but also ambassadors assigned to key capitals.[1]

From instinct rather than ratiocination, Roosevelt divined that statesmen do not make history. It is a given, like the sea, in which deep currents run: inconstant *fortuna*, unpredictable scientific innovation, blind economic forces, competitions of power oblivious to finer feeling. These lines by Henry Wadsworth Longfellow were among FDR's favorites (sent to Churchill during a dire moment for Great Britain, January 1941):

> Sail on, O ship of State!
> Sail on, O Union, strong and great!
> Humanity with all its fears,
> With all the hopes of future years,
> Is hanging breathless on thy fate![2]

The purpose of statecraft, Roosevelt gleaned, is to navigate one's nation through thickets of hazard, visible and hidden, as they thrust forward. To avoid mishap, diplomacy must be guided by the true north of prudence.

Ambassadors

Roosevelt's piloting of the ship of US state, as viewed from the angle of ambassadorial experience during the crisis years, was riddled with defects. His foreign policy mind emerges as contradictory and uneven, his reliance on personality over process and routine a pronounced trait, his supposedly forceful vision of the postwar world (modified Wilsonianism) an illusion.

Too often the president was insufficiently attentive to representatives abroad. Had he been more alert to Grew's advice, for instance, FDR might have mustered the imagination and means to avert war with Japan, thereby allowing a less distracted United States to confront Germany head on. Better support of Dodd in Berlin was surely warranted, especially in view of White House encouragement given to lesser lights, such as Long in Rome or Hurley in Chongqing. At other times, FDR was excessively casual, hence his appointment to London of Kennedy – his retention in office past expiry explicable only by reference to Roosevelt's felt need to keep a potential troublemaker abroad. On other occasions, FDR sent too-conciliatory fixers to clear alleged messes created by previous envoys. Such was the case with the dispatching of Wilson to Berlin after Dodd, a stout democratic evangelist who had tried to spread light into the gathering Nazi dusk. So, too, with Hurley's blundering into China to rescue Chiang and Sino-US relations from what was, in fact, a satisfactory Stillwell–Gauss duo. Other blots in the president's log include a readiness at one time or another to have presumptive allies (Chiang, de Gaulle) ousted by local Americans, and to accept uncritically the findings and recommendations of diplomatic missions (in France most jarringly) against deserving people trying to reach US haven. In this last instance, FDR lent his prestige and office too easily to nativist views and prejudice (in tandem with his authorizing the internment of citizens of Japanese origin).[3]

Serious as the foregoing charges are, they do not constitute an unanswerable indictment. Roosevelt understood more than he knew. He possessed an ineluctable quickness – comprising parts intellect, feeling, and shrewdness. One might reasonably call this quality of mind "intuition," were the term not so laden with connotations of pop-psychology. In any case, FDR's better judgment periodically surfaced in his handling of ambassadors and circumstances. When Berlin officialdom proved reprehensible – Kristallnacht – FDR pulled Wilson but left in country an embassy staff adequate to conduct bilateral business, such as it was, and, after 1 September 1939, to monitor developments in wartime Germany. In the wake of the Kennedy fiasco, the appointment of Winant, whose inner torments were contained for however long he operated in the harness of public duty, was a masterstroke that helped stabilize Anglo-US relations. Equally compelling, the posting of Harriman to Moscow, after Standley's elephantine clumsiness, fostered equilibrium and some confidence in the Allied partnership, hitherto in short ration.

According to Eleanor Roosevelt, empathy for people victimized by medical disabilities played a part in shaping her husband's political orientation, realized in New Deal programs to help disadvantaged citizens.[4] Perhaps so. Less open to quibble is the connection – and payoff – between FDR's brave medical struggles and the sealing of the 1942 Darlan bargain. In genuine sympathy for a fellow polio sufferer, and with encouragement from Leahy (at the time recently returned from Vichy), FDR suggested that Admiral Darlan's son, Alain, enjoy safe passage from Algiers and receive treatment at Warm Springs.

12 FDR and Admiral Claude Bloch aboard the USS *Houston*.

This gesture, albeit not decisive, further shifted Darlan senior away from resistance to TORCH.[5] The son, who secretly supported the Allied cause, was ensconced at Warm Springs when his father was assassinated on Christmas Eve 1942.

A survey of the ambassadorial crew that FDR chose confirms the following. The diplomatic service was not a mature meritocracy, despite the introduction of earlier reforms to advance professionalism over dilettantism. Social–ethnic–religious homogeneity, commonality of aesthetic–recreational preference, and an aristocratic ethos featured plainly in the appointments made by Roosevelt. None of these properties was fatal to the creating of an efficacious diplomatic corps, but in combination these tended to reinforce a sameness of mind and imagination, captured in Hugh Wilson's cloying characterization of the Foreign Service (which numbered fewer than nine hundred officers by the end of 1945): a "pretty good club."[6]

The president's envoys were white and typically from the country's eastern third. Born after the Civil War but before turn-of-the-century, they basked in the afterglow of successful reunion and were little bothered, except Winant, by the Jim Crow marring of national landscape. They were overwhelmingly Protestant, primarily Episcopalian, and politically mainstream. They tolerated Catholics (barely), preferred not to mix with Jews socially or to inquire closely into instances of intermarriage, and tended to doubt the mental competence and patriotism of Americans whose origins resided outside of northwestern Europe. Such people were to be patiently endured, their future assimilation – though not a foregone outcome – devoutly to be wished. A majority of the ambassadors possessed independent means and were educated at boarding schools (St. Paul's, Groton) and Ivy League universities. In sum, they belonged to the president's own milieu; they came from the same social and philosophical cloth as their ambassadorial predecessors.[7] Grew and Phillips might have stepped out of John Singer Sargent portraiture, or, in a Henry James novel, been sent abroad on private rescue errands. Nothing prepared such people for the age of blistering locomotion, flashing steel, belching petroleum, industrialized murder, mass mobilization, or state idolatry. Nazi and Soviet totalitarianism, plus related political malignancy, did not overwhelm this diplomatic cadre, however. Most of them coped.

Exceptions to the above profile disclose the limits of Roosevelt's broadmindedness. None of the ambassadors strayed any further to the left than Winant, whose New Hampshire program paralleled Roosevelt's own New Deal experiments to revive faltering capitalism. The extreme conservatism, bordering on reactionary mindedness, of Hurley and Standley budded only after Roosevelt had used them. Leahy's hard-right cast of mind was apparent at the time of ambassadorial office, but being compatible with the goal of wooing Vichy was lightly borne by FDR – in which case, Varian Fry and Hiram Bingham belonged to the category of expendables. Regarding obvious social outliers, Dodd's deviation from diplomatic norms and preferred background made him less than club-bable and invited ridicule. Gauss suffered a similar liability, Johnson less so owing to his effervescence. Kennedy and Bullitt occupied intermediate points between the opposite poles of Grew–Phillips and Dodd–Gauss. The Boston Irishman and the restless Philadelphian belonged to identifi-able types that FDR could stand, at least for a time. The former had a streak of cockiness and raw ambition straight out of F. Scott Fitzgerald's *The Great Gatsby*. Bullitt, whose acquaintance with Ernest Hemingway dated to 1920s Paris, could have been cast in cameo in that writer's *A Movable Feast*.[8] As for the Roman Catholicism of Caffery, it was not disapproved insofar as he dealt with the observant de Gaulle and a country, at the time, still more than nominally Catholic. Inciden-tally, Ambassador Carlton Hayes, another Catholic convert, was posted (1942–1945) to Madrid, the calculation being that his denominational affiliation reassured Franco, thus enhancing Washington's chance to dissuade Spain from joining Axis arms against the English-speaking powers (a matter of paramount concern at the time of TORCH, when Spanish forces in Morocco or near Gibraltar could have hindered the North African expedition).[9]

All of FDR's envoys were men, a condition consonant with conventional wisdom of the day; women were unsuited to international tasks. Willard Beaulac, FDR's ambassador to Paraguay, put the case succinctly: "Some jobs are too rough for women."[10] This view, how-ever prevalent, did not always tally with other perceptions or appreci-ation. Constance Harvey was a case in point. One of the original six women to enter (1930) the career Foreign Service, she was a vice consul in Lyon in 1942 and subsequently taken into custody with colleagues. The War Department awarded Harvey its Medal of Freedom for her intelligence gathering in 1941–1942 and liaison with underground activists, duties performed under the gaze of Gestapo agents and col-laborating French policemen.[11]

Despite extensive conformity in FDR's diplomatic corps, the intellectual–political tone of embassies could shift over time, depending on the man in charge – illustrated when Wilson followed Dodd, Hurley followed Johnson/Gauss, S. Pinkney Tuck succeeded Leahy, Winant replaced Kennedy, and Harriman took over after Steinhardt/Standley. Parenthetically, in this same vein: Claude Bowers in Spain, 1933–1939, strongly backed the republican cause and argued for US measures barely shy of combat during the civil war. By contrast, his successors, Alexander Weddell (1939–1942) and Hayes, put the emphasis elsewhere – on forbearance toward, and working relations with, the Franco regime, thereby countering Berlin's tug.[12] Apart from changes related to turnover in ambassadorial administration and White House tacking, there were instances of divergence in outlook across embassies. Grew differed from Johnson over policy toward the 1937 Sino-Japanese war and Dodd opposed Bullitt (during pre-Munich days) on how best to treat with Hitler. So, too, incidentally, Steinhardt in Turkey cooperated closely with the rescue work of the War Refugee Board versus Hayes who was wary of, and kept distance from, that organization.[13]

One might prefer to think that such diversity as existed in embassies over time and across locations was harmonized in the master charts and navigational skills lodged in the Oval Office. This, though, was not always true. Roosevelt, confident that things would somehow come ultimately right, frequently let matters drift, rather than set a clear course, and played for time rather than take the initiative. His was not a dynamic conception of US interests. Consequently, FDR's ambassadors enjoyed significant margins of leeway compared with the bulk of their successors, whose range of independent action has been additionally circumscribed by advances in communication/transportation undreamt in 1933–1945.

The record of FDR's ambassadors was spotty, judged by the standard they set for themselves and from the long-term perspective. Grew was anguished by his failure to prevent Japanese–US hostilities. But by his striving, he left an indelible example of diplomacy – art devoted to the peaceful resolution of outstanding problems, war only out of necessity. Dodd's hopes of cultivating common ground between the United States and Germany were not only dashed by the nature of Nazi rule. Also the ambassador's warnings went unheard or (worse) were rejected in Washington. Dodd's perspicacity and condemnation of iniquity continue, though, to stand as an inspired example. This in contrast with Hugh Wilson. That he could not sustain German–US relations was perfectly understandable. Less forgivable, he downplayed the malice and military dangers emanating from Nazi Berlin. Long and Phillips in Rome, unable to prevent or delay Italy's slide toward Germany, were neither brilliant nor notably ineffective, just middling. Yet in the case of Long, softness for Mussolini's regime assumes a sinister aspect, anticipating as it were his obduracy in supervising (1940–1944) State Department refugee policy.

Johnson and Gauss succeeded in keeping China as a going concern and then a US partner, even as that country suffered resounding blows and teetered on the brink of civil convulsion. Both men were able, their measure being the contrasting havoc wreaked by Hurley. Among his serious misdemeanors must be counted the denial to later Washington counsel of capable students of Chinese politics, among whom John Paton Davies and John Service.

Of the original and powerful anti-Axis states, only France lost significant territory to all three enemies: Germany, Italy, Japan. Only France, at one time or another, employed forces (regular) against the US, UK, and (volunteer) against the USSR. Viewed from this perspective, Bullitt's early reassurances to FDR regarding French military prowess were misplaced, just as Leahy's later estimation of Petain's merits was exaggerated. Not until Tuck reversed Leahy's policy of ignoring Vichy's human rights violations and Caffery set about to revitalize the post-occupation economy were decency and realism restored to Washington's French policy.

FDR's representation in London went from lightweight, in the case of Kennedy, whose vertiginous fall from grace has few competitors in Anglo-US history, to steady, in the person of Winant. The latter helped give meaning to the expression "special relationship," which threatened to dissolve into cliché or otherwise embarrass its principal publicist, Churchill. "Special relationship" gave cover to his instructing US colleagues, ostensibly untutored in the intricacies of power politics, on the purposes of warfare/diplomacy and allowed him dignity while the balance of world advantages slipped to the United States. Winant eased this transition by drawing the sting from British resentments, deeply stirred in June 1940–November 1941 when Americans abstained from full commitment to UK security, then exacerbated by Rooseveltian lecturing on the obsolescence of London's imperial prerogatives and decolonization's inexorableness.

The ambassadorships of Steinhardt and Standley reflected the unsettled place of the USSR in Washington's calculations. To many Americans, the Soviet regime – atheistic, despotic, collectivist – was no less despicable than Hitler's and, from August 1939 to June 1941, joined in criminal collusion with Germany. Harriman's achievement was not only his helping to salvage the fraught Soviet–US connection, but also imparting to it esprit that was crucial to Western purposes. These would not have been realized had Stalin withdrawn from the war against Germany ("separate peace"), certainly resulting in soaring Western military costs, then likely followed by sullen stalemate (until, perhaps, broken by the use of atomic weapons). Better than most of FDR's ambassadors, Harriman understood too that the job of wartime diplomats is not only to help win the war, but also to conceptualize the political meaning of violence and, as victory nears, to prepare their government for the post-hostilities era.

Regarding the ancient debate on whether career Foreign Service officers make better envoys than people drawn from other backgrounds, the evidence adduced from FDR's diplomats is inconclusive. Representing the first group were these commendable people: Grew, Johnson, Gauss. Comparably sound were these ambassadors taken from outside the Foreign Service: Dodd, Winant, Harriman. Other acceptable diplomats, if less distinguished, came equally from within and without the Foreign Service: Wilson, Phillips, Caffery versus Bullitt, Leahy, Steinhardt, Standley. All of which seems to support FDR's evaluation of his emissaries, irrespective of whether they were career officers: "I have had about as much luck with one set as with the other."[14] Still, worth pondering, the most egregious came from outside the established service: Long, Hurley, Kennedy.

The career ambassadors were no less susceptible to *déformation professionnelle* or excessive sympathy for the country of their mission than colleagues recruited from other vocations. Nobody from either group lost sight of his commission, to serve US interests as formulated in Washington, although the non-career men were more inclined to question or prod superiors. In this matter, one does not find among the Foreign Service ambassadors the outspokenness of Dodd, Long, Hurley, Bullitt, Kennedy. Difficulties in maintaining embassy order and retaining the loyalty of subordinates also afflicted non-career envoys more often than Foreign Service ambassadors. Dodd, Hurley, and Kennedy nearly provoked mutiny in their respective embassies. Such disarray was not helped in the Dodd and Kennedy cases by disquiet in the ranks over ambassadorial domestic life. George Messersmith, unlike most people in Dodd's embassy, was sympathetic to the professor, but could not abide his daughter's amorous adventures and thought them deleterious to the embassy's functioning. The military attaché in London, Raymond Lee, labeled Kennedy's oldest son and namesake a "smart aleck," putative reflection of the senior man's deficiency of character.[15] Harriman's daughter, Kathleen, by contrast, was perceived as a paragon of those qualities attaching to a well-ordered embassy – one that enjoyed particular White House favor and, concomitantly, exerted influence beyond missions headed by professional officers.

Legacy of war

Perhaps the long arc of the universe bends toward justice, mercy, and decency.[16] One cannot know but only hope. What is indisputably true, as post-1945 history shows, is that the repertoire of human depravity was not exhausted in the events – twisting from 1937 Nanjing to 1945 Nagasaki – that collectively compose the Second World War. Yet its scale of infernality remains singular while the legacy of unrestrained violence lingers still.

As both Nanjing and Nagasaki attest, the Second World War was replete with military actions that did not discriminate between legitimate and illegitimate targets, between combatant and noncombatant. Shadowy groups, like the one that struck on 11 September 2001, undertake operations that are conceptually similar to, maybe in a sense inspired by, the Axis and Allied terror-bombing campaigns. The idea in each case was to inflict maximum harm without reference to the traditional laws or norms of armed conflict, whose intended effect, as designed over generations, has been to ameliorate wartime suffering and underpin minimal standards of civilized conduct.[17] More telling still, one by one, the principal victors of World War II – USA, USSR, UK (France and China too) – not only developed weapons of mass destruction. These states also refined doctrines, exemplified by Mutually Assured Destruction (aptly MAD), and justifications pioneered in 1937–1945, premised on the idea that total conflict disallowed those moral–legal distinctions once upheld by statesmen and soldiers. In this context even the vile euphemism, "collateral damage," lost its purported analytical usefulness.

Post-1945 wars have also retained this property. War is an occasion for national leaders to discourse upon high politics and supposedly categorical causes, but to overlook or trivialize its essence: namely, war produces – above all else – vast fields of medical trauma and medical emergency. In August 1945, nurse Hashimoto of Nagasaki (that city previously associated in the popular Western mind with Puccini's *Madama Butterfly*) "was shocked to see naked bodies lying everywhere among the big and small trees that had been torn up by their roots … No one even groaned. It really was the world of the dead." She recognized the place, as medical practitioners everywhere and at all wartimes have done: "This is hell!"[18]

The metaphysical correspondence between the history of 1937–1945 and events since may be more sinuous than is the case with weapons, strategies, and the concrete experience of casualties. Still, irrespective of whether Europeans, Japanese or Chinese have been fully aware of it, their existential problem (plus that of Americans whose "good war" ended in the moral ambiguity of atomic weaponry) has centered on the difficulty of restoring affirmative purpose after enduring and inflicting varieties of inhumanity. Perhaps the beginning of political wisdom in Europe has been to understand that one can as easily be the victimizer as the victim, the guard at Auschwitz as well as the inmate.[19] In East Asia and the Pacific, the museums and memorials – in Nanjing, Pearl Harbor, Hiroshima – remind visitors of the consequences of failed diplomacy, mocking, even as they uphold, competing claims of righteousness.

The contributions made to the resolution of world crises by Grew, Dodd, Winant, Harriman, and other US diplomats will long be matters of contention. In this respect, professional historians and laity alike can profit from Churchill's reminder (uttered in November 1940 on the occasion of Neville Chamberlain's death): "In one phase men seem to have been right, in another they seem to have been wrong. Then again, a few years later, when the perspective of time has lengthened, all stands in a different setting. There is a new proportion. There is another scale of values."[20] Yet one can, while aware of the exacting tests of time and changing moods of interpretation, safely say the following: FDR's ambassadors opposed the promiscuous use of force and in that, plus other ways, were less ethically compromised than their Axis (especially German) counterparts, so enthralled to gothic conceptions of power. At the same time, the Americans – as a group – were fluent in the language of power. In this, they were on a par with Anglo-French practitioners, albeit less well drilled than they in diplomatic customs and culture. As political reporters, the Americans also enjoyed an advantage over Soviet envoys, who labored fearful of censorious Stalinist authority.[21]

Like ambassadors always and everywhere, Roosevelt's operated upon the swiftly changing surface of current events without the time or detachment of later scrutinizing generations to judge. Neither the Shoah nor the dreadfulness of atomic weaponry occupied a place in the diplomatic mind, or that of FDR, remotely comparable in prominence to latter-day observers. Only in faint outline did Dodd discern the looming genocide, most of his colleagues not at all (making all the more striking his warnings and the effort of a handful of other people to protect endangered lives). Before its use, Leahy, while Roosevelt's chair of the joint chiefs, registered doubt about the atomic bomb's feasibility. After Hiroshima and Nagasaki, he expressed revulsion for the waging of atomic war on civilian populations.[22] Years earlier, Grew – to whom diplomatic theory was housed in flesh-and-blood human beings, not abstruse treatises – had sought to prevent strife in the Pacific. But even he could not have foreseen the magnitude of impending tragedy, in which case Churchill's words again apply: "It is not given to human beings, happily for them, for otherwise life would be intolerable, to foresee or to predict to any large extent the unfolding course of events."[23]

The generic ambassador, helping the captain to navigate the ship of state and keep it afloat, must know that the sea upon which it rides is of obscure origin, the ultimate destination indistinct, and safe haven only a respite from cascading perils. Even so, statecraft and diplomacy are their own reward, the safeguarding of citizens entrusted to their care the sole raison d'être. The alternative is to allow upon one's own the gods of carnage and the accumulation of inconsolable sorrows.

NOTES

Introduction

1 See, for example, Igor Lukes, *On the Edge of the Cold War: American Diplomats and Spies in Postwar Prague* (Oxford University Press, 2012), Christopher Baxter and Andrew Stewart, eds., *Diplomats at War: British and Commonwealth Diplomacy in Wartime* (Leiden: Martinus Nijhoff Publishers, 2008), and J. Simon Rofe and Andrew Stewart, eds., *Diplomats at War: The American Experience* (Leiden: Martinus Nijhoff Publishers, forthcoming).

2 Frank Freidel, *Franklin D. Roosevelt: A Rendezvous with Destiny* (Boston: Little, Brown and Company, 1990), p. 108.

3 J. Simon Rofe, *Franklin Roosevelt's Foreign Policy and the Welles Mission* (New York: Palgrave Macmillan, 2007), p. 20. FDR would doubtless have endorsed this judgment of President Theodore Roosevelt, who declared: "The trouble with our ambassadors in stations of real importance is that they totally fail to give us real help and real information, and seem to think that the life-work of an ambassador is a kind of glorified pink tea-party." Cited in M. A. Dewolfe Howe, *George von Lengerke Meyer: His Life and Public Services* (New York: Dodd, Mead and Company, 1919), p. 111.

4 Cordell Hull, *The Memoirs of Cordell Hull* (New York: Macmillan Company, 1948), vol. II, pp. 1229–1230; Irwin Gellman, *Secret Affairs: Franklin Roosevelt, Cordell Hull, and Sumner Welles* (Johns Hopkins University Press, 1995), pp. 392–393.

5 On the diverse and conflicting centers of US wartime policy, see Jonathan Utley, *Going to War with Japan 1937–1941* (University of Tennessee Press, 1985).

6 William Faulkner, *Requiem for a Nun* (New York: Random House, 1951), p. 92. The lines are spoken by the defense lawyer, Gavin Stevens.

7 Henry Stimson and McGeorge Bundy. *On Active Service in Peace and War* (New York: Harper and Brothers, 1947), p. 633.

8 Robert Jackson, *Classical and Modern Thought on International Relations: From Anarchy to Cosmopolis* (New York: Palgrave Macmillan, 2005), p. 57.

Chapter 1: Rising Sun

1 Janis Mimuara, *Planning for Empire: Reform Bureaucrats and the Japanese Wartime State* (Cornell University Press, 2011), pp. 186–189.

2 *FRUS: Japan, 1931–1941*, vol. II, p. 125.

3 Ibid., p. 93.

4 Ibid., p. 127; *FRUS: Japan, 1931–1941*, vol. I, p. 478; Norman Graebner, "Hoover, Roosevelt, and the Japanese," in Dorothy Borg and Shumpei Okamoto, eds., *Pearl Harbor as History: Japanese–American Relations 1931–1941* (Columbia University Press, 1973), p. 41.

5 *FRUS: Japan, 1931–1941*, vol. II, p. 127.

6 Franklin Roosevelt, "Quarantine Address," in Daniel Boorstin, ed., *An American Primer* (University of Chicago Press, 1966), p. 851.

7 For a Washington assessment of the difficulties faced by US exports/investments in Japanese-dominated Manchukuo, see Hornbeck to Joseph Grew, 17 February 1939, Box 186, Stanley Hornbeck Papers. Hornbeck wrote:

> Japanese control of Manchuria has resulted in the expulsion of virtually all foreign, including American, commercial and industrial enterprises, other than Japanese, from that area. Within the last two years, and especially toward the end of 1937, the legislation enacted by "Manchukuo" establishing exchange and trade control, has been and is clearly discriminatory against all foreign trade and enterprises, except Japanese, in Manchuria.

8 FDR to Joseph Grew, 30 November 1939, Box 43, President's Secretary's File, Franklin Roosevelt Papers.

9 Joseph Grew, *Ten Years in Japan* (New York: Simon and Schuster, 1944), p. x.

10 Waldo Heinrichs, *American Ambassador: Joseph C. Grew and the Development of the United States Diplomatic Tradition* (Oxford University Press, 1966), p. 5.

11 Joseph Grew, *Turbulent Era: A Diplomatic Record of Forty Years 1904–1945*, 2 vols. (London: Hammond, Hammond and Company, 1953), vol. I, p. 12.

12 Heinrichs, *American Ambassador*, pp. 48, 158.

13 Warren Frederick Ilchman. *Professional Diplomacy in the United States 1779–1939* (University of Chicago Press, 1961), p. 224.

14 The Foreign Service was a family affair for Grew. Three of his daughters married Foreign Service officers. His Lilla Cabot Grew was wedded in 1927 to

Jay Pierrepont Moffat, minister to wartime Canada from June 1940 until his death in January 1943.

15 Heinrichs, *American Ambassador*, p. viii.

16 Ibid., p. 109; Arthur Waldron, ed., *How the Peace Was Lost: The 1935 Memorandum: Developments Affecting American Policy in the Far East Prepared for the State Department by John Van Antwerp MacMurray* (Stanford: Hoover Institution Press, 1992), pp. 22, 33.

17 Edward Bennett, "Joseph C. Grew: The Diplomacy of Pacification," in Richard Burns and Edward Bennett, eds., *Diplomats in Crisis: United States–Chinese–Japanese Relations, 1919–1941* (Santa Barbara: ABC-CLIO, 1974), p. 68.

18 Ibid., p. 66; Grew, *Turbulent Era*, vol. I, p. 9; Commodore Matthew Perry was a great-grand-uncle of Alice Grew. She was descended from Oliver Hazard Perry who achieved naval renown in the 1812 War. Benjamin Franklin was another of her famous ancestors.

19 Eugene Dooman Interview, Occupation of Japan Project, Oral History Research Office, Columbia University, 1970, p. 64; Eugene Dooman to Herbert Feis, 8 July 1949, Box 1, Eugene Dooman Papers; Grew, *Ten Years in Japan*, p. xii.

20 Charles Bohlen, *Witness to History 1929–1969* (New York: W. W. Norton and Company, 1973), pp. 106, 108; T. Michael Ruddy, *The Cautious Diplomat: Charles E. Bohlen and the Soviet Union, 1929–1969* (Kent State University Press, 1986), p. 15; John Emmerson, *The Japanese Thread: A Life in the U.S. Foreign Service* (New York: Holt, Rinehart, and Winston, 1978), p. 28.

21 Grew, *Ten Years in Japan*, p. x; Grew, *Turbulent Era*, vol. II, pp. 1267–1268.

22 Heinrichs, *American Ambassador*, pp. 25, 188, 291–292; Grew, *Ten Years in Japan*, p. 262.

23 Joseph Grew to FDR, 21 December 1939 and excerpt from Grew's diary, p. 4142, Box 204, Official File, Franklin Roosevelt Papers; Robert Butow, *Tojo and the Coming of the War* (Princeton University Press, 1961), pp. 79–80.

24 *FRUS: Japan, 1931–1941*, vol. II, p. 565; Joseph Grew, *Report from Tokyo* (New York: Simon and Schuster, 1942), p. xi; Grew, *Ten Years in Japan*, p. 322.

25 Matsukata Otohiko to FDR, nd February 1934, p. 6, Box 43, President's Secretary's File, Franklin Roosevelt Papers.

26 Heinrichs, *American Ambassador*, pp. 195, 210; Grew, *Ten Years In Japan*, p. 320.

27 Grew, *Ten Years in Japan*, pp. 204, 330.

28 Ibid., p. 144.

29 *FRUS: Japan, 1931–1941*, vol. I, p. 316.

30 Grew, *Ten Years in Japan*, pp. 207–208.

31 Ibid., p. 279.

32 Robert Craigie, *Behind the Japanese Mask* (London: Hutchinson and Company, 1946), pp. 99, 136; Herbert von Dirksen, *Moscow, Tokyo, London:*

Twenty Years of German Foreign Policy (University of Oklahoma Press, 1952), pp. 144, 166–167; Grew, *Ten Years in Japan*, pp. 107–108, 512.

33 Joseph Grew to FDR, 16 January 1940, Box 204, Official File, Franklin Roosevelt Papers; Joseph Grew to Dear Frank, 22 September 22, 1941, Box 43, President's Secretary's File, Franklin Roosevelt Papers; Grew, *Turbulent Era*, vol. II, p. 975. Also see Walter LaFeber, *The Clash: A History of U.S.–Japan Relations* (New York: W. W. Norton and Company, 1997), p. 205.

34 Jonathan Utley, *Going to War with Japan 1937–1941* (University of Tennessee Press, 1985), p. 22.

35 Grew, *Ten Years in Japan*, p. 207.

36 Ibid., p. 171.

37 Heinrichs, *American Ambassador*, p. 348; Butow, *Tojo and the Coming of the War*, p. 129.

38 Heinrichs, *American Ambassador*, pp. 241–242.

39 Akira Iriye, *The Origins of the Second World War in Asia and the Pacific* (London: Longman, 1987), p. 88.

40 Akira Iriye, *Across the Pacific: An Inner History of American–East Asian Relations* (New York: Harcourt, Brace, and World, 1967), pp. 181–182; Justus Doenecke, ed., *The Diplomacy of Frustration: The Manchurian Crisis of 1931–1933 as Revealed in the Papers of Stanley K. Hornbeck* (Stanford: Hoover Institution Press, 1981), p. 30; Heinrichs, *American Ambassador*, p. 267.

41 Emmerson, *The Japanese Thread*, p. 78. Also see Bennett, "Joseph C. Grew: The Diplomacy of Pacification," in Burns and Bennett, *Diplomats in Crisis*, pp. 76–77.

42 Grew, *Ten Years in Japan*, p. 216; Utley, *Going to War with Japan 1937–1941*, p. 13.

43 *FRUS: Japan, 1931–1941*, vol. I, p. 514.

44 Dorothy Borg, *The United States and the Far Eastern Crisis of 1933–1938* (Harvard University Press, 1964), p. 332; Grew, *Ten Years in Japan*, p. 217.

45 Heinrichs, *American Ambassador*, pp. 254, 256; *FRUS: Japan, 1931–1941*, vol. I, pp. 517–519.

46 Heinrichs, *American Ambassador*, pp. 256, 258; Akira Iriye, "The Role of the United States Embassy in Tokyo," in Borg and Okamoto, *Pearl Harbor as History*, pp. 119–120.

47 Grew, *Ten Years in Japan*, 249. Also see *FRUS: Japan, 1931–1941*, vol. I, pp. 494–495.

48 Heinrichs, *American Ambassador*, pp. 290–291.

49 *FRUS: Japan, 1931–1941*, vol. II, p. 22.

50 Ibid., p. 27.

51 Ibid., p. 29.

52 Heinrichs, *American Ambassador*, pp. 294–295; Emmerson, *The Japanese Thread*, pp. 81–82, Grew, *Ten Years in Japan*, pp. 297–298.

53 Joseph Grew to FDR, 6 November 1939, Box 43, President's Secretary's File, Franklin Roosevelt Papers.

54 Emmerson, *The Japanese Thread*, p. 86.

55 Grew, *Ten Years in Japan*, p. 335; Ian Kershaw, *Fateful Choices: Ten Decisions that Changed the World, 1940–1941* (New York: Penguin Press, 2007), pp. 118–119.

56 Grew in Tokyo had written to FDR in autumn 1939: "If we declare an embargo against Japan which can be interpreted here as an economic sanction, we must expect to see American–Japanese relations go steadily downhill thereafter." Joseph Grew to FDR, 30 November 1939, Box 43, President's Secretary's File, Franklin Roosevelt Papers.

57 Grew, *Turbulent Era*, vol. II, pp. 1224–1229.

58 Emmerson, *The Japanese Thread*, p. 90; Grew, *Ten Years in Japan*, p. 334.

59 Joseph Grew to FDR, 14 December 1940 in George Waller, ed., *Pearl Harbor: Roosevelt and the Coming of the War* (Lexington, Mass.: D.C. Heath and Company, 1976), p. 33.

60 Tripartite Pact, 27 September 1940 in J. A. S. Grenville, *The Major International Treaties 1914–1971* (London: Methuen and Company, 1974), pp. 202–203.

61 Grew, *Ten Years in Japan*, p. 333.

62 *FRUS: Japan, 1931–1941*, vol. II, p. 170.

63 On Japanese war aims, specifically those sought by Tojo Hideki, see Gerhard Weinberg, *Visions of Victory: The Hopes of Eight World War II Leaders* (Cambridge University Press, 2005), pp. 59–75.

64 David Lu, *From the Marco Polo Bridge to Pearl Harbor: Japan's Entry into World War II* (Washington: Public Affairs Press, 1961), p. 174.

65 Waldo Heinrichs, *Threshold of War: Franklin D. Roosevelt and American Entry into World War II* (Oxford University Press, 1988), pp. 35, 141.

66 Nobutaka Ike, ed. *Japan's Decision for War: Records of the 1941 Policy Conferences* (Stanford University Press, 1967), p. 246; Grew, *Turbulent Era: A Diplomatic Record of Forty Years*, vol. II, pp. 1272–1273.

67 For an account of the Maryknoll priests (Catholic Foreign Mission Society of America) and their attempt to prevent war, see Robert Butow, *The John Doe Associates: Backdoor Diplomacy for Peace, 1941* (Stanford University Press, 1974).

68 Joseph Grew to FDR, 22 September 1941, Box 43, President's Secretary's File, Franklin Roosevelt Papers; Kershaw, *Fateful Choices*, p. 338. Also see, Takeo Iguchi, *Demystifying Pearl Harbor: A New Perspective from Japan* (Tokyo: International House of Japan, 2010), pp. 107–108.

69 *FRUS: Japan, 1931–1942*, vol. II, p. 565.

70 Ibid., pp. 572–573.

71 Utley, *Going to War with Japan 1937–1941*, pp. 159–160.

72 Cordell Hull, *The Memoirs of Cordell Hull* (New York: Macmillan Company, 1948), vol. II, pp. 1024–1026.

73 Heinrichs, *Threshold of War: Franklin D. Roosevelt and American Entry into World War II*, p. 186; Kershaw, *Fateful Choices*, p. 367.

74 See, for examples, Grew's defensiveness to Hornbeck, 19 January 1938, p. 2, Box 185, Stanley Hornbeck Papers; Hornbeck's testiness to Grew, 2 May 1938, Box 185, Stanley Hornbeck Papers; Hornbeck's impatience with Grew's caution in draft of letter (to be sent under FDR's signature), January 1940, Box 187, Stanley Hornbeck Papers; Hornbeck's acid comment on Embassy Tokyo's telegram no. 219, 22 July 1937, Box 185, Stanley Hornbeck Papers.

75 Heinrichs, *Threshold of War*, pp. 187.

76 Hornbeck's comment of June 1940 on Joseph Grew's telegram no. 400, 3 June 1940, Box 187, Stanley Hornbeck Papers.

77 Richard Burns, "Stanley K. Hornbeck: The Diplomacy of the Open Door," in Burns and Bennett, *Diplomats in Crisis: United States–Chinese–Japanese Relations, 1919–1941*, pp. 111–112.

78 Iguchi, *Demystifying Pearl Harbor: A New Perspective from Japan*, p. 90.

79 Emmerson, *The Japanese Thread*, p. 118.

80 I. C. B. Dear and M. R. D. Foot, eds., *The Oxford Companion to World War II* (Oxford University Press, 1995), pp. 773, 871–872

81 Japanese internees were first placed in the Homestead Hotel in Hot Springs, Virginia. They were transferred in April 1942 to the Greenbrier Hotel in West Virginia. Their return voyage to Japan commenced in June. See the account by Iguchi in *Demystifying Pearl Harbor*, pp. 9–18. Iguchi was eleven in December 1941 and a fifth grader in Washington. His father was counselor of the Japanese embassy.

82 Bohlen, *Witness to History 1929–1969*, p. 114. For a survey of actitivities conducted by Allied POWs held in Japanese and German captivity, see Midge Gillies, *The Barbed-Wire University: The Real Lives of Prisoners of War in the Second World War* (London: Aurum, 2011).

83 Some Japanese acquaintances, notwithstanding the danger of running afoul of police authorities, sent food parcels to the interned US diplomats. Takeo Iguchi to author, 15 June 2007.

84 Eugene Dooman, "Tokyo: December 8, 1941," *Foreign Service Journal*, December 1966, pp. 45–46. Also see Craigie, *Behind the Japanese Mask*, p. 135.

85 Bohlen, *Witness to History 1929–1969*, p. 116.

86 Grew to FDR, 14 August 1942 (unsent), Joseph Grew Papers. A copy of the same is also in Box 1, Frank Schuler Papers.

87 Ibid.

88 Joseph Grew to Miss Tully, 30 April 1948, Box 21, Franklin D. Roosevelt Memorial Foundation: Records.

89 Heinrichs, *American Ambassador*, p. 363.

90 John Dower, *War Without Mercy: Race and Power in the Pacific War* (New York: Pantheon Books 1986), pp. 83, 142.

91 Rudolf Janssens, *What Future for Japan? U.S. Wartime Planning for the Postwar Era, 1941–1945* (Amsterdam: Rodopi, 1995), p. 444; Joseph Grew, *Report from Tokyo: A Message to the American People* (New York: Simon and Schuster, 1942), pp. 28, 87.

92 Grew put a number of his speeches into book form in late 1942, *Report from Tokyo*.

93 Grew to Henry Stimson, 12 February 1947, p. 2, Box 2, Eugene Dooman Papers; John Dower, *Embracing Defeat: Japan in the Wake of Word War II* (New York: W. W. Norton, 1999), pp. 217–218, 279.

94 Janssens, *What Future for Japan? U.S. Wartime Planning for the Postwar Era, 1942–1945*, p. 378; Stimson and Bundy, *On Active Service in Peace and War*, p. 626.

95 Grew, *Ten Years in Japan*, p. 369; Grew, *Turbulent Era*, vol. II, p. 1287.

96 Grew, *Turbulent Era*, vol. II, p. 1522.

97 Grew to Henry Stimson, 12 February 1947, p. 7, Box 2, Eugene Dooman Papers.

98 David Mayers, *The Ambassadors and America's Soviet Policy* (Oxford University Press, 1995), pp. 192–193.

99 For example of Dooman's prejudices, see his "The American Council on Japan and Its Influence on Relations between the United States and Japan," 25 January 1963, p. 2, Box 1, Eugene Dooman Papers.

100 Robert H. Jackson, associate justice of the Supreme Court and chief of the US prosecutorial team at the 1945–1946 Nuremberg trial, gave this incisive statement in December 1946 on what he termed "anticipatory defense," the equivalent of what President George W. Bush's administration in 2003 dubbed "preemption." The conceptual distance traveled between Jackson and Bush is plain. To military and Foreign Service officers at the National War College, Jackson explained:

I should say that the right to resort to attack as an anticipatory defense would be governed by much the same considerations as the corresponding right of an individual to do the same thing. Neither is obliged to stand idle while another destroys him. It is certain also that neither can be allowed to perpetrate an attack merely because a nation fears that at some future time it may suffer one. Between these two extremes, difficult situations may be imagined which would be decided by such factors as the imminence of the menace, the relative power of the enemy, the state of tension in their relations, and possible alternatives. Ultimate decision probably would turn on the facts of each case as to whether war was instituted in good faith in self-defense, upon reasonable grounds, or as a mere pretext to cloak aggression ... It would not be legitimate self-defense for us to use the atom bomb *now* on another country merely because of fear that at some indefinite future time it might become possessed of the secret and might use it against us. On the other hand, if a country obviously hostile to us possessed and was manufacturing atom bombs and we had clear evidence of a purpose to attack our cities, an attack in defense might be justified. An important factor in judging good faith would be the relative war potential of the parties. Then again the state of relations between two countries would shed light on the need to resort to self-defense. Good faith would also depend upon the alternative for it is quite certain that it is any country's duty to exhaust every peaceful resource before resorting to an attack by way of anticipatory self-defense.

See "War and War Crimes Trials," p. 5, 6 December 1946, Box 44, Robert Jackson Papers. Secretary Henry Stimson, a major force behind the Nuremberg trials, wrote this in *Foreign Affairs*:

In the judgment of Nuremberg there is affirmed the central principle of peace, that the man who makes or plans to make aggressive war is a criminal. A standard has been raised to which Americans at least must repair, for it is only as this standard is accepted, supported, and enforced that we can move onward to a world of peace within the law.

Cited in Robert Jackson, "The Significance of the Nuremberg Trials to the Armed Forces," *Military Affairs* (Winter 1946), p. 4.

101 Grew, *Report From Tokyo*, p. 61.
102 Ibid.

Chapter 2: Third Reich

1 Arrival Message, 8 January 1938, Box 59, and German Contribution to American Life, 6 October 1933, Box 58, William Dodd Papers; Michaela Hoenicke Moore, *Know Your Enemy: The American Debate on Nazism, 1933–1945* (Cambridge University Press, 2010), pp. 46, 80–82; William Dodd, Jr. and Martha Dodd, eds., *Ambassador Dodd's Diary 1933–1938* (New York: Harcourt, Brace and Company, 1941), pp. xiii, 400, 440, 447; *FRUS 1937*, vol. II, p. 370; Franklin Ford, "Three Observers in Berlin: Rumbold, Dodd, and François-Poncet," in Gordon Craig and Felix Gilbert, eds., *The Diplomats 1919–1939* (Princeton University Press, 1994), pp. 448–449, 475.

2 Fritz Stern, *Five Germanys I Have Known* (New York: Farrar, Straus and Giroux, 2006), p. 472.

3 M. H. Carter to Moore, 17 August 1938, Box 6, R. Walton Moore Papers.

4 Charles Beard, "Giddy Minds and Foreign Quarrels," in Robert Goldwin and Harry Clor, eds., *Readings in American Foreign Policy* (Oxford University Press, 1971), p. 133.

5 Hugh R. Wilson, Jr., *A Career Diplomat: The Third Chapter: The Third Reich* (Westport: Greenwood Press, 1960), pp. 28, 84.

6 Robert Dallek, *Democrat and Diplomat: The Life of William E. Dodd* (Oxford University Press, 1968), p. 9; Fred Bailey, *William Edward Dodd: The South's Yeoman Scholar* (University Press of Virginia, 1997), p. 17.

7 Dallek, *Democrat and Diplomat*, pp. 48–49; Bailey, *William Edward Dodd*, pp. 86–87, 114–116, 126; John Fox, "In Passion and in Hope: The Pilgrimage of an American Radical, Martha Dodd Stern and Family, 1933–1990" (Ph.D. dissertation, University of New Hampshire, 2001), p. 42.

8 See William Dodd, *The Old South: Struggles for Democracy* (New York: Macmillan Company, 1937).

9 William Dodd, "The Dilemma of Modern Civilization," in Quincy Wright, ed., *Neutrality and Collective Security* (University of Chicago Press, 1936), pp. 104, 106; Bailey, *William Edward Dodd*, pp. 104–105; Dodd to Ambassador de los Rios, 29 March 1939, Box 56, William Dodd Papers.

10 William Dodd, *Woodrow Wilson and His Work* (Garden City: Doubleday, Page and Company, 1920), p. 354.

11 Bailey, *William Edward Dodd*, p. 135; Dodd and Dodd, *Ambassador Dodd's Diary, 1933–1938*, p. 10.

12 Irwin Gellman, *Secret Affairs: Franklin Roosevelt, Cordell Hull, and Sumner Welles* (Johns Hopkins University Press, 1995), p. 157; Dallek, *Democrat and Diplomat*, pp. 187–189; Ford, "Three Observers in Berlin," p. 447; Arnold Offner, *American Appeasement: United States Foreign Policy and Germany, 1933–1938* (New York: W. W. Norton and Company, 1976), pp. 54–55.

13 Dodd and Dodd, *Ambassador Dodd's Diary 1933–1938*, p. 3.

14 Martha Dodd, *Through Embassy Eyes* (New York: Harcourt, Brace and Company, 1939), p. 12; Dodd and Dodd, *Ambassador Dodd's Diary 1933–1938*, p. 10.

15 Bailey, *William Edward Dodd*, p. 128; Moore to Dodd, 30 June 1934, Box 5, R. Walton Moore Papers.

16 Dodd and Dodd, *Ambassador Dodd's Diary 1933–1938*, pp. 5–6; Erik Larson, *In the Garden of Beasts: Love, Terror, and an American Family in Hitler's Berlin* (New York: Crown, 2011), p. 19.

17 Dodd to Moore, 3 September 1935, Box 5, R. Walton Moore Papers.

18 Dodd to Moore, 31 August 1936, President's Secretary's File, Box 32, Franklin Roosevelt Papers; Gaynor Johnson, ed., *Our Man in Berlin: The Diary of*

Sir Eric Phipps, 1933–1937 (New York: Palgrave Macmillan, 2008), p. 3; Michael Polley, "William E. Dodd," in Cathal Nolan, ed., *Notable U.S. Ambassadors since 1775* (Westport: Greenwood Press, 1997), p. 84. Like Dodd, Phipps could not abide Hitler and thought him "unbalanced." See Abraham Ascher, "Was Hitler a Riddle?" *Journal of the Historical Society*, 9(1) (2009), p. 11.

19 Dodd to Moore, 17 July 1934, Dodd to Secretary Hull, 19 May 1934, Dodd to Senator Robinson, 30 January 1935, Box 5, R. Walton Moore Papers; Dodd and Dodd, *Ambassador Dodd's Diary, 1933–1938*, pp. 16, 300–301; Gellman, *Secret Affairs*, pp. 146, 158; Bernard Burke, *Ambassador Frederic Sackett and the Collapse of the Weimar Republic, 1930–1933* (Cambridge University Press, 1994), pp. 71–72.

20 Dodd to Claude Swanson, 16 October 1934, Box 5, R. Walton Moore Papers; Dodd and Dodd, *Ambassador's Dodd's Diary 1933–1938*, pp. 151–152.

21 Dodd to Moore, 18 February 1936, Box 5, Dodd to Moore, 17 February 1937, Box 6, R. Walton Moore Papers; Dodd and Dodd, *Ambassador Dodd's Diary 1933–1938*, pp. 94, 421–422; Bailey, *William Edward Dodd*, pp. 150–151, 180–181.

22 Dodd to Moore, 14 January 1937, Box 6, R. Walton Moore Papers; William Shirer, *Berlin Diary: The Journal of a Foreign Correspondent 1934–1941* (New York: Alfred Knopf, 1941), pp. 15–16; William Shirer, *The Nightmare Years 1930–1940* (Toronto: Bantam Books, 1985), pp. 183–184; John Fox, "In Passion and in Hope," pp. 65–66.

23 Katherine Smith, "My Life: Berlin August 1935–April 1939" (unpublished book manuscript, nd), p. 203, Box 4, Truman Smith Papers.

24 Fox, "In Passion and in Hope," p. 67; Dodd, *Through Embassy Eyes*, p. 36.

25 Martha Dodd to Eleanor Roosevelt, 15 March 1939, Box 8, Martha Dodd Papers.

26 John Haynes and Harvey Klehr, *Early Cold War Spies: The Espionage Trials that Shaped American Politics* (Cambridge University Press, 2006), pp. 220–222; Allen Weinstein and Alexander Vassiliev, *The Haunted Wood: Soviet Espionage in America – the Stalin Era* (New York: Random House, 1999), pp. 50–71.

Martha Dodd's brother, William, also leaned leftward. He was courted by Soviet intelligence in the 1930s while a Ph.D. student at the University of Berlin. He did not prove an effective operator, however. He provided only "tidbits" over the years to his Soviet handlers. See Max Holland, "I. F. Stone: Encounters with Soviet Intelligence," *Journal of Cold War Studies*, 11(3) (2009), pp. 167–169.

27 Martha Dodd to Ilya Ehrenburg, 29 October 1957, Martha Dodd to William Shirer, 10 June 1969, Martha Dodd to Elmine, 23 November 1970, Box 13,

Martha Dodd Papers. Also see letters by Boris Vinogradov in the 1930s to Martha Dodd, Box 10, Martha Dodd Papers.

Martha Dodd also enjoyed American conquests. Carl Sandburg and Thomas Wolfe numbered among them.

28 John Haynes and Harvey Klehr, *Venona: Decoding Soviet Espionage in America* (Yale University Press, 2000), p. 269; Dodd to Moore, 17 August 1936, Box 5, R. Walton Moore Papers; Dodd to Moore, 31 August 1936, Box 32, President's Secretary's File, Franklin Roosevelt Papers. Archival evidence from the former USSR indicates that Martha Dodd did pass materials from her father's office to Berlin-based Soviet intelligence. See Holland, "I. F. Stone: Encounters with Soviet Intelligence," p. 169.

29 Larson, *In the Garden of Beasts*, p. 115.

30 Kenneth Weisbrode, *The Atlantic Century: Four Generations of Extraordinary Diplomats Who Forged America's Vital Alliance with Europe* (Cambridge, Mass.: Da Capo Press, 2009), p. 44.

31 Dodd to Moore, 14 December 1936, Box 5, R. Walton Moore Papers; *Documents on German Foreign Policy 1918–1945*, Series D (Washington: United States Government Printing Office, 1949), vol. I, p. 631; German amassador to the Foreign Ministry, 1 October 1937, Akten zur deutschen auswärtigen Politik 1918–1945, vol. I.

32 Moore to Dodd, 14 March 1935, Box 5, Moore to Dodd, 20 May 1937, Box 6, R. Walton Moore Papers; Offner, *American Appeasement: United States Foreign Policy and Germany 1933–1938*, p. 133.

33 Moore to Dodd, 30 June 1934, Box 5, Dodd to Moore, 3 September 1935, Box 5, Dodd to Moore, 6 July 1937, Box 6, R. Walton Moore Papers; Dodd to FDR, 31 October 1935, Box 32, President's Secretary's File, Franklin Roosevelt Papers.

34 Dodd to Moore, 8 July 1937, Box 6, R. Walton Moore Papers.

35 Dodd and Dodd, *Ambassador Dodd's Diary 1933–1938*, pp. 34, 68, 122, 154; Dodd to Moore, 14 December 1936, Box 5, R. Walton Moore Papers.

36 *FRUS 1933*, vol. II, pp. 277–280; Burke, *Ambassador Frederic Sackett*, p. 297; Richard Breitman *et al.*, eds., *Advocate for the Doomed: The Diaries and Papers of James G. McDonald 1932–1935* (Indiana University Press, 2007), pp. 79, 187; Dallek, *Democrat and Diplomat*, pp. 199–200, 209, 233; Barry Rubin, *Secrets of State: The State Department and the Struggle over U.S. Foreign Policy* (Oxford University Press, 1987), p. 31; Ford, "Three Observers in Berlin" p. 450.

37 Dodd to FDR, 27 November 1933, Box 32, President's Secretary's File, Franklin Roosevelt Papers.

38 Dodd and Dodd, *Ambassador Dodd's Diary 1933–1938*, p. 123.

39 Dodd to Moore, 5 November 1934, Box 5, R. Walton Moore Papers.

40 Dodd to FDR, 9 May 1935, Box 32, President's Secretary's File; Dodd to Moore, 27 November 1935, Box 5, R. Walton Moore Papers; Bailey, *William Edward Dodd*, p. 159; Dodd and Dodd, *Ambassador Dodd's Diary 1933–1938*, p. 296.

41 Dodd, *Through Embassy Eyes*, pp. 220, 233.

42 Ibid., pp. 350, 368; Dodd to FDR, 27 November 1933, Box 32, President's Secretary's File, Franklin Roosevelt Papers.

43 *FRUS 1933*, vol. II, pp. 396–397; Dodd to FDR, 28 October 1933, Box 1043, President's Personal File, Franklin Roosevelt Papers; Bailey, *William Edward Dodd*, pp. 156–157.

44 *FRUS 1934*, vol. II, pp. 218–221; Dallek, *Democrat and Diplomat*, p. 226.

45 Dodd and Dodd, *Ambassador Dodd's Diary 1933–1938*, p. 126.

46 David Levering Lewis, *W. E. B. Du Bois: The Fight for Equality and the American Century, 1919–1963* (New York: Henry Holt and Company, 2000), pp. 402–403. See George Eisen, "The Voices of Sanity: American Diplomatic Reports from the 1936 Berlin Olympiad," *Journal of Sport History*, 11 (1984) and Stephen Wenn, "A Tale of Two Diplomats: George S. Messersmith and Charles H. Sherrill on Proposed American Participation in the 1936 Olympics," *Journal of Sport History*, 16 (1989). More than forty percent of the American public, according to a March 1935 Gallup poll, wanted to boycott the Berlin games. See Wenn, p. 29.

47 Dodd to Moore, 19 August 1937, Box 6, R. Walton Moore Papers; *FRUS 1933*, vol. II, pp. 257–258.

48 Dodd and Dodd, *Ambassador Dodd's Diary 1933–1938*, p. 425.

49 *Documents on German Foreign Policy 1918–1945*, Series C, 1937–1945 (Washington: United States Government Printing Office, 1959), vol. II, pp. 552–554, 556–557; *FRUS 1934*, vol. II, p. 511; Offner, *American Appeasement*, p. 84; *FRUS 1937*, vol. II, pp. 368–370, 375; Dodd and Dodd, *Ambassador Dodd's Diary 1933–1938*, pp. 390, 394; Breitman, *Advocate for the Doomed*, p. 557.

50 Fox, "In Passion and in Hope," p. 144.

51 Dodd and Dodd, *Ambassador Dodd's Diary 1933–1938*, pp. 10–11.

52 Breitman, *Advocate for the Doomed*, p. 795; Bailey, *William Edward Dodd*, pp. 149–150; Larson, *In the Garden of Beasts*, pp. 83–85, 132–133.

53 *FRUS 1936*, vol. II, pp. 197–199, 201–202; Dodd to Moore, 17 September 1935, Box 5, R. Walton Moore Papers.

54 *FRUS 1937*, vol. II, pp. 395–405; Dodd and Dodd, *Ambassador Dodd's Diary 1933–1938*, pp. 402–404, 410–414; Shirer, *Berlin Diary*, pp. 74–76; Dallek, *Democrat and Diplomat*, pp. 305–306.

55 Dodd and Dodd, *Ambassador Dodd's Diary 1933–1938*, pp. 169–170.

56 Bailey, *William Edward Dodd*, p. 192. Also see Dodd, *Through Embassy Eyes*, p. 309.

57 Dodd to FDR, 15 August 1934, Box 1043, President's Secretary's File, Franklin Roosevelt Papers.

58 Dodd to Moore, 5 November 1934, Box 5, R. Walton Moore Papers; Dodd to FDR, 27 November 1933, Dodd to FDR, 9 May 1935, Dodd to FDR, 27 February 1937, Box 32, President's Secretary's File, Franklin Roosevelt Papers; Dodd and Dodd, *Ambassador Dodd's Diary 1933–1938*, pp. 252, 286, 364.

59 Dodd to FDR, 15 August 1934, Box 1043, President's Personal File, Franklin Roosevelt Papers.

60 *FRUS 1935*, vol. II, pp. 307–309; Dodd to Moore, 10 February 1936, Box 5, R. Walton Moore Papers.

61 *FRUS 1935*, vol. II, p. 321.

62 Dodd to FDR, 1 April 1936, Box 32, President's Secretary's File, Franklin Roosevelt Papers.

63 Dodd to Moore, 2 January 1936, Box 5, R. Walton Moore Papers; *FRUS 1934*, vol. II, p. 217.

64 Dodd to Moore, 29 October 1935, Dodd to Moore, 25 May 1936, Dodd to Moore, 25 November 1936, Box 5, R. Walton Moore Papers; Dodd to FDR, 7 December 1936 and FDR to Dodd, 9 January 1937 Box 32, President's Secretary's File, Franklin Roosevelt Papers; Dodd and Dodd, *Ambassador Dodd's Diary 1933–1938*, p. 310.

65 Dodd to FDR, 31 October 1935, Box 31, President's Secretary's File, Franklin Roosevelt Papers.

66 Dodd to Moore, 5 October 1934, Box 5, R. Walton Moore Papers.

67 Dodd to Senator Robinson, 30 January 1935, Box 5, R. Walton Moore Papers.

68 Dodd to FDR, 1 April 1936, Box 32, President's Secretary's File, Franklin Roosevelt Papers.

69 Dodd and Dodd, *Ambassador Dodd's Diary 1933–1938*, p. 307.

70 Ibid., pp. 407–408.

71 *Documents on German Foreign Policy 1918–1945*, Series D, vol. I, pp. 627–631; notes of Consul Freytag from the Foreign Ministry, 23 September 1937, Akten zur deutschen auswärtigen Politik 1918–1945, vol. I; Moore to Dodd, 28 September 1937, Box 6, R. Walton Moore Papers.

72 Gellman, *Secret Affairs*, pp. 158–159.

73 The Threatening German Dictatorship, 1938, Box 59, William Dodd Papers.

74 Dallek, *Democrat and Diplomat*, pp. 319–320, 323; Bailey, *William Edward Dodd*, pp. 190–192. Also see Arrival Message, 8 January 1938 and Racial-Religious Reforms in Germany (1938?), Box 59, William Dodd Papers.

75 Young Dodd received some financial aid from the USSR during his 1938 race for the Democratic nomination in Virginia's 8th congressional district. See Holland, "I. F. Stone: Encounters with Soviet Intelligence," p. 170.

76 *Documents on German Foreign Policy 1918–1945*, Series D, vol. I, pp. 679–680.

77 Eric Schroetter to Dodd, 24 October 1938, Box 56, William Dodd Papers.

78 Bailey, *William Edward Dodd*, p. 195.

79 Ibid., p. 198.

80 Dodd to Moore, 26 December 1936, Box 5, R. Walton Moore Papers. Also see Dodd to Moore, 9 April 1937, Box 6, R. Walton Moore Papers; Dodd to FDR, 29 November 1937 and Dodd to FDR, 23 December 1937, Box 32, President's Secretary's File, Franklin Roosevelt Papers.

81 Dodd to Moore, 2 November 1937, Box 6, R. Walton Moore Papers; Ralph de Bedts, *Ambassador Joseph Kennedy 1938–1940: An Anatomy of Appeasement* (New York: Peter Lang, 1985), p. 53.

82 Wilson to Louis Johnson, 10 December 1937, Box 3, Hugh Wilson Papers.

83 Arthur Bliss Lane to Wilson, 25 January 1938, Box 3, Hugh Wilson Papers.

84 Wilson to Ferdinand Mayer, 14 September 1938, Box 4, Ferdinand Mayer Papers.

85 *Documents on German Foreign Policy 1918–1945*, Series D, vol. I, p. 689; Dieckhoff to Weizsäcker, 20 December 1937, Neurath to Lammers, 5 February 1938, Akten zur deutschen auswärtigen Politik 1918–1945, vol. I.

86 *Documents on German Foreign Policy 1918–1945*, Series D, 1937–1945 (Washington: Government Printing Office, 1951), vol. IV, p. 662; Lammers to Neurath, 21 January 1938, notes of Ribbentrop, 29 April 1938 and 10 June 1938, Akten zur deutschen auswärtigen Politik 1918–1945, vol. I. Also see *FRUS 1940*, vol. I, p. 35.

87 Hugh Wilson, *The Education of a Diplomat* (London: Longmans, Green and Company, 1938), p. 191; Wilson to William Bullitt, 9 September 1937, Box 1, Hugh Wilson Papers.

88 Wilson to Welles, 20 June 1938, Box 50, Sumner Welles Papers.

89 Wilson to FDR, 3 March 1938, Box 32 President's Secretary's File, Franklin Roosevelt Papers; Wilson, *The Education of a Diplomat*, p. 65; Wilson, *A Career Diplomat*, p. 67; Offner, *American Appeasement*, p. 215. Britain's Ambassador Nevile Henderson, Phipps's immediate successor in Berlin, also admired the purported virtues of *Kraft durch Freude*. See Ascher, "Was Hitler a Riddle?" p. 16.

90 Hugh Wilson, *Diplomat Between Wars* (New York: Longmans, Green and Company, 1941), pp. 291–292.

91 Wilson to FDR, 3 March 1938, Wilson to FDR, 12 March 1938, Wilson to FDR, 2 May 1938, Box 32, President's Secretary's File, Franklin Roosevelt Papers; *FRUS 1938*, vol. I, p. 715.

92 Wilson, *A Career Diplomat*, pp. 71–72; Wilson's diary entry of 18 October 1938, Box 4, Hugh Wilson Papers; Wilson to Goering, 10 September 1938, Box 2, Hugh Wilson Papers.

93 *FRUS 1938*, vol. II, pp. 434–438, Wilson's diary entry for 8 April 1938, Box 4, Hugh Wilson Papers.

94 *Documents on German Foreign Policy 1918–1945*, Series D (Washington: Government Printing Office, 1953), vol. V, p. 895; Myron Taylor to Wilson, 24 July 1938, and Wilson to Myron Taylor, 27 July 1938 in Box 3, Hugh Wilson Papers.

95 Cordell Hull to Wilson, 21 July 1938, and Wilson to Cordell Hull, 8 August 1938, both in Box 2, Hugh Wilson Papers.

96 David Reynolds, *From Munich to Pearl Harbor: Roosevelt's America and the Origins of the Second World War* (Chicago: Ivan Dee, 2001), p. 40; *Documents on German Foreign Policy 1918–1945*, Series D, 1937–1945 (Washington: Government Printing Office, 1949), vol. II, pp. 958–959, 984–985; *FRUS 1938*, vol. I, pp. 657–658, 669–672, 684–685.

97 Wilson to Welles, 2 April 1938, Box 50, Sumner Welles Papers.

98 Wilson to Welles, 6 June 1938, Box 50, Sumner Welles Papers. Also see Wilson, *A Career Diplomat: The Third Chapter: The Third Reich*, pp. 52–53.

99 Wilson's diary entry of 15 June 1938, Box 4, Hugh Wilson Papers.

100 Wilson to Welles, 14 May 1938, Box 50, Sumner Welles Papers; Wilson telegram to Secretary Hull, 29 April 1938 and Wilson to FDR, 2 May 1938, Box 32, President's Secretary's File, Franklin Roosevelt Papers; Wilson, *A Career Diplomat*, p. 84.

101 *Documents on German Foreign Policy 1918–1945*, Series D, 1937–1945, vol. IV, p. 670; *FRUS 1938*, vol. II, pp. 380–382, 536–537; Wilson's diary entries of 24 April and 9 May 1938, Box 3, Hugh Wilson Papers.

102 Wilson to Welles, 14 August 1938, Box 32, President's Secretary's File, Franklin Roosevelt Papers.

103 Wilson to FDR, 11 July 1938, Box 32, President's Secretary's File, Franklin Roosevelt Papers; Truman Smith, Air Intelligence Activities, April 1935–April 1939, Box 1, Truman Smith Papers. Also see Wilson, *A Career Diplomat*, p. 67.

104 Wilson to FDR, 31 August 1938, Box 32, President's Secretary's File, Franklin Roosevelt Papers.

105 Martin Gilbert, *Kristallnacht: Prelude to Destruction* (New York: HarperCollins, 2006), p. 118. Also see Gerhard Weinberg, "Kristallnacht 1938: As Experienced Then and Understood Now," Weinmann Annual Lecture (Washington: United States Holocaust Memorial Museum, 2009).

106 Eckart Conze *et al.*, *Das Amt und die Vergangenheit: Deutsche Diplomaten im Dritten Reich und in der Bundesrepublik* (Munich: Karl Blessing Verlag, 2010), p. 171.

107 Wilson, *Career Diplomat*, p. 73; Wilson to Alexander Kirk, 2 September 1939, Box 3, Hugh Wilson Papers; Wilson's diary entries of 12 and 14 November 1938, Box 4, Hugh Wilson Papers.

108 "We have a great interest in preventing the United States from throwing her weight into the scales on the side of our foes," Weizsäcker testified in mid-September 1939, "and we must do everything to keep her in the group of neutral powers, of which she ... [has] constituted one of the strongest and most important members... [The] Ambassador's return to Washington would strengthen the position of those groups in the United States which are against a break with Germany." See *Documents on German Foreign Policy, 1918–1945*, Series D (Washington: Government Printing Office, 1954), vol. VIII, p. 53 and Dieckhoff to Weizsäcker, 21 December 1938, Akten zur deutschen auswärtigen Politik 1918–1945, vol. IV.

109 *FRUS 1938*, vol. II, p. 398.

110 *FRUS 1939*, vol. I, p. 23.

111 *Documents on German Foreign Policy, 1918–1945*, Series D, vol. VIII, p. 331.

112 Gilbert died from natural causes in March 1939 while acting head of the diplomatic mission.

113 On the connection between the consulates and Embassy Berlin see Christoph Strupp, "Observing a Dictatorship: American Consular Reporting on Germany, 1933–1941," *German Historical Bulletin* (Fall 2006).

114 For an account, see J. Simon Rofe, *Franklin Roosevelt's Foreign Policy and the Welles Mission* (New York: Palgrave Macmillan, 2007).

115 *FRUS 1940*, vol. I, pp. 33–58; Gellman, *Secret Affairs*, pp. 179–183; *Documents on German Foreign Policy, 1918–1945*, Series D, vol. VIII, pp. 827–829.

116 *FRUS 1940*, vol. I, pp. 159–161; William Phillips to Sumner Welles, 31 May 1940, Box 42, President's Secretary's File, Franklin Roosevelt Papers.

117 *FRUS 1941*, vol. I, p. 153.

118 Gilbert, *Kristallnacht*, p. 225; Raymond Geist to Wilson, 5 December 1938, Box 2, Hugh Wilson Papers.

119 Despite Geist–Russell efforts, the admission of German Jews to America fell far below the allotment approved by Congress of 25,957 per annum from the post-*Anschluss* Reich. See Richard Breitman and Alan Kraut, *American Refugee Policy and European Jewry, 1933–1945* (Indiana University Press, 1987), p. 9; Deborah Lipstadt, *Beyond Belief: The American Press and the Coming of the Holocaust 1933–1945* (New York: Free Press, 1986), p. 306, #10.

120 William Russell, *Berlin Embassy* (New York: Carroll and Graf, 2005), pp. 105, 119.

121 Ibid., pp. 129, 150.

122 George Kennan, *Memoirs 1925–1950* (Boston: Little, Brown and Company, 1967), pp. 119–122. Also see Freya von Moltke, *Memories of Kreisau and the German Resistance* (University of Nebraska Press, 2003) and Kennan to Inge Aicher-Scholl, 6 May 1988, Box 51, George Kennan Papers.

123 David Mayers, *George Kennan and the Dilemmas of U.S. Foreign Policy* (Oxford University Press, 1988), pp. 74–78.

His having an extramarital romance in 1941 unsettled Kennan. He told Moltke that he hoped collaboration with him would help to correct matters. "You know," he emphasized to the Count, "my personal affairs are all in a muddle just now and I did not know how to get out of it; but this work will put me right again and I hope by that way to be able to repay my debt of gratitude to Europe for the most important 15 years of my existence." See Beate Ruhm von Oppen, ed., *Helmuth James von Moltke: Letters to Freya 1939–1945* (New York: Vintage Books, 1995), p. 161.

124 See Arnold Krammer, "In Splendid Isolation: Enemy Diplomats in World War II," *Prologue*, 17(1) (1985).

125 Charles Burdick, *An American Island in Hitler's Reich: The Bad Nauheim Internment* (Menlo Park: Markgraf Publications, 1987), p. 88.

126 Very likely Kennan had another extramarital affair during his Bad Nauheim detention. See John Lewis Gaddis, *George F. Kennan: An American Life* (New York: Penguin Press, 2011), p. 454.

127 Burdick, *An American Island in Hitler's Reich*, pp. 13, 16 #21, 87. Also see Gaddis, *George F. Kennan: An American Life*, pp. 148–154 and George Kennan, "Report, the Internment and Repatriation of the American Official Group in Germany – 1941–1942," *American Foreign Service Journal*, (two parts) August and September 1942.

128 Memorandum by H. Charles Spurks, 16 December 1941, Memorandum by Breckinridge Long, 18 December 1941, Breckinridge Long to George Summerlin, 20 December 1941, Memorandum by George Summerlin, 21 March 1942, Box 206, Breckinridge Long Papers; Krammer, "In Splendid Isolation," p. 39.

Opinion in the State Department was divided on General von Boetticher's request, evidenced in this passage from Long's 18 December 1941: "We [feel] on the one hand to send the boy to Germany [would be] to turn him over to the executioner. On the other hand, the practice in Germany [is] part and parcel of the system to which General von Boetticher belong[s], whose servant he [is] and of which he must be considered an important part." Also see Alfred Beck, *Hitler's Ambivalent Attaché: Lt. Gen. Friedrich von Boetticher in*

America (Washington: Potomac Books, 2005), pp. 103, 192, 262 #28. Incidentally, Counselor Ernst Wilhelm Meyer of the German embassy had left his country's diplomatic service in 1937. He afterward stayed for a time in the United States. He opposed Hitler's policies. After the war he taught political science at two German universities: Frankfurt, Marburg. He also served as West Germany's ambassador to New Delhi and as a deputy (Social Democrat) in the Bundestag. See Frank Lambach, *Our Men in Washington* (Washington: German Information Center, 2004), p. 96.

129 Dodd and Dodd, *Ambassador Dodd's Diary 1933–1938*, p. 131; Dodd, *Through Embassy Eyes*, p. 212.

130 Timothy Snyder, *Bloodlands: Europe Between Hitler and Stalin* (New York: Basic Books, 2010), p. viii.

131 Also see for German policy toward America: Detlef Junker, "Hitler's Perception of Franklin D. Roosevelt and the United States of America," in Cornelis Minnen, ed., *FDR and His Contemporaries: Foreign Perceptions of an American President* (New York: St. Martin's Press, 1992).

132 *Documents on German Foreign Policy 1918–1945*, Series D, 1937–1945 (London: Her Majesty's Stationary Office, 1956), vol. VI, pp. 131, 1081; Dieckhoff to Weizsäcker, 19 January 1938, Akten zur deutschen auswärtigen Politik 1918–1945, vol. I; Detlef Junker, "The Continuity of Ambivalence: German Views of America, 1933–1945," in David Barclay and Elisabeth Glaser-Schmidt, eds., *Transatlantic Images and Perceptions: Germany and America since 1776* (Cambridge University Press, 1997), p. 261.

133 *Documents on German Foreign Policy 1918–1945*, Series D, 1937–1945 (Washington: Government Printing Office, 1951), vol. IV, p. 636.

134 Kennan, *Memoirs 1925–1950*, p. 139.

135 On Kennan's attitude toward Jewry, see Nicholas Thompson, *The Hawk and the Dove: Paul Nitze, George Kennan, and the History of the Cold War* (New York: Henry Holt and Company, 2009), pp. 237–239 and Gaddis, *George F. Kennan: An American Life*, pp. 43, 91, 111, 122, 126–127, 129, 143, 145–146, 156, 170, 607. The Thompson and Gaddis references indicate that Kennan had authentic friendships with prominent Jews (for example, Robert Oppenheimer and Isaiah Berlin) and he had been helpful to less well-known Jewish acquaintances in Prague and Berlin during the Nazi era. Yet he could also entertain and express – particularly in his earlier years – ungenerous views, suggesting a species of bigotry not many removes from that of Ferdinand Mayer.

136 Mayer to Hugh Wilson, 17 June 1940, Box 4, Ferdinand Mayer Papers. Mayer, incidentally, also thought black people undesirable. While head of mission in Haiti, he pronounced: "The negro race is essentially treacherous." See Mayer to Welles, 23 October 1939, Box 54, Sumner Welles Papers.

137 Peter Gay, *My German Question: Growing Up in Nazi Berlin* (New Haven: Yale University Press, 1998), p. 146; David Mayers, *Dissenting Voices in America's Rise to Power* (Cambridge University Press, 2007), p. 271.

138 Albert Einstein to Martha Dodd, 11 December 1940, Box 63, William Dodd Papers. Also see Dodd and Dodd, *Ambassador Dodd's Diary 1933–1938*, p. 209 and Dallek, *Democrat and Diplomat*, p. 325.

139 Bailey, *William Edward Dodd*, p. 161.

140 Orville Bullitt, ed., *For the President: Personal and Secret: Correspondence Between Franklin D. Roosevelt and William C. Bullitt* (Boston: Houghton Mifflin Company, 1972), p. 235; André François-Poncet, *The Fateful Years: Memoirs of a French Ambassador in Berlin, 1931–1938* (New York: Harcourt, Brace and Company, 1949), p. 213.

141 Wilson to William Bullitt, 16 October 1939, Box 1, Hugh Wilson Papers.

142 The Blücher Palace, acquired by the United States in 1930, was damaged by fire in 1931. The building was not importantly used by the Americans until spring 1939. Until then, the US diplomatic mission used other properties in the Wilhelmstrasse/Brandenburg Gate neighborhood.

Chapter 3: New Roman Empire

1 John Diggins, *Mussolini and Fascism: The View from America* (Princeton University Press, 1972), p. 244.

2 Bill Maudlin, *Up Front* (New York: Henry Holt and Company, 1945), pp. 48–50.

3 J. J. Wilhelm, *Ezra Pound: The Tragic Years 1925–1972* (Pennsylvania State University Press, 1994), pp. 178, 180; Omar Pound and Robert Spoo, eds., *Ezra and Dorothy Pound: Letters in Captivity, 1945–1946* (Oxford University Press, 1999), p. 3.

4 "Superstition," 20 July 1942, Leonard Doob, ed., *Ezra Pound Speaking: Radio Speeches of World War II* (Westport: Greenwood Press, 1978), p. 213.

5 Borden Painter, *Mussolini's Rome: Rebuilding the Eternal City* (New York: Palgrave Macmillan, 2005), p. 66.

6 Gerhard Weinberg, *Visions of Victory: The Hopes of Eight World War II Leaders* (Cambridge University Press, 2005), pp. 43–44, 46–47; H. Stuart Hughes, "The Early Diplomacy of Italian Fascism, 1922–1932," in Gordon Craig and Felix Gilbert, eds., *The Diplomats 1919–1939* (Princeton University Press, 1994), p. 212; Robert Mallett, *Mussolini and the Origins of the Second World War, 1933–1940* (New York: Palgrave Macmillan, 2003), pp. 221–222.

7 Hughes, "The Early Diplomacy of Italian Fascism, 1922–1932," p. 221.

8 See the exchange of Dodd to Long on 20 February 1936 and Long to Dodd on 4 March 1936, Box 115, Breckinridge Long Papers. At question was the length,

quality, and expense of telegrams sent by the Berlin and Rome embassies to each other and to Washington.

9 Fred Israel, ed., *The War Diary of Breckinridge Long: Selections from the Years 1939–1944* (University of Nebraska Press, 1966), p. xii.

10 Irwin Gellman, *Secret Affairs: Franklin Roosevelt, Cordell Hull, and Sumner Welles* (Johns Hopkins University Press, 1995), pp. 231–232; Israel, *The War Diary of Breckinridge Long*, p. xviii.

11 "Breckinridge Long is Dead at 77" (obituary), *New York Times*, 27 September 1958.

12 Long to Mrs. Onward Bates, 3 April 1933, Box 100, Long to Mrs. Harold Chatfield, 20 April 1933, Box 101, Long to William Logan, 9 August 1933, Box 104, Breckinridge Long Papers; Israel, *The War Diary of Breckinridge Long* p. xviii.

13 Diary entry of 3 November 1935, Box 4, Breckinridge Long Papers; Richard Lamb, *Mussolini as Diplomat: Il Duce's Italy on the World Stage* (New York: Fromm International, 1999), pp. 21, 153.

14 Long to Albert Ritchie, 21 September 1933, Box 105, Breckinridge Long Papers. Also see Long to William Logan, 9 August 1933, Box 104, Breckinridge Long Papers.

15 Long's letters to Admiral Grayson, 23 September 1933 and 28 November 1933, Box 103 Breckinridge Long Papers.

16 Long to Louis Howe, 24 November 1933, Box 103, Breckinridge Long Papers.

17 Long to Josephus Daniels, 22 October 1935, Box 112, Breckinridge Long Papers.

18 Long to James Byrnes, 24 November 1933, Brynes to Long, 7 December 1933, Long to Byrnes, 19 December 1933, Box 100, Breckinridge Long Papers.

19 Long to John Dickinson, 8 February 1935 and Dickinson to Long, 22 March 1935, Box 112, Breckinridge Long Papers.

20 Diary entry of 13 September 1935, Box 4, Breckinridge Long Papers.

21 Diary entry of 20 May 1935, Box 4, Breckinridge Long Papers.

22 Diary entry of 30 June 1940, Box 4, Breckinridge Long Papers.

23 Israel, *The War Diary of Breckinridge Long*, p. xviii; Long to Mrs. Davis Barnes, 5 April 1934, Box 108, Long to Homer Cummings, 2 June 1933, Box 102, Long to Bennett Clark, 21 September 1933, Box 101, Address to the United States Chamber of Commerce for Italy (Milan), 24 April 1934, Box 217, Breckinridge Long Papers.

24 Long to Albert Ritchie, 21 September 1933, Box 105, Breckinridge Long Papers. Also see Long to FDR, 27 June 1933, Box 447, Official File, Franklin Roosevelt Papers; Long to FDR, 14 September 1933, Box 41, President's Secretary's File, Franklin Roosevelt Papers; Israel, *The War Diary of Breckinridge Long: Selections from the Years 1939–1944*, p. xix.

25 Diggins, *Mussolini and Fascism*, pp. 48–49, 58, 172, 183–184, 209–210, 227; Mallett, *Mussolini and the Origins of the Second World War, 1933–1940*, p. 223.

26 Diggins, *Mussolini and Fascism*, pp. 27, 49, 151, 265–266.

27 FDR to Long, 15 June 1933, Box 105, Breckinridge Long Papers.

28 Long to William Logan, 9 August 1933, Box 104, Breckinridge Long Papers. Also see Long to David Lawrence, 17 November 1933, Box 104, Breckinridge Long Papers.

29 Israel, *The War Diary of Breckinridge Long*, pp. xix–xx; Long to Bennett Clark, 21 September 1933, Box 101, Long to Albert Ritchie, 21 September 1933, Box 105, Breckinridge Long Papers.

30 Long to Bennett Clark, 3 September 1933, Box 101, Breckinridge Long Papers.

31 Long to FDR, 7 July 1933, Box 41, President's Secretary's File, Franklin Roosevelt Papers.

32 Diary entry of 27 May 1935, Box 4, Breckinridge Long Papers.

33 Long to FDR, 9 June 1933 and 10 June 1933, Box 447, Official File, Franklin Roosevelt Papers.

34 *FRUS 1933*, vol. II, pp. 587–589; *FRUS 1934*, vol. II, pp. 589–593.

35 Long to FDR, 30 October 1935, Box 42, President's Secretary's File, Franklin Roosevelt Papers.

36 Joseph Harris, *African-American Reactions to War in Ethiopia 1936–1941* (Louisiana State University Press, 1994), pp. 34–62. See also Thomas Simmons, *The Brown Condor: The True Adventures of John C. Robinson* (Silver Springs: Bartleby Press, 1988).

37 *FRUS 1936*, vol. III, p. 115; *FRUS 1935*, vol. I, p. 761; Diary entry of 24 September 1935, Box 4, Breckinridge Long Papers.

38 Long to FDR, 30 October 1935 and Long to FDR, 8 November 1935, Box 41, President's Secretary's File, Franklin Roosevelt Papers.

39 *FRUS 1935*, vol. I, p. 836; Diary entry of 23 December 1935, Box 4, Breckinridge Long Papers; Long to FDR, 29 November 1935, Box 41, President's Secretary's File, Franklin Roosevelt Papers.

40 Diary entry of 26 October 1935, Box 4, Breckinridge Long Papers; *FRUS 1935*, vol. I, p. 668.

41 Address to the Kansas City Bar Association (not delivered because of illness), 6 June 1936 and draft of address on foreign relations, p. 11, 1936 or 1937, Box 217, Breckinridge Long Papers.

42 Long to John Corrigan, 19 March 1936, Box 115, Breckinridge Long Papers.

43 FDR to Breckinridge Long, 22 February 1936, Long to FDR, 13 March 1936, Long to FDR, 23 June 1936, Box 41, President's Secretary's File, Franklin Roosevelt Papers.

44 FDR and Caroline Drayton were second cousins. She and William Phillips were married in 1910 while he was first secretary in London,

serving under Ambassador Whitelaw Reid. The Drayton–Phillips marriage produced six children.

45 Harold Nicolson, *Diplomacy* (Oxford University Press, 1980), p. 62.

46 Paul Henry Reuter, "William Phillips and the Development of American Foreign Policy, 1933–1947" (Ph.D. dissertation, University of Southern Mississippi, 1979), p. 52. Also see Claude Bowers, *My Life* (New York: Simon and Schuster, 1962), p. 262 and Erik Larson, *In the Garden of Beasts: Love, Terror, and an American Family in Hitler's Berlin* (New York: Crown, 2011), p. 217.

47 The Reminiscences of William Phillips, Columbia University Oral History Project, p. 43; Robert Schulzinger, *The Making of the Diplomatic Mind: The Training, Outlook, and Style of United States Foreign Service Officers, 1908–1931* (Wesleyan University Press, 1975), p. 56.

48 Reuter, *William Phillips and the Development of American Foreign Policy*, pp. 49–50.

49 Gellman, *Secret Affairs*, p. 121; The Reminiscences of William Phillips, p. 112.

50 William Phillips, *Ventures in Diplomacy* (Portland, ME: Anthoensen Press, 1952), pp. 184, 186–187.

51 Phillips to Welles, 26 May 1938, Box 47, Sumner Welles Papers.

52 The Reminiscences of William Phillips, p. 112; *FRUS 1937*, vol. II, p. 467; *FRUS 1939*, vol. II, p. 634; Reuter, *William Phillips and the Development of American Foreign Policy, 1933–1947*, pp. 157–159.

53 Memorandum, 7 October 1936, William Phillips Papers; Phillips to FDR, 26 May 1939, Box 42, President's Secretary's File, Franklin Roosevelt Papers; Phillips, *Ventures in Diplomacy*, p. 191.

54 Memoranda of 29 October 1937 and 12 May 1938, William Phillips Papers; Phillips to FDR, 5 January 1939, Box 42, President's Secretary's File, Franklin Roosevelt Papers; Ray Moseley, *Mussolini's Shadow: The Double Life of Count Ciano* (Yale University Press, 1999), pp. 26, 42.

55 Ian Kershaw, *Fateful Choices: Ten Decisions that Changed the World, 1940–1941* (New York: Penguin Press, 2007), p. 153; Phillips to FDR, 25 August 1939, Box 41, President's Secretary's File, Franklin Roosevelt Papers; Phillips, *Ventures in Diplomacy*, p. 325; The Reminiscences of William Phillips, p. 118.

56 Harold Tittman III, ed., *Inside the Vatican of Pius XII: The Memoirs of an American Diplomat During World War II: Harold H. Tittmann, Jr.* (New York: Doubleday, 2004), pp. 5, 124.

57 *FRUS 1940*, vol. II, p. 687; Phillips, *Ventures in Diplomacy*, pp. 229, 237, 260–261; Memorandum of 9 June 1938, William Phillips Papers; Phillips to FDR, 22 April 1937, Box 42, President's Secretary's File, Franklin Roosevelt Papers.

58 Phillips to FDR, 17 March 1938 and 6 September 1939, Box 42, President's Secretary's File, Franklin Roosevelt Papers.

59 Phillips, *Ventures in Diplomacy*, p. 242.

60 Andreas Mayor, ed., *Ciano's Hidden Diary, 1937–1938* (New York: E. P. Dutton and Company, 1953), p. 93.

61 Phillips to FDR, 5 January 1939 with memorandum of 3 January 1939, and Benito Mussolini to FDR, 11 January 1939, Box 41, President's Secretary's File, Franklin Roosevelt Papers; Memorandum of 25 June 1937, William Phillips Papers; Joshua Zimmerman, ed., *Jews in Italy under Fascist and Nazi Rule, 1922–1945* (Cambridge University Press, 2005), pp. 3–4.

62 Phillips, *Ventures in Diplomacy*, p. 225; Phillips to FDR, 1 September 1938, Box 42, President's Secretary's File, Franklin Roosevelt Papers; Memoranda of 28 July 1938 and 25 December 1938, William Phillips Papers; *FRUS 1938*, vol. II, pp. 587–588, 591, 598–599; *FRUS 1939*, vol. II, pp. 649, 653–654.

63 Nicky Mariano, *Forty Years with Berenson* (New York: Alfred Knopf, 1966), pp. 276–277; Dario Biocca, ed., *A Matter of Passion: Letters of Bernard Berenson and Clotilde Marghieri* (University of California Press, 1989), pp. xiii, 221; A. K. McComb, ed., *The Selected Letters of Bernard Berenson* (New York: Houghton Mifflin Company, 1964), pp. 153–156, 227–231, 260; Meryle Secrest, *Being Bernard Berenson: A Biography* (New York: Holt, Rinehart and Winston, 1979), pp. 355–356.

64 Liliana Picciotto, "The Shoah in Italy: Its History and Characteristics," in Zimmerman, *Jews in Italy under Fascist and Nazi Rule*, p. 219.

65 Phillips, *Ventures in Diplomacy*, p. 310.

66 General Alfried Jodl testified in 1946: "During the whole of the war Italy was no help to us, only a burden." Cited in Telford Taylor, *The Anatomy of the Nuremberg Trials: A Personal Memoir* (New York: Alfred A. Knopf, 1992), p. 437. Also see Christopher Dodd, ed. *Letters from Nuremberg: My Father's Narrative of a Quest for Justice* (New York: Crown Publishing, 2007), p. 97.

67 Phillips to FDR, 25 March 1941, Box 42, President's Secretary's File, Franklin Roosevelt Papers; diary entry of 15 July 1941, William Phillips Papers; Phillips to Sumner Welles, 26 June 1941, Box 41, President's Secretary's File, Franklin Roosevelt Papers.

68 Phillips to FDR, 16 September 1941, Box 42, President's Secretary's File, Franklin Roosevelt Papers.

69 Kershaw, *Fateful Choices*, p. 197; Lamb, *Mussolini as Diplomat*, p. 279; Malcolm Muggeridge, ed., *Ciano's Diplomatic Papers* (London: Odhams Press, 1948), pp. 337–338; *FRUS 1940*, vol. I, pp. 12–13, 17–19, 21–33, 92–116; Phillips to FDR, 1 March 1940, Box 42, President's Secretary's File, Franklin Roosevelt Papers.

70 Phillips to Welles, 25 June 1940, Box 63, Sumner Welles Papers.

71 Phillips to Welles, 2 July 1940, Box 63, Sumner Welles Papers.

72 Phillips to FDR, 2 October 1940 and FDR to Phillips, 24 September 1940, Box 41, President's Secretary's File, Franklin Roosevelt Papers; Phillips, *Ventures in Diplomacy*, pp. 290–291, 310; Reuter, *William Phillips and the Development of American Foreign Policy*, pp. 250–251.

73 Diary entry of 12 August 1941, William Phillips Papers. The embassy as of early October 1941 consisted of 138 people, from ambassador to doorman.

74 Hugh Gibson, *The Ciano Diaries 1939–1943* (Garden City: Doubleday and Company, 1946), p. 417; Phillips to FDR, 25 June 1941, Box 42, President's Secretary's File, Franklin Roosevelt Papers; diary entries of 22 April 1941 and 18 August 1941, William Phillips Papers; Reuter, *William Phillips and the Development of American Foreign Policy*, p. 229.

75 Phillips, *Ventures in Diplomacy*, pp. 292–293; diary entry of 23 January 1941, William Philips Papers.

76 Diary entries of 2 September 1941 and 21 September 1941, William Phillips Papers.

77 Phillips to FDR, 21 January 1941, Box 41, and Phillips to FDR, 14 April 1941, Box 42, President's Secretary's File, Franklin Roosevelt Papers.

78 Phillips to FDR, 20 June 1940, Box 42, President's Secretary's File, Franklin Roosevelt Papers.

79 Phillips to Sumner Welles, 28 January 1941, Box 41, President's Secretary's File, Franklin Roosevelt Papers.

80 Diary entry of 15 March 1941, William Phillips Papers.

81 Phillips, *Ventures in Diplomacy*, p. 324.

82 Gibson, *The Ciano Diaries 1939–1943*, p. 417.

83 George Wadsworth to Secretary of State, 29 January 1942 (124.653/542) and 31 January 1942 (124.653/581), Record Group 59.

84 Harold Tittmann to Secretary of State, 12 May 1942 (124.653/573 1/2), Record Group 59.

85 *FRUS 1942*, vol. I, pp. 323–324; Long to Mr. Green, 12 January 1942, Box 206, Breckinridge Long Papers; diary entry of 2 June 1942, Caroline Astor Drayton Phillips Papers.

86 Leland Harrison to Secretary of State, 28 May 1942 (124.653/576), Record Group 59.

87 Clipping of "Farewell Salute" from File April 1942-August 1942 (date and source not indicated), Box 3, Caroline Astor Drayton Phillips Papers.

88 Memorandum of Conversation with Swiss Minister representative of Italian interests, 12 January 1942, Box 206, Breckinridge Long Papers; Arnold Krammer, "In Splendid Isolation: Enemy Diplomats in World War II," *Prologue*, 17(1) (1985), pp. 35, 38–39.

89 Phillips, *Ventures in Diplomacy*, p. 327.

90 Phillips to Welles, 25 June 1940, Box 63, Sumner Welles Papers.

91 Phillips to FDR, 14 April 1941, Box 42, President's Secretary's File, Franklin Roosevelt Papers.

92 *FRUS 1935*, vol. I, pp. 749–751, 752–761; Israel, *The War Diary of Breckinridge Long*, pp. xxiii–xxiv; diary entry of 12 September 1935, Box 4, Breckinridge Long Papers; Long to FDR, 29 November 1935, Box 41, President's Secretary's File, Franklin Roosevelt Papers.

93 Max Paul Friedman, *Nazis and Good Neighbors: The United States Campaign against the Germans of Latin America in World War II* (Cambridge University Press, 2003), pp. 156–157; Kenneth Weisbrode, *The Atlantic Century: Four Generations of Extraordinary Diplomats Who Forged America's Vital Alliance with Europe* (Cambridge, Mass.: Da Capo Press, 2009), pp. 71–75.

94 Fabio Rizi, *Benedetto Croce and Italian Fascism* (University of Toronto Press, 2003), p. 247.

Chapter 4: Middle Kingdom

1 Tang Tsou, *America's Failure in China 1941–1950* (University of Chicago Press, 1969 edition), pp. 49–50.

2 Russell Buhite and David Levy, eds., *FDR's Fireside Chats* (University of Oklahoma Press, 1992), pp. 222, 263, 276.

3 Michael Schaller, "FDR and the China Question," in David Woolner, Warren Kimball, and David Reynolds, eds., *FDR's World: War, Peace, and Legacies* (New York: Palgrave Macmillan, 2008), p. 151.

4 *United States Relations with China with Special Reference to the Period 1944–1949* (Washington: Government Printing Office, 1949) [hereafter *China White Paper*], p. 37.

   Chiang was gratified when at Cairo pledges were made to restore to China territories taken by Japan: Taiwan, Manchuria, the Pescadores.

5 Winston Churchill, *The Hinge of Fate* (Boston: Houghton Mifflin, 1950), p. 562.

6 Barbara Tuchman, *Stilwell and the American Experience in China, 1911–45* (New York: Macmillan Company, 1971), p. 239.

7 *FRUS 1942: China*, pp. 27–28; Tuchman, *Stilwell and the American Experience in China*, p. 262; Christopher Thorne, *Allies of a Kind: The United States, Britain and the War against Japan, 1941–1945* (Oxford University Press, 1978), p. 181.

8 *FRUS 1942: China*, pp. 44, 104–105. Japanese forces numbered an additional one million in Manchuria; many were stationed along the Soviet frontier. More than nine hundred thousand puppet troops operated in parts of China and Manchuria. See Herbert Feis's durable *The China Tangle: The American Effort in China from Pearl Harbor to the Marshall Mission* (Princeton University Press, 1953), pp. 355–356.

9 Stilwell had a vulgar streak. He referred (in his diary) to the polio-afflicted FDR as "Rubberlegs." See Tuchman, *Stilwell and the American Experience in China*, p. 398.

10 Patrick Hurley once reflected: "China was the most disagreeable service of my career." See Hurley to Grace Tully, 30 July 1948, Box 22, Franklin D. Roosevelt Memorial Foundation, Franklin Roosevelt Papers.

11 Russell Buhite, *Nelson T. Johnson and American Policy Toward China 1925–1941* (Michigan State University Press, 1968), pp. 1, 6–8; John Paton Davies, *Dragon by the Tail* (New York: W. W. Norton and Company, 1972), p. 164; David Mayers, *Dissenting Voices in America's Rise to Power* (Cambridge University Press, 2007), pp. 257–258.

12 Nelson Johnson, Oral History, pp. 231, 367, 462–463, 676, 720; Herbert Wood, "Nelson Trusler Johnson: The Diplomacy of Benevolent Pragmatism," in Richard Burns and Edward Bennett, eds., *Diplomats in Crisis: United States–Chinese–Japanese Relations, 1919–1941* (Santa Barbara: ABC-CLIO, 1974), pp. 8–10.

13 *FRUS 1939*, vol. III, p. 188; Michael Schaller, *The U.S. Crusade in China, 1938–1945* (Columbia University Press, 1979), p. 7; Tuchman, *Stilwell and the American Experience in China*, p. 148; Dorothy Borg, *The United States and the Far Eastern Crisis of 1933–1938* (Harvard University Press, 1964), p. 59.

14 Jay Taylor, *The Generalissimo: Chiang Kai-shek and the Struggle for Modern China* (Cambridge, Mass.: Belknap Press, 2009), p. 117.

15 Johnson to Stanley Hornbeck, 22 December 1937, Box 66, Nelson Johnson Papers.

16 Johnson to Stanley Hornbeck, 27 September 1937, Box 66, Nelson Johnson Papers; Johnson to FDR, 27 February 1939, Box 27, President's Secretary's File, Franklin Roosevelt Papers.

17 Nelson Johnson to FDR, 27 February 1939, Box 27, President's Secretary's File, Franklin Roosevelt Papers.

18 Johnson to Stanley Hornbeck, 10 February 1938, Box 66, Nelson Johnson Papers; *FRUS 1937*, vol. III, pp. 256–258, 620; *FRUS 1938*, vol. III, pp. 64–65, 153–154, 161, 177, 384; *FRUS, 1939*, vol. III, p. 175; *FRUS 1940*, vol. IV, p. 424; *FRUS 1941*, vol. V, p. 493.

19 Johnson to Stanley Hornbeck, 27 September 1937, Box 66, Nelson Johnson Papers.

20 FDR to Cordell Hull, 18 December 1937, Box 26, President's Secretary's File, Franklin Roosevelt Papers.

21 Marcia Ristaino, *The Jacquinot Safe Zone: Wartime Refugees in Shanghai* (Stanford University Press, 2008), pp. 2, 103.

22 Johnson's two letters to Stanley Hornbeck, 22 December 1937 and 29 December 1937, Box 66, Nelson Johnson Papers; *FRUS 1938*, vol. III, pp. 52, 54.

23 *FRUS 1938*, vol. IV, pp. 221–222, 227–228, 232–233; Erwin Wickert, ed. *The Good Man of Nanking: The Diaries of John Rabe* (New York: Alfred Knopf, 1998), pp. 28, 40, 50, 58, 94, 162; Iris Chang, *The Rape of Nanking: The Forgotten Holocaust of World War II* (New York: Basic Books, 1997), p. 120; John Allison, *Ambassador from the Prairie or Allison Wonderland* (Boston: Houghton Mifflin Company, 1973), p. 40.

24 Johnson to Stanley Hornbeck, 14 January 1938, Box 66, Nelson Johnson Papers. Also see Kemp Tolley, *Yangtze Patrol: The U.S. Navy in China* (Annapolis: Naval Institute Press, 1971), pp. 249–251.

25 Eric Sevareid, *Not So Wild a Dream* (New York: Atheneum, 1976), pp. 207, 310–312; Theodore White and Annalee Jacoby, *Thunder Out of China* (New York: William Sloane Associates, 1946), pp. 9–12, 16; Gary May, *China Scapegoat: The Diplomatic Ordeal of John Carter Vincent* (Washington: New Republic Books, 1979), pp. 63–64; Ellis Briggs, *Proud Servant: The Memoirs of a Career Ambassador* (Kent State University Press, 1998), p. 207. The US compound in Chongqing was vulnerable even during peaceful days. A landslide on 30 September 1945 made the ambassadorial residence uninhabitable. See Walter Robertson to Hurley, 19 October 1945, Box 98, Patrick Hurley Papers.

26 Domestic Troubles in the Chiang Household, 10 May 1944, Box 27, President's Secretary's File, Franklin Roosevelt Papers; Taylor, *The Generalissimo*, pp. 217–218.

27 *FRUS 1940*, vol. IV, p. 887.

28 Johnson to Stanley Hornbeck, 1 June 1940, Box 66, Nelson Johnson Papers.

29 Johnson to Cordell Hull, 27 May 1938, Box 34, Nelson Johnson Papers.

30 Johnson to Stanley Hornbeck, 10 February 1938, Box 66, Nelson Johnson Papers.

31 Norman Davis to FDR, 12 September 1940, Box 150, Official File, Franklin Roosevelt Papers.

32 Johnson to Stanley Hornbeck, 27 September 1937, Box 66, Nelson Johnson Papers.

33 Johnson to Clarence Gauss, 1 March 1941, Box 39, Johnson to Stanley Hornbeck, 13 March 1941, Box 66, Nelson Johnson Papers; *FRUS 1941*, vol. V, pp. 605–608.

34 *FRUS 1940*, vol. IV, pp. 679–682; *FRUS 1941*, vol. V, pp. 635–637; Schaller, "FDR and the China Question," p. 149; Martha Bird, *Chennault: Giving Wings to the Tiger* (University of Alabama Press, 1987), pp. 107–108; Buhite, *Nelson T. Johnson and American Policy Toward China*, p. 141.

35 *FRUS 1940*, vol. IV, pp. 678–679; *FRUS 1941*, vol. V, pp. 629–630.

36 Johnson to Stanley Hornbeck, 16 January 1941, Box 66; Johnson to Roy Howard, 4 February 1941 and 15 April 1941, Box 39, Nelson Johnson Papers; *FRUS 1940*, vol. IV, pp. 450–453.

37 Johnson to Stanley Hornbeck, 11 December 1941, Box 66, Nelson Johnson Papers.

38 Nelson Johnson Oral History, pp. 23, 673; May, *China Scapegoat*, p. 170.

39 John Service Oral History, pp. 158, 174, 264; Lynne Joiner, *Honorable Survivor: Mao's China, McCarthy's America, and the Persecution of John S. Service* (Annapolis: Naval Institute Press, 2009), p. 52; Harvey Klehr and Ronald Radosh, *The Amerasia Spy Case: Prelude to McCarthyism* (University of North Carolina Press, 1996), p. 22; James Durrence, "Ambassador Clarence E. Gauss and United States Relations with China, 1941–1944" (Ph.D. dissertation, University of Georgia, 1971), p. 233; Joseph Esherick, ed., *Lost Chance in China: The World War II Despatches of John S. Service* (New York: Random House, 1974), p. 8; E. J. Kahn, *The China Hands: America's Foreign Service Officers and What Befell Them* (New York: Viking Press, 1975), pp. 64–65; Davies, *Dragon by the Tail*, pp. 233, 342–343.
    Service, after soul-searching, chose to remain with his American wife, Caroline Shultz. He had known her since Oberlin College years.

40 John Service, Oral History, pp. 171, 189; Durrence, *Ambassador Clarence E. Gauss and United States Relations with China*, p. 232; Davies, *Dragon by the Tail*, pp. 163–164.

41 *FRUS 1942: China*, p. 120; *FRUS 1943: China*, pp. 171, 358; Taylor, *The Generalissimo*, p. 602 #81; Schaller, *The U.S. Crusade in China*, p. 89.

42 Jonathan Fenby, *Chiang Kai Shek: China's Generalissimo and the Nation He Lost* (New York: Carroll and Graf Publishers, 2003), p. 341; Durrence, *Ambassador Clarence E. Gauss and United States Relations with China*, p. 234.

43 FDR considered two other men, in addition to Gauss, for the China post. They both had East Asian experience, but being older than Gauss were thought unsuited to the rigors of Chongqing: Admiral Harry Yarnell (b. 1875), commander of the Asiatic Fleet in 1936–1939; John Van Antwerp MacMurray (b. 1881), a seasoned diplomat who knew China and Japan from first-hand experience. MacMurray had served as chief of the State Department's Far Eastern Division (1919–1924) and US minister to China, 1925–1929.

44 Johnson to Stanley Hornbeck, 16 January 1941, Box 66, Nelson Johnson Papers.

45 John Service, Oral History, p. 245; John Emmerson, *The Japanese Thread: A Life in the U.S. Foreign Service* (New York: Holt, Rinehart and Winston, 1978), p. 162; Davies, *Dragon by the Tail*, pp. 246–247; Kahn, *The China Hands*, p. 99 #13.

46 See Wendell Willkie's chronicle of travels through Asia, USSR, the Middle East, and South America – *One World* (New York: Simon and Schuster, 1943).

47 Currie volunteered to take over from Gauss. Roosevelt, Welles, and Hull evidently ignored the suggestion.

48 Thorne, *Allies of a Kind*, pp. 173, 197 #24.

49 Hull's Memorandum for the President: Ambassador Gauss's dispatch No. 1693 on China's War Effort, 2 December 1943, Box 27, President's Secretary's File, Franklin Roosevelt Papers; Brian Crozier, *The Man Who Lost China* (New York: Charles Scribner's Sons, 1976), p. 253; Xiaoyuan Liu, *A Partnership for Disorder: China, the United States and Their Policies for the Postwar Disposition of the Japanese Empire, 1941–1945* (Cambridge University Press, 1996), p. 20.

50 Robert Dallek, *Franklin D. Roosevelt and American Foreign Policy, 1932–1945* (Oxford University Press, 1979), p. 330.

51 Gauss to Cordell Hull, Telegram 2361 (Section Two), 9 December 1943, Box 27, President's Secretary's File, Franklin Roosevelt Papers; *FRUS 1943: China*, pp. 168–176.

52 Hull's Memorandum for the President: Draft of Telegram to Ambassador Gauss, 7 September 1944 and Hull's Memorandum for the President: Situation in China, 25 September 1944, Box 27, President's Secretary's File, Franklin Roosevelt Papers; *FRUS 1944: China*, pp. 544–551, 594; *China White Paper*, p. 64; Bevin Alexander, *The Strange Connection: U.S. Intervention in China, 1944–1972* (New York: Greenwood Press, 1992), p. 9.

53 Theodore White, ed., *The Stilwell Papers* (New York: William Sloane Associates, 1948), pp. 327, 335; Richard Aldrich, *Intelligence and the War against Japan: Britain, America and the Politics of Secret Service* (Cambridge University Press, 2000), p. 269; Taylor, *The Generalissimo*, pp. 257–259. Also see John Service, *The Amerasia Papers: Some Problems in the History of U.S.–China Relations* (Berkeley: Center for Chinese Studies, 1971), p. 163 and Oliver Caldwell, *A Secret War: Americans in China, 1944–1945* (Southern Illinois University Press, 1972), pp. 94–95.

54 Tuchman, *Stilwell and the American Experience in China*, p. 323, 460; Albert Wedemeyer, *Wedemeyer Reports!* (New York: Henry Holt and Company, 1958), p. 295; *FRUS 1944: China*, pp. 125–126; Durrence, *Ambassador Clarence E. Gauss and United States Relations with China*, p. 134.

55 George Atcheson to Johnson, 30 November 1944, and Johnson to Atcheson, 12 December 1944, Box 66, Nelson Johnson Papers; Service, *The Amerasia Papers*, pp. 73–74.

   Gauss left the Foreign Service in May 1945. At Truman's request, he served as director of the Export-Import Bank, from which he retired in 1952. He received the Medal of Freedom from the State Department before his death in 1960.

56 FDR to Clarence Gauss, 14 March 1945, Official File 3874, Franklin Roosevelt Papers.

57 Clarence Gauss to FDR, 6 February 1945, Official File 3874, Franklin Roosevelt Papers.

58 May, *China Scapegoat*, p. 112.

59 Tsou, *America's Failure in China 1941–1950*, p. 114.

60 Carolle Carter, *Mission to Yenan: American Liaison with the Chinese Communists 1944–1947* (University Press of Kentucky, 1997), p. 127.

61 Russell Buhite, *Patrick J. Hurley and American Foreign Policy* (Cornell University Press, 1973), pp. 6–9, 33, 94–99.

62 Ibid., pp. 39–40, 44–45; Henry Stimson and McGeorge Bundy, *On Active Service in Peace and War* (New York: Harper and Brothers, 1948), p. 243.

63 Patrick Hurley to Grace Tully, 30 July 1948, Box 22, Franklin D. Roosevelt Memorial Foundation, Franklin Roosevelt Papers.

64 Johnson to George Atcheson, 12 December 1944, Box 66, Nelson Johnson Papers.

65 Hurley wrote to Henry Wallace: "The quality that I liked most in [FDR] was his cheerfulness and the fact that whenever he took an open swing at me he never resented my swinging back at him." Wallace was himself impressed by how "very close" FDR felt to Hurley. See Wallace to Hurley, 23 June 1951 and Hurley to Wallace, 25 June 1951, Box 104, Patrick Hurley Papers.

66 Memorandum of Conversation at Ambassador Hurley's House, 18 June 1945, Box 94, Patrick Hurley Papers; John Melby, *The Mandate of Heaven: Record of a Civil War: China 1945–49* (University of Toronto Press, 1968), p. 22; Briggs, *Proud Servant*, p. 215.

67 Kahn, *The China Hands*, p. 145; Arthur Ringwalt, Oral History, pp. 9–10.

68 Wedemeyer, *Wedemeyer Reports!*, pp. 306–307, 312–313; Carter, *Mission to Yenan*, pp. 143–144.

69 Albert Wedemeyer to Hurley, 10 July 1945, Box 95, Patrick Hurley Papers.

70 Briggs, *Proud Servant*, pp. 206, 316–317; Kahn, *The China Hands*, p. 160. Robertson served as Assistant Secretary of State for Far Eastern Affairs, 1953–1959.

71 Thorne, *Allies of a Kind*, pp. 573–574.

72 Charles Hood, "The China Hands' Experience: Journalists and Diplomacy," in Paul Gordon Lauren, ed., *The China Hands' Legacy: Ethics and Diplomacy* (Boulder: Westview Press, 1987), pp. 151–152.

73 White and Jacoby, *Thunder Out of China*, pp. 244, 246.

74 David Barrett, *Dixie Mission: The United States Army Observer Group in Yenan, 1944* (Berkeley: Center for Chinese Studies, 1970), p. 57.

75 Mao Tse-tung, *Selected Works* (Peking: Foreign Language Press, 1967), vol. III, pp. 273, 281.

76 Hurley to Edward Stettinius, 31 January 1945, Box 91, Patrick Hurley Papers; *FRUS 1945*, vol. VII, pp. 192–197; *China White Paper*, pp. 74–75; Kai-yu Hsu, *Chou En-lai: China's Gray Eminence* (Garden City: Doubleday and Company, 1968), p. 162.

77 Thorne, *Allies of a Kind*, p. 574; Buhite, *Patrick J. Hurley and American Foreign Policy*, pp. 38–39. On subjects Jewish, Hurley wrote General George Van Horn Moseley: "My experience ... has shown me that the Jews are against fundamental American principles, both at home and abroad ... Always I could have had their support if I had agreed to serve them instead of my country." Hurley to Van Horn Moseley, 12 January 1949, Box 100, Patrick Hurley Papers.

78 Schaller, *The U.S. Crusade in China*, pp. 221–222.

79 Hurley to Homer Ferguson, 4 January 1945, Box 91, Patrick Hurley Papers; Emmerson, *The Japanese Thread*, p. 204; Barrett, *Dixie Mission*, p. 57.

80 Hurley to FDR, 20 November 1943, Box 86, Patrick Hurley Papers; Hurley to Edward Stettinius, 12 February 1945, Box 92, Patrick Hurley Papers; *China White Paper*, pp. 71–72.

81 Chiang was not surprised by Hurley's revelations in June 1945 about the Soviet–US accord reached at Yalta. They simply confirmed information – flowing from leaks – previously known to him. The Sino-Soviet treaty of 14 August 1945 recapitulated the Yalta understanding, a "sellout" from the standpoint of *both* Chiang and Mao. See Taylor, *The Generalissimo*, pp. 302–303 and Schaller, *The U.S. Crusade in China*, p. 260.

82 Kenneth Shewmaker, *Americans and Chinese Communists, 1927–1945* (Cornell University Press, 1971), p. 175.

83 Thorne, *Allies of a Kind*, p. 575.

84 Chiang Kai-shek, *China's Destiny* (New York: Macmillan Company, 1947), p. 217.

85 *FRUS 1945*, vol. VII, pp. 242–246.

86 Barrett, *Dixie Mission*, p. 91.

87 Notes on conference between Hurley and Sir Horace Seymour, 3 November 1944, Box 88; Hurley to FDR, 26 November 1944, Box 89; Hurley to Sir Horace Seymour, November or December 1944, Box 89, Patrick Hurley Papers. Also see *FRUS 1945*, vol. VII, pp. 107–114 and Aldrich, *Intelligence and the War against Japan*, pp. 176–177; Buhite, *Patrick J. Hurley and American Foreign Policy*, pp. 241, 252.

88 SACO stood for Sino-American Cooperative Organization.

89 Aldrich, *Intelligence and the War against Japan: Britain, America and the Politics of Secret Service*, p. 270; Frederic Wakeman, *Spymaster: Dai Li and the Chinese Secret Service* (University of California Press, 2003), pp. 348–349; Milton Miles, *A Different Kind of War* (Garden City: Doubleday and Company, 1967), pp. 200, 468; Schaller, *The U.S. Crusade in China*, pp. 204–206; Dick Wilson, *Zhou Enlai: A Biography* (New York: Viking, 1984), p.166.

90 Statement without title, 2 June 1950, Box 104; excerpt from a report of staff meeting at the embassy on US policy in China, no day/month 1945, Box 91, Patrick Hurley Papers.

91 Harry Truman to Chiang Kai-shek, 19 October 1945, Box 99, Patrick
    Hurley Papers; Buhite, *Patrick J. Hurley and American Foreign Policy*,
    pp. 258–259; Davies, *Dragon by the Tail*, p. 337.
92 *China White Paper*, pp. 582–583.
93 Testimony from investigation of Far Eastern Policy, 5 December 1945, Box 98,
    Patrick Hurley Papers.
94 McNaughton to David Hubbard, 7 December 1945, Box 10, Frank
    McNaughton Papers.
95 John Paton Davies to Hurley, 26 November 1944, Hurley to FDR, 26
    November 1944, Davies to Hurley, 29 November 1944, Box 89; Davies,
    China and the Kremlin, 4 January 1945, Box 91, Patrick Hurley Papers.
96 Hurley to Ruth Hurley, 17 November 1943, Box 216, James Byrnes to Hurley,
    28 November 1945, Box 98, Statement without title, 2 June 1950, Box 104,
    Patrick Hurley Papers; May, *China Scapegoat*, p. 123; McNaughton to David
    Hubbard, 6 December 1945, Box 10, Frank McNaughton Papers.
97 Buhite, *Patrick J. Hurley and American Foreign Policy*, p. 271.
98 Ibid., pp. 263–266.
99 Hurley to Walter Robertson, 31 January 1946, Box 100, Patrick Hurley Papers.
100 Hurley became a fixture on the right wing of the GOP. He held conspiracy
    theories about the Yalta conference and viewed himself a victim of
    State Department intriguers, among whom he counted Dean Acheson.
    Hurley's career was celebrated in a biography by Don Lohbeck: *Patrick
    J. Hurley* (Chicago: Henry Regnery, 1956). Lohbeck's book amounts to
    hagiography and is without scholarly value. Not until Russell Buhite's work
    on Hurley was published in 1973 did the reading public have a judicious
    account of his life.
101 *China White Paper*, p. xvi.
102 Hurley to Robert Richards, 3 December 1954, Box 58, Patrick Hurley Papers.
    Also see Joiner, *Honorable Survivor*, p. 223.
103 John Service, Oral History, p. 179; Esherick, *Last Chance in China*,
    pp. xvi–xvii; Kahn, *The China Hands*, p. 52 #4; Joiner, *Honorable Survivor*,
    pp. 30, 180, 253.
104 Robert McNamara, *In Retrospect: The Tragedy and Lessons of Vietnam*
    (New York: Random House, 1995), p. 33.
105 Schaller, *The U.S. Crusade in China*, pp. 149, 191.
106 John Paton Davies, China and the Kremlin, 4 January 1945, Box 91, Patrick
    Hurley Papers.
        I have taken liberties in selectively quoting from this Davies document
    that was primarily centered on Soviet perceptions of America's China policy.
    Still, my presentation amounts to a fair depiction of Davies's astute realpolitik
    orientation.

107 Another version of Wallace and the Chongqing incident appears in Brigg's *Proud Servant: Memoirs of a Career Ambassador*, p. 207 #4. Briggs, who was not in China in 1944 and recorded the tale five decades after the event, believes that Wallace refused service by chair bearers (not rickshaw drivers). Instead of getting to carry him, they had to bear the burdens of "lost face" and lost revenue.

    I have reproduced the Wallace story as told by Claire Chennault in his *Way of a Fighter* (New York: G. P. Putnam's Sons, 1949), p. 231. Chennault was in China in 1944 and at the time of his writing closer to events. Still, caution is required. Chennault disliked liberals of the New Deal type and could have embellished to make Wallace look silly. Chennault was also unfriendly to the State Department and its China hands. He described them as "incompetent scrubs" and "left wingers."

108 *FRUS 1944: China*, p. 520.

109 Nelson Johnson Oral History, p. 694; Johnson to Quincy Wright, 31 March 1947, Box 68, Nelson Johnson Papers.

110 Chang, *The Rape of Nanking*, p. 129.

111 Wickert, *The Good Man of Nanking*, p. 46.

Chapter 5: France Agonistes

1 Ernest May, *Strange Victory: Hitler's Conquest of France* (New York: Hill and Wang, 2000), p. 6; Tony Judt, *Reappraisals: Reflections on the Forgotten Twentieth Century* (New York: Penguin Books, 2008), p. 212.

2 Raoul Aglion, *Roosevelt and de Gaulle: Allies in Conflict: A Personal Memoir* (New York: Free Press, 1988), p. 120.

3 Marc Bloch, *Strange Defeat: A Statement of Evidence Written in 1940* (New York: W. W Norton and Company, 1999), p. 25.

4 Irène Némirovsky, *Suite Française* (New York: Vintage Books, 2007), p. 156.

5 Germaine Bree and George Bernauer, eds., *Defeat and Beyond: An Anthology of French Wartime Writing, 1940–1945* (New York: Pantheon Books, 1970), p. 148.

6 Bloch, *Strange Defeat*, p. 25; Thomas Christofferson, *France During World War II: From Defeat to Liberation* (Fordham University Press, 2006), p. 22.

7 Georges Suarez, *Pétain ou la démocratie? Il faut choisir* (Paris: Bernard Grasset, 1941), p. 87.

8 Mark Mazower, *Hitler's Empire: How the Nazis Ruled Europe* (New York: Penguin Press, 2008), p. 107.

9 *FRUS 1940*, vol. II, pp. 469–470.

10 *FRUS 1940*, vol. I, p. 239.

11 Christofferson, *France During World War II*, p. 79.

12 Charles de Gaulle, *War Memoirs* (New York: Carroll and Graf Publishers, 1998), p. 84.

13 Henry Rousso, *The Vichy Syndrome: History and Memory in France since 1944* (Harvard University Press, 1991), pp. 5–8.

14 Richard Vinen, *The Unfree French: Life under the Occupation* (Yale University Press, 2006), p. 144. Also see Samuel Kalman, *The Extreme Right in Interwar France: The Faisceau and the Croix de Feu* (Aldershot: Ashgate, 2008) and Alan Riding, *And the Show Went On: Cultural Life in Nazi-Occupied Paris* (New York: Alfred Knopf, 2010).

15 OSS Intelligence Report, 27 July 1944, Political Adviser to SHAEF (William Phillips), Subject Files 1943–1944, Box 5, RG 84.

16 Tony Judt, *The Burden of Responsibility: Blum, Camus, Aron and the French Twentieth Century* (University of Chicago Press, 1998), p. 111; Marc Ferro, *Resentment in History* (Cambridge: Polity Press, 2010), p. 71.

17 FDR to Churchill, 17 June 1943, Political Adviser to SHAEF (William Phillips), Subject Files 1943–1944, Box 5, RG 84; *FRUS 1943*, vol. II, pp. 155–157.

18 See William Bullitt and Sigmund Freud, *Thomas Woodrow Wilson, Twenty-Eighth President of the United Sates: A Psychological Study* (Boston: Houghton Mifflin, 1967).

19 Charles Glass, *Americans in Paris: Life and Death under Nazi Occupation* (New York: Penguin Books, 2011), p. 14.

20 While ambassador to France, Bullitt played a part in securing Freud's release (June 1938) from Nazi Vienna and reaching safety in London. See Will Brownell and Richard Billings, *So Close to Greatness: A Biography of William C. Bullitt* (New York: Macmillan Publishing Company, 1987), p. 213. Also useful is Memorandum [re Bullitt's 1938 aid to Freud], nd [circa 1956], Box 30, William Bullitt Papers.

21 William Bullitt, *The Great Globe Itself: A Preface to World Affairs* (New York: Charles Scribner's Sons, 1946), p. 193.

22 Gordon Wright, "Ambassador Bullitt and the Fall of France," *World Politics* (October 1957), p. 66, #15.

23 Brownell and Billings, *So Close to Greatness*, p. 202.

24 Robert Murphy, *Diplomat among Warriors* (Garden City: Doubleday and Company, 1964), p. 38.

25 Brownell and Billings, *So Close to Greatness*, p. 191; Edouard Daladier, *Prison Journal 1940–1945* (Boulder: Westview Press, 1995), pp. 47, 331; Orville Bullitt, ed., *For the President: Personal and Secret: Correspondence Between Franklin D. Roosevelt and William C. Bullitt* (Boston: Houghton Mifflin Company, 1972), pp. 168, 246 (hereafter *For the President*). Also see Edouard Daladier to Bullitt, 24 December 1940, Box 24, William Bullitt Papers: "The memory of our friendship is one of the finest things in my life." Bullitt counted

Léon Blum "one of my closest personal friends." See Bullitt's 1950 eulogy of Blum, Box 10, William Bullitt Papers.

26 William Dodd to Bullitt, 5 October 1936; Bullitt to Dodd, 8 October 1936; Bullitt to Dodd, 5 March 1937, Box 25, William Bullitt Papers; Bullitt to FDR, 10 May 1937 and Bullitt to FDR, 7 December 1937, Box 30, President's Secretary's File, Franklin Roosevelt Papers; Bullitt, *For the President*, pp. 239, 242.

27 Wright, "Ambassador Bullitt and the Fall of France," p. 70; William Keylor, "France and the Illusion of American Support, 1919–1940," in Joel Blatt, ed., *The French Defeat of 1940* (Providence: Berghahn Books, 1998), p. 227; Henry Blumenthal, *Illusion and Reality in Franco-American Diplomacy 1914–1945* (Louisiana State University Press, 1986), p. 227.

28 Bullitt to Hugh Wilson, 19 July 1938, Box 91, William Bullitt Papers; Bullitt, *For the President*, pp. 200, 262.

29 Bullitt to Hugh Wilson, 23 June 1938, Box 91, William Bullitt Papers; William Kaufmann, "Two American Ambassadors: Bullitt and Kennedy," in Gordon Craig and Felix Gilbert, eds. *The Diplomats 1919–1939* (Princeton University Press, 1994), p. 661.

30 Brownell and Billings, *So Close to Greatness*, p. 232; Bullitt, *For the President*, pp. 306, 321.

31 Wright, "Ambassador Bullitt and the Fall of France," p. 73.

32 Mario Rossi, *Roosevelt and the French* (Westport: Praeger, 1993), p. 38.

33 Bullitt, *For the President*, p. 383; *FRUS 1939*, vol. I, p. 270.

34 *FRUS 1939*, vol. I, p. 410.

35 William Bullitt to FDR, 4 October 1939, Box 2, President's Secretary's File, Franklin Roosevelt Papers; Bullitt, *For the President*, p. 379.

36 Bullitt, *For the President*, pp. 192–193, 269–270; Edouard Daladier to FDR, 4 April 1940, Box 31, President's Secretary's File, Franklin Roosevelt Papers; *FRUS 1938*, vol. I, p. 2.

37 Blumenthal, *Illusion and Reality in Franco-American Diplomacy 1914–1945*, pp. 205–206; Brownell and Billings, *So Close to Greatness*, p. 128; Bullitt, *For the President*, pp. 234–236, 315–317. Léon Blum had earlier discussed ways by which France might have secured loans from the United States and circumvented the Johnson Act. See *FRUS 1937*, vol. I, pp. 848–850.

38 Bullitt, *For the President*, p. 410.

39 *FRUS 1939*, vol. I, p. 460.

40 William Bullitt to FDR, 13 June 1938, Box 30, President's Secretary's File, Franklin Roosevelt Papers; Bullitt, *For the President*, pp. 267–272.

41 Bullitt, *For the President*, p. 298.

42 William Bullitt to Welles, 28 November 1939, Box 51, Sumner Welles Papers; *FRUS 1939*, vol. I, pp. 445, 475.

43 Keylor, "France and the Illusion of American Support, 1919–1940," p. 242; François Duchêne, *Jean Monnet: The First Statesman of Interdependence* (New York: W. W. Norton and Company, 1994), pp. 65, 68–70; Bullitt, *For the President*, pp. 391–392.

44 Bullitt, *For the President*, pp. 372–374.

45 *FRUS 1940*, vol. I, p. 225.

46 Wright, "Ambassador Bullitt and the Fall of France," pp. 83–84; *FRUS 1940*, vol. I, p. 237; Bullitt, *For the President*, p. 446.

47 Bullitt, *For the President*, p. 447.

48 Irwin Gellman, *Secret Affairs: Franklin Roosevelt, Cordell Hull, and Sumner Welles* (Johns Hopkins University Press, 1995), pp. 240–241; Kenneth Weisbrode, "The Master, the Maverick, and the Machine: Three Wartime Promoters of Peace," *Journal of Policy History*, 21 (2009), p. 368; Brownell and Billings, *So Close to Greatness*, p. 297; Bullitt, *For the President*, pp. 512–514.

49 LeHand's duty encompassed work as de facto White House chief of staff. She loved Bullitt, whose failure to marry her may have been interpreted by FDR as evidence of a character flaw. LeHand suffered a stroke in June 1941 that ended her White House career. She died three years later. Evidence, albeit inconclusive, suggests that FDR at one time had fastened his romantic yearnings on Lehand. See Frank Costigliola, "Broken Circle: The Isolation of Franklin D. Roosevelt in World War II," *Diplomatic History*, 32 (2008), pp. 677, 686–694; Brownell and Billings, *So Close to Greatness*, p. 267; Bullitt, *For the President*, p. 398.

50 Bullitt, *For the President*, p. 184; Don Kladstrup and Petie Kladstrup, *Wine and War: The French, the Nazis, and the Battle for France's Greatest Treasure* (New York: Broadway Books, 2001), p. 33.

51 William Bullitt to FDR, 31 August 1938, Box 30, President's Secretary's File, Franklin Roosevelt Papers.

52 Bullitt, *For the President*, p. 410. Also see *FRUS 1940*, vol. I, pp. 58–72, 91–92; Marvin Zahniser, *Then Came Disaster: France and the United States, 1918–1940* (Westport: Praeger, 2002), p. 76; Blumenthal, *Illusion and Reality in Franco-American Diplomacy 1914–1945*, p. 257.

53 William Bullitt to FDR, 31 August 1938, Box 30, President's Secretary's File, Franklin Roosevelt Papers.

54 Kenneth Weisbrode, *The Atlantic Century: Four Generations of Extraordinary Diplomats Who Forged America's Vital Alliance with Europe* (Cambridge, Mass.: Da Capo Press, 2009), p. 69; John Lewis Gaddis, *George F. Kennan: An American Life* (New York: Penguin Press, 2011), p. 98; Bullitt, *For the President*, p. 216; Brownell and Billings, *So Close to Greatness*, pp. 195–196, 204; Zahniser, *Then Came Disaster*, p. 64.

Offie's homosexual liaisons apparently did not upset Bullitt. His tolerance of them fueled rumors that Bullitt's own sexual preferences were unresolved. Bullitt and Offie lived in the same quarters in Moscow, Paris, and Washington. See Costigliola, "Broken Circle: The Isolation of Franklin D. Roosevelt in World War II," p. 703; Gellman, *Secret Affairs*, p. 245.

55 FDR to William Bullitt, 10 April 1939 and Bullitt to FDR, 23 April 1939, Box 30, President's Secretary's File, Franklin Roosevelt Papers.

56 Vicki Caron, "The Path to Vichy: Antisemitism in France in the 1930s," Shapiro Lecture (Washington: United States Holocaust Memorial Museum, 2005), p. 11.

57 Andre Brissaud, *Canaris* (New York: Grosset and Dunlap, 1974), pp. 318–319; Heinz Hohne, *Canaris* (Garden City: Doubleday and Company, 1979), pp. 466, 488–489, 507; John Waller, *Europe: Espionage and Conspiracy in the Second World War* (New York: I. B. Tauris, 1996), p. 308; Michael Mueller, *Canaris: The Life and Death of Hitler's Spymaster* (Annapolis: Naval Institute Press, 2007), pp. 226–227.

58 William Bullitt to FDR, 27 August 1939, Box 30, President's Secretary's File, Franklin Roosevelt Papers.

59 Russell Buhite and David Levy, eds., *FDR's Fireside Chats* (University of Oklahoma Press, 1992), p. 161; Zahniser, *Then Came Disaster*, p. 65.

60 Hanna Diamond, *Fleeing Hitler: France in 1940* (Oxford University Press, 2007), p. 110; Murphy, *Diplomat among Warriors*, p. 48.

61 Cordell Hull, *The Memoirs of Cordell Hull* (New York: Macmillan Company, 1948), vol. I, pp. 789–791.

62 Bullitt, *For the President*, p. 468.

63 Ibid., pp. 434, 441, 455.

64 De Gaulle, *War Memoirs*, p. 61.

65 René Pleven to Bullitt, 1 August 1940, Box 66, William Bullitt Papers.

66 Matthews to Father Luke [father-in-law], p. 4, 14 August 1940, H. Freeman Matthews Papers.

67 Harold Ickes, *The Secret Diary* (New York: Simon and Schuster, 1954), vol. III, p. 209

68 Douglas MacArthur II, Foreign Affairs Oral History, pp. 12, 16–17.

69 Matthews to Father Luke, pp. 12–13, 14 August 1940, H. Freeman Matthews Papers.

70 Paul Deutschman, "Mission Extraordinary" (unpublished manuscript), pp. 311–312, 369, Box 71, Jefferson Caffery Papers. Charles Anderson and Frank Delisio – both responsible for upkeep of embassy offices and residences – were arrested by the Germans on 7 January 1942 and interned at Bad Nauheim, where they remained until repatriated with other Americans in May. Consular personnel and their families had been obliged by the Germans to quit the Paris embassy and leave France in summer 1941.

71 Vinen, *The Unfree French*, pp. 51, 381 #13. Ambassador Alexander Bogomolov led the Soviet embassy. Vichy–Soviet relations ended with Germany's invasion of the USSR. Several thousand volunteers from the occupied zone served in the *Légion des Volontaires françois contre le Bolchevisme* and saw action in eastern Europe.

72 De Gaulle, *War Memoirs*, p. 87.

73 Julian Hurtsfield, *America and the French Nation, 1939–1945* (University of North Carolina Press, 1986), pp. 10–11.

74 Aglion, *Roosevelt and de Gaulle*, p. 120.

75 Bullitt, *For the President*, pp. 483–485, 489.

76 William Bullitt to FDR, 1 July 1941, #1124, President's Personal File, Franklin Roosevelt Papers.

77 Matthews to William Shirer, 20 March 1968, H. Freeman Matthews Papers; MacArthur II, Foreign Affairs Oral History, p. 15.

78 Bullitt, *For the President*, p. 487.

79 "Ambassador Bullitt's Remarkable Report to His People," *Bangor Daily News*, 20 August 1940.

80 Bullitt, *For the President*, pp. 505–506.

81 Glass, *Americans in Paris*, p. 413.

82 Henry Adams, *Witness to Power: The Life of Fleet Admiral William D. Leahy* (Annapolis: Naval Institute Press, 1985), p. 135.

83 William Leahy, *I Was There* (New York: Whittlesey House, 1950), p. 3; "President Roosevelt's Ear at Vichy," *Oberlaendisches Voklsblatt*, 26 August 1941, pp. 1–4, Box OVS, William Leahy Papers.

84 Adams, *Witness to Power*, pp. 26, 49, 124, 328.

85 Memorandum of Interview with Fleet Admiral William D. Leahy, 24 May, 1948, pp. 5–6, Frank Freidel, Oral History, Franklin Roosevelt Papers.

86 *FRUS 1940*, vol. II, 425–429; Leahy, *I Was There*, pp. p. 8–9, 443–446; Adams, *Witness to Power*, p. 5.

87 Adams, *Witness to Power*, p. 147.

88 Murphy, *Diplomat among Warriors*, pp. 56–57; Hal Vaughan, *FDR's 12 Apostles: The Spies Who Paved the Way for the Invasion of North Africa* (Guilford: Lyons Press, 2006), p. 12.

89 About twenty-five officers and clerks, some with accompanying spouses and children, staffed the Vichy embassy. See Leahy, *I Was There*, p. 62; MacArthur II, Foreign Affairs Oral History, p. 21.

90 Matthews to Father Luke, 14 August 1940, pp. 31–33, H. Freeman Matthews Papers.

91 "Memoirs" [unpublished] p. 399, H. Freeman Matthews Papers.

92 *FRUS 1940*, vol. II, pp. 565–568; Diamond, *Fleeing Hitler*, p. 166.

93 Matthews to Jefferson Caffery, 4 July 1941, p. 5, H. Freeman Matthews Papers.

94 Entry of 2 February 1941, Diary, William Leahy Papers; Leahy, *I Was There,*
    p. 33.

95 Adams, *Witness to Power,* p. 168; Leahy, *I Was There,* pp. 455, 465, 470;
    Hubert Cole, *Laval: A Biography* (New York: G. P. Putnam's Sons, 1963),
    p. 192.

96 Leahy, *I Was There,* p. 374; Herbert Lottman, *Pétain: Hero or Traitor: The
    Untold Story* (New York: William Morrow and Company, 1985), pp. 360, 366.

97 Leahy, *I Was There,* p. 462; Hurtsfield, *America and the French Nation
    1939–1945,* pp. 74–77, 82.

98 Entries of 9 October 1941 and 13 February 1942, Diary, William Leahy
    Papers; François Kersaudy, *Churchill and de Gaulle* (New York: Atheneum,
    1982), p. 268.

99 Kersaudy, *Churchill and de Gaulle,* p. 295; Adams, *Witness to Power,* p. 153;
    Matthews to Jefferson Caffery, 4 July 1941, H. Freeman Matthews Papers.

100 *FRUS 1941,* vol. II, pp. 93–96; Leahy to FDR, 21 April 1941, reproduced
    in Diary, William Leahy Papers; Murphy to William Leahy, 1 January 1943,
    Box 45, Robert Murphy Papers. On US food aid to France, also see Robert
    Murphy to Bullitt, 16 September 1940, Box 60, William Bullitt Papers.

101 William Leahy to Secretary of State, French officials associated with Admiral
    Darlan's policy of collaboration with Germany, 21 June 1941, p. 4, France:
    US Embassy, Vichy 1940–1942, Box 5, RG 84; William Langer, *Our Vichy
    Gamble* (New York: Alfred Knopf, 1947), p. 387; Leahy, *I Was There,*
    pp. 70, 76.

102 Geoffrey Warner, *Pierre Laval and the Eclipse of France* (New York:
    Macmillan Company, 1969), p. 292.

103 *FRUS 1941,* vol. II, pp. 461–466; *FRUS 1942,* vol. II, pp. 128–133; Langer,
    Our Vichy Gamble, pp. 402–412; Leahy, *I Was There,* pp. 18, 455–457.

104 Eckart Conze *et al., Das Amt und die Vergangenheit: Deutsche Diplomaten im
    Dritten Reich und in der Bundesrepublik* (Munich: Blessing, 2010), pp. 227–236.

105 Leahy, *I Was There,* pp. 15, 33–36; Adams, *Witness to Power,* pp. 149, 159.

106 Leahy, *I Was There,* p. 479; FDR to Leahy, Diary, n.d. February 1942, William
    Leahy Papers.

107 Leahy, *I Was There,* p. 85.

108 Aglion, *Roosevelt and de Gaulle,* pp. 65–66; Hurtsfield, *America and the
    French Nation, 1939–1945,* pp. 48–49, 114, 130, 147, 153–154.

109 Janet Malcolm, *Two Lives: Gertrude and Alice* (Yale University Press, 2007),
    p. 24.

110 Leahy, *I Was There,* p. 51; *FRUS 1941,* vol. II, pp. 503–511; Adam Nossiter,
    The Algeria Hotel: France, Memory, and the Second World War
    (Boston: Houghton Mifflin Company, 2001), p. 151; entry of 5 March 1942,
    Diary, William Leahy Papers.

111 Entry of 23 September 1941, Diary, William Leahy Papers; MacArthur II, Foreign Affairs Oral History, p. 21.

112 Varian Fry, *Surrender on Demand* (New York: Random House, 1945), p. x.

113 Yvonne Cossu, "Le Nazisme et l'art," *Mémoire Vivante*, 62 (2009), p. 15; Jewish-German Albert Hirschman ("Beamish") was Fry's closest collaborator in France. Hirschman enjoyed a distinguished postwar career as economist in the United States.

114 Ronald Weber, *The Lisbon Route: Entry and Escape in Nazi Europe* (Lanham: Ivan Dee, 2011), pp. 64–65. Also see *Transit Visa* (Boston: Little, Brown, 1944), a novel by Anna Seghers. Based on her Marseille saga and escape to the New World, the book conveys something of the danger and uncertainty that plagued intellectual-political-artistic fugitives from the German/Vichy net.

115 Mordecai Paldiel, *The Righteous among the Nations: Rescuers of Jews During the Holocaust* (New York: Collins, 2007), pp. 127–128; Susan Subak, *Rescue and Flight: American Relief Workers Who Defied the Nazis* (University of Nebraska Press, 2010), p. 116; Andy Marino, *A Quiet American: The Secret War of Varian Fry* (New York: St. Martin's Press, 1999), p. 189; Rosemary Sullivan, *Villa Air-Bel: World War II, Escape, and a House in Marseille* (New York: HarperCollins, 2006), pp. 290–292; Fry, *Surrender on Demand*, p. 81.

116 Eleanor Roosevelt to Mrs. Fry, 13 May 1941, Box 1, Varian Fry Papers. Also see Alfred Barr to Archibald MacLeish, 9 May 1941, Box 8, Varian Fry Papers.

117 Marino, *A Quiet American*, p. 335.

118 Sheila Isenberg, *A Hero of Our Own: The Story of Varian Fry* (New York: Random House, 2001), pp. 229, 242, 247–248, 253; Marino, *A Quiet American*, pp. 322–323

119 Diary entry or draft of a letter by Fry, 8 February 1941: "Bullitt said that I would find the Embassy staff very cooperative and helpful. I wonder how he could have been so wrong ... how thin [is] the ice under my feet." Box 7, Varian Fry Papers.

120 Fry to William Leahy, 8 January, 1941, Fry to Leahy, 15 January 1941, Douglas MacArthur II to Fry, 15 January 1941, Fry to Leahy, 29 January 1941, Box 7; Fry to Otto Hirschman, 30 November 1941, Box 8, Varian Fry Papers; Isenberg, *A Hero of Our Own*, p. 212; Marino, *A Quiet American*, p. 311.

121 Fry to H. Freeman Matthews, 13 November 1940 and Matthews to Fry, 9 January 1941, Box 7, Varian Fry Papers.

122 Fry to Frank Kingdon, 24 June 1941, Box 8, Varian Fry Papers.

123 Hugh Fullerton to Fry, 21 January 1941, Fry to Mr. Sholes, 14 February 1941, Fry to Felix Cole, 14 February 1941, Fry to Clark Husted, 17 February 1941, Fry to Fullerton, 25 February 1941, Fullerton to Fry, 28 February 1941, Box 7, Varian Fry Papers; Hugh Fullerton to H. Freeman Matthews, 26 May 1941, France US Embassy, Vichy 1940–1942, Box 5, RG 84; Isenberg, *A Hero of Our Own: The Story of Varian Fry*, p. 141.

124 Clark Husted to Fry, 1 March 1941. Also see this correspondence: Fry to Husted, 4 March 1941, Husted to Fry, 7 March 1941, Fry to Husted, 10 April 1941, Husted to Fry, 26 April 1941, Box 7, Varian Fry Papers. More on Coperman is in Marino, *A Quiet American*, p. 299, 329.

125 Robert Dexter to Cordell Hull, 2 January 1941, Breckinridge Long to Dexter, 11 January 1941, Long to Hugh Fullerton, 11 January 1941, 123 Bingham, Hiram/190, Decimal File 1940–1944, Box 331, RG 59.

126 Mordecai Paldiel, *Diplomat Heroes of the Holocaust* (Jersey City: KTAV Publishing House, 2007), pp. 203–204; Subak, *Rescue and Flight*, pp. 48–50, 89–90, 93–94, 252 #8, 254 #36; Sullivan, *Villa Air-Bel*, p. 204; Robert Bingham, *Courageous Dissent: How Harry Bingham Defied His Government to Save Lives* (Greenwich: Triune Books, 2007), pp. 4, 11, 22. Also see Ellen Rafshoon, "Harry Bingham: Beyond the Call of Duty," *Foreign Service Journal* (June 2002).

127 Speech by Hiram Bingham at American Consular Corps Dinner, Buenos Aires, 6 December 1943, 123 Bingham, Hiram/252, Decimal File 1940–1944, Box 331, RG 59.

128 Fry, *Surrender on Demand*, p. 215.

129 H. Freeman Matthews to Ray Atherton, 6 March 1943, Box 45, Robert Murphy Papers.

130 Nossiter, *The Algeria Hotel: France, Memory, and the Second World War*, p. 158; William Bullitt to FDR, 5 July 1937, FDR to Bullitt, 17 July 1937, Bullitt to FDR, 25 April 1939, President's Secretary's File, Box 30, Franklin Roosevelt Papers.

131 S. Pinkney Tuck to H. Freeman Matthews, 20 August 1942, U.S. Embassy, Vichy, Supplemental Records, Box 1, RG 84.

132 S. Pinkney Tuck to Bullitt, 13 May 1942, Box 82, William Bullitt Papers. Also see Ferro, *Resentment in History*, p. 65.

133 *FRUS 1942*, vol. II, pp. 160–161, 170–171; Leahy, *I Was There*, p. 90; Carlton Hayes, *Wartime Mission in Spain 1942–1945* (New York: Macmillan Company, 1945), p. 15.

134 *FRUS 1942*, vol. II, pp. 187–189.

135 S. Pinkney Tuck to Ray Atherton, 2 March 1942, US Embassy, Vichy, Supplemental Record, Box 1, RG 84.

136 J. Webb Benton to Tyler Thompson, 12 August 1942 with Leslie Bell's Memorandum to Mr. Sparrow, 7 August 1942, US Embassy, Vichy, Box 18, RG 84.

137 Michael Marrus and Robert Paxton, *Vichy France and the Jews* (Stanford University Press, 1995), pp. 260–262.

138 J. Webb Benton to Tyler Thompson, 12 August 1942, Benton to S. Pinkney Tuck, 17 August 1942, Walter Orebaugh to Tuck, 27 August 1942, Orebaugh to Tuck, 1 September 1942, Benton to Tuck, 4 September 1942, Benton to Tuck, 14 September 1942, Orebaugh to Tuck, 18 September 1942, Benton to Tuck, 30 October 1942, US Embassy Vichy, Box 18, RG 84.

139 Walter Orebaugh to S. Pinkney Tuck, 21 August 1942, US Embassy Vichy, Box 18, RG 84.

140 S. Pinkney Tuck to Secretary of State, 10 September 1942, US Embassy Vichy, France, Box 18, RG 84.

141 *FRUS 1942*, vol. II, p. 712.

142 S. Pinkney Tuck to Secretary of State, 4 September 1942, US Embassy, Vichy, Box 18, RG 84.

143 *FRUS 1942*, vol. II, pp. 710–716; Donald Lowrie, Conversation with Mr. Bousquet, 16 October 1942, US Embassy, Vichy, Box 18, RG 84; "U.S. Rebukes Vichy on Deporting Jews," *New York Times*, 5 September 1942; entry of 7 September 1942, Diary, William Leahy Papers; Vicki Caron, *Uneasy Asylum: France and the Jewish Refugee Crisis, 1933–1942* (Stanford University Press, 1999), pp. 338–341; Marrus and Paxton, *Vichy France and the Jews*, pp. 266–267; Yehuda Bauer, *American Jewry and the Holocaust: The American Jewish Joint Distribution Committee, 1939–1945* (Wayne State University Press, 1981), pp. 174–176, 260–262.

144 Secretary of State to S. Pinkney Tuck, 18 June 1942, US Embassy, Vichy, Box 17, RG 84.

145 Small numbers of children were able to escape from German-occupied France. James Mann of the War Refugee Board met a few in Portugal in 1944. He wrote:

I called at the house of the refugee children one afternoon and talked with several of the children, whom we picked at random. The children described the details of their escape, which are interesting. It appears that they had all been in Toulouse and their parents had been taken by the Germans. These children had come into Spain in two groups. In each case (groups of 6 and 7), they had been told that they were going for a walk and after they had walked from the home in which they were stationed, they were picked by truck and told that they were going to Palestine. They proceeded for a distance by truck until they were met by guides, who took them across the border in a trip which lasted better than two days. The children stopped regularly at cottages along the way and were fed. Sometimes, they slept a while at night, but never got a full night's sleep. In fact, most of their travel was at night and it seems they walked along the railroad and through railroad tunnels. Just before they

arrived at the French border, they were met by some women and men who
took them across by train, giving the appearance of a family. After they had
crossed the border, the men disappeared and the women turned them over to a
person who took them to Barcelona ... [another designated person]
clandestinely took them into Portugal. After they entered Portugal, their
entrance was legalized ... The oldest of the children at the reception center is
14 and the youngest is 5.

    James Mann, "Report on Trip to Portugal and Spain" (May–July 1944),
pp. 26–27, Box 78, War Refugee Board Papers.

146 *FRUS 1942*, vol. II, pp. 430–432; Lottman, *Pétain: Hero or Traitor*,
pp. 289–290; Malcolm, *Two Lives: Gertrude and Alice*, pp. 182, 186.

147 Diary entries of 10–11 January and 11 March 1943, Box 5, Breckinridge
Long Papers; *FRUS 1942*, vol. I, pp. 374–377; *FRUS 1943*, vol. I, pp. 76–78,
81–83, 115–117.

148 Memorandum by Harvey, 21 January 1947, Box 1, Constance Harvey Papers.

149 Ralph Heinzen, "Inside Germany Today", *Collier's*, 10 June 1944, p. 62.
For details of the Lourdes–Baden Baden captivity, see the four-part account by
Woodruff Walner, a third secretary at Embassy Vichy: "Report of the Internment
and Repatriation of the Official American Group in France, 1942, 1943, 1944"
American Foreign Service Journal, May, June, July, August 1944. Also useful
are Harvey to Betty [Tucker], 3 September 1943, Box 1, Constance Harvey
Papers, and "Repatriates," *Life*, 27 March 1944, pp. 41–44.

150 MacArthur II, Foreign Affairs Oral History, p. 22.

151 "Repatriates Tell of Bombings and Hell Train Ride," *Buffalo Evening News*,
16 March 1944.

152 Walter Orebaugh, *Guerrilla in Striped Pants: A U.S. Diplomat Joins the
Italian Resistance* (New York: Praeger, 1992), p. 239.

153 Deutschman, *Mission Extraordinary*, pp. 355–356.

154 Vinen, *The Unfree French*, p. 318; Blumenthal, *Illusion and Reality in Franco-
American Diplomacy 1924–1945*, p. 299; Vaughan, *FDR's 12 Apostles:
The Spies Who Paved the Way for the Invasion of North Africa*, p. xv #6.

155 De Gaulle had, in FDR's language, a "Messianic complex"; the Allied cause
would be better served were he in the "Oasis of Somewhere" or made
governor of Madagascar. See *FRUS 1943*, vol. II, pp. 24, 111–112.

156 Christofferson, *France During World War II*, p. 140; Hurtsfield, *America and
the French Nation*, p. 209.

157 David Haglund, "Roosevelt as Friend of France – But Which One?"
Diplomatic History, 31 (2007), p. 896.

158 Murphy, *Diplomat among Warriors*, pp. 76, 102; Alistair Horne, *Harold
Macmillan*, vol. I, pp. 1894–1965 (New York: Viking, 1989), p. 162; *FRUS
1943*, vol. II, p. 189.

159 See H. Freeman Matthews to Leahy, Diary, 10 December 1942, William Leahy Papers and Anthony Verrier, *Assassination in Algiers: Churchill, Roosevelt, de Gaulle, and the Murder of Admiral Darlan* (New York: W. W. Norton and Company, 1990), p. 258.

160 Abrogation of Crémieux effectively canceled rights of French citizenship to Algerian Jews, placing them on a footing with Algerian Moslems.

161 Murphy to Charles Mast, 2 February 1970, Box 118, Robert Murphy Papers.

162 Christofferson, *France During World War II*, p. 135; Vinen, *The Unfree French: Life under the Occupation*, p. 320.

163 Although not ultimately adopted, the State Department plan for the administration of Allied-occupied France (AMGOT) deeply rankled de Gaulle. See the account by Charles Robertson, *When Roosevelt Planned to Govern France* (University of Massachusetts Press, 2011).

164 Rossi, *Roosevelt and the French*, p. 141. For later discussion of aid to French forces, see FDR to Charles de Gaulle, 24 March 1945, Box 30, President's Secretary's File, Franklin Roosevelt Papers.

165 Elmer Davis and Propaganda Plan for France to FDR, 22 June 1944, Office of War Information, President's Secretary's File, Franklin Roosevelt Papers.

166 Robert Corrigan, "An Appreciation of a Diplomat," *Foreign Service Journal* (November 1967), pp. 22, 24–25; Steven Sapp, "Jefferson Caffery, Cold War Diplomat: American-French Relations 1944–1949," *Louisiana History*, 23 (1982), pp. 180–181; Weisbrode, *The Atlantic Century: Four Generations of Extraordinary Diplomats Who Forged America's Vital Alliance with Europe*, p. 98; Philip Dur "Jefferson Caffery of Louisiana: Highlights of His Career," Part 1: 1911–1933, *Louisiana History*, 15 (1974), pp. 6–8; Philip Dur, "Jefferson Caffery of Louisiana: Highlights of His Career," Part 2: 1933–1944, 15 (1974), pp. 385–387, 390; "Careerist to Paris," *Time*, 2 October 1944, p. 20; "Envoy to Paris," *Newsweek*, 2 October 1944, p. 44; MacArthur II, Foreign Affairs Oral History, p. 28.

167 During his pre-Brazil career, Caffery had served as chief of mission in three countries: El Salvador, Colombia, Cuba. He had also served in various capacities in Stockholm, Tehran, Athens, Tokyo, Madrid, Paris, Berlin. His last ambassadorial assignment would be to Egypt, 1949–1955.

168 Walter Lippmann worried that however free Caffery was from Vichy taint, Embassy Paris was staffed with too many of the previous officers. They included Hugh Fullerton as Consul General, Tyler Thompson, and Douglas MacArthur II. See Department of State, *News Digest*, No. 289, 2 December 1944, pp. 3–4, Box 52 Jefferson Caffery Papers.

169 Steven Sapp, "The United States, France and the Cold War: Jefferson Caffery and American–French Relations, 1944–1946" (Kent State University, Ph.D. dissertation, 1978), p. 19.

170 De Gaulle, *War Memoirs*, pp. 758–770; Rossi, *Roosevelt and the French*, pp. 150–151; Aglion, *Roosevelt and de Gaulle*, pp. 198–199; Sapp, *The United States, France and the Cold War*, pp. 26–27, 34–35.

171 *FRUS 1945*, vol. IV, p. 764.

172 Jefferson Caffery to FDR, 26 February 1945, Box 30, President's Secretary's File, Franklin Roosevelt Papers.

173 Jefferson Caffery to FDR, 1 March 1945, Box 30, President's Secretary's File, Franklin Roosevelt Papers.

174 Notes on Memoirs #13, "Adventures in Diplomacy" (unpublished manuscript), Box 69, Jefferson Caffery Papers; De Gaulle, *War Memoirs*, p. 769.

175 Sapp, *The United States, France and the Cold War*, pp. 37–49, 61–67.

176 *FRUS 1944*, vol. III, pp. 773, 780; Notes on Memoirs #9, *Adventures in Diplomacy*, Box 69, Jefferson Caffery Papers; Sapp, *The United States, France and the Cold War*, pp. 51, 172–173, 198, 318–320, 328–329.

177 Christofferson, *France During World War II*, p. 199; Alistair Horne, *La Belle France: A Short History* (New York: Vintage Books, 2006), p. 367; Vinen, *The Unfree French: Life under the Occupation*, p. 215.

178 *FRUS 1946*, vol. V, pp. 413.

179 Sapp, *The United States, France and the Cold War*, pp. 23–24, 73–74, 107–110; Sapp, "Jefferson Caffery, Cold War Diplomat", pp. 183, 188–189.

180 Hurtsfield, *America and the French Nation*, pp. 223–224; MacArthur II, Foreign Affairs Oral History, p. 28; Horne, *La Belle France: A Short History*, p. 358.

181 See Notes on Memoirs (number not indicated): "Breck is a very loyal friend and a great gentleman." Box 69, Jefferson Caffery Papers. Also see Caffery to Ellis Briggs regarding H. Freeman Matthews, 6 May 1949, Box 51, Jefferson Caffery Papers.

182 Speech at the Dedication of the ORT Building at Montreuil, 15 July 1948, Box 56, Jefferson Caffery Papers; "Caffery Attends Rites for Jewish Orphans," *New York Herald Tribune*, 12 December 1947, p. 3.

183 MacArthur II, Foreign Affairs Oral History, p. 16.

184 Jean de Lustrac to Matthews, 12 December 1962, H. Freeman Matthews Papers.

185 Entry of 23 May 1942, Diary, William Leahy Papers.

186 The War Refugee Board (WRB) ceased operations on 15 September 1945. Its Washington staff never numbered more than thirty people. The WRB had personnel assigned as special attachés to embassies/legations in Turkey, Switzerland, Sweden, Portugal, Italy, Great Britain, and North Africa.

187 *FRUS: The Conferences at Washington, 1941–1942, and Casablanca, 1943*, p. 608.

188 Paldiel, *The Righteous among the Nations*, p. 129; Isenberg, *A Hero of Our Own: The Story of Varian Fry*, pp. 272–273; Sullivan, *Villa Air-Bel*, p. 417.

189 Bingham, *Courageous Dissent: How Harry Bingham Defied His Government to Save Lives*, pp. 91–92, 131.

190 The 39-cent stamp series also honored these people: Charles Bohlen (ambassador to USSR, Philippines, France), Philip Habib (ambassador to South Korea, Undersecretary of State for Political Affairs), Clifton Wharton (first African American Foreign Service officer, ambassador to Norway, minister to Romania), Frances Willis (first female career diplomat to achieve ambassadorial rank, ambassador to Switzerland, Norway, Sri Lanka).

On 28 March 2011 in New York the Simon Wiesenthal Center conferred its Medal of Valor posthumously on Bingham. Other people recognized at the same awards ceremony included Winston Churchill and Pope John Paul II.

191 Cordell Hull to Murphy, 18 March 1943, Murphy to State Department, 21 March 1943, Hull to Murphy, 29 March 1943, Hull to Murphy, 3 April 1943, Jean Monnet to Felix Frankfurter, 7 April 1943, Murphy to State Department, 17 April 1943, Hull to Murphy, 24 April 1943, Murphy to State Department, 29 April 1943, Box 162; William Bird to Murphy, 31 May 1945, Box 58; Murphy to Jacques Weygand, 12 December 1945, statement by Murphy on Maxime Weygand, 25 April 1946, Murphy to Maxime Weygand, 5 June 1946, Box 59; Murphy to Charles Mast, 2 October 1974, Box 118, Robert Murphy Papers.

192 Vaughan, *FDR's 12 Apostles: The Spies Who Paved the Way for the Invasion of North Africa*, pp. 237–239.

193 De Gaulle, *War Memoirs*, pp. 314, 540.

194 Murphy, *Diplomat Among Warriors*, pp. 147–148.

195 Gerhard Weinberg, *Germany, Hitler, and World War II* (Cambridge University Press, 1995), p. 220.

196 Pierre Laval, *The Diary of Pierre Laval* (New York: Charles Scribner's Sons, 1948), p. 56.

197 Sarah Farmer, *Martyred Village: Commemorating the 1944 Massacre at Oradour-sur-Glane* (University of California Press, 1999), p. 1; Telford Taylor, *The Anatomy of the Nuremberg Trials: A Personal Memoir* (New York: Alfred A. Knopf, 1992), p. 302.

198 Hannah Arendt, *The Origins of Totalitarianism* (New York: World Publishing, 1972), p. 93.

199 Horne, *La Belle France: A Short History*, p. 395.

200 Raymond Aron, *Mémoires* (Paris: Julliard, 1983), pp. 184–186, 234.

201 Bloch, *Strange Defeat*, p. 175.

202 De Gaulle speech of 25 August 1944, "France Forever," 2 September 1944, Box 30, William Bullitt Papers. Also see Raymond Aron, *Chroniques de guerre: la France libre* (Paris: Gallimard, 1990), p. 38.

Chapter 6: Britannia

1 David Reynolds, *From World War to Cold War: Churchill, Roosevelt, and the International History of the 1940s* (Oxford University Press, 2007), p. 109; I. C. B. Dear and M. R. D. Foot, eds., *The Oxford Companion to World War II* (Oxford University Press, 1995), p. 680.

2 Ian Kershaw, *Fateful Choices: Ten Decisions That Changed the World, 1940–1941* (New York: Penguin Press, 2007), pp. 298–299. See War Office, *Notes on German Preparations for the Invasion of the United Kingdom: War Office 1942* (London: Military Library Research Services, 2006).

3 *Public Papers of the Presidents of the United States, 1963* (Washington: Government Printing Office, 1964), pp. 315–316.

4 Mark Stoler, "FDR and the Origins of the National Security Establishment," in David Woolner, Warren Kimball, and David Reynolds, eds., *FDR's World: War, Peace, and Legacies* (New York: Palgrave Macmillan, 2008), p. 63; Kershaw, *Fateful Choices*, p. 241.

5 Joseph Kennedy to FDR, 30 September 1939, Box 37, President's Secretary's File, Franklin Roosevelt Papers.

6 Gerhard Weinberg, *Visions of Victory: The Hopes of Eight World War II Leaders* (Cambridge University Press, 2005), p. 139; Notes – 10 June 1940 Conference with Churchill, Box 100, Joseph Kennedy Papers.

7 Farewell Dinner to Mr. J. G. Winant at Lancaster House, 23 April 1946, p. 2, Box 196, John Winant Papers at Franklin D. Roosevelt Presidential Library (FDRL).

8 Ralph de Bedts, *Ambassador Joseph Kennedy 1938–1940: An Anatomy of Appeasement* (New York: Peter Lang, 1985), p. 13.

9 Kennedy to FDR, 13 January 1936, Amanda Smith, ed. *Hostage to Fortune: The Letters of Joseph P. Kennedy* (New York: Viking, 2005), p. 236.

10 David Koskoff, *Joseph P. Kennedy: A Life and Times* (Englewood Cliffs: Prentice Hall, 1974), p. 116.

11 Robert Dallek, *An Unfinished Life: John F. Kennedy 1917–1963* (Boston: Little, Brown and Company, 2003), p. 54; Michael Beschloss, *Kennedy and Roosevelt: The Uneasy Alliance* (New York: W. W. Norton and Company, 1980), p. 157.

12 Laurence Leamer, *The Kennedy Men* (New York: William Morrow, 2001), p. 112; Koskoff, *Joseph P. Kennedy*, p. 117.

13 FDR to Boettiger, 3 March 1941, Box 21, John Boettiger Papers.

14 Richard Whalen, *The Founding Father: The Story of Joseph P. Kennedy* (New York: New American Library, 1964), pp. 212–213; Smith, *Hostage to Fortune: The Letters of Joseph P. Kennedy*, p. 230.

15 Max Hastings, *Finest Years: Churchill as Warlord 1940–1945* (London: Harper Press, 2009), p. 360; Will Swift, *The Kennedys Amidst the Gathering Storm:*

A Thousand Days in London, 1938–1940 (New York: Collins, 2008), pp. 3–4; Beschloss, *Kennedy and Roosevelt*, p. 154; De Bedts, *Ambassador Joseph Kennedy 1938–1940*, p. 35.

16 FDR to Joseph Kennedy, 22 March 1938, Box 37, President's Secretary's File, Franklin Roosevelt Papers.

17 Kennedy to Lady Astor, 8 December 1938, Box 101, Joseph Kennedy Papers.

18 Diary entry of 9 November 1940, Smith, *The Letters of Joseph P. Kennedy*, p. 493. Also see Kennedy's supportive letter to Neville Chamberlain, 22 October 1940, Box 104, Joseph Kennedy Papers.

19 *FRUS 1938*, vol. I, pp. 44, 86.

20 Memorandum, 19 December 1938, Box 100, Joseph Kennedy Papers; William Kaufmann, "Two American Ambassadors: Bullitt and Kennedy," in Gordon Craig and Felix Gilbert, eds., *The Diplomats 1919–1939* (Princeton University Press, 1994), pp. 665–666; Beschloss, *Kennedy and Roosevelt*, pp. 181–182.

21 Wayne Cole, *Roosevelt and the Isolationists 1932–1945* (University of Nebraska Press, 1983), pp. 282–283.

22 *FRUS 1938*, vol. I, p. 73.

23 Memoranda of 26 and 27 September 1938, Box 165, Joseph Kennedy Papers; De Bedts, *Ambassador Joseph Kennedy 1938–1940*, p. 94.

24 *FRUS 1938*, vol. I, p. 693.

25 Stephen Wise to FDR, 4 March 1938, Box 37, President's Secretary's File, Franklin Roosevelt Papers; Anthony Biddle to Kennedy, 19 November 1938, Box 103, Kennedy to Mrs. Ogden Reid, 8 December 1938, Box 163, Memorandum, 2 December 1938 and answer of 5 December 1938 regarding "fog-piercing lamp," Box 163, Dr. Rudolf Prister to Kennedy, 16 February 1939 and Edward Moore to Prister, 21 February 1939, Box 163, Joseph Kennedy Papers; Koskoff, *Joseph P. Kennedy*, pp. 175–181; De Bedts, *Ambassador Joseph Kennedy 1938–1940*, pp. 114–119; Swift, *The Kennedys Amidst the Gathering Storm*, pp. 25, 115–119, 137; Francis Russell, *The President Makers: From Mark Hanna to Joseph P. Kennedy* (Boston: Little, Brown and Company, 1976), p. 356.

26 Diary entry of 20 July 1938, Smith, *Hostage to Fortune: The Letters of Joseph P. Kennedy*, p. 267.

27 For more analysis, see Fred Leventhal, "Essential Democracy: The 1939 Royal Visit to the United States," in George Behlmer and Fred Leventhal, eds., *Singular Continuities: Tradition, Nostalgia, and Identity in Modern British Culture* (Stanford University Press, 2000).

28 Koskoff, *Joseph P. Kennedy*, pp. 206–207.

29 Leamer, *The Kennedy Men*, p. 140; Warren Kimball, *Forged in War: Roosevelt, Churchill, and the Second World War* (New York: William Morrow and Company, 1997), p. 29.

30 De Bedts, *Ambassador Joseph Kennedy 1938–1940*, p. 162; Irwin Gellman, *Secret Affairs: Franklin Roosevelt, Cordell Hull, and Sumner Welles* (Johns Hopkins University Press, 1995), p. 170.

31 Koskoff, *Joseph P. Kennedy*, p. 128; Leamer, *The Kennedy Men*, pp. 113–114.

32 Kennedy to Cordell Hull, 17 October 1938, Smith, *Hostage to Fortune: The Letters of Joseph P. Kennedy*, p. 295.

33 Martin Gilbert, *Churchill and America* (New York: Free Press, 2005), pp. 171–173.

34 "Whose Ambassador is Mr. Kennedy?" *The New Republic*, 21 June 1939.

35 Beschloss, *Kennedy and Roosevelt*, pp. 185–186; Smith, *Hostage to Fortune: The Letters of Joseph P. Kennedy*, p. 228; Nancy Hooker, ed., *The Moffat Papers: Selections from the Diplomatic Journals of Jay Pierrepont Moffat 1919–1943* (Harvard University Press, 1956), pp. 220–221; De Bedts, *Ambassador Joseph Kennedy 1938–1940*, p. 67.

36 Kershaw, *Fateful Choices*, p. 210.

37 Kennedy to Cordell Hull, 15 May 1940, Box 3, President's Secretary's File, Franklin Roosevelt Paper.

38 Beschloss, *Kennedy and Roosevelt*, p. 192; William Stevenson, *A Man Called Intrepid: The Secret War* (New York: Brace Jovanovich, 1976), p. 67.

39 Hooker, *The Moffat Papers*, p. 298; Harold Nicolson, "People and Things," *The Spectator*, 8 March 1940, p. 327; Harold Laski, "British Democracy and Mr. Kennedy," *Harper's Magazine*, April 1941, p. 470.

40 Mr. Whitehead, Minute, 6 March 1940, and Mr. Perowne, Minutes, 22 August 1940 and 3 September 1940, and Mr. J. Balfour, Minute, 7 October 1940, PO371/24251, Foreign Office Records; Stevenson, *A Man Called Intrepid*, pp. 77, 84, 147, 166; Kimball, *Churchill and Roosevelt: The Complete Correspondence* (Princeton University Press, 1984), vol. I, p. 26; Koskoff, *Joseph P. Kennedy*, p. 240; Leamer, *The Kennedy Men*, pp. 146, 150.

41 Reynolds, *From World War to Cold War*, p. 184.

42 Alexander Kendrick, *Prime Time: The Life of Edward R. Murrow* (Boston: Little, Brown and Company, 1969), pp. 176–177, 193, 222, 447; A. M. Sperber, *Murrow: His Life and Times* (New York: Freundlich Books, 1986), p. 605. Also see Edward R. Murrow, *This is London* (New York: Schocken Books, 1969) and Edward Bliss, ed., *In Search of Light: The Broadcasts of Edward R. Murrow 1938–1961* (New York: Alfred Knopf, 1967).

43 Gellman, *Secret Affairs*, p. 172.

44 Entry of 17 September 1940, James Leutze, ed., *The London Journal of General Raymond E. Lee 1940–1941* (Boston: Little, Brown and Company, 1971), p. 62.

45 Neville Chamberlain selected Churchill as First Lord of the Admiralty on 3 September 1939. He remained in that office until he became prime minister on 10 May 1940.

46 Ray Bearse and Anthony Read, *Conspirator: The Untold Story of Tyler Kent* (New York: Doubleday, 1991), pp. xiv, 3, 5, 277–297; Stevenson, *A Man Called Intrepid*, pp. 80, 87–90; Kimball, *Churchill and Roosevelt: The Complete Correspondence*, vol. I, pp. 40–41.

47 Kimball, *Churchill and Roosevelt: The Complete Correspondence*, vol. I, p. 63; Kimball, *Forged in War*, p. 58.

48 Gellman, *Secret Affairs: Franklin Roosevelt, Cordell Hull, and Sumner Welles*, p. 174.

49 *FRUS 1940*, vol. I, pp. 72–91.

50 Entry of 3 August 1940, Leutze, *The London Journal of General Raymond E. Lee*, p. 28.

51 De Bedts, *Ambassador Joseph Kennedy 1938–1940*, pp. 206–209; Koskoff, *Joseph P. Kennedy*, pp. 243–245, 255–256.

52 Robert Murphy, *Diplomat among Warriors* (Garden City: Doubleday and Company, 1964), p. 38. Also see Kennedy to Anthony Biddle, 23 April 1940, Box 103, Joseph Kennedy Papers.

53 Beschloss, *Kennedy and Roosevelt*, p. 229.

54 Entry of 11 October 1940, Fred Israel, ed., *The War Diary of Breckinridge Long: Selections from the Years 1939–1944* (University of Nebraska Press, 1966), pp. 141–142.

55 Koskoff, *Joseph P. Kennedy*, p. 298.

56 Entry of 6 November 1940, Israel, *The War Diary of Breckinridge Long*, p. 147.

57 Telegram to Lord Lothian from J. B(alfour), ? November 1940, PO371/24251 Foreign Office Records.

58 Bernard Bellush, *He Walked Alone: A Biography of John Gilbert Winant* (The Hague: Mouton, 1968), p. 118.

59 Ibid., pp. 41–50.

60 Lynne Olson, *Citizens of London: The Americans Who Stood with Britain in Its Darkest, Finest Hour* (New York: Random House, 2010), pp. 13–14. Constance Winant raised show dogs. She enjoyed horse-races, shopping expeditions, and luxury spas. Her husband was censorious on the subject of her gambling.

61 Leon Anderson, untitled "sketch" of John Gilbert Winant, 15 January 1970, John Winant Papers at New Hampshire Historical Society (NHHS). For an unflattering view of Winant in Geneva, see Geoffrey Partington, "John Gilbert Winant at Geneva: The Testimony of Sir Walter Crocker," *National Observer*, Spring 2003.

62 Entry of 15 February 1941, Israel, *The War Diary of Breckinridge Long*, p. 181; Mr. R. Butler, Minute, 23 January 1941, FO371/26224 (File 409), Foreign Office Records; W. Averell Harriman and Elie Abel, *Special Envoy to Churchill and Stalin 1941–1946* (New York: Random House, 1975), p. 5; Reynolds, *From World War to Cold War*, pp. 150–162.

63 John Winant, *Our Greatest Harvest: Selected Speeches* (London: Hodder and Stoughton, 1950), p. 58.

64 Robert Sherwood, *Roosevelt and Hopkins: An Intimate History* (New York: Harper and Brothers, 1948), pp. 839–840; Farewell Dinner to Mr. J. G. Winant at Lancaster House, 23 April 1946, p. 4, Box 196, John Winant Papers at FDRL.

65 Charles Rumford Walker, "Winant of New Hampshire," *The Atlantic* (May 1941), p. 553.

66 Winant, *Our Greatest Harvest: Selected Speeches*, p. 4.

67 Bert Whittemore, "A Quiet Triumph: The Mission of John Gilbert Winant to London, 1941," *Historical New Hampshire*, 30 (1975), p. 7.

68 Nigel Nicolson, ed., *Harold Nicolson: Diaries and Letters 1939–1945* (London: Collins, 1967), pp. 186, 263.

69 John Colville, *The Fringes of Power: 10 Downing Street Diaries 1939–1955* (New York: W. W. Norton and Company, 1985), pp. 372, 773; Bellush, *He Walked Alone*, pp. 168, 180; John Winant, *Letter from Grosvenor Square: An Account of a Stewardship* (Boston: Houghton Mifflin Company, 1947), pp. 61–62; Ethel Johnson, "The Mr. Winant I Knew," *South Atlantic Quarterly* (January 1949), 37; Farewell Dinner to Mr. J. G. Winant at Lancaster House, 23 April 1946, p. 2, Box 196, John Winant Papers at FDRL.

70 Mr. T. North Whitehead, Minute, 22 January 1941 and Mr. R. Butler, Minute, 23 January 1941, FO371/26224 (File 409), Foreign Office Records.

71 Interview of Winston Churchill, p. 2, 4 July 1951, Box 1, interview of Virginia Crawley, p. 4, 3 July 1951, interview of Anthony Eden, pp. 15–17, 7 and 8 July 1951, Box 2, Bernard Bellush Papers; Johnson, "The Mr. Winant I Knew," p. 38; Winant, *Letter from Grosvenor Square*, pp. 92, 96–97; Bellush, *He Walked Alone*, p. 178; David Reynolds, *In Command of History: Churchill Fighting and Writing the Second World War* (New York: Random House, 2005), pp. 263–264.

   Winant's John survived German prison and the war. A younger son, Rivington, survived Pacific combat with the Marine Corps.

72 Edward R. Murrow to Winant, 10 November 1941, Box 209, John Winant Papers at FDRL; Sperber, *Murrow: His Life and Times*, p. 189; entries of 14 April and 3 August 1941, Leutze, *The London Journal of General Raymond E. Lee 1940–1941*, pp. 241, 361; Bellush, *He Walked Alone*, p. 166.

73 Notes made from diary of Maurine Mulliner, p. 3, Box 7, Bernard Bellush Papers. Also Winant to Howard Braucher, 12 November 1941, Box 186, John Winant Papers at FDRL.

74 Robert St. John to NBC, 15 January 1943, John Winant Papers at NHHS.

75 Winant, *Our Greatest Harvest: Selected Speeches*, pp. 56–57.

76 Ibid., pp. 26–27, 102–103; Maisky, *Memoirs of a Soviet Ambassador* (New York: Charles Scribner's Sons, 1968), p. 214; Reynolds, *From World War to Cold War*, pp. 187–188.

77 Winant, *Our Greatest Harvest*, p. 198; Bellush, *He Walked Alone*, p. 163.

78 Colville, *The Fringes of Power*, pp. 434–43; entry of 29 August 1941, Leutze, *The London Journal of General Raymond E. Lee 1940–1941*, p. 382.

79 Bellush, *He Walked Alone*, p. 173.

80 Olson, *Citizens of London*, pp. 169–170; Sherwood, *Roosevelt and Hopkins*, pp. 269, 311, 919; Rudy Abramson, *Spanning the Century: The Life of W. Averell Harriman, 1891–1986* (New York: William Morrow and Company, 1992), pp. 302–304; Harriman and Abel, *Special Envoy to Churchill and Stalin 1941–1946*, p. 26; entries of 14 and 27 April, 15 and 25 and 30 July, 29 August 1941 in Leutze, *The London Journal of General Raymond E. Lee 1940–1941*, pp. 241, 259, 340, 353, 359, 382; Bellush, *He Walked Alone*, p. 175; interview of Virginia Crawley, 3 July 1951, pp. 7–8, Box 2, Bernard Bellush Papers.

81 Winant to Hopkins, 16 October 1943, Box 257, Harry Hopkins Papers; memorandum, 9 August 1943, Secretary of State, Northern Department, FO371/34121, Foreign Office Records; Sherwood, *Roosevelt and Hopkins*, pp. 754–756.

82 Churchill explained: "My relationship with President Roosevelt superseded both the Foreign Office of my nation and the American Embassy." Cited in interview of Winston Churchill, p. 1, 4 July 1951, Box 1, Bernard Bellush Papers.

83 Churchill to FDR, 1 April 1942, Kimball, *Churchill and Roosevelt: The Complete Correspondence*, vol. I, p. 439.

84 William Phillips to FDR, 13 August 1942, Box 38, President's Secretary's File, Franklin Roosevelt Papers; George Marshall to FDR, 9 September 1942 and FDR to John Winant, 10 September 1941, Box 38, President's Secretary's File, Franklin Roosevelt Papers; Paul Kellogg to Winant, 16 May 1944, Box 211, John Winant Papers at FDRL; Henry Morgenthau to Winant, 19 August 1944, Box 209, John Winant Papers at FDRL; interview of General Dwight David Eisenhower, 8 August 1951, p. 2, Box 2, Bernard Bellush Papers; Leutze, *The London Journal of General Raymond E. Lee 1940–1941*, p. 338; Olson; *Citizens of London*, pp. 288–289; Bellush, *He Walked Alone*, p. 215.

85 John Winant, "How Britain Controls Its Manpower," *The Atlantic*, May 1942, p. 63.

86 Article for American Red Cross Booklet to be Given to American Soldiers and Sailors in the British Isles, 6 June 1942, Box 181, John Winant Papers at FDRL.

87 Frances Perkins to Winant, 8 December 1944 and Winant to Perkins, 16 January 1945, Box 214, John Winant Papers at FDRL.

88 Gilbert, *Churchill and America*, p. 345; Eleanor Roosevelt, *This I Remember* (New York: Harper, 1949), p. 266.

89 Winant to Hopkins, 16 October 1943, Box 257, Harry Hopkins Papers.

90 Churchill to FDR, 4 June 1942, Kimball, *Churchill and Roosevelt: The Complete Correspondence*, vol. I, p. 505. Also see pp. 393–394 in ibid.

91 Winant, *Letter from Grosvenor Square: An Account of a Stewardship*, pp. 207–209; Maisky, *Memoirs of a Soviet Ambassador*, pp. 180–181, 268; Bellush, *He Walked Alone*, pp. 189–190; Kimball, *Forged in War*, p. 223.

92 *FRUS: The Conferences at Cairo and Tehran 1943*, pp. 301–303.

93 Winant to John McCloy, 24 February 1945, Box 195, John Winant Papers at FDRL.

94 Murphy, *Diplomat among Warriors*, pp. 230–233.

95 Lord Strang, *Home and Abroad* (London: André Deutsch, 1956), pp. 205, 225.

96 *FRUS 1944*, vol. III, pp. 3–6: *FRUS: The Conferences at Cairo and Tehran 1943*, pp. 883–884; Bellush, *He Walked Alone*, pp. 192, 204.

97 Winant to Hopkins, 19 December 1944, Box 257, Harry Hopkins Papers.

98 Winant to FDR, 28 January 1945 and Winant to John McCloy, 24 February 1945, Box 195, John Winant Papers at FDRL.

99 Winant to FDR, 21 January 1944, Box 257, Harry Hopkins Papers; Murphy, *Diplomat among Warriors*, p. 232; George Kennan, *Memoirs: 1925–1950* (Boston: Little, Brown and Company, 1967), pp. 164–180; Bellush, *He Walked Alone*, pp. 192–210.

100 Reynolds, *From World War to Cold War*, p. 312.

101 Winant, *Our Greatest Harvest*, p. 65.

102 Colville, *The Fringes of Power*, pp. 391, 528; Gilbert, *Churchill and America*, pp. 318–319.

103 Nicolson, *Harold Nicolson: Diaries and Letters 1939–1945*, p. 263.

104 *FRUS 1939*, vol. I, pp. 603–604; Edward Maney, Memorandum re. Immigration Visa Work at Embassy London from March 1938 to Date, 11 October 1940, Box 167, Joseph Kennedy Papers; entry of 7 September 1939, Israel, *The War Diary of Breckinridge Long*, p. 10.

105 Herschel Johnson to Welles, 28 April 1939 and Welles to Johnson, 15 May 1939, Box 53, Sumner Welles Papers.

106 See Joseph Kennedy and James Landis, *The Surrender of King Leopold* (New York: Joseph P. Kennedy Memorial Foundation, 1950).

107 Niebuhr cited in Detleff Junker's "Roosevelt and the National Socialist Threat to the United States," in Frank Tommler and Joseph McVeigh, eds., *America and the Germans: An Assessment of a Three-Hundred-Year History* (University of Pennsylvania Press, 1985), vol. II, p. 43.

108 R. Douglas Stuart to Kennedy, 19 December 1940 and Kennedy to Stuart, 23 December 1940, Box 118, Joseph Kennedy Papers; Douglas Fairbanks to FDR, 19 November 1940, Box 37, President's Secretary's File, Franklin Roosevelt Papers.

109 Koskoff, *Joseph P. Kennedy*, pp. 315–318; Leamer, *The Kennedy Men*, p. 180; Beschloss, *Kennedy and Roosevelt*, pp. 172, 245.

110 Beschloss, *Kennedy and Roosevelt*, p. 162.

111 Dallek, *An Unfinished Life: John F. Kennedy 1917–1963*, p. 82.

112 Manfred Jonas, *Isolationism in America 1935–1941* (Cornell University Press, 1966), p. 278.

Kennedy's orientation in the 1950s did not deviate from this thought penned in his 1940 diary: "How fortunate it might be for civilization if, instead of making enemies of every country in the world for the United States, we had made some friends; then our influence would have amounted to something. As it is ... they all regard us as a terrific influence but in their hearts no country likes us at all." See 24 September 1940, Diary, Box 100, Joseph Kennedy Papers.

113 Alonzo Hamby, *Man of the People: A Life of Harry S. Truman* (Oxford University Press, 1995), p. 280; interview of Anthony Eden, 7 and 8 July 1951, p. 19, Box 2, Bernard Bellush Papers; John Allison, *Ambassador from the Prairie or Allison Wonderland* (Boston: Houghton Mifflin Company, 1973), p. 102; Frances Perkins, *The Roosevelt I Knew* (New York: Viking Press, 1946), p. 392.

114 Winant and Truman met only once, briefly and informally while FDR was still alive. Winant had hoped to meet Truman at the time of the Potsdam conference. Winant's request for a meeting with the president either went unanswered or, more likely, was simply refused. See Roger Tubby to Alvin Knepper, 23 December 1952, Box 1359, Official File and John Winant to Truman, 13 June 1945, Box 9, Naval Aide File, Papers of Harry Truman.

115 Winant, *Our Greatest Harvest*, pp. 98–99.

116 Winant had been in love with Churchill's married daughter Sarah. They conducted a discreet affair during the days of his ambassadorship. He later entertained notions of marrying her, but she did not go along. See Olson, *Citizens of London*, pp. 113, 370–371, 385.

Maurine Mulliner was a devoted friend of Winant and special assistant. Perhaps, they too were romantically attracted to each other. See the suggestive Notes from the Diary of Mulliner, Box 7, Bernard Bellush Papers.

117 John Winant, "Fundamental Freedoms," *Conference: The Magazine of Human Relations* (Winter 1947), p. 5.

118 Louis Fischer, "John G. Winant: Casualty of the Peace," *The Saturday Review*, 6 December 1947, p. 21; editorial by James Langley, *Concord Monitor* (New Hampshire), 4 November 1947; Sperber, *Murrow*, p. 298.

119 Bellush, *He Walked Alone*, pp. 227–228.

120 Speech by Robert Sherwood at dedication of Winant House in London, 5 July 1951, item 2237, Robert Sherwood Papers; Dedication and Presentation of Winant House (pamphlet), 5 July 1951, Box 7, Bernard Bellush Papers.

121 The Anglo-American Committee for War Refugees in Great Britain to Lady Abingdon, 30 June 1941, John Winant Papers at NHHS.

122 Winant to FDR, 17 October 1942, Box 38, President's Secretary's File, Franklin Roosevelt Papers.

Chapter 7: Great Patriotic War

1 Roberta Reeder, ed. *The Complete Poems of Anna Akhmatova* (Somerville: Zephyr Press, 1990), vol. II, pp. 185, 187.

2 Sharon Leiter, *Akhmatova's Petersburg* (University of Pennsylvania, 1983), p. 3.

3 I. C. B. Dear and M. R. D. Foot, eds., *The Oxford Companion to World War II* (Oxford University Press, 1995), p. 683.

4 Reeder, *The Complete Poems of Anna Akhamatova*, vol. II, p. 191.

5 Abraham Ascher, "Was Hitler a Riddle?" *Journal of the Historical Society*, 9 (1) 2009, p. 13.

6 Mark Mazower, *Hitler's Empire: How the Nazis Ruled Europe* (New York: Penguin Press, 2008), pp. 161, 178.

7 Geoffrey Roberts, *Stalin's Wars: From World War to Cold War, 1939–1953* (Yale University Press, 2006), pp. 170–172.

8 Dennis Dunn, *Caught Between Roosevelt and Stalin: America's Ambassadors to Moscow* (University Press of Kentucky, 1998), p. 121; Ralph Stackman, "Laurence A. Steinhardt: New Deal Diplomat, 1933–45" (Ph.D. dissertation, Michigan State University, 1967), p. 254.

9 Roberts, *Stalin's Wars*, pp. 10–11.

10 *FRUS: The Conferences at Washington and Quebec 1943*, p. 625.

11 Statement of W. Averell Harriman to the Committee on Armed Services and Foreign Relations of the Senate, 13 July 1951, File 6207, President's Personal File, Franklin Roosevelt Papers; John Lukacs, *The Legacy of the Second World War* (Yale University Press, 2010), p. 62.

12 George Herring, *Aid to Russia 1941–1946: Strategy, Diplomacy, the Origins of the Cold War* (Columbia University Press, 1973), p. xiii.

13 Rudy Abramson, *Spanning the Century: The Life of W. Averell Harriman 1891–1986* (New York: William Morrow and Company, 1992), pp. 383, 395.

14 Hans von Herwarth, *Zwischen Hitler und Stalin: Erlebte Zeitgeschichte 1931 bis 1945* (Frankfurt: Ullstein Verlag, 1982), pp. 175, 181; Eckart Conze *et al.*, *Das Amt und die Vergangenheit: Deutsche Diplomaten im Dritten Reich und in der Bundesrepublik* (Munich: Karl Blessing, 2010), pp. 364–365.

15 Charles Bohlen, *Witness to History 1929–1969* (New York: W. W. Norton and Company, 1973), p. 85.

16 Susan Butler, ed., *My Dear Mr. Stalin: The Complete Correspondence of Franklin D. Roosevelt and Joseph V. Stalin* (Yale University Press, 2005), p. 23; Keith Eagles, "Laurence Adolphe Steinhardt," in Cathal Nolan, ed., *Notable U.S. Ambassadors since 1775* (Westport: Greenwood Press, 1997), p. 328.

17 Stackman, "Laurence A. Steinhardt", p. 33; David Mayers, *The Ambassadors and America's Soviet Policy* (Oxford University Press, 1995), pp. 125–126.

18 Stackman, "Laurence A. Steinhardt," pp. 10–11, 16–17; Barry Rubin, *Istanbul Intrigues* (New York: McGraw-Hill publishing, 1989), p. 122.

19 Steinhardt to John Browning, 26 September 1939, Box 27, Steinhardt to William Cochran, 23 June 1939, Box 78, Steinhardt to Hinkie Steinhardt, 6 June 1940, Box 79, Laurence Steinhardt Papers; Joseph O'Connor, "Laurence A. Steinhardt and American Policy toward the Soviet Union, 1939–1941" (Ph.D. dissertation, University of Virginia, 1968), p. 27; Mayers, *The Ambassadors and America's Soviet Policy*, p. 284 #64.

20 Cordell Hull, *The Memoirs of Cordell Hull* (New York: Macmillan Company, 1948), vol. I, pp. 603–604; Dunn, *Caught Between Roosevelt and Stalin*, pp. 93, 100–101.

21 Gabriel Gorodetsky, *Stafford Cripps' Mission to Moscow, 1940–42* (Cambridge University Press, 1984), p. 47.

22 George Baer, ed., *A Question of Trust: The Origins of U.S.–Soviet Diplomatic Relations: The Memoirs of Loy W. Henderson* (Stanford: Hoover Institution Press, 1986), pp. 520–522.

23 Igor Lukes, "Ambassador Laurence Steinhardt: From New York to Prague," *Diplomacy and Statecraft*, 17 (2006), 524; Dunn, *Caught Between Roosevelt and Stalin*, p. 103; Bohlen, *Witness to History 1929–1969*, pp. 88–89, 95, 108.

24 Andrew Nagorski, *The Greatest Battle: Stalin, Hitler, and the Desperate Struggle for Moscow that Changed the Course of World War II* (New York: Simon and Schuster, 2007), p. 149. Maxim Litvinov, himself Jewish, also did not care for Steinhardt. See memorandum (author not indicated, perhaps Sumner Welles), 8 January 1942, Box 49 (file confidential), President's Secretary's File, Franklin Roosevelt Papers.

25 *FRUS: The Soviet Union, 1933–1939*, pp. 778–779.

26 O'Connor, "Laurence A. Steinhardt," pp. 54–55; Lukes, "Ambassador Laurence Steinhardt: From New York to Prague," p. 529; Baer, *A Question of Trust*, pp. 556–568; Dunn, *Caught Between Roosevelt and Stalin*, pp. 98, 294 #5.

27 Bohlen, *Witness to History 1929–1969*, pp. 44–45.

28 Mary Glantz, *FDR and the Soviet Union: The President's Battles over Foreign Policy* (University Press of Kansas, 2005), p. 43; *FRUS 1940*, vol. III, p. 403.

29 Glantz, *FDR and the Soviet Union*, p. 44; Stackman, *Laurence A. Steinhardt*, pp. 181–183; O'Connor, "Laurence A. Steinhardt," pp. 41–43.

30 *FRUS: The Soviet Union, 1933–1939*, p. 868.

31 Stackman, "Laurence A. Steinhardt," pp. 191–193; O'Connor, "*Laurence A. Steinhardt*", pp. 66–70; Bohlen, *Witness to History 1929–1969*, p. 96.

32 Mayers, *The Ambassadors and America's Soviet Policy*, p. 126. No evidence indicates that Steinhardt was aware of Polish pogroms against Jews during the German occupation, such as that recounted by Jan Gross in his *The Neighbors: The Destruction of the Jewish Community in Jedwabne, Poland* (Princeton University Press, 2001).

33 Steinhardt to J. L. Magnes, 21 March 1940, Box 79, and Steinhardt to Stephen Wise, 20 May 1941, Box 96, Laurence Steinhardt Papers.

34 Richard Breitman *et al.*, eds., *Refugees and Rescue: The Diaries and Papers of James G. McDonald 1935–1945* (Indiana University Press, 2009), pp. 216–217; Kenneth Weisbrode, *The Atlantic Century: Four Generations of Extraordinary Diplomats Who Forged America's Vital Alliance with Europe* (Cambridge, Mass.: Da Capo Press, 2009), p. 75.

35 Steinhardt to Breckinridge Long, 8 May 1941, Box 92, Laurence Steinhardt Papers.

36 Philip Cannistraro *et al.*, eds., *Poland and the Coming of the Second World War: The Diplomatic Papers of A. J. Drexel Biddle, Jr. United States Ambassador to Poland 1937–1939* (Ohio State University Press, 1976), pp. 30–31; Lukes, "Ambassador Laurence Steinhardt," p. 530.

   Another interpretation holds that Grzybowski was not expelled by the Soviets, but was recalled by his government to protest words by Molotov to this effect: Poland, ugly bastard of the Versailles system, was knocked out by punches administered by the Wehrmacht and Red Army. Igor Lukes to author, 2 August 2011.

37 Steinhardt to Hageman Hilty, 7 October 1939, Box 78, Laurence Steinhardt Papers.

38 *FRUS: The Soviet Union, 1933–1939*, p. 793.

39 *FRUS 1940*, vol. I, pp. 281–282, 284–286.

40 Steinhardt to Alvin Untermyer, 5 March 1940, Box 79, Laurence Steinhardt Papers.

41 Benson Lee Grayson, ed., *The American Image of Russia 1917–1977* (New York: Frederick Ungar, 1978), p. 151.

42 Stackman, "Laurence A. Steinhardt," p. 205.

43 Ibid., pp. 234–235.

44 Loy Henderson to Steinhardt, 13 December 1940, Box 29, Laurence Steinhardt Papers; O'Connor, "Laurence A. Steinhardt," pp. 121–122.

45 *FRUS 1941*, vol. I, pp. 906–907; Baer, *A Question of Trust*, p. 327; Lukes, "Ambassador Laurence Steinhardt," p. 532.

46 *FRUS 1940*, vol. I, p. 586; *FRUS 1941*, vol. I, p. 755.

47 *FRUS 1941*, vol. I, pp. 711–712. Also Gustav Hilger and Alfred Meyer, *The Incompatible Allies: A Memoir of German–Soviet Relations 1918–1941* (New York: Macmillan Company, 1953), pp. 331–332.

48 The desperation of Stalin was evident in his willingness, conveyed in summer 1941 to Harry Hopkins, to let an independently commanded US army operate – in conjunction with Red forces – on Soviet territory against the German invasion. Stalin also invited Churchill to spare twenty-five army divisions, under British command, for service in the USSR. See *FRUS 1941*, vol. I, p. 814 and Lukacs, *The Legacy of the Second World War*, p. 62.

49 William Shirer, *The Rise and Fall of the Third Reich: A History of Nazi Germany* (New York: Simon and Schuster, 1960), p. 843; Adam Ulam, *Expansion and Coexistence: Soviet Foreign Policy 1917–73* (New York: Holt, Rinehart and Winston, 1974), p. 284.

50 *FRUS 1941*, vol. I, p. 137.

51 John Lukacs, *June 1941: Hitler and Stalin* (Yale University Press, 2006), p. 73.

52 *FRUS 1941*, vol. I, pp. 177, 874, 880; Henry Cassidy, *Moscow Dateline 1941–1943* (Boston: Houghton Mifflin Company, 1943), p. 57; Steinhardt to Angus Ward, 3 June 1941, Box 95, Laurence Steinhardt Papers; Herwarth, *Zwischen Hitler und Stalin*, p. 223.

53 Gorodetsky, *Stafford Cripps' Mission to Moscow 1940–1942*, p. 196.

54 Glantz, *FDR and the Soviet Union*, p. 56.

55 Joseph Davies, *Mission to Moscow* (New York: Simon and Schuster, 1941), p. 493.

56 Loy Henderson in Washington reported to Steinhardt: "Military people here were convinced that Moscow would fall before the first of August." Henderson to Steinhardt, 18 August 1941, Box 33, Laurence Steinhardt Papers.

57 Hull, *The Memoirs of Cordell Hull*, vol. II, p. 967.

58 William Leahy, *I Was There* (New York: Whittlesey House, 1950), pp. 37–38

59 Glantz, *FDR and the Soviet Union*, pp. 80, 84, 205 #123.

60 O'Connor, "Laurence A. Steinhardt," p. 180; Dunn, *Caught Between Roosevelt and Stalin: America's Ambassadors to Moscow*, p. 126; William Standley and Arthur Ageton, *Admiral Ambassador to Russia* (Chicago: Henry Regnery Company, 1955), p. 63.

61 Cassidy, *Moscow Dateline*, p. 76.

62 Steinhardt to Hull, 3 November 1941, Box 33, Laurence Steinhardt Papers; O'Connor, "Laurence A. Steinhardt," pp. 199–201.

63 Loy Henderson to Steinhardt, 26 November 1941, Box 33, Laurence Steinhardt Papers.

64 Ira Hirschmann, *Life Line to a Promised Land* (New York: Vanguard Press, 1946), pp. 42, 64, 169; Ronald Florence, *Emissary of the Doomed: Bargaining*

for *Lives in the Holocaust* (New York: Viking, 2010), pp. 104–105, 131–132; Barry Rubin, "Ambassador Laurence A. Steinhardt: The Perils of a Jewish Diplomat, 1940–1945," *American Jewish History*, 70 (1981), 331, 335, 344; Stackman, "Laurence A. Steinhardt," pp. 373–374, 381–382; Nahum Goldmann to Steinhardt, 14 October 1944, Box 91, Ira Hirschmann to Steinhardt, 19 October 1944 and 28 December 1944, M. Shertok to Steinhardt, 10 January 1945, Box 92, Laurence Steinhardt Papers; Steinhardt to Cordell Hull, 20 February 1944, John Pehle to Steinhardt, 22 April 1944, Steinhardt to Pehle, 10 May 1944, Ira Hirschmann to Pehle, 4 October 1944, Box 31, War Refugee Board Papers.

65 Steinhardt to Breckinridge Long, 8 May 1941, Box 92, Steinhardt to Nahum Goldmann, 11 November 1944, Box 91, Laurence Steinhardt Papers. Also see Eric Jabotinky, Report on the work in Turkey in 1944 for the Emergency Committee to Save the Jewish People of Europe, 13 February 1945, Box 92, Laurence Steinhardt Papers.

66 Instead of election to the governor's office in Albany, Steinhardt became ambassador to Czechoslovakia, serving there from 1945 to 1948. Truman later appointed him to Canada, where he served from 1949 to his death (plane crash) in March 1950. For more on Steindhardt's post-WW II career, see Igor Lukes, *On the Edge of the Cold War: American Diplomats and Spies in Postwar Prague* (Oxford University Press, 2012).

67 Glantz, *FDR and the Soviet Union*, p. 104.

68 Mayers, *The Ambassadors and America's Soviet Policy*, p. 140.

69 Dunn, *Caught Between Roosevelt and Stalin*, pp. 152–153.

70 Kemp Tolley, *Caviar and Commissars: The Experiences of a U.S. Naval Officer in Stalin's Russia* (Annapolis: Naval Institute Press, 1983), p. 154.

71 Standley and Ageton, *Admiral Ambassador to Russia*, p. 3.

72 "John Young" by Standley, n.d. (1951?), William Standley Papers. Also see Standley and Ageton, *Admiral Ambassador to Russia*, p. 111.

73 Butler, *My Dear Mr. Stalin*, p. 66.

74 Memorandum of Stalin–Standley Conversation, 23 April 1942, William Standley Papers. Also see Standley and Ageton, *Admiral Ambassador to Russia*, pp. 151–158.

75 Memorandum of Stalin–Standley Conversation, 2 July 1942, and Standley to Major E. J. York, 22 March 1943, William Standley Papers; *FRUS 1942*, vol. III, p. 606.

76 Memorandum of Admiral Kuznetsov–Standley Conversation, 18 August 1942 and Memorandum of Molotov–Standley Conversation, 13 January 1943, William Standley Papers; Standley and Ageton, *Admiral Ambassador to Russia*, pp. 221–234.

77 Dunn, *Caught Between Roosevelt and Stalin*, p. 162.

78 Memorandum of Molotov–Standley Conversation, 3 July 1942, and Major General Follett Bradley to Standley, 12 November 1951, William Standley Papers.

79 Tolley, *Caviar and Commissars*, p. 63; Standley and Ageton, *Admiral Ambassador to Russia*, p. 288.

80 Standley and Ageton, *Admiral Ambassador to Russia*, p. 407.

81 Memorandum of Molotov–Standley Conversation, 3 July 1942. Also see Memoranda of Vyshinsky–Standley Conversation, 27 May 1942, and Lozovsky–Standley Conversation, 9 September 1942, William Standley Papers.

82 Memorandum of Molotov–Standley Conversation, 26 April 1943, Memorandum of Stalin–Molotov–Standley–Clark Kerr and Aide Memoire, 11 August 1943, William Standley Papers; *FRUS 1943*, vol. III, pp. 381–382.

83 *FRUS 1943*, vol. III, pp. 344–347, 432–434.

84 Ibid., p. 435.

85 Standley and Ageton, *Admiral Ambassador to Russia*, p. 252.

86 Standley to Senator Pat McCarran, 6 September 1951, William Standley Papers; Glantz, *FDR and the Soviet Union*, pp. 112, 116–117.

87 Glantz, *FDR and the Soviet Union*, pp. 125–126. Also see Standley and Ageton, *Admiral Ambassador to Russia*, pp. 364–382.

88 Standley and Ageton, *Admiral Ambassador to Russia*, p. 372.

89 Ibid., p. 373.

90 Conversations of Admiral Standley, 5 November 1942, and Standley to Kenneth Roberts, 2 April 1951, William Standley Papers; Herring, *Aid to Russia 1941–1946*, p. 84; Tolley, *Caviar and Commissars*, p. 104; Standley and Ageton, *Admiral Ambassador to Russia*, pp. 350–363; Glantz, *FDR and the Soviet Union*, pp. 135–137.

91 *FRUS 1943*, vol. III, p. 631.

92 Ibid., p. 632.

93 *FRUS 1942*, vol. III, p. 461.

94 Mayers, *The Ambassadors and America's Soviet Policy*, pp. 145–146.

95 Glantz, *FDR and the Soviet Union*, p. 121.

96 See File 4770 [Standley, Adm. William H. 1940–1943], Official File, Franklin Roosevelt Papers; Robert Sherwood, *Roosevelt and Hopkins: An Intimate History* (New York: Harper and Brothers, 1948), p. 706.

97 Glantz, *FDR and the Soviet Union*, p. 123.

98 Standley to Allan Kirk, 30 May 1949, William Standley Papers.

99 *FRUS 1942*, vol. III, p. 454.

100 *FRUS 1943*, vol. III, p. 565.

101 Standley to Frank Storm, 30 May 1950, William Standley Papers.

102 Our Post-War Relations with Russia, p. 5, 13–19 April 1945, William Standley Papers.

103 Glantz, *FDR and the Soviet Union*, p. 118; Sherwood, *Roosevelt and Hopkins*, p. 733.

104 Butler, *My Dear Mr. Stalin*, p. 22.

105 Abramson, *Spanning the Century*, p. 348.

106 Standley and Ageton, *Admiral Ambassador to Russia*, p. 490.
    At his first ambassadorial news conference in Moscow, Harriman put conceptual distance between himself and Standley with this statement: "The American people have the greatest of sympathy for the Russian people, who have suffered so much, and it is in their hearts to attempt to be of the greatest assistance." See Memorandum for Press Conference, 4 November 1943, Box 747, W. Averell Harriman Papers.

107 Vladimir Pechatnov, "Moskovskoe posolstvo Averella Garimana, 1943–1946," *Novaia i noveshaia istoriia*, Part 2, No. 4 (2002).

108 Abramson, *Spanning the Century*, pp. 268–269; Herring, *Aid to Russia 1941–1946*, p. 15.

109 Harriman's Press Statement, 4 November 1943, Box 747, W. Averell Harriman Papers; John Deane, *The Strange Alliance: The Story of Our Efforts at Wartime Co-operation with Russia* (New York: Viking Press, 1947), pp. 9–12.

110 David Fogelsong, *The American Mission and the Evil Empire: The Crusade for a Free Russia since 1881* (Cambridge University Press, 2007), pp. 102–103; Robert Newman, *The Cold War Romance of Lillian Hellman and John Melby* (University of North Carolina Press, 1989), p. 27; Bohlen, *Witness to History 1929–1969*, p. 133; Harriman and Abel, *Special Envoy to Churchill and Stalin 1941–1946* (New York: Random House, 1975), p. 301.

111 Newman, *The Cold War Romance of Lillian Hellman and John Melby*, p. 27.

112 Bohlen, *Witness to History 1929–1969*, p. 127; Mayers, *The Ambassadors and America's Soviet Policy*, pp. 151, 287 #40.

113 George Kennan, *Memoirs: 1925–1950* (Boston: Little, Brown and Company, 1967), pp. 231, 233. Also see John Lewis Gaddis, *George F. Kennan: An American Life* (New York: Penguin Books, 2011), p. 627.

114 Answers to questions submitted by John Lewis Gaddis regarding George Kennan, 23–24 September 1982, Box 1010, W. Averell Harriman Papers.

115 Diary entry, September 1945, p. 4, Box 231, George Kennan Papers.

116 Gaddis, *George F. Kennan*, pp. 173–174, 184.

117 Abramson, *Spanning the Century*, pp. 348, 350; Harriman and Abel, *Special Envoy to Churchill and Stalin 1941–1946*, pp. 226–228; *FRUS 1944*, vol. IV, p. 874.

118 Harriman and Abel, *Special Envoy to Churchill and Stalin 1941–1946*, pp. 294–295, 298; Deane, *The Strange Alliance*, pp. 55–56, 60–63.

119 Glen Infield, *The Poltava Affair: A Russian Warning: An American Tragedy* (New York: Macmillan Publishing, 1973), pp. 226–227.

120 Kathleen Harriman to Mary Harriman, 4 June 1944, Box 6, W. Averell Harriman Papers.

121 Infield, *The Poltava Affair*, pp. xiv, 162–163.

122 Press Conference (Anglo-American Correspondents), 27 June 1944, Box 748, W. Averell Harriman Papers.

123 Abramson, *Spanning the Century*, p. 383; Harriman and Abel, *Special Envoy to Churchill and Stalin 1941–1946*, pp. 296–297, 341; Deane, *The Strange Alliance*, pp. 107–125, 296; Infield, *The Poltava Affair*, p. 225; Robert Storey, *The Final Judgment? Pearl Harbor to Nuremberg* (San Antonio: Naylor Company, 1968), pp. 33–35.

124 Vladimir Pechatnov, "Moskovskoe posolstvo Averella Garimana, 1943–1946," *Novaia i noveshaia istoriia*, Part 1, No. 3 (2002).

125 Dear and Foot, eds., *The Oxford Companion to World War II*, p. 1262. Also see Timothy Snyder, *Bloodlands: Europe Between Hitler and Stalin* (New York: Basic Books, 2010), p. 416. Snyder gives a lower number of Polish fatalities at Warsaw, speaking of "more than one hundred thousand."

126 Message of the Soviet Government in Reply to Message of the British Government of 5th September 1944, 9 September 1944, Box 1070, W. Averell Harriman Papers; Roberts, *Stalin's Wars*, pp. 214–215.

127 Message from His Majesty's Government to the People's Commissar for Foreign Affairs, 4 September 1944 (delivered 5 September), Box 1070 W. Averell Harriman Papers.

128 Butler, *My Dear Mr. Stalin*, p. 252–254.

129 Kennan, *Memoirs: 1925–1950*, pp. 211, 267; Dunn, *Caught Between Roosevelt and Stalin*, p. 230.

130 Press Conference, 20 June 1944, p. 4, Box 748, W. Averell Harriman Papers. For additional remarks on the London Poles and Harriman's skepticism of them see Press Conference for American Correspondents, 19 January 1944, pp. 2–3, Box 747, W. Averell Harriman Papers.

131 Harriman to FDR and Cordell Hull, 25 January 1944, John Melby, Trip to Smolensk and the Katyn Forest, 21–23 January 1944, Kathleen Harriman, Report on Inspection Tour of Katyn, 23 January 1944, Box 1070, W. Averell Harriman Papers.

132 Answers to questions submitted by John Lewis Gaddis regarding George Kennan, 23–24 September 1982, Box 1010, W. Averell Harriman Papers; Infield, *The Poltava Affair*, pp. 197–198.

133 Harriman to Hopkins, 10 September 1944, Box 157, Harry Hopkins Papers; *FRUS 1944*, vol. IV, p. 989.

134 David Wyman and Rafael Medoff, *A Race Against Death: Peter Bergson, America, and the Holocaust* (New York: New Press, 2002), pp. 10–11; Andrew Preston, *Sword of the Spirit, Shield of Faith: Religion in American War and Diplomacy* (New York: Alfred A. Knopf, 2012), pp. 336–337.

135 Concerning the treatment of Poles, Hitler had earlier advised senior German army officers along these lines: "Our strength is in our quickness and brutality. Genghis Khan had millions of women and children killed with a gay heart. History sees in him only a great state builder ... Thus, for the time being, I have sent to the East only my 'Death's Head Units' with the order to kill without pity or mercy all men, women and children of Polish race or language. Only in such a way will we win the vital space that we need."

Of Jewish resistance in the Warsaw ghetto, SS Major General Jürgen Stroop, the officer in charge of its 1943 suppression, reported that his men had achieved their object "with utter ruthlessness and merciless tenacity." He also allowed: "Jews usually left their hideouts but frequently remained in the burning buildings and jumped out of the windows only when the heat became unbearable. Then they tried to crawl with broken bones across the street into buildings which were not afire ... Countless numbers of Jews were liquidated in sewers and bunkers with blasting."

Cited in Robert H. Jackson, "Nurnberg in Retrospect," *The Canadian Bar Review*, 27 (1949), 774–775. See also Robert Jackson, *The Case Against the Nazi War Criminals* (New York: Alfred A. Knopf, 1946), p. 46.

136 *FRUS 1944*, vol. IV, pp. 1208–1209.

137 *FRUS 1943*, vol. III, p. 606.

138 Kathleen Harriman to Mary Harriman, 30 August 1944, Box 6, W. Averell Harriman Papers.

Timothy Snyder has placed the number of Jews killed at Majdanek at 50,000. According to him, roughly 10,000 non-Jewish Poles also perished there. Of the 6,000,000 Jews who died at the hands of the Germans and their helpers, he estimated that 300,000 were murdered by the Third Reich's Romanian ally. See Snyder, *Bloodlands: Europe Between Hitler and Stalin*, pp. 275, 293 and his "Hitler vs. Stalin: Who Killed More?" in *New York Review of Books*, 10 March 2011, p. 36.

139 Averell Harriman to Secretary of State, 30 December 1944 and Edward Stettinius to Embassy Moscow, 22 January 1945, Box 7, George Kennan to Secretary of State, 6 February 1945, Box 37, War Refugee Board Papers.

140 Nicholas Bethell, *The Last Secret: The Delivery to Stalin of over Two Millions Russians by Britain and the United States* (New York: Basic Books, 1974), pp. 36–37; Butler, *My Dear Mr. Stalin*, pp. 301–302.

141 *FRUS 1945*, vol. V, pp. 1097–1098.

142 Bethell, *The Last Secret*, pp. x, 1, 28–29.

143 Fraser Harbutt, *Yalta 1945: Europe and America at the Crossroads* (Cambridge University Press, 2010), pp. 299–300.

144 Gerhard Weinberg, *A World at Arms: A Global History of World War II* (Cambridge University Press, 1994), p. 808.

145 Harriman, Oral History, p. 257, Columbia University, Box 615, W. Averell Harriman Papers.

146 Harriman and Abel, *Special Envoy to Churchill and Stalin 1941–1946*, p. 358.

147 Max Hastings, *Finest Years: Churchill as Warlord 1940–1945* (London: Harper Press, 2009), pp. 571–577.

148 Roberts, *Stalin's Wars*, pp. 263–264.

149 Henry Stimson and McGeorge Bundy, *On Active Service in Peace and War* (New York: Harper and Brother, 1948), p. 606; Walter Millis, ed. *The Forrestal Diaries* (New York: Viking Press, 1951), pp. 47, 55–58.

150 Harry Truman, *Memoirs: Year of Decisions* (Garden City: Doubleday, 1955), pp. 71, 395; *FRUS 1945*, vol. V, p. 819.

151 Quentin Reynolds interview of Harriman, p. 7, 3 March 1946 and Address to American Association of Advertising Agencies, p. 2, 10 April 1946, Box 748, W. Averell Harriman Papers.

152 John Lewis Gaddis, *The United States and the Origins of the Cold War 1941–1947* (Columbia University Press, 1971), p. 204.

153 *FRUS 1944*, vol. IV, pp. 951, 1054–1055; Herring, *Aid to Russia 1941–1946*, pp. 150, 153–154, 196; Harriman and Abel, *Special Envoy to Churchill and Stalin 1941–1946*, p. 386; Harbutt, *Yalta 1945*, p. 367.

154 Speech for Smolensk Dedication, 17 August 1945, Box 748, W. Averell Harriman Papers.

155 Pechatnov, "Moskovskoe posolstvo Averella Garimana, 1943–1946."

156 Ibid. Also see Wilson Miscamble, *The Most Controversial Decision: Truman, the Atomic Bombs, and Defeat of Japan* (Cambridge University Press, 2011), pp. 101–102.

157 Abramson, *Spanning the Century*, pp. 401, 403–404; Dunn, *Caught Between Roosevelt and Stalin*, p. 258; Harriman and Abel, *Special Envoy to Churchill and Stalin 1941–1946*, pp. 499–501.

158 David Holloway, *Stalin and the Bomb: The Soviet Union and Atomic Energy 1939–1956* (Yale University Press, 1994), pp. 128–129, 154; *FRUS 1945*, vol. V, pp. 922–924.

159 Diary entry, 26 November 1945, Box 231, George Kennan Papers.

160 Harriman and Abel, *Special Envoy to Churchill and Stalin 1941–1946*, p. 536.

161 *FRUS 1945*, vol. V, p. 849; Kennan, *Memoirs: 1925–1950*, p. 241; Roberts, *Stalin's War*, p. 265; Deane, *The Strange Alliance*, p. 180.

162 Reeder, *The Complete Poems of Anna Akhmatova*, vol. II, p. 613.

163 In brief, Stalin's "two world" analysis rested on the alleged irreconcilability of capitalism and communism. Kennan's "long telegram" pivoted on the Kremlin's worldview as anchored in a "traditional" Russian suspicion of the

West, born of insecurity and a sense of inferiority. Churchill's "iron curtain" speech emphasized the need for Anglo-US unity to check Soviet aggrandizement in a divided Europe.

164 David Mayers, *Wars and Peace: The Future Americans Envisioned 1861–1991* (New York: St. Martin's Press, 1998), p. 83. For an alternative interpretation of the Cold War's origins, one placing greater emphasis on personalities and relationships among top Allied leaders, see Frank Costigliola, *Roosevelt's Lost Alliances: How Personal Politics Helped Start the Cold War* (Princeton University Press, 2012).

165 A second Polish disaster at Katyn occurred on 10 April 2010. The jet, carrying dozens of Warsaw dignitaries to commemorate the seventieth anniversary of the killings, crashed while trying to land at Smolensk airport. All passengers died, including President Lech Kaczynski, Ryszard Kaczorowski (former president in exile), Jerzy Szmajdzinski (deputy speaker of Parliament), Aleksander Szczyglo (head of the National Security Bureau), Andrzej Kremer (deputy foreign minister), General Franciszek Gagor (army chief of staff), and Slawomir Skrzypek (president of the National Bank of Poland). Katyn "is a damned place," said Aleksander Kwasniewski (former president), upon learning of the fatal accident. "It sends shivers down my spine." *New York Times*, 11 April 2010, p. 1.

166 Infield, *The Poltava Affair*, p. 211; Ronald Florence, *Emissary of the Doomed: Bargaining for Lives in the Holocaust* (New York: Viking, 2010), pp. 193–194; David Mayers, *Dissenting Voices in America's Rise to Power* (Cambridge University Press, 2007), pp. 270–274.

167 Pechatnov, "Moskovskoe posolstvo Averella Garimana, 1943–1946," Part 1, No. 3, 2002; Pavel Sudoplatov and Anatoli Sudoplatov, *Special Tasks: The Memoirs of an Unwitting Witness – A Soviet Spymaster* (Boston: Little, Brown and Company, 1994), pp. 225–226.

168 Diary entry of 26 July 1944, Box 231, George Kennan Papers.

169 Citizens' Foreign Relations Committee to Dwight D. Eisenhower, September 1957, Standley to Eisenhower, 1 May 1950, Standley to Herbert Hoover, n.d. (1951?), Roosevelt Jewish Ancestry, n.d., William Standley Papers; "Standley Sticks to Guns Re Communistic Influence," *La Mesa Scout* (La Mesa, California), 4 March 1948.

170 Steinhardt to Alvin Untermyer, 19 December 1939, Box 78, Laurence Steinhardt Papers. Also see Steinhardt to Hageman Hilty, 25 August 1939, Steinhardt to Louise and Frederic Partridge, 1 November 1939, Steinhardt to Fred Sterling, 14 November 1939, Box 78, Steinhardt to Alvin Untermyer, 5 March 1940, Box 79, Laurence Steinhardt Papers.

171 Harriman and Abel, *Special Envoy to Churchill and Stalin 1941–1946*, p. 377.

172 Grayson, *The American Image of Russia 1917–1977*, p. 175.

173 Anatoly Dobrynin, *In Confidence: Moscow's Ambassador to America's Six Cold War Presidents* (New York: Times Books, 1995), p. 379.

Chapter 8: Conclusions

1 Niccolò Machiavelli can be invoked as authority in support of this method. That one-time Florentine diplomat advised his readers: "The first thing one does to evaluate the intelligence of a ruler is to examine the men he has around him; and when they are capable and loyal, he can always be considered wise, for he has known how to recognize their capability and maintain their loyalty. But when they are otherwise, one can always form an unfavorable opinion of him in all other things; because the first mistake he makes, he makes in this choice of ministers." See Mark Musa, ed., *Machiavelli's The Prince* (New York: St. Martin's Press, 1964), p. 195.

2 Winston Churchill, *The Grand Alliance* (Boston: Houghton Mifflin, 1950), pp. 23–24. Longfellow's "The Building of the Ship" was published in 1849 and recited during moments of national crisis, particularly in the Civil War era. See Richard Marius, ed., *The Columbia Book of Civil War Poetry* (Columbia University Press, 1994), p. 85.

3 FDR's administration was not alone. Japanese-Canadians were confined (in British Columbia) by their government. Suspect minorities in the USSR were severely mistreated. Roughly 3.5 million people were deported to the east. Fatalities were high. Crimean Tartars, Volga Germans, Chechens, Turks, Greeks, and Bulgarians were among the relocated. See John Lukacs, *The Legacy of the Second World War* (Yale University Press, 2010), pp. 45–46 and I. C. B. Dear and M. R. D. Foot, eds., *The Oxford Companion to World War II* (Oxford University Press, 1995), pp. 295–296.

4 Interviews of Eleanor Roosevelt, 3 September 1952 and 13 July 1954, Frank Freidel, Oral History, Franklin Roosevelt Papers.

5 Alain Darlan to Murphy, 21 November 1955, Murphy to Darlan, 25 November 1955, Murphy statement on Darlan, 30 November 1955, Box 88, Robert Murphy Papers; Robert Murphy, *Diplomat among Warriors* (Garden City: Doubleday and Company, 1964), p. 114.

6 Erik Larson, *In the Garden of Beasts: Love, Terror, and an American Family in Hitler's Berlin* (New York: Crown, 2011), p. 355.

7 Of the ambassadors reviewed in this book, three went to Harvard as undergraduates: Grew, Phillips, Kennedy. Three went to Yale: Wilson, Bullitt, Harriman. Two went to Princeton: Long, Winant (did not graduate). One went to Columbia: Steinhardt.

Of the rest, two attended the US Naval Academy (Annapolis): Leahy, Standley. One attended Tulane: Caffery. Two men had only marginal or no university education: Johnson (one year at George Washington University), Gauss (high school graduate). Hurley earned a law degree at George Washington University. Dodd was the only ambassador with an advanced degree from a non-English language institution (Ph.D., University of Leipzig).

Mentioned in connection to Spain: like Dodd, Hayes was a respected historian and was elected (1945) president of the American Historical Association. Hayes earned his undergraduate degree and Ph.D. at Columbia. Weddell, as an undergraduate, attended George Washington University. Bowers started, but did not finish, legal studies.

Dodd was a lapsed Baptist. Three of the above were Catholics: Kennedy, Caffery (convert), Hayes (convert). Steinhardt was the only Jew, though Bullitt was of Jewish background on his mother's side. The rest, with allowance for gradations of commitment, were Episcopalian. The Hyde Park (New York)-born FDR attended Groton, Harvard, Columbia Law School, and was a thoroughgoing Episcopalian. On FDR's religious beliefs, see Andrew Preston, *Sword of the Spirit, Shield of Faith: Religion in American War and Diplomacy* (New York: Alfred A. Knopf, 2012), pp. 315–326.

Enhanced ambassadorial diversity – along racial, ethnic, religious, gender, and educational lines – waited until well after 1945. The same point holds for the Foreign Service.

8 Charles Glass, *Americans in Paris: Life and Death under Nazi Occupation* (New York: Penguin Books, 2011), p.14.

9 Vehemently opposed to the USSR, Francoist Spain in March 1939 joined the anti-Comintern Pact and later sent airmen and soldiers – Blue Division – to the eastern front. In June 1940, as French power crumbled, Franco declared that his country had moved from "neutral" to "nonbelligerent," presumably a small step away from openly joining the Axis in hostilities. German submarines and surface raiders, meanwhile, enjoyed safety and re-supply in Spanish ports. German aviators and sailors, who washed up on Spanish territory, were promptly repatriated. Tens of thousands of republican supporters were executed by Franco's regime during the World War II years; elements of the Gestapo, on loan from Germany, helped maintain Franco's version of justice and domestic tranquility. Spain also conducted trade with the Third Reich, exporting valuable wolfram to it. However, despite this cooperation and ideological affinity ("spiritual alliance"), Franco managed to resist Hitler's attempt – combining warm promises with threats – to enlist Spain fully on the Axis side. The Caudillo knew that Spain, impoverished and damaged by the civil war, must abstain from hostilities, the alternative being the country's ruin.

Hayes meant to keep Franco true to this neutralist vocation, which entailed "preemptive" buying of Spanish goods and sundry economic considerations (plus American Red Cross and food aid). In 1944, to Hayes's gratification,

Madrid agreed to curtail drastically wolfram sales to Germany, expel German espionage agents from Spain, withdraw remaining elements of the Blue Division (its redeployment to Spain begun in 1943) from the east, release interned Italian merchant ships, and suppress the German Consulate General in Tangier. Most US pundits and political figures held Franco's Spain no better than Hitler's Germany or Mussolini's Italy. They damned Hayes ("fascist sympathizer") for being too indulgent of his hosts, a charge compounded by his publicly stated post-1945 appreciations of Franco.

See Murphy to Carlton Hayes, 18 April 1944 and Carlton Hayes to Murphy, 2 May 1944, Box 45, Robert Murphy Papers; Willard Beaulac, *Franco: Silent Ally in World War II* (Southern Illinois University Press, 1986), p. 161; Jerrold Packard, *Neither Friend Nor Foe: The European Neutrals in World War II* (New York: Charles Scribner's Sons, 1992), pp. 191, 338; Carlton Hayes, *The United States and Spain: An Interpretation* (New York: Sheed and Ward, 1951), pp. 172, 179, 183, 186, 191.

10 Willard Beaulac, *Career Diplomat: A Career in the Foreign Service of the United States* (New York: Macmillan Company, 1964), p. 51.

11 Harvey to Miss Snow, 30 September 1947, Box 1, Constance Harvey Papers; Ruth White, "From Sea to Shining Sea," *Independent Woman* (February 1952), p. 64.

12 Joan Maria Thomas, *Roosevelt and Franco During the Second World War: From the Spanish Civil War to Pearl Harbor* (New York: Palgrave Macmillan, 2008), p. 52; Claude Bowers, *My Mission to Spain: Watching the Rehearsal for World War II* (New York: Simon and Schuster, 1954), pp. vi, 418–419, 421; Claude Bowers, *My Life* (New York: Simon and Schuster, 1962), pp. 283–284; Stanley Payne. *Franco and Hitler: Spain, Germany, and World War II* (Yale University Press, 2008), p. 105; Charles Halstead, "Diligent Diplomat: Alexander W. Weddell as American Ambassador to Spain, 1939–1942," *Virginia Magazine of History and Biography*, 82 (1974), pp. 18, 24; Hayes, *The United States and Spain: An Interpretation*, pp. 164–165, 175, 186; Carlton Hayes, *Wartime Mission in Spain 1942–1945* (New York: Macmillan Company, 1945), p. 16.

13 The activities of the War Refugee Board (WRB), in the view of Hayes, compromised ambassadorial reputation and threatened to confound Allied relations with Spain. He did not allow any WRB representative to join the Madrid embassy. The WRB's James Mann wondered whether Hayes was anti-Semitic and was stunned by his saying that the WRB sought its own "glory" in wanting to facilitate refugees across Spain. Representative Emanuel Celler of New York's tenth congressional district demanded (summer 1944) that Hayes be recalled from Madrid for obstinately refusing to assist the WRB.

See James Mann's Report on Trip to Portugal and Spain (May–July 1944), 30 August 1944, pp. 77, 85, Box 78, War Refugee Board Papers. Several memoranda (by Mann and other personnel) in Box 31 of the War Refugee Board Papers attest to the WRB's alarm over Hayes. Also see John Paul Wilson, "Carlton J. H. Hayes in Spain, 1942–1945" (Ph.D. dissertation, Syracuse University, 1969), pp. 205, 218, 226–228; Kenneth Weisbrode, *The Atlantic Century: Four Generations of Extraordinary Diplomats Who Forged America's Vital Alliance with Europe* (Cambridge, Mass.: Da Capo Press, 2009), p. 73.

14 David Reynolds, *From World War to Cold War: Churchill, Roosevelt, and the International History of the 1940s* (Oxford University Press, 2007), p. 163.

15 Larson, *In the Garden of Beasts*, pp. 249–250; James Leutze, ed., *The London Journal of General Raymond E. Lee 1940–1941* (Boston: Little, Brown and Company, 1971), p. 208.

16 Martin Luther King famously said: "The arc of the moral universe is long, but it bends toward justice." The origin of King's statement resides in phrasing made by Theodore Parker, a nineteenth-century abolitionist and Unitarian minister based in Boston.

17 Michael Walzer, *Just and Unjust Wars: A Moral Argument with Historical Illustrations* (New York: Basic Books, 2000), p. 198.

18 Takashi Nagai, *The Bells of Nagasaki* (Tokyo: Kodansha International 1984), p. 13.

19 Of Europeans who had direct experience of World War II, and while in executive office subsequently wrestled with fundamental questions, two people stand out: Charles de Gaulle, who understood his responsibility as primarily based in France, and Pope John Paul II, accountable to a larger constituency.

De Gaulle was no more able than other mortals to check the periodic recrudescence of reaction and bigotry, against which Albert Camus once warned, lest the "rats" be sent forth again to plague humankind. Impressively, though, postwar France has usually prevailed "in the never ending fight against terror and its relentless onslaughts" (Camus again), despite moments reminiscent of Vichy: viciousness against Tonkinese peasants and Algerian resistants in the 1950s; more recently in demands from Jean-Marie Le Pen and his daughter Marine (leaders of the National Front party) for revivification of "traditional French values"; Nicholas Sarkozy's 2010 campaign to expel the Roma, and stigmatization of Muslims (prohibition on full veils in public). De Gaulle himself was not immune to thinking in racialist categories, as when in 1967 he derided Jews as "an elite people, self-assured and domineering." But at his best, he – bane of FDR and abominated by Leahy's embassy – remained committed to France's repudiating the "dark years." Even while the war's outcome was undecided, and abashed that national manpower was not fully engaged against Germany, he celebrated France: agent of liberty, eternally devoted to humane civilization.

John Paul II could not redeem the murder of unaided innocence that stained his native Poland, where as the seminarian Karol Wojtyla he had escaped Nazi vindictiveness and aided fugitive Jews. No hopeful interpretation could be retrieved from German actions in Warsaw (1943, 1944), or from Auschwitz, or Majdanek, or Treblinka, or any other horrid site of familiar recitation. Yet John Paul represented an irrepressible moral force, once familiar even to Stalin when a young Orthodox (Georgian) Christian seminarian. Meaningful history had not ended, the pope asserted in words and deeds. Hence his pilgrimage to Yad Vashem in 2000 to honor the Shoah's victims and to spur Christian–Jewish understanding. Earlier he established (1994) formal diplomatic connection between the Holy See and Israel. Earlier still, he prayed (1979) at Auschwitz. Moreover, John Paul helped, by virtue of his counterexample, to bring about the demise of the communist order in Poland and, by extension, in the remainder of Eastern Europe (USSR too). He did not thereby repeal the Stalinist past or impart life to the guiltless that died in Soviet deportations or at Katyn. But he gave Stalin's heirs a moral chance on which they made good, thus confirming Harriman's own postwar expectation – that Kremlin bosses also yearned for a better future, the USSR's stranglehold on Eastern Europe would prove temporary.

See Albert Camus, *The Plague*, (New York: Vintage Books, 1972), p. 287; Tony Judt, *The Burden of Responsibility: Blum, Camus, Aron and the French Twentieth Century* (University of Chicago Press, 1998), p. 176; *FRUS 1944*, vol. III, p. 660; Charles de Gaulle, *War Memoirs* (New York: Carroll and Graf Publishers, 1998), p. 461.

20 Churchill delivered his remarks on 12 November 1940: www.winstonchurchill.org/learn/speeches/speeches-of-winston-churchill/104-neville-chamberlain.

21 For an unblinking account of the Third Reich's foreign ministry and diplomatic corps, see Eckart Conze *et al.*, *Das Amt und die Vergangenheit: Deutsche Diplomaten im Dritten Reich und in der Bundesrepublik* (Munich: Karl Blessing Verlag, 2010). This book was originally commissioned as a report by Joschka Fischer, Germany's foreign minister in 1998–2005. Its release in 2010 sparked debates in Germany and was reviewed in such publications as the *Frankfurter Allgemeine, Die Zeit, Die Welt, Frankfurter Allgemeine Sonntags-Zeitung (FAS)*, and on television and raidio.

Some German diplomats did oppose Hitler from early-on, including Count Friedrich von Prittwitz who served as ambassador to Washington in 1928–1933. He resigned to protest Hitler's coming to power. Jeremy Black, *A History of Diplomacy* (London: Reaktion Books, 2010), p. 194.

22 William Leahy, *I Was There* (New York: McGraw-Hill Book Company, 1950), pp. 431, 441. Also see Wilson Miscamble, *The Most Controversial Decision: Truman, the Atomic Bombs, and the Defeat of Japan* (Cambridge University Press, 2011), pp. 33, 78, 115 and Michael Bess, *Choices under Fire: Moral Dimensions of World War II* (New York: Alfred A. Knopf, 2006), pp. 198–253.

23 www.winstonchurchill.org/learn/speeches/speeches-of-winston-churchill/104-neville-chamberlain.

BIBLIOGRAPHY

Manuscript Collections

Akten zur deutschen auswärtigen Politik 1918–1945 aus dem Archiv des Deutschen Auswärtigen Amtes (Berlin).

Bellush, Bernard, 1917–. Franklin D. Roosevelt Presidential Library (Hyde Park, New York).

Boettiger, John, 1900–1950. Franklin D. Roosevelt Presidential Library.

Bullitt, William, 1891–1967. Yale University (New Haven, Connecticut).

Caffery, Jefferson, 1886–1974. University of Louisiana (Lafayette, Louisiana).

Dodd, Martha E., 1908–1990. Library of Congress (Washington, DC).

Dodd, William Edward, 1869–1940. Library of Congress.

Dooman, Eugene Hoffman, 1890–1969. Hoover Institution (Stanford, California); Oral History Research Project, Columbia University (New York, New York).

Foreign Office Records. National Archives (London [Kew]).

France, Record Group-43. Center for Advanced Holocaust Studies, United States Holocaust Memorial Museum (Washington, DC).

Franklin D. Roosevelt Memorial Foundation. Franklin D. Roosevelt Presidential Library.

Fry, Varian, 1907–1947. Columbia University.

Grew, Joseph, 1880–1965. Houghton Library, Harvard University (Cambridge, Massachusetts).

Harriman, W. Averell, 1891–1986. Library of Congress.

Harvey, Constance, 1904–1997. Smith College (Northampton, Massachusetts).

Hopkins, Harry, 1890–1946. Franklin D. Roosevelt Presidential Library.

Hornbeck, Stanley, 1883–1966. Hoover Institution.

Hurley, Patrick, 1883–1963. University of Oklahoma (Norman, Oklahoma).

Jackson, Robert H., 1892–1954. Library of Congress.

Johnson, Nelson Trusler, 1887–1954. Library of Congress; Oral History Research Project, Columbia University.

Kennan, George, 1904–2005. Mudd Manuscript Library, Princeton University (Princeton, New Jersey).

Kennedy, Joseph Patrick, 1888–1969. John F. Kennedy Presidential Library (Boston, Massachusetts).

Kent, Tyler, 1911–1988. Boston University (Boston, Massachusetts); Franklin D. Roosevelt Presidential Library.

Leahy, William, 1875–1959. Library of Congress.

Long, Breckinridge, 1881–1958. Library of Congress.

MacArthur II, Douglas, 1909–1997. Foreign Affairs Oral History, Library of Congress.

Matthews, H. Freeman, 1899–1986. Oral History, Harry S. Truman Presidential Library (Independence, Missouri); Mudd Manuscript Library, Princeton University.

Mayer, Ferdinand, 1887–1966. Herbert Hoover Presidential Library (West Branch, Iowa).

McNaughton, Frank, 1906–1978. Harry S. Truman Presidential Library.

Morgenthau, Henry, Jr., 1891–1967. Franklin D. Roosevelt Presidential Library.

Mulliner, Maurine, 1906–2002. Oral History Research Project, Columbia University.

Murphy, Robert, 1894–1978 Hoover Institution.

Moore, R. Walton, 1859–1941. Franklin D. Roosevelt Presidential Library.

Pell, Herbert, 1884–1961. Franklin D. Roosevelt Presidential Library.

Phillips, Caroline Astor Drayton, 1880–1965. Schlesinger Library, Harvard University.

Phillips, William, 1878–1968. Houghton Library, Harvard University; Oral History Research Project, Columbia University.

Record Groups (RG) 59, 84. National Archives (College Park, Maryland).

Roosevelt, Anna Eleanor, 1884–1962. Franklin D. Roosevelt Presidential Library.

Roosevelt, Franklin D., 1882–1945. Alphabetical File, Frank Freidel Oral History, Official File, President's Personal File, President's Secretary's File, Franklin D. Roosevelt Presidential Library.

Roosevelt, James, 1907–1991. Franklin D. Roosevelt Presidential Library.

Schuler, Frank, 1908–1996. Franklin D. Roosevelt Presidential Library.

Sherwood, Robert, 1895–1955. Houghton Library, Harvard University.

Smith, Truman, 1893–1970. Herbert Hoover Presidential Library.

Standley, William, 1872–1963. University of Southern California (Los Angeles, California).

Steinhardt, Laurence, 1892–1950. Library of Congress.

Truman, Harry S., 1884–1972. Naval Aide File, Official File, Oral Histories (O. Edmund Clubb, W. Averell Harriman, Arthur Ringwalt, John Service), President's Personal File, President's Secretary's File. Harry S. Truman Presidential Library.

War Refugee Board. Franklin D. Roosevelt Presidential Library.

Welles, Sumner, 1892–1961. Franklin D. Roosevelt Presidential Library.

Wilson, Hugh, 1885–1946. Herbert Hoover Presidential Library.

Winant, John Gilbert, 1889–1947. Franklin D. Roosevelt Presidential Library; New Hampshire Historical Society (Concord, New Hampshire).

Published Government Documents

Documents on German Foreign Policy, 1918–1945 (Washington: Government Printing Office, series).

Esherick, Joseph, ed. Lost Chance in China: The World War II Despatches of John S. Service (New York: Random House, 1974).

Foreign Relations of the United States (Washington: Government Printing Office, series).

France During the German Occupation 1940–1944: A Collection of 292 Statements on the Government of Marshal Pétain and Pierre Laval (Stanford University Press, 1958), 3 vols.

Grenville, J. A. S., ed. The Major International Treaties 1914–1973 (London: Methuen and Company, 1974).

Ike, Nobutaka. Japan's Decision for War: Records of the 1941 Policy Conferences (Stanford University Press, 1967).

Jackson, Robert. The Case Against the Nazi War Criminals (New York: Alfred A. Knopf, 1946).

Public Papers of the Presidents of the United States, 1963 (Washington: Government Printing Office, 1964).

Principal Officers of the Department of State and United States Chiefs of Mission 1778–1988 (Washington: Department of State Publication, 1988).

United States Relations with China: With Special Reference to the Period 1944–1949 (Washington: Government Printing Office, 1949).

Waldron, Arthur, ed. How the Peace Was Lost: The 1935 Memorandum: Developments Affecting American Policy in the Far East Prepared for the State Department by John Van Antwerp MacMurray (Stanford: Hoover Institution Press, 1992).

War Office. Notes on German Preparations for the Invasion of the United Kingdom: War Office 1942 (London: Military Library Research Service, 2006).

Autobiographies, Diaries, Edited Collections, Memoirs, Speeches

Aglion, Raoul. *Roosevelt and de Gaulle: Allies in Conflict: A Personal Memoir* (New York: Free Press, 1988).

Allison, John. *Ambassador from the Prairie or Allison Wonderland* (Boston: Houghton Mifflin Company, 1973).

Aron, Raymond. *Mémoires* (Paris: Julliard, 1983).

Baer, George, ed. *A Question of Trust: The Origins of U.S.–Soviet Diplomatic Relations: The Memoirs of Loy W. Henderson* (Stanford: Hoover Institution Press, 1986).

Barrett, David. *Dixie Mission: The United States Army Observer Group in Yenan, 1944* (Berkeley: Center for Chinese Studies, 1970).

Beaulac, Willard. *Career Ambassador* (New York: Macmillan Company, 1951).

Biocca, Dario, ed. *A Matter of Passion: Letters of Bernard Berenson and Clotilde Marghieri* (University of California Press, 1989).

Bliss, Edward, ed. *In Search of Light: The Broadcasts of Edward R. Murrow 1938–1961* (New York: Alfred A. Knopf, 1967).

Blum, John Morton, ed. *From the Morgenthau Diaries: Years of War 1941–1945* (Boston: Houghton Mifflin Company, 1967).

Bohlen, Charles. *Witness to History 1929–1969* (New York: W. W. Norton and Company, 1973).

Bowers, Claude. *My Mission to Spain: Watching the Rehearsal for World War II* (New York: Simon and Schuster, 1954).

Bowers, Claude. *My Life* (New York: Simon and Schuster, 1962).

Breitman, Richard *et al.*, eds. *Advocate for the Doomed: The Diaries and Papers of James G. McDonald 1932–1935* (Indiana University Press, 2007).

Breitman, Richard *et al.*, eds. *Refugees and Rescue: The Diaries and Papers of James G. McDonald 1935–1945* (Indiana University Press, 2009).

Briggs, Ellis. *Farewell to Foggy Bottom: The Recollections of a Career Diplomat* (New York: David McKay Company, 1964).

Briggs, Ellis. *Proud Servant: The Memoirs of a Career Ambassador* (Kent State University Press, 1998).

Buhite, Russell and David Levy, eds. *FDR's Fireside Chats* (University of Oklahoma Press, 1992).

Bullitt, Orville, ed. *For the President: Personal and Secret: Correspondence Between Franklin D. Roosevelt and William C. Bullitt* (Boston: Houghton Mifflin Company, 1972).

Butler, Susan, ed. *My Dear Mr. Stalin: The Complete Correspondence of Franklin D. Roosevelt and Joseph V. Stalin* (Yale University Press, 2005).

Caldwell, Oliver. *A Secret War: Americans in China, 1944–1945* (Southern Illinois University Press, 1972).

Campbell, Thomas and George Herring, eds. *The Diaries of Edward R. Stettinius, 1943–1946* (New York: New Viewpoints, 1975).

Cannistraro, Philip *et al.*, eds. *Poland and the Coming of the Second World War: The Diplomatic Papers of A. J. Drexel Biddle, Jr. United States Ambassador to Poland 1937–1939* (Ohio State University, 1976).

Chennault, Claire Lee. *Way of a Fighter* (New York: G. P. Putnam's Sons, 1949).

Churchill, Winston. *The Second World War* (Boston: Houghton Mifflin, 1948–1953), 6 vols.

Ciano, Edda Mussolini. *My Truth* (New York: William Morrow and Company, 1977).

Clubb, O. Edmund. *The Witness and I* (Columbia University Press, 1974).

Colville, John. *The Fringes of Power: 10 Downing Street Diaries 1939–1955* (New York: W. W. Norton and Company, 1985).

Craigie, Robert. *Behind the Japanese Mask* (London: Huchinson and Company, 1946).

Daladier, Edouard. *Prison Journal 1940–1945* (Boulder: Westview Press, 1995).

Davies, Joseph. *Mission to Moscow* (New York: Simon and Schuster, 1941).

Davis, Elmer, ed. *This Is London* (New York: Schocken Books, 1985).

Deane, John. *The Strange Alliance: The Story of Our Efforts at Wartime Co-operation with Russia* (New York: Viking Press, 1947).

Dirksen, Herbert von. *Moscow, Tokyo, London: Twenty Years of German Foreign Policy* (University of Oklahoma Press, 1952).

Dobrynin, Anatoly. *In Confidence: Moscow's Ambassador to America's Six Cold War Presidents* (New York: Times Books, 1995).

Dodd, Christopher, ed. *Letters From Nuremberg: My Father's Narrative of a Quest for Justice* (New York: Crown Publishing, 2007).

Dodd, Martha. *Through Embassy Eyes (New York*: Harcourt, Brace and Company, 1939).

Dodd, Jr., William and Martha Dodd, eds. *Ambassador's Dodd's Diary 1933–1938* (New York: Harcourt, Brace and Company, 1941).

Doenecke, Justus, ed. *The Diplomacy of Frustration: The Manchurian Crisis of 1931–1933 as Revealed in the Papers of Stanley K. Hornbeck* (Stanford: Hoover Institution Press, 1981).

Doob, Leonard, ed. *Ezra Pound Speaking: Radio Speeches of World War II* (Westport: Greenwood Press, 1978).

Emmerson, John. *The Japanese Thread: A Life in the U.S. Foreign Service (New York*: Holt, Rinehart and Winston, 1978).

Feuchtwanger, Lion. *The Devil in France: My Encounter with Him in the Summer of 1940* (New York: Viking Press, 1941).

François-Poncet, André. *The Fateful Years: Memoirs of a French Ambassador in Berlin, 1931–1938* (New York: Harcourt, Brace and Company, 1949).

Fry, Varian. *Surrender on Demand* (New York: Random House, 1945).

Gaulle, Charles de. *War Memoirs* (New York: Carroll and Graf Publishers, 1998).

Gay, Peter. *My German Question: Growing Up in Nazi Berlin* (Yale University Press, 1998).

Gibson, Hugh, ed. *The Ciano Diaries 1939–1943* (New York: Doubleday and Company, 1946).

Grayson, Benson. *The American Image of Russia 1917–1977* (New York: Frederick Ungar Publishing, 1978).

Grew, Joseph. *Report From Tokyo: A Message to the American People* (New York: Simon and Schuster, 1942).

Grew, Joseph. *Ten Years in Japan* (New York: Simon and Schuster, 1944).

Grew, Joseph. *Turbulent Era: A Diplomatic Record of Forty Years 1904–1945* (London: Hammond, Hammond and Company, 1953), 2 vols.

Gromyko, Andrei. *Memoirs* (New York: Doubleday, 1990).

Harriman, W. Averell and Elie Abel. *Special Envoy to Churchill and Stalin 1941–1946* (New York: Random House, 1975).

Hayes, Carlton. *Wartime Mission in Spain 1942–1945* (New York: Macmillan Company, 1945).

Herwarth, Hans von. *Zwischen Hitler und Stalin: Erlebte Zeitgeschichte 1931 bis 1945* (Frankfurt: Ullstein Verlag, 1982).

Hessen, Robert, ed. *Berlin Alert: The Memoirs and Reports of Truman Smith* (Stanford: Hoover Institution Press, 1984).

Hilger, Gustav and Alfred Meyer. *The Incompatible Allies: A Memoir-History of German–Soviet Relations 1918–1941* (New York: Macmillan Company, 1953).

Hirschmann, Ira. *Life Line to a Promised Land* (New York: Vanguard Press, 1946).

Hooker, Nancy, ed. *The Moffat Papers* (Harvard University Press, 1956).

Hull, Cordell. *The Memoirs of Cordell Hull* (New York: Macmillan Company, 1948), 2 vols.

Ickes, Harold. *The Secret Diary* (New York: Simon and Schuster, 1954), vol. III.

Israel, Fred, ed. *The War Diary of Breckinridge Long* (University of Nebraska Press, 1966).

Johnson, Gaynor, ed. *Our Man in Berlin: The Diary of Sir Eric Phipps, 1933–1937* (New York: Palgrave Macmillan, 2008).

Kennan, George. *Memoirs 1925–1950* (Boston: Little, Brown and Company, 1967).

Kimball, Warren, ed. *Churchill and Roosevelt: The Complete Correspondence* (Princeton University Press, 1984), 3 vols.

Knatchbull-Hugessen, Hughe. *Diplomat in Peace and War* (London: John Murray, 1949).

Krock, Arthur. *Memoirs: Sixty Years on the Firing Line* (New York: Funk and Wagnalls, 1968).

Lattimore, Owen. *Ordeal by Slander* (Boston: Little, Brown and Company, 1950).

Laval, Pierre. *The Diary of Pierre Laval* (New York: Charles Scribner's Sons, 1948).

Leahy, William. *I Was There* (New York: Whittlesey House, 1950).

Leutze, James, ed. *The London Journal of General Raymond E. Lee 1940–1941* (Boston: Little, Brown and Company, 1971).

Loewenheim, Francis *et al.*, eds. *Roosevelt and Churchill: Their Secret Wartime Correspondence* (New York: Saturday Review Press, 1975).

MacArthur, Brian, ed. *The Penguin Book of Twentieth-Century Speeches* (London: Penguin Books, 1999).

Maisky, Ivan. *Memoirs of a Soviet Ambassador: The War: 1939–1943* (New York: Charles Scribner's Sons, 1968).

Mao Tse-tung. *Selected Works* (Peking: Foreign Languages Press, 1967 and 1969), vols. III, IV.

Mariano, Nicky. *Forty Years with Berenson* (New York: Alfred Knopf, 1966).

Marius, Richard, ed. *The Columbia Book of Civil War Poetry* (Columbia University Press, 1994).

Mayor, Andreas, ed. *Ciano's Hidden Diary 1937–1938* (New York: E. P. Dutton and Company, 1953).

McComb, A. K., ed. *The Selected Letters of Bernard* Berenson (Boston: Houghton Mifflin Company, 1963).

McNamara, Robert. *In Retrospect: The Tragedy and Lessons of Vietnam* (New York: Times Books, 1995).

Melby, John. *The Mandate of Heaven: Record of a Civil War: China 1945–49* (University of Toronto Press, 1968).

Miles, Milton. *A Different Kind of War* (Garden City: Doubleday and Company, 1967).

Millis, Walter, ed. *The Forrestal Diaries* (New York: Viking Press, 1951).

Moats, Alice Leone. *Blind Date with Mars* (Garden City: Doubleday, Doran and Company, 1943).

Moltke, Freya von. *Memories of Kreisau and the German Resistance* (University of Nebraska Press, 2003).

Moore, Frederick. *With Japan's Leaders: An Intimate Record of Fourteen Years as Counsellor to the Japanese Government, Ending December 7, 1941* (New York: Charles Scribner's Sons, 1942).

Muggeridge, Malcolm, ed. *Ciano's Diplomatic Papers* (London: Odhams Press, 1948).

Murphy, Robert. *Diplomat among Warriors* (Garden City: Doubleday and Company, 1964).

Nicolson, Nigel, ed. *Harold Nicolson: Diaries and Letters 1939–1945* (London: Collins, 1967).

Oppen, Beate Ruhm von, ed. *Helmuth James von Moltke: Letters to Freya 1939–1945* (New York: Vintage Books, 1995).

Orebaugh, Walter. *Guerrilla in Striped Pants: A U.S. Diplomat Joins the Italian Resistance* (New York: Praeger, 1992).

Papen, Franz von. *Memoirs* (New York: E. P. Dutton and Company, 1953).

Perkins, Frances. *The Roosevelt I Knew* (New York: Viking Press, 1946).

Phillips, William. *Ventures in Diplomacy* (Portland, ME: Anthoensen Press, 1952).

Pound, Omar and Robert Spoo, eds. *Ezra and Dorothy Pound: Letters in Captivity, 1945–1946* (Oxford University Press, 1999).

Reeder, Roberta. *The Complete Poems of Anna Akhmatova* (Somerville: Zephyr Press, 1990), vol. II.

Roosevelt, Eleanor. *This I Remember* (New York: Harper, 1949).

Russell, William. *Berlin Diary* (New York: Carroll and Graff, 2005).

Sevareid, Eric. *Not So Wild a Dream* (New York: Atheneum, 1976).

Shirer, William. *Berlin Diary: The Journal of a Foreign Correspondent 1934–1941* (New York: Alfred A. Knopf, 1941).

Smith, Amanda, ed. *Hostage to Fortune: The Letters of Joseph P. Kennedy* (New York: Viking, 2001).

Standley, William and Arthur Ageton. *Admiral Ambassador to Russia* (Chicago: Henry Regnery Company, 1955).

Stern, Fritz. *Five Germanys I Have Known* (New York: Farrar, Straus and Giroux, 2006).

Stimson, Henry and McGeorge Bundy. *On Active Service in Peace and War* (New York: Harper and Brothers, 1948).

Storey, Robert. *The Final Judgment? Pearl Harbor to Nuremberg* (San Antonio: Naylor Company, 1968).

Strang, Lord. *Home and Abroad* (London: André Deutsch, 1956).

Sudoplatov, Pavel and Anatoli Sudoplatov. *Special Tasks: The Memoirs of an Unwanted Witness – A Soviet Spymaster* (Boston: Little, Brown and Company, 1994).

Taylor, Fred, ed. *The Goebbels Diaries 1939–1941* (New York: G. P. Putnam's Sons, 1983).

Taylor, Myron, ed. *Wartime Correspondence Between President Roosevelt and Pope Pius XII* (New York: Da Capo Press, 1975).

Taylor, Telford. *The Anatomy of the Nuremberg Trials: A Personal Memoir* (New York: Alfred A. Knopf, 1992).

Tittmann, Harold H. (the third), ed. *Inside the Vatican of Pius XII: The Memoir of an American Diplomat During World War II: Harold H. Tittmann, Jr.* (New York: Doubleday 2004).

Togo, Shigenori. *The Cause of Japan* (New York: Simon and Schuster, 1956).

Tolley, Kemp. *Caviar and Commissars: The Experiences of a U.S. Naval Officer in Stalin's Russia* (Annapolis: Naval Institute Press, 1983).

Truman, Harry. *Memoirs: Year of Decisions* (Garden City: Doubleday, 1955).

Wedemeyer, Albert. *Wedemeyer Reports!* (New York: Henry Holt and Company, 1958).

Welles, Sumner. *Seven Decisions that Shaped History* (New York: Harper and Row, 1950).

White, Theodore, ed. *The Stilwell Papers* (New York: William Sloane Associates, 1948).

Wickert, Erwin, ed. *The Good Man of Nanking: The Diaries of John Rabe* (New York: Alfred Knopf, 1998).

Wilson, Hugh. *The Education of a Diplomat* (London: Longmans, Green and Company, 1938).

Wilson, Hugh. *Diplomat Between Wars* (New York: Longmans, Green and Company, 1941).

Winant, John Gilbert. *Letter from Grosvenor Square: An Account of a Stewardship* (Boston: Houghton Mifflin Company, 1947).

Winant, John Gilbert. *Our Greatest Harvest: Selected Speeches 1941–1946* (London: Hodder and Stoughton, 1950).

Zhou Enlai. *Selected Works* (Beijing: Foreign Languages Press, 1981).

Books, Journal Articles, Unpublished Manuscripts

Abramson, Rudy. *Spanning the Century: The Life of W. Averell Harriman 1891–1986* (New York: William Morrow and Company, 1992).

Adams, Henry. *Witness to Power: The Life of Fleet Admiral William D. Leahy* (Annapolis: Naval Institute Press, 1985).

Aldrich, Richard. *Intelligence and the War Against Japan: Britain, America and Politics of Secret Service* (Cambridge University Press, 2008).

Alexander, Bevin. *The Strange Connection: U.S. Intervention in China, 1944–1972* (New York: Greenwood Press, 1992).

Arendt, Hannah. *The Origins of Totalitarianism* (New York: World Publishing, 1972).

Aron, Raymond. *Chroniques de guerre: la France libre, 1940–1945* (Paris: Gallimard, 1990).

Ascher, Abraham. "Was Hitler a Riddle?" *Journal of the Historical Society*, 9 (1) (2009).

Atkin, Nicholas. *Pétain* (London: Longman, 1998).

Baer, George. *Test Case: Italy, Ethiopia, and the League of Nations* (Stanford: Hoover Institution Press, 1976).

Bailey, Fred Arthur. *William Edward Dodd: The South's Yeoman Scholar* (University Press of Virginia, 1997).

Barclay, David and Elisabeth Glaser-Schmidt, eds. *Transatlantic Images and Perceptions: Germany and America since 1776* (Cambridge University Press, 1997).

Barclay, Glen. *The Rise and Fall of the New Roman Empire: Italy's Bid for World Power, 1890–1943* (London: Sidgwick and Jackson, 1973).

Bassow, Whitman. *The Moscow Correspondents: Reporting on Russia from the Revolution to Glasnost* (New York: William Morrow and Company, 1988).

Bauer, Yehuda. *American Jewry and the Holocaust: The American Jewish Joint Distribution Committee, 1939–1945* (Wayne State University Press, 1981).

Baxter, Christopher and Andrew Steward, eds. *Diplomats at War: British and Commonwealth Diplomacy in Wartime* (Leiden: Martinus Nijhoff Publishers, 2008).

Beard, Charles. *President Roosevelt and the Coming of the War 1941* (Yale University Press, 1948).

Bearse, Ray and Anthony Read. *Conspirator: The Untold Story of Tyler Kent* (New York: Doubleday, 1991).

Beaulac, Willard. *Career Diplomat: A Career in the Foreign Service of the United States* (New York: Macmillan Company, 1964).

Beaulac, Willard. *Franco: Silent Ally in World War II* (Southern Illinois University Press, 1986).

Beck, Alfred. *Hitler's Ambivalent Attaché: Lt. Gen. Friedrich von Boetticher in America* (Washington: Potomac Books, 2005).

Behlmer, George and Fred Leventhal, eds. *Singular Continuities: Tradition, Nostalgia, and Identity in Modern British Culture* (Stanford University Press, 2000).

Bellush, Bernard. *He Walked Alone: A Biography of John Gilbert Winant* (The Hague: Mouton, 1968).

Beschloss, Michael. *Kennedy and Roosevelt: The Uneasy Alliance* (New York: W. W. Norton and Company, 1980).

Bess, Michael. *Choices under Fire: Moral Dimensions of World War II* (New York: Alfred Knopf, 2006).

Bethell, Nicholas. *The Last Secret: The Delivery to Stalin of over Two Million Russians by Britain and the United States* (New York: Basic Books, 1974).

Bingham, Robert Kim. *Courageous Dissent: How Harry Bingham Defied His Government to Save Lives* (Greenwich: Triune Books, 2007).

Bird, Kai. *The Chairman: John J. McCloy: The Making of the American Establishment* (New York: Simon and Schuster, 1992).

Black, Jeremy. *A History of Diplomacy* (London: Reaktion Books, 2010).

Blatt, Joel, ed. *The French Defeat of 1940* (Providence: Berghahn Books, 1998).

Bloch, Marc. *Strange Defeat: A Statement of Evidence Written in 1940* (New York: W. W. Norton and Company, 1999).

Blumenthal, Henry. *Illusion and Reality in Franco-American Diplomacy 1914–1945* (Louisiana State University Press, 1986).

Borg, Dorothy. *The United States and the Far Eastern Crisis of 1933–1938* (Harvard University Press, 1964).

Borg, Dorothy and Shumpei Okamoto, eds. *Pearl Harbor as History: Japanese–American Relations 1931–1941* (Columbia University Press, 1973).

Boyle, John Hunter. *China and Japan at War: The Politics of Collaboration* (Stanford University Press, 1972).

Bree, Germaine and George Bernauer, eds. *Defeat and Beyond: An Anthology of French Wartime Writing, 1940–1945* (New York: Pantheon Books, 1970).

Breitman, Richard and Alan Kraut. *American Refugee Policy and European Jewry, 1933–1945* (Indiana University Press, 1987).

Brissaud, André. *Canaris* (New York: Grosset and Dunlap, 1974).

Brogi, Alessandro. *A Question of Self-Esteem: The United States and the Cold War Choices in France and Italy, 1944–1958* (Westport: Praeger, 2002).

Brownell, Will and Richard Billings. *So Close to Greatness: A Biography of William C. Bullitt* (New York: Macmillan Publishing Company, 1987).

Buhite, Russell. *Nelson T. Johnson and American Policy Toward China 1925–1941* (Michigan State University Press, 1968).

Buhite, Russell. *Patrick J. Hurley and American Foreign Policy* (Cornell University Press, 1973).

Bullitt, William. *The Great Globe Itself: A Preface to World Affairs* (New York: Charles Scribner's Sons, 1946).

Bullitt, William and Sigmund Freud. *Thomas Woodrow Wilson, Twenty-Eighth President of the United States: A Psychological Study* (Boston: Houghton Mifflin Company, 1967).

Burdick, Charles. *An American Island in Hitler's Reich: The Bad Nauheim Internment* (Menlo Park: Markgraf Publications, 1987).

Burgwyn, H. James. *Italian Foreign Policy in the Interwar Period 1918–1940* (Westport: Praeger, 1997).

Burke, Bernard. *Ambassador Frederic Sackett and the Collapse of the Weimar Republic, 1930–1933: The United States and Hitler's Rise to Power* (Cambridge University Press, 1994).

Burns, Richard and Edward Bennett, eds. *Diplomats in Crisis: United States–Chinese–Japanese Relations, 1919–1941* (Santa Barbara: ABC-CLIO, 1974).

Burrin, Philippe. *France under the Germans: Collaboration and Compromise* (New York: New Press, 1993).

Butow, Robert. "The Hull–Nomura Conversations: A Fundamental Misconception," *American Historical Review*, 65 (1960).

Butow, Robert. *Tojo and the Coming of the War* (Princeton University Press, 1961).

Butow, Robert. *The John Doe Associates: Backdoor Diplomacy for Peace, 1941* (Stanford University Press, 1974).

Byrd, Martha. *Chennault: Giving Wings to the Tiger* (University of Alabama Press, 1987).

Camus, Albert. *The Plague* (New York: Vintage Books, 1972).

Cardoza, Anthony. *Benito Mussolini: The First Fascist* (New York: Pearson Longman, 2006).

Caron, Vicki. *Uneasy Asylum: France and the Jewish Refugee Crisis, 1933–1942* (Stanford University Press, 1999).

Caron, Vicki. "The Path to Vichy: Anti-Semitism in France in the 1930s," Shapiro Lecture (Washington: United States Holocaust Memorial Museum, 2005).

Carter, Carolle. *Mission to Yenan: American Liaison with the Chinese Communists 1944–1947* (University Press of Kentucky, 1997).

Cassidy, Henry. *Moscow Dateline 1941–1943* (Boston: Houghton Mifflin Company, 1943).

Chambrun, René de. *Pierre Laval: Traitor or Patriot?* (New York: Charles Scribner's Sons, 1984).

Chang, Iris. *The Rape of Nanking: The Forgotten Holocaust of World War II* (New York: Basic Books, 1997).

Chiang Kai-shek. *China's Destiny* (New York: Macmillan Company, 1947).

Christofferson, Thomas. *France During World War II: From Defeat to Liberation* (New York: Fordham Press, 2006).

Churchill, Winston. *The Grand Alliance* (Boston: Houghton Mifflin, 1950).

Cohen, Warren. "Who Fought the Japanese in Hunan? Some Views of China's War Effort," *Journal of Asian Studies*, 27 (1967).

Cole, Hubert. *Laval: A Biography* (New York: G. P. Putnam's Sons, 1963).

Cole, Wayne. *Roosevelt and the Isolationists 1932–1945* (University of Nebraska Press, 1983).

Colvin, Ian. *Master Spy* (New York: McGraw-Hill Book Company, 1951).

Conze, Eckart *et al. Das Amt und die Vergangenheit: Deutsche Diplomaten in Dritten Reich und in der Bundesrepublik* (Munich: Karl Blessing Verlag, 2010).

Corrigan, Robert Foster. "An Appreciation of a Diplomat," *Foreign Service Journal* (November 1967).

Cossu, Yvonne. "Le Nazisme et L'Art," *Mémoire Vivante* (September 2009).

Costigliola, Frank. "Broken Circle: The Isolation of Franklin D. Roosevelt in World War II," *Diplomatic History*, 32 (2008).

Costigliola, Frank. *Roosevelt's Lost Alliances: How Personal Politics Helped Start the Cold War* (Princeton University Press, 2012).

Craig, Gordon and Felix Gilbert, eds. *The Diplomats 1919–1939* (Princeton University Press, 1994).

Craig, Gordon and Francis Loewenheim, eds. *The Diplomats 1939–1979* (Princeton University Press, 1994).

Crozier, Eric. *The Man Who Lost China* (New York: Charles Scribner's Sons, 1976).

Dallek, Robert. *Democrat and Diplomat: The Life of William E. Dodd* (Oxford University Press, 1968).

Dallek, Robert. *Franklin D. Roosevelt and American Foreign Policy, 1932–1945* (Oxford University Press, 1979).

Dallek, Robert. *The American Style of Foreign Policy: Cultural Politics and Foreign Affairs* (Oxford University Press, 1983).

Dallek, Robert. *An Unfinished Life: John F. Kennedy 1917–1963* (Boston: Little, Brown and Company, 2003).

Dalton, Kathleen. "Nighthawks of 1942: William and Caroline Phillips and their friends Eleanor and Franklin Roosevelt," presented to Boston University's History Department, 14 November 2007.

Davies, John Paton. *Foreign and Other Affairs* (New York: W. W. Norton and Company, 1966).

Davies, John Paton. *Dragon by the Tail: American, British, Japanese, and Russian Encounters with China and One Another* (New York: W. W. Norton and Company, 1972).

Dear, I. C. B. and M. R. D. Foot, eds. *The Oxford Companion to World War II* (Oxford University Press, 1995).

De Bedts, *Ralph. Ambassador Joseph Kennedy: An Anatomy of Appeasement* (New York: Peter Lang, 1985).

Diamond, Hanna. *Fleeing Hitler: France 1940* (Oxford University Press, 2007).

Diggins, John. *Mussolini and Fascism: The View from America* (Princeton University Press, 1972).

Dodd, William E. *Woodrow Wilson and His Work* (Garden City: Doubleday, Page and Company, 1920).

Dodd, William E. *The Old South: Struggles for Democracy* (New York: Macmillan Company, 1937).

Doerr, Wilhelm. *Semper Apertus: Sechshundert Jahre Ruprecht-Karls-Universität Heidelberg 1386–1986* (Berlin: Springer-Verlag, 1985), vol. III.

Dower, John. *War Without Mercy: Race and Power in the Pacific War* (New York: Pantheon Books, 1986).

Dower, John. *Embracing Defeat: Japan in the Wake of World War II* (New York: W. W. Norton and Company, 1999).

Duchêne, François. *Jean Monnet: The First Statesman of Interdependence* (New York: W. W. Norton and Company, 1994).

Dugan, James and Laurence Lafore. *Days of Emperor and Clown: The Italo-Ethiopian War 1935–1936* (Garden City: Doubleday and Company, 1973).

Dunn, Dennis. *Caught Between Roosevelt and Stalin: America's Ambassadors to Moscow* (University Press of Kentucky, 1998).

Dur, Philip. "Jefferson Caffery of Louisiana: Highlights of His Career," Part I: 1911–1933 and Part II: 1933–1944, *Louisiana History*, 15(1) and 15(4) (1974).

Durrence, James Larry. "Ambassador Clarence E. Gauss and United States Relations with China, 1941–1944" (University of Georgia, Ph.D. dissertation, 1971).

Eisen, George. "The Voices of Sanity: American Diplomatic Reports from the 1936 Berlin Olympiad," *Journal of Sport History*, 11 (1984).

Elegant, Robert. *Mao vs. Chiang: The Battle for China, 1925–1949* (New York: Grosset and Dunlap, 1972).

Farmer, Sarah. *Martyred Village: Commemorating the 1944 Massacre at Oradour-sur-Glane* (University of California Press, 1999).

Faulkner, William. *Requiem for a Nun* (New York: Random House, 1951).

Feis, Herbert. *The Spanish Story: Franco and the Nations at War* (New York: Alfred Knopf, 1948).

Feis, Herbert. *The China Tangle: The American Effort in China from Pearl Harbor to the Marshall Mission* (Princeton University Press, 1953).

Fenby, Jonathan. *Chiang Kai Shek: China's Generalissimo and the Nation He Lost* (New York: Carroll and Graf Publishers, 2004).

Ferro, Marc. *Resentment in History* (Cambridge: Polity Press, 2010).

Fischer, Louis. "The Essence of Gandhiism," *Saturday Review*, 6 December 1947.

Florence, Ronald. *Emissary of the Doomed: Bargaining for Lives in the Holocaust* (New York: Viking, 2010).

Foglesong, David. *The American Mission and the "Evil Empire"* (Cambridge University Press, 2007).

Ford, Daniel. *Flying Tigers: Claire Chennault and the American Volunteer Group* (Washington: Smithsonian Institution Press, 1991).

Fox, Annette Baker. *The Power of Small States: Diplomacy in World War II* (University of Chicago Press, 1959).

Fox, John Francis. "In Passion and in Hope: The Pilgrimage of an American Radical, Martha Dodd Stern and Family, 1933–1990" (University of New Hampshire, Ph.D. dissertation, 2001).

Freidel, Frank. *Franklin D. Roosevelt: A Rendezvous with Destiny* (Boston: Little, Brown and Company, 1990).

Friedman, Max Paul. *Nazis and Good Neighbors: The United States Campaign against the Germans of Latin America in World War II* (Cambridge University Press, 2003).

Friedman, Max Paul. "Berlin Holocaust Memorial an Ironic, Postmodern Playground," *Jewish Bulletin of Northern California*, October 2005.

Funk, Arthur. *The Politics of Torch: Allied Landings and the Algiers Putsch 1942* (University Press of Kansas, 1974).

Gaddis, John Lewis. *The United States and the Origins of the Cold War 1941–1947* (Columbia University Press, 1972).

Gaddis, John Lewis. *George F. Kennan: An American Life* (New York: Penguin Press, 2011).

Gao Wenqian. *Zhou Enlai: The Last Perfect Revolutionary* (New York: Public Affairs, 2007).

Gellman, Irwin. *Secret Affairs: Franklin Roosevelt, Cordell Hull, and Sumner Welles* (Johns Hopkins University Press, 1995).

Gilbert, Martin. *Churchill and America* (New York: Free Press, 2005).

Gilbert, Martin. *Kristallnacht: Prelude to Destruction* (New York: HarperCollins, 2006).

Gillies, Donald. *Radical Diplomat: The Life of Archibald Clark Kerr, Lord Inverchapel, 1882–1951* (London: I. B. Tauris Publishers, 1999).

Gillies, Midge. *The Barbed-Wire University: The Real Lives of Prisoners of War in the Second World War* (London: Aurum, 2011).

Glantz, Mary. *FDR and the Soviet Union: The President's Battles over Foreign Policy* (University Press of Kansas, 2005).

Glass, Charles. *Americans in Paris: Life and Death under Nazi Occupation* (New York: Penguin Books, 2011).

Goldwin, Robert and Harry Clor, eds. *Readings in American Foreign Policy* (Oxford University Press, 1971).

Gordon, Bertram, ed. *Historical Dictionary of World War II France: The Occupation, Vichy, and the Resistance, 1938–1946* (Westport: Greenwood Press, 1998).

Gorodetsky, Gabriel. *Stafford Cripps' Mission to Moscow, 1940–42* (Cambridge University Press, 1984).

Griffiths, Richard. *Marshal Pétain* (London: Constable and Company, 1970).

Gross, Jan. *The Neighbors: The Destruction of the Jewish Community in Jedwabne, Poland* (Princeton University Press, 2001).

Haglund, David. "Roosevelt as Friend of France – But Which One?" *Diplomatic History*, 31 (2007).

Halstead, Charles. "Diligent Diplomat: Alexander W. Weddell as American Ambassador to Spain, 1939–1942," *Virginia Magazine of History and Biography*, 82 (1974).

Hamby, Alonzo. *Man of the People: A Life of Harry S. Truman* (Oxford University Press, 1995).

Harbutt, Fraser. *Yalta 1945: Europe and America at the Crossroads* (Cambridge University Press, 2010).

Harris, Joseph. *African-American Reactions to War in Ethiopia 1936–1941* (Louisiana State University Press, 1994).

Hastings, Max. *Finest Years: Churchill as Warlord 1940–1945* (London: Harper Press, 2009).

Hayes, Carlton. *The United States and Spain: An Interpretation* (New York: Sheed and Ward, 1951).

Haynes, John Earl and Harvey Klehr. *Venona: Decoding Soviet Espionage in America* (Yale University Press, 1999).

Haynes, John Earl and Harvey Klehr. *Early Cold War Spies: The Espionage Trials that Shaped American Politics* (Cambridge University Press, 2006).

Heinrichs, Waldo. *American Ambassador: Joseph C. Grew and the Development of the United States Diplomatic Tradition* (Oxford University Press, 1966).

Heinrichs, Waldo. *Threshold of War: Franklin D. Roosevelt and American Entry into World War II* (Oxford University Press, 1988).

Heinzen, Ralph. "Inside Germany Today," *Collier's*, 10 June 1944.

Herring, George. *Aid to Russia 1941–1946: Strategy, Diplomacy, the Origins of the Cold War* (Columbia University Press, 1973).

Hoenicke Moore, Michaela. *Know Your Enemy: The American Debate on Nazism, 1933–1945* (Cambridge University Press, 2010).

Hohne, Heinz. *Canaris* (Garden City: Doubleday and Company, 1979).

Holland, Max. "I. F. Stone: Encounters with Soviet Intelligence," *Journal of Cold War Studies*, 11(3) (2009).

Holloway, David. *Stalin and the Bomb: The Soviet Union and Atomic Energy 1939–1956* (Yale University Press, 1994).

Hornbeck, Stanley. *The United States and the Far East: Certain Fundamentals of Policy* (Boston: World Peace Foundation, 1942).

Horne, Alistair. *To Lose a Battle: France 1940* (New York: Penguin Books, 1979).

Horne, Alistair. *Harold Macmillan*, vol. 1, 1894–1956 (New York: Viking, 1989).

Horne, Alistair. *La Belle France: A Short History* (New York: Vintage Books, 2006).

Howe, M. A. Dewolfe. *George von Lengerke Meyer: His Life and Public Services* (New York: Dodd, Mead and Company, 1919).

Hughes, H. Stuart. *The United States and Italy* (Harvard University Press, 1979).

Hurtsfield, Julian. *America and the French Nation, 1939–1945* (University of North Carolina Press, 1986).

Iguchi, Takeo. *Demystifying Pearl Harbor: A New Perspective from Japan* (Tokyo: International House of Japan, 2010).

Ilchman, Warren Frederic. *Professional Diplomacy in the United States 1779–1939* (University of Chicago Press, 1961).

Infield, Glenn. *The Poltava Affair: A Russian Warning: An American Tragedy* (New York: Macmillan Publishing, 1973).

Iriye, Akira. *Across the Pacific: An Inner History of American–East Asian Relations* (New York: Harcourt, Brace and World, 1967).

Iriye, Akira. *Power and Culture: The Japanese–American War, 1941–1945* (Harvard University Press, 1981).

Iriye, Akira. *The Origins of the Second World War in Asia and the Pacific* (London: Longman, 1987).

Isenberg, Sheila. *A Hero of Our Own: The Story of Varian Fry* (New York: Random House, 2001).

Jackson, Robert. *Classical and Modern Thought on International Relations: From Anarchy to Cosmopolis* (New York: Palgrave Macmillan, 2005).

Jackson, Robert H. "The Significance of the Nuremberg Trials to the Armed Forces," *Military Affairs* (Winter 1946).

Jackson, Robert H. "Nürnberg in Retrospect," *The Canadian Bar Review* (August–September 1949).

Janssens, Rudolf. *What Fate for Japan? U.S. Wartime Planning for the Postwar Era, 1942–1945* (Amsterdam: Rodopi, 1995).

Johnson, Ethel. "The Mr. Winant I Knew," *The South Atlantic Quarterly* (January 1949).

Johnson, Gaynor, ed. *The International Context of the Spanish Civil War* (Newcastle: Cambridge Scholars Publishing, 2009).

Joiner, Lynne, *Honorable Survivor: Mao's China, McCarthy's America, and the Persecution of John S. Service* (Annapolis: Naval Institute Press, 2009).

Jonas, Manfred. *Isolationism in America 1935–1941* (Cornell University Press, 1966).

Judt, Tony. *The Burden of Responsibility: Blum, Camus, Aron and the French Twentieth Century* (University of Chicago Press, 1998).

Judt, Tony. *Reappraisals: Reflections on the Forgotten Twentieth Century* (New York: Penguin Books, 2008).

Kahn, Ely. *The China Hands: America's Foreign Service Officers and What Befell Them* (New York: Viking Press, 1975).

Kalman, Samuel. *The Extreme Right in Interwar France: The Faisceau and the Croix du Feu* (Aldershot: Ashgate, 2008).

Keith, Ronald. *The Diplomacy of Zhou Enlai* (New York: St. Martin's Press, 1989).

Kendrick, Alexander. *Prime Time: The Life of Edward R. Murrow* (Boston: Little, Brown and Company, 1969).

Kennan, George. "Report, the Internment and Repatriation of the American Official Group in Germany-1941–1942," *American Foreign Service Journal* (two parts) (August 1942 and September 1942).

Kennan, George. *American Diplomacy 1900–1950* (University of Chicago Press, 1951).

Kennedy, John F. *Why England Slept* (New York: Wilfred Funk, 1961).

Kennedy, Joseph. *I'm for Roosevelt* (New York: Reynal and Hitchcock, 1936).

Kennedy, Joseph and James Landis. *The Surrender of King Leopold* (New York: Joseph P. Kennedy Memorial Foundation, 1950).

Kersaudy, François. *Churchill and de Gaulle* (New York: Atheneum, 1982).

Kershaw, Ian. *Fateful Choices: Ten Decisions that Changed the World, 1940–1941* (New York: Penguin Press, 2007).

Kimball, Warren. *The Juggler: Franklin Roosevelt as Wartime Statesman* (Princeton University Press, 1991).

Kimball, Warren. *Forged in War: Roosevelt, Churchill, and the Second World War* (New York: William Morrow and Company, 1997).

Kladstrup, Don and Petie Kladstrup. *Wine and War: The French, the Nazis, and the Battle for France's Greatest Treasure* (New York: Broadway Books, 2001).

Klehr, Harvey, John Earl Haynes, and Fridrikh Igorevich Firsov. *The Secret World of American Communism* (Yale University Press, 1995).

Klehr, Harvey and Ronald Radosh. *The Amerasia Spy Case: Prelude to McCarthyism* (University of North Carolina Press, 1996).

Knox, MacGregor. *Mussolini Unleashed 1939–1941: Politics and Strategy in Fascist Italy's Last War* (Cambridge University Press, 1982).

Koskoff, David. *Joseph P. Kennedy: A Life and Times* (Englewood Cliffs: Prentice Hall, 1974).

Krammer, Arnold. "In Splendid Isolation: Enemy Diplomats in World War II," *Prologue*, 17(1) (1985).

LaFeber, Walter. *The Clash: A History of U.S.–Japan Relations* (New York: W. W. Norton and Company, 1997).

Lamb, Richard. *Mussolini as Diplomat: Il Duce's Italy on the World Stage* (New York: Fromm International, 1999).

Lambach, Frank. *Our Men in Washington* (Washington: German Information Center, 2004).

Langer, William. *Our Vichy Gamble* (New York: Alfred A. Knopf, 1947).

Larson, Erik. *In the Garden of Beasts: Love, Terror, and an American Family in Hitler's Berlin* (New York: Crown, 2011).

Laski, Harold. "British Democracy and Mr. Kennedy," *Harper's Magazine* (April 1941).

Laub, Thomas. *After the Fall: German Policy in Occupied France, 1940–1944* (Oxford University Press, 2010).

Lauren, Paul Gordon, ed. *The China Hands' Legacy: Ethics and Diplomacy* (Boulder: Westview Press, 1987).

Leamer, Laurence. *The Kennedy Men* (New York: William Morrow, 2001).

Leiter, Sharon. *Akhmatova's Petersburg* (University of Pennsylvania Press, 1983).

Lewis, David Levering. *W. E. B. Du Bois: The Fight for Equality and the American Century, 1919–1963* (New York: Henry Holt and Company, 2000).

Liang, Chin-tung. *General Stilwell in China 1942–1944: The Full Story* (St. John's University Press, 1972).

Lipstadt, Deborah. *Beyond Belief: The American Press and the Coming of the Holocaust 1933–1945* (New York: Free Press, 1986).

Liu, Xiaoyuan. *A Partnership for Disorder: China, the United States, and their Polices for the Postwar Disposition of the Japanese Empire, 1941–1945* (Cambridge University Press, 1996).

Lohbeck, Don. *Patrick J. Hurley* (Chicago: Henry Regnery Company, 1956).

Lottman, Herbert. *Pétain: Hero or Traitor: The Untold Story* (New York: William Morrow and Company, 1985).

Lu, David. *From the Marco Polo Bridge to Pearl Harbor: Japan's Entry into World War II* (Washington: Public Affairs Press, 1961).

Lu, David. *Agony of Choice: Matsuoka Yosuke and the Rise and Fall of the Japanese Empire, 1880–1946* (Lanham: Lexington Books, 2002).

Lukacs, John. *Five Days in London: May 1940* (Yale University Press, 1999).

Lukacs, John. *June 1941: Hitler and Stalin* (New Haven: Yale University Press, 2006).

Lukacs, John. *The Legacy of the Second World War* (Yale University Press, 2010).

Lukes, Igor. "Ambassador Laurence Steinhardt: From New York to Prague," *Diplomacy and Statecraft*, 17 (2006).

Lukes, Igor. *On the Edge of the Cold War: American Diplomats and Spies in Postwar Prague* (Oxford University Press, 2012).

Luthi, Lorenz. *The Sino-Soviet Split: Cold War in the Communist World* (Princeton University Press, 2008).

Lynn, Madeleine, ed. *Yangtze River: The Wildest, Wickedest River on Earth* (Oxford University Press, 1997).

Malcolm, Janet. *Two Lives: Gertrude and Alice* (Yale University Press, 2007).

Mallett, Robert. *Mussolini and the Origins of the Second World War, 1933–1940* (New York: Palgrave Macmillan, 2003).

Marino, Andy. *A Quiet American: The Secret War of Varian Fry* (New York: St. Martin's Press, 1999).

Marrus, Michael and Robert Paxton. *Vichy France and the Jews* (Stanford University Press, 1995).

Maudlin, Bill. *Up Front* (New York: Henry Holt and Company, 1945).

May, Ernest. *Strange Victory: Hitler's Conquest of France* (New York: Hill and Wang, 2001).

May, Gary. *China Scapegoat: The Diplomatic Ordeal of John Carter Vincent* (Washington: New Republic Books, 1979).

Mayers, David. *George Kennan and the Dilemmas of U.S. Foreign Policy* (Oxford University Press, 1988).

Mayers, David. *The Ambassadors and America's Soviet Policy* (Oxford University Press, 1995).

Mayers, David. *Wars and Peace: The Future Americans Envisioned 1861–1991* (New York: St. Martin's Press, 1998).

Mayers, David. *Dissenting Voices in America's Rise to Power* (Cambridge University Press, 2007).

Mazower, Mark. *Hitler's Empire: How the Nazis Ruled Europe* (New York: Penguin Press, 2008).

McJimsey, George. *Harry Hopkins: Ally of the Poor and Defender of Democracy* (Harvard University Press, 1987).

Mimura, Janis. *Planning for Empire: Reform Bureaucrats and the Japanese Wartime State* (Cornell University Press, 2011).

Minnen, Cornelis, ed. *FDR and His Contemporaries: Foreign Perceptions of an American President* (New York: St. Martin's Press, 1992).

Miscamble, Wilson. *From Roosevelt to Truman: Potsdam, Hiroshima, and the Cold War* (Cambridge University Press, 2007).

Miscamble, Wilson. *The Most Controversial Decision: Truman, the Atomic Bombs, and the Defeat of Japan* (Cambridge University Press, 2011).

Morgan, Philip. *The Fall of Mussolini: Italy, the Italians, and the Second Word War* (Oxford University Press, 2007).

Moseley, Ray. *Mussolini's Shadow: The Double Life of Count Galeazzo Ciano* (Yale University Press, 1999).

Mueller, Michael. *Canaris: The Life and Death of Hitler's Spymaster* (Annapolis: Naval Institute Press, 2007).

Musa, Mark, ed. *Machiavelli's The Prince* (New York: St. Martin's Press, 1964).

Nagai, Takashi. *The Bells of Nagasaki* (Tokyo: Kodansha International, 1984).

Nagorski, Andrew. *The Greatest Battle: Stalin, Hitler, and the Desperate Struggle for Moscow that Changed the Course of World War II* (New York: Simon and Schuster, 2007).

Némirovsky, Irène. *Suite Française* (New York: Vintage Books, 2007).

Newman, Robert. *The Cold War Romance of Lillian Hellman and John Melby* (University of North Carolina Press, 1989).

Newman, Robert. *Owen Lattimore and the "Loss" of China* (University of California Press, 1992).

Nicolson, Harold. *Diplomacy* (Oxford University Press, 1980).

Nossiter, Adam. *The Algeria Hotel: France, Memory, and the Second World War* (Boston: Houghton Mifflin, 2001).

O'Connor, Joseph. "Laurence A. Steinhardt and American Policy Toward the Soviet Union, 1939–1941" (University of Virginia, Ph.D. dissertation, 1968).

Offner, Arnold. *American Appeasement: United States Foreign Policy and Germany, 1933–1938* (New York: W. W. Norton and Company, 1976).

Olson, Lynne. *Citizens of London: The Americans Who Stood with Britain in Its Darkest, Finest Hour* (New York: Random House, 2010).

Packard, Jerrold. *Neither Friend Nor Foe: The European Neutrals in World War II* (New York: Charles Scribner's Sons, 1992).

Painter, Borden. *Mussolini's Rome: Rebuilding the Eternal City* (New York: Palgrave Macmillan, 2005).

Paldiel, Mordecai. *The Righteous among the Nations: Rescuers of Jews During the Holocaust* (New York: Collins, 2007).

Partington, Geoffrey. "John Gilbert Winant at Geneva: The Testimony of Sir Walter Crocker," *National Observer* (Spring 2003).

Paxton, Robert. *Vichy France: Old Guard and New Order, 1940–1944* (New York: Alfred A. Knopf, 1972).

Payne, Stanley. *The Spanish Revolution* (New York: W. W. Norton and Company, 1970).

Payne, Stanley. *The Collapse of the Spanish Republic, 1933–1936* (Yale University Press, 2006).

Payne, Stanley. *Franco and Hitler: Spain, Germany, and World War II* (Yale University Press, 2008).

Pechatnov, Vladimir. "Moskovskoe posolstvo Averella Garimana, 1943–1946," *Novaia i noveshaia istoriia*, 1(3) and 2(4) (2002).

Pell, Herbert. "None More Genuinely American," *Saturday Review*, 6 December 1947.

Pound, Ezra. *Jefferson and/or Mussolini* (New York: Liveright Publishing, 1936).

Pratt, Julius. *Cordell Hull* (New York: Cooper Square Publishers, 1964), 2 vols.

Preston, Andrew. *Sword of the Spirit, Shield of Faith: Religion in American War and Diplomacy* (New York: Alfred A. Knopf, 2012).

Qing, Simei. *From Allies to Enemies: Visions of Modernity, Identity, and U.S.–China Diplomacy, 1945–1960* (Harvard University Press, 2007).

Rafshoon, Ellen. "Harry Bingham: Beyond the Call of Duty," *Foreign Service Journal* (June 2002).

Rayski, Adam. *The Choice of the Jews under Vichy: Between Submission and Resistance* (University of Notre Dame Press, 2006).

Redman, Tim. *Ezra Pound and Italian Fascism* (Cambridge University Press, 1991).

Reuter, Paul Henry. "William Phillips and the Development of American Foreign Policy, 1933–1947" (University of Southern Mississippi, Ph.D. dissertation, 1979).

Reynolds, David. *From Munich to Pearl Harbor: Roosevelt's America and the Origins of the Second World War* (Chicago: Ivan R. Dee, 2001).

Reynolds, David. *In Command of History: Churchill Fighting and Writing the Second World War* (New York: Random House, 2005).

Reynolds, David. *From World War to Cold War: Churchill, Roosevelt, and the International History of the 1940s* (Oxford University Press, 2006).

Riding, Alan. *And the Show Went On: Cultural Life in Nazi-Occupied Paris* (New York: Alfred Knopf, 2010).

Ristaino, Marcia. *The Jacquinot Safe Zone: Wartime Refugees in Shanghai* (Stanford University Press, 2008).

Rizi, Fabio. *Benedetto Croce and Italian Fascism* (University of Toronto Press, 2003).

Roberts, Andrew. *The Storm of War: A New History of the Second World War* (New York: HarperCollins, Publishers, 2011).

Roberts, Geoffrey. *Stalin's Wars: From World War to Cold War, 1939–1953* (Yale University Press, 2006).

Robertson, Charles. *When Roosevelt Planned to Govern France* (University of Massachusetts Press, 2011).

Robertson, David. *Sly and Able: A Political Biography of James F. Byrnes* (New York: W. W. Norton and Company, 1994).

Rofe, J. Simon. *Franklin Roosevelt's Foreign Policy and the Welles Mission* (New York: Palgrave Macmillan, 2007).

Romanus, Charles and Riley Sunderland. *Stilwell's Mission to China* (Washington: Department of the Army, 1953).

Romanus, Charles and Riley Sunderland. *Time Runs Out in CBI* (Washington: Department of the Army, 1959).

Roseman, Mark. *The Villa, the Lake, the Meeting: Wannsee and the Final Solution* (London: Penguin Books, 2003).

Rosenbaum, Robert. *Waking to Danger: Americans and Nazi Germany, 1933–1941* (Santa Barbara: Praeger, 2010).

Rossi, Mario. *Roosevelt and the French* (Westport: Praeger, 1993).

Rousso, Henry. *The Vichy Syndrome: History and Memory in France since 1944* (Harvard University Press, 1991).

Rubin, Barry. "Ambassador Laurence A. Steinhardt: The Perils of a Jewish Diplomat 1940–1945," *American Jewish History*, 70 (1981).

Rubin, Barry. *Secrets of State: The State Department and the Struggle over U.S. Foreign Policy* (Oxford University Press, 1987).

Rubin, Barry. *Istanbul Intrigues* (New York: McGraw-Hill Publishing, 1989).

Ruddy, T. Michael. *The Cautious Diplomat: Charles E. Bohlen and the Soviet Union, 1929–1969* (Kent State University Press, 1986).

Russell, Francis. *The President Makers: From Mark Hanna to Joseph P. Kennedy* (Boston: Little, Brown and Company, 1976).

Sapp, Steven. "The United States, France, and the Cold War: Jefferson Caffery and American–French Relations, 1944–1949" (Kent State University, Ph.D. dissertation, 1978).

Sapp, Steven. "Jefferson Caffery, Cold War Diplomat: American–French Relations 1944–49," *Louisiana History*, 23 (1982).

Sarfatti, Michele. *The Jews in Mussolini's Italy: From Equality to Persecution* (University of Wisconsin Press, 2006).

Schaller, Michael. *The U.S. Crusade in China, 1938–1945* (Columbia University Press, 1979).

Schapiro, Leonard, ed. *Political Opposition in One Party States* (London: Macmillan, 1972).

Schulzinger, Robert. *The Making of the Diplomatic Mind: The Training, Outlook, and Style of United States Foreign Service Officers, 1908–1931* (Wesleyan University Press, 1975).

Scott, Robert Lee. *Flying Tiger: Chennault of China* (Garden City: Doubleday and Company, 1959).

Secrest, Meryle. *Being Bernard Berenson: A Biography* (New York: Holt, Rinehart and Winston, 1979).

Seghers, Anna. *Transit Visa* (Boston: Little, Brown, 1944).

Service, John. *The Amerasia Papers: Some Problems in the History of U.S.–China Relations* (Berkeley: Center for Chinese Studies, 1971).

Sherwood, Robert. *Roosevelt and Hopkins: An Intimate History* (New York: Harper and Brothers, 1948).

Shewmaker, Kenneth. *Americans and Chinese Communists, 1927–1945: A Persuading Encounter* (Cornell University Press, 1971).

Shirer, William. *The Rise and Fall of the Third Reich: A History of Nazi Germany* (New York: Simon and Schuster, 1960).

Shirer, William. *The Collapse of the Third Republic: An Inquiry into the Fall of France in 1940* (New York: Simon and Schuster, 1969).

Shirer, William. *The Nightmare Years 1930–1940* (Toronto: Bantam Books, 1985).

Simmons, Thomas. *The Brown Condor: The True Adventures of John C. Robinson* (Sliver Spring: Bartleby Press, 1988).

Smith, Gaddis. *American Diplomacy During the Second World War, 1941–1945* (New York: Alfred A. Knopf, 1985).

Smith, Michel Joseph. *Realist Thought from Weber to Kissinger* (Louisiana State University Press, 1986).

Snow, Edgar. *Red Star over China* (New York: Random House, 1938).

Snyder, Timothy. *Bloodlands: Europe Between Hitler and Stalin* (New York: Basic Books, 2010).

Snyder, Timothy. "Hitler vs. Stalin: Who Killed More?" *New York Review of Books*, 10 March 2011.

Sperber, A. M. *Murrow: His Life and Times* (New York: Freundlich Books, 1986).

Stackman, Ralph Robert. "Laurence A. Steinhardt: New Deal Diplomat, 1933–1945" (Michigan State University, Ph.D. dissertation, 1967).

Stevenson, William. *A Man Called Intrepid: The Secret War* (New York: Harcourt Brace Jovanovich, 1976).

Stiller, Jesse. *George S. Messersmith: Diplomat of Democracy* (University of North Carolina Press, 1987).

Strupp, Christoph. "Observing Dictatorship: American Consular Reporting on Germany, 1933–1942," *German Historical Institute Bulletin* (Fall 2006).

Stueck, William. *The Wedemeyer Mission: American Politics and Foreign Policy during the Cold War* (University of Georgia Press, 1984).

Suarez, Georges. *Pétain ou la démocratie? Il faut choisir* (Paris: Bernard Grasset, 1941).

Subak, Susan. *Rescue and Flight: American Relief Workers Who Defied the Nazis* (University of Nebraska, 2010).

Sullivan, Rosemary. *Villa Air-Bel: World War II, Escape, and a House in Marseille* (New York: HarperCollins, 2006).

Sweets, John. *Choices in Vichy France: The French under Nazi Occupation* (Oxford University Press, 1986).

Swift, Will. *The Kennedys Amidst the Gathering Storm: A Thousand Days in London, 1938–1940* (New York: HarperCollins, 2008).

Tanaka, Yuki. *Hidden Horrors: Japanese War Crimes in World War II* (Boulder: Westview Press, 1996).

Taylor, Jay. *The Generalissimo: Chiang Kai-shek and the Struggle for Modern China* (Harvard University Press, 2009).

Thomas, Hugh. *The Spanish Civil War* (New York: Harper and Row Publishers, 1961).

Thomas, Joan Maria. *Roosevelt and Franco During the Second World War: From the Spanish Civil War to Pearl Harbor* (New York: Palgrave Macmillan, 2008).

Thompson, Nicholas. *The Hawk and the Dove: Paul Nitze, George Kennan, and the History of the Cold War* (New York: Henry Holt and Company, 2009).

Thorne, Christopher. *Allies of a Kind: The United States, Britain and the War against Japan, 1941–1945* (Oxford University Press, 1978).

Tolley, Kemp. *Yangtze Patrol: The U.S. Navy in China* (Annapolis: Naval Institute Press, 1971).

Trommler, Frank and Joseph McVeigh, eds. *America and the Germans: An Assessment of a Three-Hundred-Year History* (University of Pennsylvania Press, 1985), vol. II.

Tsou, Tang. *America's Failure in China 1941–1950* (University of Chicago Press, 1969 edition).

Tuchman, Barbara. *Stilwell and the American Experience in China, 1911–45* (New York: Macmillan Company 1971).

Tuchman, Barbara. *Notes from China* (New York: Collier Books, 1972).

Ulam, Adam. *Expansion and Coexistence: Soviet Foreign Policy, 1917–73* (New York: Praeger Publishers, 1974).

U.S. Week. Vol. I: Number 5, 12 April 1941; Number 9, 10 May 1941; Number 13, 7 June 1941; Number 33, 25 October 1941.

Utley, Freda. *Last Chance in China* (Indianapolis: Bobbs-Merrill Company, 1947).

Utley, Jonathan. *Going to War with Japan, 1937–1941* (University of Tennessee Press, 1985).

Vaughan, Hal. *FDR's 12 Apostles: The Spies Who Paved the Way for the Invasion of North Africa* (Guilford: Lyons Press, 2006).

Verrier, Anthony. *Assassination in Algiers: Churchill, Roosevelt, de Gaulle, and the Murder of Admiral Darlan* (New York: W. W. Norton and Company, 1990).

Vinen, Richard. *The Unfree French: Life under the Occupation* (Yale University Press, 2006).

Wakeman, Frederic. *Spymaster: Dai Li and the Chinese Secret Service* (University of California Press, 2003).

Walker, Charles Rumford. "Winant of New Hampshire," *The Atlantic* (May 1941).

Waller, George, ed. *Pearl Harbor: Roosevelt and the Coming of the War* (Lexington, Mass.: D.C. Heath and Company, 1976).

Waller, John. *Europe: Espionage and Conspiracy in the Second World War* (New York: I. B. Tauris, 1996).

Wallner, Woodruff. "Report of the Internment and Repatriation of the Official American Group in France, 1942, 1943, 1944," *American Foreign Service Journal* (4 installments) (May, June, July, August 1944).

Walzer, Michael. *Just and Unjust Wars: A Moral Argument with Historical Illustrations* (New York: Basic Books, 2000).

Warner, Geoffrey. *Pierre Laval and the Eclipse of France* (New York: Macmillan Company, 1968).

Watt, Donald Cameron. *How War Came: The Immediate Origins of the Second World War, 1938–1939* (New York: Pantheon Books, 1989).

Weber, Frank. *The Evasive Neutral: Germany, Britain and the Quest for a Turkish Alliance in the Second World War* (University of Missouri Press, 1979).

Weber, Ronald. *The Lisbon Route: Entry and Escape in Nazi Europe* (Lanham: Ivan R. Dee 2011).

Weinberg, Gerhard. *A World at Arms: A Global History of World War II* (Cambridge University Press, 1994).

Weinberg, Gerhard. *Germany, Hitler, and World War II* (Cambridge University Press, 1995).

Weinberg, Gerhard. *Visions of Victory: The Hopes of Eight World War II Leaders* (Cambridge University Press, 2005).

Weinberg, Gerhard. "Kristallnacht 1938: As Experienced Then and Understood Now," Weinmann Annual Lecture (Washington: United States Holocaust Memorial Museum, 2009).

Weinstein, Allen and Alexander Vassiliev. *The Haunted Wood: Soviet Espionage in America – the Stalin Era* (New York: Random House, 1999).

Weisbrode, Kenneth. *The Atlantic Century: Four Generations of Extraordinary Diplomats Who Forged America's Vital Alliance with Europe* (Cambridge, Mass.: Da Capo Press, 2009).

Weisbrode, Kenneth. "The Master, the Maverick, and the Machine: Three Wartime Promoters of Peace," *Journal of Policy History*, 21 (4) (2009).

Welles, Benjamin. *Sumner Welles: FDR's Global Strategist* (New York: St. Martin's Press, 1997).

Welles, Sumner. *The Time for Decision* (New York: Harper and Brothers Publishers, 1944).

Wenn, Stephen. "A Tale of Two Diplomats: George S. Messersmith and Charles H. Sherrill on Proposed American Participation in the 1936 Olympics," *Journal of Sport History*, 16 (1989).

Whalen, Richard. *The Founding Father: The Story of Joseph P. Kennedy* (New York: New American Library, 1964).

White, Dorothy. *Seeds of Discord: De Gaulle, Free France and the Allies* (Syracuse University Press, 1964).

White, Ruth Beeler. "From Sea to Shining Sea," *Independent Woman* (February 1952).

White, Theodore and Annalee Jacoby. *Thunder out of China* (New York: William Sloan Associates, 1946).

Whittam, John. *Fascist Italy* (Manchester University Press, 1995).

Whittemore, Bert. "A Quiet Triumph: The Mission of John Gilbert Winant to London, 1941," *Historical New Hampshire*, 30 (1975).

Wilhelm, J. J. *Ezra Pound: The Tragic Years, 1925–1972* (Pennsylvania State University Press, 1994).

Willkie, Wendell. *One World* (New York: Simon and Schuster, 1943).

Willson, John Paul. "Carlton J. H. Hayes in Spain, 1942–1945" (Syracuse University, Ph.D. dissertation, 1969).

Wilson, Dick. *Zhou Enlai* (New York: Viking, 1984).

Wilson, Hugh R. *Diplomacy as a Career* (Cambridge, Mass.: Riverside Press, 1941).

Wilson, Jr., Hugh R. *For Want of a Nail: The Failure of the League of Nations in Ethiopia* (New York: Vantage Press, 1959).

Wilson, Jr., Hugh R. *A Career Diplomat: The Third Chapter: The Third Reich* (Westport: Greenwood Press, 1960).

Winant, John. "How Britain Controls Its Manpower," *The Atlantic* (May 1942).

Winant, John. "Fundamental Freedoms," *Conference* (Winter 1947).

Wolfers, Arnold. *Britain and France Between Two Wars: Conflicting Strategies of Peace from Versailles to World War II* (New York: W. W. Norton and Company, 1966).

Woolner, David, Warren Kimball, and David Reynolds, eds. *FDR's World: War, Peace, and Legacies* (New York: Palgrave Macmillan, 2008).

Wright, Gordon. "Ambassador Bullitt and the Fall of France," *World Politics* (October 1957).

Wright, Quincy, ed. *Neutrality and Collective Security* (University of Chicago Press, 1936).

Wyman, David and Rafael Medoff, *A Race Against Death: Peter Bergson, America, and the Holocaust* (New York: New Press, 2002).

Yoshima, Yoshiaki. *Comfort Women: Sexual Slavery in the Japanese Military During Word War II* (Columbia University Press, 2000).

Zahniser, Marvin. *Then Came Disaster: France and the United States, 1918–1940* (Westport: Praeger, 2002).

Zimmerman, Joshua, ed. *Jews in Italy under Fascist and Nazi Rule, 1922–1945* (Cambridge University Press, 2005).

INDEX